A
Minority
of Members

WOMEN IN THE U.S. CONGRESS

Hope Chamberlin

PRAEGER PUBLISHERS
New York · Washington · London

To my mother and father

PRAEGER PUBLISHERS

111 Fourth Avenue, New York, N.Y. 10003, U.S.A.
5, Cromwell Place, London SW7 2JL, England

Published in the United States of America in 1973
by Praeger Publishers, Inc.

Library of Congress Cataloging in Publication Data
Chamberlin, Hope.
   A minority of members.
   1. United States. Congress—Biography.   2. Women in the United States
—Biography.   3. Women and politics—United States—History.   I. Title.
JK1030.A2C5   328.73'092'2 [B]   73-151950

Printed in the United States of America

Contents

Contents v

A *section of photographs follows page* 118.

Acknowledgments

The names of some of the people who helped me with this book are scattered through the text and may be easily detected. In addition, I want to invite the reader's attention to other individuals whose encouragement and assistance were indispensable.

Many relatives of deceased congresswomen drew freely on their memories to provide firsthand observations, which have been incorporated in the word portraits. A particular debt of gratitude is due the following: Lowell B. Mason, brother of Winnifred Mason Huck, and a two-term Illinois state senator in the 1920s; Charles M. Huck, her grandson; San Francisco Attorney Julius Kahn, Jr., elder son of Florence Prag Kahn; Rudd Owen Brown, younger daughter of Ruth Bryan Owen and twice the Democratic Party nominee for Congress from the 21st California District; Blanche Wingo Sawyer, only daughter of Effiegene Locke Wingo; Willa Fulmer Reed, youngest daughter of Willa Lybrand Fulmer; Jane Buchanan Thomas, twin daughter of Vera D. Buchanan; and Louise Reece Marthens, only child of Louise Goff Reece.

Those who contributed specialized knowledge based on their Capitol Hill experience as key aides to former congresswomen include Irene Lewis, administrative assistant to Frances P. Bolton; Dorothy D. Jessup, secretary to Cecil M. Harden; Helen B. Gladwell, administrative assistant to Jessica McCullough Weis; and Doris Lovett, secretary to Irene B. Baker.

Parker Westbrook, special assistant to Senator J. William Fulbright and longtime student of Arkansas political history, gave me unique insight into the life and times of the late Senator Hattie W. Caraway. For factual information concerning the 2d South Carolina District in general and the election of Congresswoman Corinne Boyd Riley in particular I am indebted to W. A. Cook, who served as legislative assistant to the late Representative John Jacob Riley.

Staff members in the offices of the fifteen women in the 92d Congress cooperated wholeheartedly in arranging appointments and providing essential records. Deserving of special mention are Irene M. Peterson, administrative assistant to Leonor K. Sullivan; Michael C. Bennett, press secretary and legislative assistant to Julia Butler Hansen; Joseph H. Macaulay, administrative assistant to Charlotte T. Reid; Edward J. Forand, Jr., press aide to Ella T. Grasso, and Thomas M. Gilbert, administrative assistant to Elizabeth B. Andrews.

Within the national political parties, Harriet Cipriani, director of women's activities for the Democratic National Committee, offered many helpful suggestions. Moreover, she made available for study the answers to a questionnaire submitted to women candidates defeated for public office in the 1968 elections. These personal accounts were enlightening in that they revealed the mood and the frustrations, the weariness, and the uncertainties of modern-day women bent on a career in politics.

In the course of doing research for the book, I received valuable guidance from a select group of specialists, all of whom showed great patience and generosity: Georgia C. Cowan, chief of the Biography Division at the District of Columbia Public Library; William G. Sartain, head of the Reader Service Section in the Library of Congress; Jeanne Spiegel, director of the Business and Professional Women's Foundation Library; Dr. John L. Ferguson, state historian of the Arkansas History Commission; Manon B. Atkins of the Oklahoma Historical Society; and Jay Williar of the California Historical Society.

A number of friends gave me assistance in the form of consultation or took time to search local archives for specific data: Lucy Rogers Hawkins, former lecturer at the Medill School of Journalism, Northwestern University; Rita Harmer Kellogg, a teacher in the Portland, Oregon public school system; Ruth Tyo, former chairman of the Hancock (Ohio) County Republican Women's Organization; Ed. J. Dooley, editor of the *San Francisco Examiner*; Robert C. Ingalls, editor and publisher of the *Corvallis Gazette-Times* and 10th District Representative in the

Oregon Legislature; and Bruce Merkle, administrative assistant to Representative William G. Bray of Indiana.

Certified election statistics were furnished by the Secretary of State in the thirty-seven states that have sent women to Congress. To those in the election bureaus who went widely out of their way to locate old records, especially Eleanor Edwards in Albany, New York, I owe special thanks.

Lois Decker O'Neill, senior editor in the Washington, D.C., office of Praeger Publishers, is deserving of appreciation for her excellent editorial counsel and humane attitude toward deadlines.

Finally, I am grateful to all present and former congresswomen who replied so candidly and sincerely to my questions, either by letter or in person. Without their individual contributions, this book would have been entirely impossible.

HOPE CHAMBERLIN

Washington, D.C.
December, 1972

A MINORITY OF MEMBERS

Introduction

By whatever unstated, immeasurable, invisible standards the American people apply to candidates for Congress, women have seldom been their choice. From 1917—when Montana voters sent Jeannette Rankin to Capitol Hill—through 1972, only 80 women occupied congressional seats: 11 in the Senate (6 Democrats and 5 Republicans) and 70 in the House (43 Democrats and 27 Republicans.* (Five more were elected November 7, 1972, to serve in the 93d Congress.)

Although their proportion has never exceeded 3.7 per cent in any Congress, women have demonstrated that, when imbued with a particular kind of motivation, drive, and luck, they can win seats, sustain the support of their constituencies, and exert commendable leadership. By so doing they have helped shape the course of government and thus the course of the nation.

Most members of this numerically select group were reared in modest economic circumstances; almost all attended college; only a few never married. The majority have been white, Anglo-Saxon, and Protestant. Beyond hard work and the gift of intuition, however, they have had little else in common. The laws of chance, if nothing else, argue against parallels. Their geographical heritage embraces 38 of the 50 states; their precongressional careers, if any, span a broad spectrum: teaching, stenography,

* Margaret Chase Smith, the Maine Republican who served in both the House and the Senate, is counted twice.

3

journalism, social work, broadcasting, the theater, law—even cow-punching.

As might be expected, the quality of their on-the-job performance has also differed. Some have sought little more than a political flirtation. Amid the flash of cameras they have swept up the Capitol steps, tried a few lesislative whirls, and departed. Others, however, have brought to Congress practical minds, integrity, dedication to duty, and the courage to challenge the system in the interest of better government. They have established seniority, headed committees, and introduced meaningful, relevant legislation. Among them have been a significant number of pacesetters. As they earned reputations as able lawmakers, they simultaneously lost their identity as women, becoming, in the eyes of colleagues and constituents alike, Members of Congress. With the passage of time and altering of customs, the way women have gained national political office has undergone changes. Whereas in the beginning most of those who came to Congress were widows of deceased congressmen, nowadays the path usually has been mapped out in advance. Currently there are fewer widows and more wives; more, too, with legislative orientation.

But, despite this promising trend, there is as yet no sign of a large-scale movement by women in the direction of high-level political careers. It is true that it took 72 years following the Declaration of Independence before women actively sought the right to vote and another 72 years before they attained their objective. Yet, in the more than half a century since, a mere handful have reached the top echelon of legislative government.

Why?

The nature of the chosen few and their peculiar history may provide an answer—or at least a clue.

Plight of a Dove

JEANNETTE RANKIN
REPUBLICAN OF MONTANA

"Go! Go! Go! It makes no difference where just so you go! go!
go! Remember at the first opportunity go!"

This diary notation, which Jeannette Rankin made in 1902, was
an ultimatum to herself. Recently graduated from the University
of Montana, she was tired of dabbling in odd jobs around the
house, tired of accompanying her father on trips to his lumber
camp, where she sometimes cooked for crews of fifty or sixty,
tired of not having "anything definite to do."

Go, she did: from teaching ("awful") to dressmaking ("bor-
ing") to studying furniture design by correspondence ("frustrating"). In the East to visit her brother, she toured Boston and
was shocked by its slums. In San Francisco, she worked briefly
among the poor in the Latin Quarter. On the East Coast again
in 1908, she spent a year at the New York School of Philanthropy, a progressive institution whose philosophy was that wom-
en "in the underside of life" suffered because they had no civic
voice "in creating the power that ruled over them." Back home,
she plunged into the suffrage movement, eventually moving to
the forefront as a lobbyist in a dozen states and on Capitol Hill.
With time out for a brief vacation, she was off to New Zealand,
where she "went out sewing by the day . . . to learn about
the living and working conditions of the people."

Finally, in 1916, four years before the 19th Amendment assured all American women the ballot, Montana voters, teetering

5

between reason and sentiment, elected her to the U.S. House of Representatives, and Miss Rankin, symbol and early harvester of the long, bittersweet struggle for women's rights, went to the nation's capital. Sworn in on April 2, 1917, she became the first woman to serve in the Congress of the United States.

A robust Western feeling of equality, as much as anything, was responsible for Jeannette Rankin's going to Washington. "We got the vote in Montana," she said, "because the spirit of pioneer days was still alive. Men thought of women in the same terms as they thought of themselves." Clearly she counted her father among this special breed. John Rankin, the son of Scottish immigrants, had made his way by flatboat and oxcart from his native Ontario, Canada, in the 1860s, to cast his lot, at age 29, with other adventurous hopefuls in the wild Bitter Root Valley below the mountain range that forms a natural boundary with Idaho.

Olive Pickering, whom he married in 1879, was in her mid-20s when the Pickerings began a westward trek from New Hampshire that ended in Missoula County. There she became the second schoolteacher in a territory that was admitted to the Union in 1889 as the 41st state. From Olive Rankin, described as "kind, firm, and in a mild way domineering," the seven Rankin children (all but one of whom reached adulthood) acquired their intellectual bent. Each, in turn, was graduated from the state university. Three of the girls went on to Wellesley. The lone son, Wellington Duncan Rankin, finished Harvard Law School and spent a winter studying at Oxford.

The family, according to Lita Barnett, a Missoula teacher, was "forward-thinking and democratic." The Rankins were also politically minded. The head of the household, a Republican, ran successfully for county commissioner, an office he held for six years before his untimely death in 1904, the victim of Rocky Mountain spotted fever. Wellington, active in the Progressive Party, was destined to be elected state attorney general. After Jeannette, the oldest, entered the GOP congressional race, "it was beautiful to see the way the Rankin family pulled together," Peter Clark MacFarlane reported in *Collier's*:

> One of the sisters was a bride of but two months, yet she kissed her husband good-by and sailed out to campaign for Jeannette; another had a child two years old, but she too went campaigning for Jeannette, taking the baby with her; a third left her children at home and went out on the hustings, while the youngest sister of all, a student in law school, threw down her *Greenleaf on Evidence,* abandoned torts for retorts and the lecture hall for the po-

litical stump. Even that school-teacher from New Hampshire whom the builder had married, now a gray-haired, home-keeping woman and a little dazed by all this swift onrush of new ideas, put aside her knitting and went out among the neighbors and old-time ranch friends offering hopeful, motherish reasons for sending her daughter to Congress.

Wellington managed Jeannette's campaign. Cautiously optimistic about the outcome, he suggested she might be ahead of her time. "I am shocked," he said, "at the prejudice that exists against a woman going to Congress. . . . The biggest campaign of education that is going to be required is to the effect that a woman can . . . do the work there and should be sent there, rather than the question of you, individually going." Were it not for "the prejudice," he thought, "there would be nothing to it. That prejudice, however, is substantial."

Her brother reckoned without the statewide organization Jeannette Rankin had kept intact from the successful 1914 suffrage drive. Each county and every precinct had at least one woman leader willing to lay aside party labels and press for her election. Moreover, she was well known throughout the state—if not personally, by reputation. During her exhausting crusade for women's rights, she had toured Montana many times, visiting every city, village, and hamlet.

Even those Republican spokesmen who were reluctant to endorse Miss Rankin publicly conceded privately that they had been favorably impressed with her prowess as a lobbyist on Capitol Hill. More than a few agreed that it "could be advantageous to the party" to be represented by a woman—especially one as familiar as she was with congressional procedures.

Because Montana elected its two representatives at large, she had to cover the entire state. The speaking tour that Wellington charted was based on an estimate that there were 183,000 more voters east of Bozeman than west; therefore, she would have to spend most of her time traversing the plains. By train, buggy, and car and on horseback, she carried her platform to the people. If elected, she promised to work for a federal suffrage amendment, an eight-hour day for women, improved health care for mothers and infants, tax law reform, Prohibition, and a stronger national defense.

To those who asked why a woman should sit in Congress, she replied, "There are hundreds of men to care for the nation's tariff and foreign policy and irrigation projects. But there isn't a single woman to look after the nation's greatest asset: its children."

Jeannette Rankin won the August GOP primary handily. She captured 33 of the 41 counties and led a field of seven male contenders by 7,080 votes. In the November election, marked by a Democratic landslide in the state, her victory was even more impressive: 76,932 against 66,974 for George W. Farr, a Miles City attorney who carried only 5 counties.

Newspapers vied with one another to give readers a glimpse of the nation's first congresswoman. Miss Rankin, however, on the advice of the party hierarchy, refused to be photographed or to grant interviews. Consequently, what got into print in the days immediately following her election was a hodgepodge of conjecture and imagination.

She was reported to be about 33 years of age (she was 36), tall (she was not), and blue-eyed (her eyes were hazel). One writer described her as a "cowgirl." Another, nicknaming her "Jenny," suggested she must be an "Amazon." In the *Literary Digest* she was headlined "The Girl of the Golden West."

Only after she appeared on the opening day of the 65th Congress—amid applause and cheers from colleagues on the floor and suffragettes who filled the gallery—did the public receive a full-blown, accurate physical description.

"In spite of Jeannette Rankin's unusual position and surroundings, she remains the typical woman from top to toe," the Tattler wrote in the *Nation*.

> The top is especially prominent, crowned as it is with a mass of brown hair slightly streaked with gray, worn *à la Pompadour* in a fashion that emphasizes its abundance. The next most noticeable feature is the nose, which is large, straight in outline, and fairly dominates the face, particularly in profile. The chin stands out well, but is round and reduced in conspicuousness by a fullness of the cheeks which extends down to the line of the jaw. Her small, rather slight figure, clad in well-fitting garments . . . adds to her thoroughly feminine effect. The V-shaped opening at the neck, and the use of lace and tulle wherever a man would use flat linen stiff with starch, differentiate her completely from the background against which she is projected. . . . Her face is mobile, her motions lithe, and her manner has all the vivacity comportable with her obvious seriousness of purpose.

It was characteristic of Miss Rankin, who limited her biographical entry in the *Congressional Directory* to half a line, to give brief answers to questions from the press, particularly if they dealt with trivia. "It makes no difference how anyone addresses me," she told a magazine reporter. "I was elected from my state as one of its two congressmen." When asked if she attached any significance to the fact she had been assigned an office across the hall from one of the most eligible House bachelors, she replied, "I expect to put in my time here learning the ropes."

As to her position on U.S. involvement in the war in Europe, she insisted her stand was well known. In a prepared statement submitted to the *New York Times* after her election, she had stated that she did not think "war could continue for any considerable length of time without the support of women." In reporting her viewpoint, the *Times* had suggested that it "may be questioned by those who think that the present war is continuing despite the weariness and protests of the women [but] she will have plenty of time between now and her first appearance in Congress to think many things over."

' Suffrage, not war, preoccupied Miss Rankin during the ensuing months. Nevertheless, she would write at a later date that she "had been *thinking peace*"—had, in fact, "built up a peace-thinking habit." Consequently, nothing that President Woodrow Wilson said in his request for a declaration of war on Germany before a historic joint session of Congress on the night of April 2 convinced her that the United States should commit troops to European battlefields.

Three days later, when Senate Joint Resolution Number One, declaring that "a state of war exists between the Imperial German Government and the Government of the people of the United States," was placed before the House, Jeannette Rankin knew precisely how she would cast her first vote. Yet she did not respond to the first roll call. In the course of the long debate, Wellington had pressured her to change her mind. He followed his argument that she might be committing political suicide with an appeal that she dispel the myth about all women being alike. "Vote a man's vote," he pleaded.

"It was easy to stand against the propaganda and the militarists," she explained later, "but very difficult to go against friends and dear ones who felt that I would make a needless sacrifice by voting against war, since my vote would not be a decisive one. I decided . . . not to vote until the last opportunity."

Toward three o'clock on Good Friday morning the clerk called "Rankin" a second time. She half rose and, disregarding the House rule that forbids comment during a roll call, said in a distraught, barely audible voice, "I wish to stand by my country, but I cannot vote for war. I vote 'No.'"

The final tally showed that 49 colleagues had joined her in rejecting Wilson's plea. Some of them, like the Montana congresswoman, had wept. Yet the newspapers credited the tears to the solitary woman. Moreover, she, not the antiwar men, was singled out for insinuations of cowardice and disloyalty.

"This beginning of Miss Rankin's career as a national legislator is most unfortunate for her" was the view offered in a *New York Times* editorial entitled "Patriotism with a But." "She starts wrong, for she has justified distrust of her judgment and of her opinions." The consensus was perhaps best summed up in the *Nation*: "It is regrettable that her first important vote on the floor should have been one in which she could not with an easy conscience voice the prevailing sentiment of her own district or of the country at large, for her attitude on the war issue can never be expunged from the record, however earnestly she may devote her energies hereafter to the national cause."

As a legislator in the 65th Congress, Jeannette Rankin made her greatest impact in promoting suffrage. Early in the first session, she cosponsored a resolution for a constitutional amendment granting this right to women. When it became apparent that the House Judiciary Committee intended to pigeonhole the measure, she successfully introduced legislation creating a 13-member Woman Suffrage Committee. Because she was the acknowledged authority in this area, the Republican caucus endorsed her as the ranking minority member.

Most House opposition to suffrage came from Southerners who argued that, where there were large Negro populations, the amendment would double the ignorant electorate. They also raised the question of states' rights. When one witness before the committee charged that suffragists were trying to change the constitutions of the various states, "which were adopted by the people," Miss Rankin interjected, "May I ask who are the people?"

Chosen to lead the floor debate, which began on January 10, 1918, the Montana congresswoman focused her appeal on fairness. Within the country as a whole, she reminded fellow members, there was precedence for implementing reforms on a nationwide basis. Prohibition was about to be enforced as a national measure. Child welfare was being supervised by the U.S. Children's Bureau. "Shall our women, our home defense," she asked, "be our only fighters in the struggle for democracy who shall be denied federal action?" Declaring that democracy was the "national religion of America," she urged Congress to prove to the American people that "the war is being fought for democracy . . . by granting this small measure of democracy to the women of our country."

Antisuffragists employed all of the well-known arguments, in-

cluding a suggestion that the franchise would lead to the mas-
culinizing of females and the feminizing of males and, eventually, to the decay of American civilization. In the end, however—
by precisely the two-thirds vote required—the House agreed
to the amendment. But, when the Senate refused to concur, the
issue was dead as far as the 65th Congress was concerned.

Not so along the 1918 campaign trail. There it remained very
much alive. By leading an assault against antisuffrage senators
seeking re-election, women succeeded in shifting the balance of
power. In mid-1919 the Woman Suffrage Amendment went to
the states for ratification.

Ironically, Jeannette Rankin was not a member of the consent-
ing Congress. A complicated chain of events over which she had
no control contributed to her defeat in 1918. The Montana Legislature had created two congressional districts, thereby eliminating the at-large posts. If she had sought re-election to the House,
she would have had to run in the 1st District, the western third
of the state, which was largely Democratic. Rather than be
boxed in geographically, she filed for the Senate.

The move was bold and risky. Although none of the three men
entered in the GOP primary were considered unbeatable, the
Senate was viewed as such an impregnable male bastion that the
likelihood of a woman's being admitted was remote. Predictably,
she lost, but not by as large a margin as had been expected.
Oscar M. Lanstrum, a Helena physician and onetime titular head
of Montana Republicans, defeated her by only 1,714 votes.
The Democrats renominated Thomas J. Walsh, an ally of suffrage.

A less-determined person than Miss Rankin might at this point
have given up. Wellington, again her manager, urged her to
withdraw. So did others. But she stayed in the race, using as
the vehicle for her candidacy the National Party, a newly formed
coalition of Socialists, Prohibitionists, Progressives, and farmers.

At the outset, her prospects were brightened by an endorsement from the Montana branch of the Nonpartisan League. Its
rank and file, primarily sheep and wheat ranchers in the northeastern part of the state, were impressed by her voting record
on farm legislation. And many, like Miss Rankin, were opposed
to the war. "They have the idea that Wall Street and the muni-
tions manufacturers in the East have done a great deal to bring it
on," explained one observer. Backing came also from several ethnic groups: the Irish, because she had introduced a resolution
in Congress to recognize Ireland's right to political independence, and the Scandinavians, because they were largely pacifists.

In appealing to women, Miss Rankin emphasized her accomplishments in Congress. She had sponsored the first maternity and infancy bill to provide, among other things, free hygiene instruction. On the issue of the eight-hour workday for women, she had made an impressive beginning by threatening a congressional inquiry unless Secretary of the Treasury William A. McAdoo ordered an end to the 12-hour schedule in effect at the Bureau of Engraving and Printing. The upshot was McAdoo's compliance.

Her record on women's rights, said opponents, was fine. But the question that went to the heart of her suitability to continue to represent Montana was that of the stand she had taken against the war. Although she had spoken publicly on behalf of the state Liberty Loan drive and the American Red Cross and had adopted as a campaign slogan "Win the War, and Make the World Safe for Humanity," there were those who doubted her patriotism. Some citizen groups denied her the right to speak. In Butte, for instance, she arrived to find the high school auditorium doors locked; Deer Lodge turned her away.

Jeannette Rankin's cause was not helped when Carrie Chapman Catt, national leader of suffrage forces, publicly endorsed Senator Walsh. Mrs. Catt's unexpected political preference for a male candidate over a female (both of them ardently supported suffrage) was based on her belief that Walsh could win. Clearly, she did not want to be identified with a loser—particularly with one whose defeat could, in her opinion, give men a chance to say, "We told you so!"

The election took place less than a week before the signing of the armistice in Compiègne. An influenza epidemic and a snow-and-sleet storm significantly reduced the voter turnout. Walsh collected 46,160 votes to win re-election; Dr. Lanstrum was second, with 40,229; and Jeannette Rankin trailed with 26,-013. She made a good showing in Mineral County, north of Missoula. running a mere 20 votes behind Walsh there. However, the only three counties she carried were in the northeastern corner of the state, where Nonpartisan League membership was high.

In view of Democratic Party strength in Montana and Walsh's popularity (he was re-elected to two more, successive terms and died in office), did Miss Rankin ever really have a chance of going to the Senate in 1918? She thinks not. Years later she told an interviewer that the campaign "had been hopeless from the start."

Nearly a quarter of a century was to pass before Jeannette Rankin made a congressional comeback. She began her second term in January 1941—ironically a year when another and a greater war in Europe was threatening to involve the United States.

Not the lone female legislator this time, but one of eight, including a lady senator, Miss Rankin made no headlines when she was sworn in at the opening of the 77th Congress. This is not to say, however, that the media ignored her. It was widely reported that she had re-entered politics because "the people desire peace and it is the business of legislators to protect the people's wishes." As a congresswoman, she would be able to say on the House floor: "America should be ready to defend its own shores, but foreign wars are no part of the American way of life."

Throughout the two decades following her involuntary retirement from the political mainstream, she had spent more time in the legislative halls on Capitol Hill than anywhere else. As field secretary of the reform-minded National Consumers League, she lobbied for federal wage-and-hour laws, for a child labor amendment, and for the Sheppard-Towner bill, the maternity and infancy measure she had introduced under her own name in 1918. When it became law in 1921, most of the credit went to her thoroughness and competence, characteristics that had won praise from fellow congressmen during the 65th Congress.

Despite the modest success she achieved in the social welfare field, it was the peace movement that eventually captured and held her undivided attention. With the Women's International League for Peace and Freedom, she worked as lobbyist, educator, and speechmaker to mobilize public opinion. In 1929, after leading the Georgia Peace Society crusade on behalf of the Kellogg-Briand Pact, she joined the Women's Peace Union and lobbied for a constitutional amendment "forbidding the United States from preparing for, or engaging in war." When this effort failed, she became legislative secretary of the National Council for the Prevention of War (NCPW) and spent the 1930s urging Congress to adopt a policy of neutrality.

Miss Rankin's philosophy (humanitarian considerations perhaps aside) was "America First." Her thinking coincided with that of Senator Gerald P. Nye of North Dakota, Senator Burton K. Wheeler of her own state, and, on the sidelines, famed aviator Charles A. Lindbergh. Like most isolationists, she distrusted President Franklin D. Roosevelt. In a 1938 speech, she charged FDR with "preparing the people for war" and suggested that "if we define our defense boundaries, which are roughly from the

Aleutian Islands to Hawaii, from the Panama Canal to Maine and Labrador . . . we can prevent a dictator from taking us into a foreign war." Even after the Germans crossed the Polish border on September 1, 1939, and England and France honored their commitments to aid Poland, she retained this view. On a visit to Montana at the time, she met head on the argument that America was morally committed to defend its allies. "Instead of taking sides with one group of nations against another," she said, "the United States should help, by its example, the men and women in every country to abolish war and build democracy."

Now white-haired and not as quick of step as she had once been, Miss Rankin approaching 60 was, nevertheless, in robust health and vigorous voice. With her 1940 announcement that she would seek the 1st District seat in the House, she said that her major platform plank would be "Prepare to the limit for defense; keep our men out of Europe." Fiorello LaGuardia, mayor of New York and a former U.S. representative, wrote for her handbills an emphatic sentence: "This woman has more courage and packs a harder punch than a regiment of regular line politicians." During the primary contest she discovered that her biggest obstacle was not the GOP incumbent, Dr. Jacob Thorkelson (also an isolationist), but her prolonged absences from the state. Many voters had to be reminded that she had never given up her legal residence in Montana.

Except for party labels, there were no fundamental differences in political ideology between Miss Rankin and her Democratic opponent, Jerry J. O'Connell of Butte, who was also a former member of Congress (1937–39). No wonder that she looked on her campaign as one of the rich adventures of her life.

The November election results in Montana were amazingly similar to those of 1916: Jeannette Rankin was the single Republican national-office winner. Out of nearly 104,000 ballots cast in the 1st District, she lost only four counties and chalked up a plurality of more than 9,000 votes. Commenting on her victory, the *Christian Century* engaged in serious speculation: "One cannot but wonder whether she will again be called upon to vote on the question of America's entrance into the war. The certainty as to how her vote would be cast must have had some weight with the voters who supported her. Unless there is a tremendous reversal of popular sentiment she will not be voting with the minority this time—if Congress gets a chance to vote."

Congress did. On December 8, 1941, the day after Japan stunned and outraged the nation by wantonly bombing Pearl Harbor, President Roosevelt arrived at the Capitol at 12:12 P.M.,

to ask the assembled members "to declare that since the unprovoked and dastardly attack . . . a state of war has existed
between the United States and the Japanese Empire."

Within the hour, the Senate acted 82-to-0 upon his request.
In the House, John McCormack, Massachusetts Democrat, moved
to suspend the rules and pass the resolution. One member objected: Miss Rankin. A few minutes before the clerk began to
intone the lawmakers' names, she was on her feet, waving her
hand, seeking recognition from Speaker Sam Rayburn on a point
of order. But a roll call was being demanded, so he ignored her.
From the back of the chamber, when her name was called, she
cast a firm "No."

Of what happened afterward, the *Washington Post* gave this
account:

> There was a small procession of solemn-faced colleagues back
> up the aisle to her seat. They spoke earnestly to her in the benign
> manner of men who strive to change a woman's mind. Miss Rankin
> spoke excitedly to Everett Dirksen of Illinois, George Bender of
> Ohio, and Karl Stefan of Nebraska, all Republicans. At the end
> of each conversation, she always shook her head.

Thus, at 1:32 P.M., with one dissenting vote, Congress declared
war on Japan.

Leaving the floor, Jeannette Rankin encountered a barrage of
flash bulbs and reporters' questions. She made her way to a telephone booth in the cloakroom and dialed a number. The Capitol
police who responded escorted her to the Cannon Building,
where she spent the afternoon behind the locked doors of her
office, a uniformed officer on guard in the corridor. Before the
day ended, in reply to a telegram from the Republican National
Committeeman in Missoula "urging and beseeching" her "to redeem Montana's honor and loyalty" by changing her vote "as
early as possible," she released the text of a statement to 1st
District constituents:

> While I believed with the other members of the House that
> the stories which had come over the radio were probably true,
> still I believed that such a momentous vote—one which would
> mean peace or war for our country—should be based on more
> authentic evidence than the radio reports now at hand.
> Sending our boys to the Orient will not protect this country.
> We are all for every measure which will mean defense for our
> land, but taking our army and navy across thousands of miles
> to fight and die certainly cannot come under the head of pro-
> tecting our shores.

"What one decides to do in a crisis," she told a friend, "depends upon one's philosophy of life, and that philosophy cannot be changed by an incident. If one hasn't any philosophy in crises, others make the decision. The most disappointing feature of working for a cause," she added, "is that so few people have a philosophy of life. We used to say, in the suffrage movement, that we could trust the woman who believed in suffrage, but we could never trust the woman who just wanted to vote."

However divergent the viewpoints on war before the attack on Pearl Harbor, the overwhelming majority of American citizens quickly closed ranks after it took place. Jeannette Rankin's decision to stand to the last for peace received considerable attention, but no praise—although a few commended her courage. Two days after the war declaration, William Allen White, publisher of the *Emporia* (Kansas) *Gazette* wrote:

> Probably a hundred men in Congress would have liked to do what she did. Not one of them had the courage to do it. The *Gazette* entirely disagrees with the wisdom of her position. But, Lord, it was a brave thing! And its bravery someway discounted its folly.
>
> When, in a hundred years from now, courage, sheer courage based upon moral indignation is celebrated in this country, the name of Jeannette Rankin, who stood firm in folly for her faith, will be written in monumental bronze not for what she did but for the way she did it.

Other Rankin-watchers remembered that not once during the long, heated debates preceding the day of infamy had she deviated from her position that it was the duty of Congress to reflect the will of the people. That will, she had staunchly maintained, stood for peace. She had been one of a small minority to vote against the lend-lease bill, arguing that "Congress is abdicating its responsibilities to the President." The legislation she had initiated before Pearl Harbor was designed to force the House to commit itself to purely defensive military policies.

Contending that "people never make war; it is always governments," she set out to prove that Roosevelt had conspired with British Prime Minister Winston Churchill, during their historic meeting at sea off Newfoundland in August 1941, to preserve European empires in Asia by instigating war between Japan and the United States. "Was it not strange," she asked, "that Mr. Roosevelt, who by refusing for years to enforce the Neutrality Act of 1936 to prevent shipments of war supplies to Japan . . .

had largely contributed to supplying that nation with the raw
material for the armaments now being used against our own
troops . . . then, after the Atlantic Conference, suddenly
changed his policy and not only cut off war supplies, but virtually everything required by the civilian population of Japan
as well?"

The results of her investigation, carried on with the help of
two secretaries and one stenographer, appeared in the *Congressional Record* in 1942. Entitled "Some Questions About Pearl
Harbor," the report represented one of the earliest published attempts to cast doubt on the Administration's avowal that the
Japanese bombing raids had been an act of "unprovoked aggression." (Thirty years later, when secret British wartime documents were made public, it was revealed that President Roosevelt indeed was so eager to get America into the war in 1941
that he went out of his way to provoke "incidents" which could
be represented as German aggression against America. Roosevelt was "obviously determined" to come into the war, Churchill
stated. "The President said that he would wage war but not
declare it. . . . If the Germans did not like it, they could
attack the American forces.")

It has been written that Miss Rankin's second term "ended
for all practical purposes on December 8, 1941." True or not, she
recognized that as a "shameless isolationist" she could not be re-
elected. Besides, she was tired and not in the best of financial
health. She had had to use her share of John Rankin's $125,000
legacy during the Depression, when she often worked for only
a token salary or for no salary at all. In a letter to a former associate in the peace movement, she explained her decision to
retire voluntarily from politics: "The women are for me now,
[but] since there is no way to know about the war situation in
the future I'm not willing to risk all I have and take a chance on
having a debt and no office."

Nonagenarian Jeannette Rankin is living out her life as an activist and pacifist. Her aged but still resonant voice continues
to be heard, proclaiming the right to dissent and attacking the
Vietnam War. In 1968, she lent her name to the Jeannette Rankin Brigade and led a parade of several thousand women for
peace onto the steps of the nation's Capitol. During moratorium
marches in other cities at other times, she has fairly shouted,
"No one can let up in this effort to bring about peace. Real
peace. A lasting peace. We have to get it into our heads once and

for all that we cannot settle disputes by eliminating human beings."

Miss Rankin believes, as she did while campaigning for the
suffrage amendment, that women are more concerned with humanitarian goals than are men, and that women should make
themselves more conspicuous politically. "The men have taught
women not to trust their emotions," she says, "but women have
an emotional ideal to contribute, and if they organized we could
have peace in one year."

As she travels—between an earthen-floored house in Watkins-
ville, Georgia, a "smallish" ranch in Montana, and an apartment
in Carmel Valley, California, or to South America, the Middle
East, or India—her curiosity focuses on two issues: the status of
women and peace.

On her 90th birthday, in 1970, the Montana State Society of
Washington, D.C., toasted her at a champagne reception in the
Rayburn House Office Building. Although confined to a wheel-
chair (she had suffered a broken hip in a fall while preparing
for a trip to Russia), she radiated zest as she described her newest crusade: a direct preferential vote for the Presidency. The
key to peace, she asserted, lies in electoral reform.

One legislator present referred to her as the "original dove
in Congress." "Look at the record now," he added. "We're voting
your way, Jeannette."

A prayer written by Miss Rankin's great-nephew Erik S. Ron-
hovde of the State Department expressed the sentiment of the
celebrants: "The whole world may feel and see that things that
were cast down are being raised up, and things which had grown
old are being made new."

Jeannette Rankin has indicated that she is thankful to have
seen the fruits of some of her reform efforts. She has also made
it clear that she has faith in her spiritual descendants. "You," she
said in acknowledging personal tributes, "can go on from where
I leave off."

Benefit of the Doubt

REBECCA LATIMER FELTON

DEMOCRAT OF GEORGIA

Securely locked forever in recorded annals of American political history is the fact that the first woman to take the oath of office as a U.S. senator was Rebecca Latimer Felton, Democrat of Georgia. Almost lost to history, however, is the fact that on October 3, 1922—the date affixed by seal to her senatorial commission—the likelihood that Mrs. Felton would be accorded this unprecedented honor was singularly unlikely.

The sudden death on September 26, 1922, of influential but controversial Georgia Senator Thomas E. Watson gave Governor Thomas W. Hardwick an opportunity rarely afforded even the most powerful politician. While a member of the 65th Congress, he had aroused female ire by voting against the 19th Amendment. Now, if he were to name a woman to the Senate, he might, he hoped, recapture favor with the newly enfranchised ladies. And, because the election to be held before the 67th Congress reconvened would surely return a male to the post, he was confident his action would not be questioned by any man.

When the *Atlanta Journal* reported that Hardwick was considering Tom Watson's widow for the interim appointment, the governor spoke for himself. He announced Mrs. Felton, also a widow, as his choice and said he would be a candidate for the unexpired term in the October 17 primary. Then he explained that he had offered the commission to Mrs. Watson and, when she had refused because of poor health, he had turned to "another noble Georgia woman, now in the sunset of a splendid, useful life." Almost as an afterthought, he added, "It is unfortunate that an elected successor will prevent her from being sworn in."

The governor's press statement upset but did not unnerve Mrs. Felton. As one who had been in the front ranks of the campaign to elect Hardwick, she was accustomed to gentlemanly power plays. The telegram of acceptance she sent to the governor gave no clue that she had already made up her mind to reach the Senate floor. She simply expressed appreciation "on behalf of the thousands of Georgia women who will reward you at the ballot box."

Almost everybody in "Mother" Felton's hometown of Cartersville turned out on the rainy, cold night of October 7 to witness the official ceremony at which she received her certificate of appointment. Her 87 years reinforced her reputation as a remarkably talented and courageous human being. She was proud of her Southern heritage and equally proud that she had long ago cast off the shackles of tradition to step beyond the hearthstone and walk boldly—even belligerently—into the political arena beside her husband.

Among the courthouse crowd was author Corra Harris, who had used Rebecca Felton as the prototype for the strong-minded, politically ambitious heroine of her novel *The Co-Citizens*. She assured the many well-wishers that her longtime friend "could have been elected as easily as she has been appointed."

The governor spoke in a different key. He admitted that he had been against suffrage for women, but, inasmuch as it was now the law of the land, he believed "it was *right*." Therefore, he had selected Mrs. Felton to prove that Georgia had accepted the enfranchisement of women as a fact. He regretted that her tenure must end before she could serve. However, she could derive satisfaction from knowing that her name would appear on the official and permanent roster of U.S. senators.

Rebecca Felton, parchment scroll in hand, expressed her appreciation in roseate phrases. "The biggest part of this appointment," she said, "lies in the recognition of women in the government of our country. It means, as far as I can see, there are now no limitations upon the ambitions of women. They can be elected or appointed to any office in the land. The word 'sex' has been obliterated entirely from the Constitution."

Newspapers north and south of the Mason-Dixon line acclaimed Mrs. Felton a woman of exceptional ability and character, a lady blessed with the love and veneration of her people. But, on the matter of the governor's motives, editors were not complimentary. Calling his act "merely a pretty sentiment . . . an empty gesture," the *Pittsburgh Gazette-Times* stated, "He did not appoint a woman because he has respect for women in politics, but actually to smooth his own path to the Senate." The *St. Louis Star* was subtler, yet no less critical: "Other Governors who may be studying the health charts of U.S. Senators should take full note of Governor Hardwick's strategy."

Suffragists from across the land began to insist—in letters and telegrams—that Mrs. Felton be officially seated among her peers in the U.S. Capitol. They did not seek her permission for their effort, because they knew they had it. She was an unwavering advocate of the political advancement of women. To anyone who asked, she had confided that "this belated recognition of women in government" must be acknowledged on the national stage. But how to unblock the road to Washington? Either the President would have to be persuaded to call a special session of Congress or the Senate must consent to her being sworn in before the elected successor took his seat.

Among the most dedicated of Mrs. Felton's protagonists was Helen Dortch Longstreet, vociferous widow of a celebrated Confederate general. The two women had been allies since Civil War days, and in 1915 Mrs. Longstreet had publicly predicted that Rebecca Felton would be the first Georgia woman elected to Congress. Moving to the forefront of the drive, she issued a call to *all* women to make their wishes known "where it counts." The response was overwhelming. President Warren Gamaliel Harding was inundated with messages beseeching him to permit "the Grand Old Lady from Georgia" to have her day in the Senate of the United States. Helen Longstreet, writing in the *New York Times,* lobbied with candor: "President Harding has a rare opportunity to offer a bouquet to millions of American women." His refusal was curt: "It would be too expensive to summon Congress just to seat a single senator."

When, in the mid-October primary (in 1922, tantamount to election in Georgia), the voters chose Walter Franklin George, a former justice of the State Supreme Court, the women shifted their pressure tactics. Subtly at first, then not so subtly, they tried to elicit from George a promise that he would defer presentation of his credentials. He assured them that he would be glad to help Mrs. Felton; however, he believed an act of Congress would be required before she could qualify. By law, he counseled, the 17th Amendment ruled that the term of an appointed senator ends the day a successor is elected—in this case, the date would be November 7. Furthermore, seating her could conceivably create a serious fiscal problem. There would be *three* Georgia senators on the congressional payroll.

In late October a throat ailment sent Mrs. Felton to an Atlanta hospital. From her sickbed she wrote the President, whom she had met in 1920 when, at his invitation, she attended a conference in St. Augustine, Florida. She was the only woman and only Southerner from whom he sought guidance and advice on domestic matters. In her note she asked him to reconsider his decision against calling a special session. On November 9, Harding issued a proclamation to convene Congress on November 20—not to seat her, but to urge immediate passage of the Administration-sponsored ship subsidy bill.

From drowsy Cartersville a few days later, Mrs. Felton talked by long distance with Senator-elect George. He said he would have to be present on opening day, but, if she was willing to take the risk of rejection, she could present her credentials first. He warned her, however, that the objection of a single senator could deny her the seat. Subsequently, Georgia's Secretary of State, S. G. McLendon, told her that he had mailed the official certificate of appointment to Washington and that, if she was in the Senate when it convened, he knew of no reason why she could not be sworn in. She began to pack a suitcase.

Mr. Felton's decision to set out for the nation's capital to occupy, if only briefly, Tom Watson's vacant seat surprised no one who knew her. For 50 years people had been telling her what she could not do. Usually she had done what *she* chose: stumping with her husband to fight graft, bribery, and the state Democratic bosses, skirmishing with state legislators who were slow to consider her proposals for a "bone-dry" state, prison reform, compulsory school attendance, vocational education, care for expectant mothers, and suffrage. Her successes were legendary—and not always unexpected.

Born in 1835 near the close of Andrew Jackson's second Administration, Rebecca Ann Latimer entered life during Georgia's "Golden Age." Her childhood world was unique in both time and place. She grew up on a large farm through which ran the main road between Decatur and Augusta. Because there was a stagecoach stop on the property (adjacent to an inn called Latimer's Tavern) she had been privy to a wider-than-usual view of the Old South—one not limited by the boundaries of an antebellum plantation.

Her parents, Charles and Eleanor Swift Latimer, as Rebecca was to recall in her memoirs, were a wonderful blending. . . . "My father was one of the staunchest and strongest of men, very much ahead of the time as to theories and thought—which accounts for my force of character and advanced ideas. Mother was the gentlest and most devout of women, imparting [to me] a religious ardor and stand in the temperance movement."

In newly carved DeKalb County, Latimer had helped clear the large timber tract 10 miles south of Decatur on which stood not only the home and tavern but also a country store and a frame schoolhouse. A year before the birth of Rebecca, first of the couple's three children, his resolute loyalty to the Whig Party had earned him an appointment as postmaster of Latimer's Crossroads. Aided by slave labor, the family prospered.

Rebecca, who from infancy exhibited precocity, was not yet five when she began to attend classes in the one-room building on the family acreage. Of this early experience, she wrote, "I immediately became devoted to Webster's blue backed spelling book. Everyone brought goose quills from home to fashion into pens . . . and I had a small slate on which I drew pictures of cows, cats, and dogs. . . . It was reading, writing, and ciphering from eight in the morning to five or six in the afternoon."

When lessons ended, she sometimes forsook riding her pony to wait under the gold-lettered tavern sign, listening for the sound of the stagecoach horn and watching for the conveyance to come into view—lumbering when rains had drenched the road and the wheel ruts showed or showered by dust in dry spells. While one team of horses was exchanged for another, she would talk to the travelers or go into the store to enjoy the flurry of excitement that always surrounded the opening of the mailbag. After the stagecoach resumed its journey, according to her memoirs, "it was the most natural thing in the world for my father to read aloud from the *Southern Recorder,* which was coming to my home when I could first remember and continued as long as it was in existence before the [Civil] War. The eager people who listened learned all they knew of national politics in that way. I became familiar also with Tippecanoe and Tyler too!"

Although she was only nine years old when the fiercely partisan Polk-Clay campaign took place in 1844, Rebecca found herself caught up in the frenzy that infected the entire household:

> I read the paper diligently. It assured me that Henry Clay's election was a foregone conclusion; that his defeat was unthinkable. . . . I was certain that the country would go to the

"demnition bow-wows," if James Polk happened to get in. Perhaps I did not lose much sleep, but I certainly kept busy—with a comparison of the records of the opposing candidates—and while I could do very little, I could show my father there was one loyal heart on his side in politics.

It was some time after the election before news of Clay's defeat reached Latimer's Crossroads. "I have always understood since that day how the soldiers felt at Thermopylae or at Waterloo!" she wrote later. "For weeks afterward it kinder made me weak to hear the stage horn blow—and I lost some of my exuberant faith in the *Southern Recorder.*"

Not long after the Whig disaster, the "field" school burned to the ground. Rebecca was sent to board with a minister's family in Oxford, where she attended Miss Hayes's classes. So eager was her father to have her obtain the best education available that he built a second home, Panola Plantation, only one mile from Decatur, where there was an academy administered by John S. Wilson. It was in this school that she had to face the first serious personal disappointment in her young life. She loved to dance. The Virginia Reel was the popular step of the time. Dr. Wilson, however, a Presbyterian minister unutterably opposed to dancing, forbade his pupils to attend dancing parties. Rebecca begged her parents to intercede in her behalf. They refused. "Little girl," her father said, "Dr. Wilson is trying to educate your mind and I must help him. After a while there will be time aplenty to educate your heels."

There was "time aplenty"—but not for dancing. Before her 16th birthday, she was enrolled in Madison Female College, a strict Methodist institution, which her mother had attended. Graduating with honors in 1852, the youngest in her class, she served on the committee that selected the commencement speaker, William Harrell Felton. A Methodist minister widely praised for his eloquence in the pulpit, a medical doctor who had given up his practice for health reasons, and a member of the State Legislature, he was also, at 30, a widower with a small daughter. His address inspired all 12 girl graduates, but particularly Rebecca Latimer. "No country can reach true greatness," he said, "without educated mothers. Christian homes graced with intelligent, devout wives have given America its supremacy over all other nations."

Fifteen months later—on October 11, 1853—diminutive, dark-eyed Misss Latimer and tall, deacon-like Dr. Felton were married in her parents' white-columned plantation home overlooking South River. They left immediately for the 100-mile journey northwest to her husband's modest farmhouse in Cass County (later renamed Bartow), three miles from Cartersville, a small station on the Western and Atlantic (W. & A.) Railroad. Those who knew the couple believe that Dr. Felton's love for Rebecca stemmed from her active mind and independent spirit. She, in turn, admired him primarily because of his temperament—one not unlike that of her confidently combative father, whom she adored. Then, too, Dr. Felton was willing to permit women more freedom than most men of his day.

In the bleak Piedmont region where they went to live, something of the aura of the frontier lingered. Fortunately, the soil along the banks of the Etowah River in northwestern Georgia was rich. While her husband oversaw the tilling of this fertile land, Rebecca Felton busied herself supervising the Negro household staff. For her leisure hours there were books and music. At 19 she gave birth to a son, who was named John. Two years later Mary Eleanor arrived, but died in infancy.

When, in January 1861, Georgia, the 13th colony to join the United States, seceded from the Union, the sound of cannons echoing over the hills from Rome was heard in Cartersville. For the Feltons the crisis was one of the mind as well as the heart. Dr. Felton was a secessionist. She was not. He volunteered as a surgeon. Sadly, she worked by his side, feeding and nursing the soldiers whose bleeding, broken bodies filled the W. & A. charnel cars bound for hospitals in Atlanta and beyond. Even though she steadfastly clung to her conviction that secession could—and should—have been avoided, she gradually accepted it as fact. "Like General Lee," she said, "I could not fight against our kindred in a struggle that meant life or death to them."

As the fighting in the spring of 1864 reached Dalton, 50 miles to the north, the Feltons left their home in the care of 15 slaves and fled south with their two sons, "Johnny," now 10, and 5-year-old William Harrell, Jr., to a barnlike house in an isolated pine grove on the Monticello Road near Clinton. They were not to return until the late summer of 1865, four months after the surrender at Appomattox. To finance their homeward journey by rail and to cover the cost of transporting the caskets containing the bodies of the boys, both of whom had succumbed to infectious diseases, Mrs. Felton sold the handsome paneled family carriage. Before the war it had cost $600 in gold; at auction it brought a mere $100 in greenbacks.

"When I reached the gate of our house, I picked up the springs that had been a part of my dead baby's fine carriage; then the arm of a mahogany chair that had been also burned. Desolation and destruction were everywhere; bitter, grinding poverty—slaves all gone, money too" is the way Rebecca Felton described what had happened because of a war she still believed should never have been allowed to begin.

In adversity and grief, the Feltons faced the raw truth that the Old South was forever gone. Together they opened a school in the Cartersville Methodist Church and sought other people willing to help them teach 80 pupils. Their objectives were twofold: to do something for young people who had been deprived of formal education during most of the conflict and to earn enough capital to restore their home and acquire farm labor.

Despite the travails of Reconstruction, which every day tore into the lives of men, women, and children, Mrs. Felton drew from her nature the will to wage a constant campaign against what she believed to be the evil of strong drink—an obsession unquestionably derived from her mother's dedication to the temperance cause. In 1869 she gave birth to a third son, Howard Erwin. Paul Aiken followed in 1871, but died a few months later.

As the fabric of Georgia society, shredded first by "Reb" invaders and looters, then by rapacious carpetbaggers, was gradually rewoven, sectional prejudices—particularly the fear of Negro domination—seemed still to blind the political judgment of both officeholders and officeseekers. In 1874, dissident Democrats in the 7th Congressional District, searching for a strong, progressive leader, persuaded Dr. Felton to run as an Independent. With his candidacy Mrs. Felton's political career began.

In an interview with Irma Dooly of the *Atlanta Constitution,* Rebecca Felton described how she "was shot into politics":

> From the beginning to the end, I was in the thick of my husband's campaign. Without a daily newspaper and [with] only two little weeklies, that hot convass was made by Dr. Felton on the stump and my individual work with my pen. I wrote hundreds of letters all over fourteen counties. I wrote night and day, and for two months before the close kept a man and a horse at the door to catch every mail train three miles away. . . . The like of this campaign was never known before or since in Georgia. At one time my health broke down, but I was propped up in bed with pillows and wrote ahead. I made appointments for speaking, recruited speakers, answered newspaper attacks, contracted for the printing and distribution of circulars and sample ballots, and more than all, kept a brave face to the foe and a smiling face to the almost exhausted candidate.

The congressional count was in doubt three entire days. Dr.

Felton "won" and "lost" time and again, and the wires were kept hot to know the result. At last he came in, in spite of all, with an eighty-two majority.

Success proved a great tonic. It was all Mrs. Felton needed to "be up and ready" for what became six years of part-time duty in "Washington City." As her husband's private secretary and clerk, she worked from their comfortable rooms in the Victorian-style National Hotel three blocks from the Capitol—"the Pennsylvania Avenue hostelry," she reminded the folks back home, "where Henry Clay once lived." She answered mail, kept track of the House calendar and the committees and legislation in which her husband was particularly interested, edited his speeches, and reported on life in Washington for two Atlanta newspapers. Gaining confidence in her professional capacities, she welcomed the opportunity to display her efficiency and government connections, especially to constituents. Constant attention to their wishes earned her the title "our Second Representative from the Seventh." It was a verity, for she became so proficient in handling matters that it was difficult to tell where her work ended and Dr. Felton's began.

During the fiery campaign for re-election that Dr. Felton waged through the searing summers and into the autumns of 1876 and 1878, her role turned out to be almost more controversial than the issues. She spent many months traversing the district with her husband. In a roomy, made-to-order buggy, she went with him into almost every county. Political rallies were rough, coarse affairs not considered fit for the eyes or ears of Georgia ladies. Consequently, her presence at the "all-day speakings" was denounced by the overwhelmingly Democratic press. Bluntly, editorials called her attendance a "disgusting spectacle" and insinuated she should take to heart the old maxim that "the dirty work of politics should be confined to men."

"I did not stop to think what a change this was for a young woman considered only an ornament and household mistress," she confessed. Comparing herself with Madame Roland, the intellectual Girondist whose frequent public appearances with her husband were a powerful inspiration to French revolutionists, she offered no apology for her activism. Rather, she told her detractors that they should look upon "the presence of ladies at the hustings" as the "crowning poetical feature of the male feasts."

During both campaigns, Mrs. Felton set another precedent— the prototype of modern-day teas and coffee hours presided over by wives of candidates. When her husband was tired and needed rest, she met his friends in hotel parlors or piazzas and gave them quotable facts to pass on to neighbors and other potential voters.

Dr. Felton's re-elections to the 45th and 46th congresses were due in no small measure to the counsel and aid he received from his talented, zealous wife. She had a special flair for sharp, slashing prose. Her sentences cut like razor strokes; in editorial controversy she was a deft and deadly foe. Dr. Felton's enemies were frequently the butt of unladylike epithets, which she felt they deserved: "political gymnast," "dirty dog," "fourth-rate lawyer." Her eyes would flash and her thin lips tighten as she retaliated against party-line Democrats, the anti-Felton newspapers, and the political bosses who denounced her husband as a "Yankee ally," a "disgrace to his clerical calling," or a "hospital rat who never wore the grey uniform." Labeling the allegations "slander," she called each perpetrator a "consummate liar."

In an attempt to silence her, the Democratic press announced that her signed articles had deprived her of a Southern lady's immunity to criticism. "There is a nobler, higher sphere for women," editors said. "Fill it!" One editorial asked sarcastically, "Which Felton Is the Congressman and Which the Wife?"

When Dr. Felton lost in 1880 to a Democrat who did not campaign, some said it was because his wife had no target at which to toss her stinging barbs. There was a modicum of truth in the statement, for the Democrats, aware they could not prevail against her husband's unassailable record in Congress, his thundering oratory, and Rebecca's powerful pen, later admitted they had gone out of their way to avoid a "mud-slinging contest with the parson and a woman" by choosing a political unknown. (Dr. Felton lost again in 1882—the year marked by the end of the Independent Party in Georgia.)

To expose what Mrs. Felton called the "whirling, howling dervishes" of the graft-infected Democratic hierarchy, the couple had launched a newspaper, the weekly *Cartersville Free Press* (the name was later changed to the *Courant*). In its columns she attacked corruption of many kinds, as well as the inhuman conditions in prison camps ("I'll shame my state until it closes these halls of Calcutta"). What she condemned most vehemently was the confining of female and juvenile lawbreakers in institutions housing hardened male criminals. At this time in Georgia history, babies were being born "on the chain," the offspring of convict mothers forced to submit to brutal guards and overseers. Although almost everyone in the state was afraid to encounter the vengeance of the political bosses responsible for the degrading and disgraceful prison practices, Mrs. Felton was not. Some years later, when the state finally began to segregate men and women prisoners and to place youthful offenders in reformatories, she considered these changes a personal victory.

Dr. Felton was chosen as a candidate for the Georgia Assembly and ran unopposed in October 1884. Suffering from palsy, he leaned more heavily than ever on Mrs. Felton, now generally accepted as his comrade in politics. Gradually she became more prominent than he—with political influence in her own right.

"When his enemies were training their guns on him, I obtained his permission to 'sharp shoot' them," she boasted. "It was a physical impossibility for him to draw a 'bead on his gun' every day in the week, but I enjoyed the *gunning,* and I kept my 'powder dry.' Whenever they showed their heads above the ramparts, this sharp-shooter deliberately picked them off for public amusement and feminine revenge."

During the three terms Dr. Felton served in the Statehouse, the fusillades aimed at his wife exploded with great frequency —in the form of sneers from the pulpit and jeers in print. Probably the worst billingsgate heaved at her came from Assemblyman E. G. Simmons of Sumter. While arguing against the prison reform bill on the floor of the House, he directed his invective almost solely in her direction. Rebecca Felton, for the specific purpose of rallying "numbers" to wage war on the notorious convict lease system, had sought and obtained the endorsement of the Woman's Christian Temperance Union for a resolution that Dr. Felton introduced in the legislature. This effort on her part, together with a by-line magazine article freighted with indictments against the convict lessees, so infuriated the Democrats that they decided to hit back hard. Assemblyman Simmons climaxed his attack with a reference to "the hand of the political *she* of Georgia," an obvious and only thinly veiled comparison of Mrs. Felton with the infamous *She* of Rider Haggard's novel.

It was only natural that when Dr. Felton retired from political life (he died in 1909), Mrs. Felton would decide to travel the reformer's route alone. With more opportunities for women appearing on the horizon as the 19th century faded into the 20th, she disregarded friendly advice to "avoid collisions" and sallied forth over the next two decades to speak forthrightly on issues big and small:

Motherhood: "We are told that 'the hand which rocks the

cradle rules the world.' I have lived in this world for over fifty years, but I find no evidence of rulership in the act of cradle-rocking. If it had been recorded that 'the hand which rocks the cradle' bears the burdens in the world, the connection between the truth and poetry would have been self-evident." —Address before the National Mothers' Congress, Washington, D.C., February 1897

Labor: "To leave the hundreds of women working in the factories like mere machines of manual labor while men are given the advantages of superior training is incongruous with laws of progress, relegating laboring women to a condition scarcely removed from slavery." —Interview in the *Atlanta Constitution,* 1899.

Women's Rights: "If husbands want everything neat and cheerful, let them pitch in and do some work and smiling of their own."—*Atlanta Journal,* 1900

Genetics: "It is a shame we take more pains in breeding cattle than in mating human beings. Men go a thousand miles to get the best grafts for orchards, but they allow the veriest scrubs to be grafted on the family tree." —"Message to the Twentieth Century," Atlanta Woman's Club, April 1901

Education: "You have patched and poulticed the system for thirty years. Why not try a remedy that will save the patient?" —"Infirmities of Our Public School System," address before a joint session of the Georgia General Assembly, Atlanta, November 1901

Marriage: "Our young women about to step into matrimony know less of themselves and what is involved in parental relations than any other subject. Why should [mothers] not instruct their daughters, aye, their sons, as the king's chamberlain tutored Esther before she was wedded to Ahasuerus?" —"The Problems That Interest Motherhood," Georgia Sociological Society, Atlanta, June 1902

Conscription: "As a result of what I saw during the Civil War, I am opposed to conscription for Georgia boys. I have no objection to volunteers going to France, but I am against forcing our soldiers into airships or sending them across the Atlantic Ocean to dictate to foreign governments or fight for kings or queens." —*Atlanta Journal,* 1917

Suffrage: "The Bible saying that 'a man and his wife are one' reads correctly, for man is the only one. . . . With education, property rights, and the ballot conferred on all Negro men who are not idiots or criminals, [why are] Southern women still [not permitted] to be enfranchised?" —*Country Life in Georgia in the Days of My Youth* (Atlanta: Index Printing Company, 1919)

At one point this woman who had grown up in the care of slaves and had owned them as a young homemaker also spoke on race. She told the *Atlanta Sun-American,* "Over fifty years of hard experience since the Civil War demonstrates one fact only: that the Negro is in the United States to stay, and according as he is dealt with depends our own peace or disaster in his association with the whites."

Although Mrs. Felton did not win every cause she championed, the firmness and fire of her relentless performance aroused a reasonable share of respect among many of the men who counted. They sent her as an official delegate to the Chicago Columbian Exposition (1892), to the Cotton States and International Exposition in Atlanta (1895), to the Tennessee Centennial in Nashville (1897), and to the St. Louis Exposition (1904). Had she not felt "too old to travel" in 1915 (she was 80), she would have represented Georgia at the San Francisco Exposition.

An invitation to address the State Legislature—the first ever extended to a woman in Georgia—reflected the esteem in which lawmakers held her. Unabashed pride welled within as she was welcomed by a standing ovation and heard Assembly President Clark Howell overrule one protesting member ("The time of this body is too precious and expensive to waste on permitting a female to speak.") and extol her intellectual competence: "There is a great deal of discussion and contention as to who is the smartest man in Georgia, but it is universally conceded that the woman who is to address you today is the brightest and smartest woman in the state."

Aboard the train enroute to Washington, D.C., and what she hoped would be her finest hour, Mrs. Felton recalled the long mental and physical miles she had traveled. White-haired, bespectacled, wrinkled of face and fragile of body, she had some regrets ("I am practical or I am nothing"). The last time she had made this northward journey (1919) was to celebrate congressional passage of the Woman Suffrage Amendment—only to return home to find the Legislature hurriedly assembling so that Georgia could be the first state to refuse ratification. As a counterbalance, she reviewed some of the successes. Particularly satisfying was the reputation she had earned as a formidable firing-line opponent of male domination in public life. She had met and matched the adversaries at her gate, and, if she had not totally bested them, she had at least achieved a tolerable stand-off.

What would be the disposition of those members of the Senate present for the third session of the 67th Congress? At the moment no one was sure. The *New York Times* had reported that a few senators planned to oppose her taking the oath because of the precedent it might set. On the other hand, the *Atlanta Journal* quoted a Republican as saying, "It will be a brave man that objects. I'm not a candidate for the job."

Vice President Calvin Coolidge gaveled the assembled 61 senators to order precisely at noon on November 20, 1922. Rebecca Felton, who had arrived more than an hour earlier amid cheers from the gallery crowded with women, occupied an absent member's chair alongside senior Georgia Senator William J. Harris. Adjournment came exactly 12 minutes later "out of respect to the memory of the deceased Tom Watson."

"I felt quite at home," Mrs. Felton told waiting reporters, "and I'll be back tomorrow." Smiling and peering through gold-rimmed spectacles glinting from under her black silk bonnet, she posed for photographers, holding aloft the certificate of confirmation she had carefully rolled in brown paper before leaving Cartersville.

Before returning to the Senate chamber the following day, she walked the short distance from the Lafayette Hotel to the White House to pay her respects to President Harding. Alone, they chatted about the St. Augustine conference and discussed some of the pressing problems in the South. She asked him, as a personal favor, to exercise caution with respect to his own safety. In her lifetime, three chief executives had been assassinated, and she frankly admitted she was "worried about him."

In Coolidge's absence, the second-day proceedings were opened by the President pro tempore, Albert B. Cummins of Iowa. Again all the gallery seats were occupied by women wearing the colors of their various feminine-rights organizations. Her only surviving son, Howard, recuperating from surgery, was also there. As she walked down the aisle, this time to occupy Watson's vacant seat, she turned and blew the onlookers a kiss.

She heard the commissions of two new senators from Pennsylvania and one from Delaware read, then listened intently as Harris solemnly stated her case: "I hope no senator will object to [Mrs. Felton's] taking the oath of office [which] will not in any way prejudice Mr. George's claim to the seat to which the people of Georgia have elected him."

Cummins ordered Senator Harris "to present the certificate of appointment."

"It is in the possession of the Secretary of the Senate," Harris replied.

"Mr. President" came a voice from the Democratic side of the floor. Cummins recognized Thomas J. Walsh of Montana, a man with a passion for facts and for the intricacies of law. Harris sat down.

Walsh spoke slowly, seriously:

> I am very sure there is no member of the Senate who does not desire to accord to this estimable and worthy woman the high honor of sitting even for a brief period as a member of this body, if he can do so consistently with his sense of duty. It would do very little credit, however, to this body or to her to admit her to membership if the Constitution, which we have all sworn to support by the oath she must subscribe to, forbids it. As very grave doubt has been cast upon her present right to take the oath by the public statement of the governor of her state, I venture to submit for the consideration of the Senate some reflections upon the subject.

Before he could continue, a message came from the House that the President was ready to speak. As the members left the floor to hear Harding plead for operational changes in the merchant marine, the women poured out of the galleries in a fighting mood. They were suspicious of Walsh's motives.

Mrs. Felton seemed unperturbed. During the President's address she sat near the center aisle between Harris and George, sometimes glancing at the acceptance-speech notes written on two small cards that she had withdrawn from her handbag.

The joint session having ended, Henry Cabot Lodge of Massachusetts proposed that those senators whose "commissions will provoke no discussion" be inducted. His motion carried. Then Walsh rose, only to be asked to yield by the stellar Republican from Idaho, William E. Borah, who wanted to insert a brief remark pertaining to Pueblo Indian land claims in New Mexico. Next, a lesser-known colleague asked to be heard. Walsh balked: "No; I object to the transaction of any business whatever until the pending matter shall have been disposed of. It is a question of high privilege."

The Senator from Montana steadily built up an argument against seating Mrs. Felton, citing first Clause 2 of the 17th Amendment, to which Senator-elect George had referred weeks ago in Georgia. Next, he read a ruling by Vice President Thomas R. Marshall in a 1918 letter to the financial secretary of the Senate. It stipulated that "the right of an appointee of the governor to the office, at least so far as the salaries of the clerks were concerned, expired on the night of a successor's election. Equitably, it would seem that an incumbent ought to be permitted to hold until the successor elected has been sworn in. . . . Such, however, is not the law."

Walsh then switched to the other side of the question: "While I have the very highest respect for the opinion of the late Vice President upon a subject like this, and we all know that his views upon similar questions were characterized by saving good sense, it is quite evident that he passed upon the question without consideration of the precedents of the Senate, which seem to me all important, indeed, controlling."

Explaining that "the province of the original Constitution was quite ambiguous as to the time when the right of an appointee ceased," Walsh cited a long list of cases, dating from the beginning of the federal government, that illustrated that "the uniform practice and course of the Senate" had been to uphold the right of an appointee "to sit until an elected successor presented his credentials." To further substantiate his argument, Walsh quoted Thomas Hart Benton, a U.S. senator for 30 years (1821–51) and a member of the Judiciary Committee:

I have been accustomed to see Senators who hold appointments . . . wait in their seats until their successors arrived. And I have seen them when their successors arrived, introduce them, get up and give them their seats and go out. It corresponds to what I think is due every State, what is due to the system of representation, that if there be any doubt at all in a question of this kind, the *benefit of that doubt* should be given to the State. She [the State] should have the benefit of a full representation up to the last moment. There should be no gap or interval. [Italics added.]

In conclusion, Walsh held up a volume entitled *Senate Election Cases.* "There is no instance since 1850," he said, "that any controversy was ever raised as to the right of the governor's appointee to sit and participate in the deliberations of the Senate until his or her successor appeared with the proper credentials."

Walsh emphasized to his colleagues that he had taken time to recall history and precedent because he did not want it to appear that, "if the lady is sworn in, the Senate had so far departed from its duty as to extend so grave a right to her as a favor, or as a mere matter of courtesy or being moved by the spirit of gallantry, but rather that the Senate, being fully advised about it, decided she was entitled to take the oath."

Silence. Not a single senator moved to rise.

The President pro tem asked the clerk to read Mrs. Felton's credentials. Mrs. Felton sighed, almost audibly, and a smile of satisfaction passed across her lips. Directed to proceed to the rostrum to be sworn in, she stood, lifted her floor-length black gown slightly and took Senator Harris's arm. Silence persisted throughout the chamber.

Her "I do" as she swore to uphold and defend the Constitution was clear and distinct. A burst of applause from the galleries followed, with the senators joining in. Cummins chose to ignore the Senate rule forbidding this kind of outburst. He ignored it again when, just before adjournment, hand-clapping followed a comment by Senator B. P. (Pat) Harrison of Mississippi that "It augurs well for this session of Congress that so soon after some of the recent political cyclones we should begin as we have today by seating a distinguished lady as the Senator from Georgia."

On her first day as a full-fledged senator there were no quorum calls and no matters calling for a vote, so Mrs. Felton did not have the opportunity to place her name in the "Yea" or "Nay" records. She wanted to speak, but the Senate was bent on finishing unfinished business. Well, after weeks of biding her time, she could wait another day.

At the Wednesday session, Senator Felton sat prim and erect in a seat now officially hers. She answered the roll call, crisply replying "Present" in contrast to the men's perfunctory "Here." She listened carefully to a message from the House about the signing of three enrolled bills. Then she rose and addressed the chair. Without a moment's hesitation, President pro tem Cummins recognized "The junior Senator from Georgia."

Looking like a tintype come to life, she began what was to be the first and last speech of her senatorial career:

Mr. President, in my very remarkable campaign in Georgia which, contrary to precedent, all came along after I was selected, one of the very amusing things that came to me by mail was a cartoon from San Antonio, Texas. The cartoon represented the United States Senate in session. The seats seemed to be fully occupied and there appeared in the picture the figure of a woman who had evidently entered without sending in her card. The gentlemen of the Senate took the situation variously. Some seemed to be a little bit hysterical, but most of them occupied their time looking at the ceiling. Over the cartoon was written "Will They Ask the Lady to Take a Chair?" I want to return my thanks to-day for the beautiful, hospitable welcome that you have ac-corded to the lady when you gave her a chair.

I also want to return thanks to the sober men of Georgia. Georgia was very slow in her promises with reference to wom-en's suffrage. She has been rapid to perform. For the first State in the Union of the forty-eight, one chivalric Governor went to the front and said: "Send that old lady there and let her look at the Senate for a short time." The Senator-elect from Georgia said: "She shall have her day there." And I want to thank him in his presence.

As she spoke, her voice reached all parts of the chamber. She held the note cards in her hand but ignored them, even when she forsook the somewhat whimsical for the very serious. Calling herself a "remnant of the old South who has never flick-ered in loyalty to her country," she assured her colleagues that she would not disgrace her commission. And she mentioned that millions of women voters had been heartened by the "romantic . . . historic event."

Addressing herself to the future, she looked intently at the senators and said gravely, "When the women of the country come in and sit with you, though there may be but a very few in the next few years, I pledge you that you will get ability, you will get integrity of purpose, you will get exalted patriotism, and you will get unstinted usefulness."

The applause was instant, spirited, and a long time dwin-dling. When it ended, Senator Harris presented the credentials of Walter F. George. He was sworn in immediately.

The last item of business before the morning session ended was the submission by Harris of Senate Resolution 366 direct-ing the Secretary of the Senate "to pay the Honorable Rebecca Latimer Felton the amount due her as a Senator from the State of Georgia: $287.67 for compensation from November 8 to 21, and $280 for mileage."

Home again in Georgia, ex-Senator Felton had no intention of sitting idly in front of the fire in her little gray house tucked away among the mountains. She became as concerned with young World War I veterans as she had been with old Con-federates. She campaigned against future involvement in for-eign alliances. She traveled—even to Washington again. She voted in every election, state and national, and urged other women to do likewise. She sorted and sifted her voluminous collection of diaries, letters, and other documents she planned to will to the University of Georgia. Among them, only one had never been made public.

It was discovered by a university archivist after Mrs. Felton's death from pneumonia on January 24, 1930, at age 94 in Atlanta, where she had gone earlier in the month on business related to the Georgia Training School for Girls. Labeled "this speech I never made," it consisted of remarks she had prepared in the event the Senate ruled against her taking the oath of office.

I have not the slightest intention to dictate to this honorable body as to the qualifications of its members, but I do feel inclined to say that I would like to rest a spell in one of your everyday, plain chairs, because it will mean so much to the women of America in the years yet to come. The voting women are intensely patriotic, but they are likewise blessed with long memories.

With ninety-five Senators on the roll of the Senate, the temporary presence of one woman Senator, who asks nothing but a hearty welcome and is pledged to hand you nothing more hostile than a cheerful good-bye, should be granted: not as a favor or a compliment, not as a bequest to a charity patient, not as a tribute to personal vanity, but as a tribute to the integrity, the patriotism and the womanhood of the blessed wives and mothers of our common country.

Then There Were Three

Considering the bruised state in which the 19th Amendment emerged after a trip through 36 all-male state legislatures, it was difficult to believe that anything less than getting women elected to the U.S. House and Senate would lead to realistic political equality. No matter how far-reaching the changes might be under the new law, they would not perform the miracles that suffragists had led the citizenry to expect. Yet the puzzling fact was that, almost as soon as the enfranchisement victory had been properly celebrated, all but a fraction of Carrie Chapman Catt's followers seemed indifferent to the question of female representation in Congress. Between 1920 and 1924, for example, fewer than a dozen women sought congressional seats. Of these, only three— Alice M. Robertson, Winnifred Mason Huck, and Mae E. Nolan —were successful, and not one of them was re-elected.

ALICE M. ROBERTSON
REPUBLICAN OF OKLAHOMA

The political wonder of the 1920 congressional elections was Alice Mary Robertson, a Republican. Scoring a stunning upset in consistently Democratic Oklahoma, she dislodged incumbent William W. Hastings to become the second woman to be seated in the House.

What set Miss Robertson apart from other female aspirants was her antisuffrage position. Exchanging a woman's privileges for a man's rights, she maintained, was too much like "bartering the birthright for a mess of pottage." But, once the issue had been settled by law, she decided to test it. "The men have thrust the vote on us and now I am going to see whether they mean it," she said in announcing her intention to enter the 2d District race.

An audacious approach perhaps, but Miss Alice, as she was affectionately called, had the pluck and backbone to do anything to which she had set her mind. When the Muskogee daily newspapers refused to support her candidacy, she bought space in the classified columns to publicize her positions on the issues. Her messages, printed in agate type, combined homely philosophy with not so mild partisanship:

> I'm glad not to see the wondrous beauty of flower-like cotton-fields today, nor gins with long processions of waiting wagons heaped with snowy fleece, for you may not see one without seeing also the haunting, almost hunted look of the farmer who is meeting sore disappointment in the price he gets. As a Republican I am glad that it is under a Democratic administration that this comes to pass, but after all, the fact that we are not responsible does not help the farmer. When he suffers, the whole foundation of our national life is assailed.

Weeks before the election, readers were turning first to the want-ad section to learn "what the woman candidate has to say tonight."

Miss Robertson hewed to an informal style of campaigning. "It's the handshaking that counts," she said. Many of the hands she shook were those of patrons in the Sawokla Cafeteria, the downtown Muskogee eatery she owned. If her appearance did not excite the voters, she clearly aroused their curiosity as she moved among the tables, remembering names, introducing herself, and passing out small cards bearing her signature and a homespun appeal for votes: "There are already more lawyers and bankers in Congress than are needed. The farmers need a farmer. I am a farmer. The women need a woman to look after their new responsibilities. The soldier boys need a proven friend. I promise few speeches, but faithful work. You can judge by past performance."

That performance was impressive. In her 66 years, college-educated Alice Robertson had been the first female clerk in the Indian Office of the Department of the Interior, a secretary at the Carlisle Indian School in Pennsylvania, an interpreter and a stenographer at tribal peace negotiations in Indian Territory (later eastern Oklahoma), founder of a school for children of the

Five Civilized Tribes (Cherokees, Chickasaws, Choctaws, Creeks, and Seminoles), a recruiter of cavalrymen for the Rough Riders of Spanish-American War fame, supervisor of all Creek schools, the postmaster of Muskogee, the architect of plans culminating in round-the-clock canteen service for transient World War soldiers, and the owner-manager of a successful 50-acre farm. She had also been saluted by President Theodore Roosevelt as "one of the great women of America."

Befitting one whose bloodline could be traced through 10 generations of Presbyterian ministers to Pilgrim, Puritan, and Scotch convenanters, Alice Robertson lived by a simple credo: She feared only God. Tullahassee Mission, where she was born in 1854 and grew up as one of four white children among nearly a hundred Creek students, was a parochial boarding school. Here, in Indian Territory, her morally exacting and spiritually stern missionary parents literally gave their lives serving the Lord. Of their offspring, only the lone son did not heed their admonition "to go forth and spread the Gospel among the Indians."

In Washington as in Oklahoma, Alice Robertson revealed herself for what she was: a spinster of spartan habits, compassionate yet uncompromising. Her face, a seamed reflection of prairie hardships, was framed by white hair brushed back and tightly knotted; it was considered newsworthy in the nation's capital that "she scorns the false and wears no switch." She was tall and stout. "Built on similar architectural lines as former Representative Champ Clark, she moves with the same deliberate tread," a *Washington Herald* reporter wrote. "One never knows quite what Miss Alice has on. Her costume is always black, and of a cut behind the prevailing mode."

Asked if she intended to shorten her skirts to conform with the new style of the twenties, she replied that all of her dresses would remain the same length—to the ankles. As for silk stockings, she had never owned a pair and never intended to. Nor did she aspire to "georgette waists."

For a freshman congresswoman, Miss Robertson had an unusual impact in the House, if for no other reason than because she had run on the campaign slogan "I cannot be bought, I cannot be sold, I cannot be intimidated" and was, therefore, free to speak and vote as her conscience dictated. Although loyal to her constituency, willing to listen and to change her mind, she was immovable when convinced she was right, not afraid to stick by an unpopular decision.

At the outset she incurred the wrath of the most esteemed

national women's organizations, including the Daughters of the American Revolution, of which she was a member, because of her refusal to support the Sheppard-Towner bill. This measure, originally authored by Jeannette Rankin, was allegedly designed to reduce the number of deaths of mothers and newborn infants —at an annual cost to the taxpayers of $1 million.

Miss Robertson shocked the bill's proponents by calling it "a lie of the sort that Ananias and Sapphira told—truth, but not the whole truth." To document her allegation, she cited the lack of adequate statistics:

> The "sob-stuff" claim that 680 babies die every day from the failure in enacting this bill . . . is absurd . . . quite in keeping with comparing Congressmen to Herod. A bill that does not provide medical or nursing attendance, or milk or baby clothes, or anything that would give immediate aid is not tangible help of the kind that the general public infer would be given, but the establishment of an autocratic, undefined, practically uncontrolled yet Federally authorized center of propaganda.

Like all conservative Republicans, she wanted the federal government to mind its own business. This philosophy prompted her to vote against the creation of a U.S. Department of Education. "Massachusetts does not object to colored children sitting in the same school seats with white," she said, "but Mississippi does." If a strong centralized power were to control educational affairs, she suggested, it would "not be long until we have a state church."

Her unqualified endorsement of some other important issues— higher tariff rates and stricter immigration quotas, for example —won bipartisan approval in Oklahoma, where many citizens had felt the economic pinch of the free-trade legislation enacted in 1913 and where, as in most other parts of the country, near hysteria was spreading against anything and everything foreign. She also endeared herself to the people back home by helping to obtain authorization for a veterans' hospital in Muskogee.

And Oklahoma Republicans beamed on learning she had been chosen to welcome Lord and Lady Astor when they paid an official visit to the nation's capital. When her supporters saw the newspaper photographs of Viscountess Astor, England's only woman member of Parliament, and Miss Robertson, America's only woman member of Congress, clasping hands at the National Press Club, it did not seem important that Miss Alice, in an ankle-length dress, sensible shoes, and unflattering turban, looked out of place beside Nancy Astor, the epitome of fashion in crepe gown, matching pumps, and plumed picture hat.

Although Alice Robertson passed a number of crucial tests, there was no assurance that she could be re-elected. The women's clubs had not forgiven her for the recalcitrant stand she had taken on the maternity and infancy bill; furthermore, Hastings was determined to reclaim the 2d District for the Democrats. Still, until the startling revelation that she would oppose payment of a bonus to World War veterans, there was general agreement that she had a "fighting chance."

Under heavy fire from everyone who remembered her promise to work in Washington "for our boys," Miss Robertson rushed to Muskogee to mend her political fences. She summarized her position this way:

> We cannot measure what veterans have done, least of all in money. We can give them a quit-claim deed if they want it, [but] the men of my ancestry didn't want it and didn't ask for it. I have been in close touch with those who know the finances of the country, and I know that the Treasury is practically empty. I voted against the Sheppard-Towner bill and I voted against the millions to Russia because I am against every appropriation we can do without. If a bank is broke, why give a check on it and make the check bad?

Her enemies were not placated. They continued their litany of censure. The Women's Auxiliary of the American Legion published a resolution condemning her as "unworthy of American womanhood." One veteran, who signed his letter "A Cripled [sic] Soldier," wrote, "A woman like you should not be a representative in Congress . . . it is time that the voters pricked up their ears."

They did. At the polls on November 7, 1922, 56-year-old William Hastings of Tahlequah, the Cherokee attorney she had defeated two years earlier, was elected by a plurality of 8,445 votes.

Satisfied that she had "kept the faith committed to me," Miss Robertson looked to the future: "I've been a Cinderella at 68," she said, "but now the pumpkin is round the corner waiting to whisk me back. God has better work for me, I am sure."

She addressed the House for the last time on March 3, 1923, the final day of the 67th Congress. Speaking as a member of the Indian Affairs Committee, she roundly criticized the federal government for failing to live up to its moral obligations to the Indians. Recalling her own participation in one of the tribal rituals that followed peace negotiations between the United States and the Five Civilized Tribes, she said, "As I could not smoke the resplendently decorated peace pipe . . . I was directed to lay it above my heart instead. I have kept watch through the years of the tribesmen with whom I took the peace obligation so long ago—an obligation never broken. I believe I am the sole remaining survivor."

During Miss Robertson's first campaign for office, she had remarked somewhat proudly, "I have always done a man's work, carried a man's burden, and paid a man's bills. Whenever I needed help in money matters, I got a man to advise me."

It is problematical whether a man's advice could have stemmed the tide of financial reverses she suffered during her postcongressional years. The bonus issue plagued her; it was the reason given for her ouster as a welfare worker at Muskogee Veterans' Hospital, a post to which she had been appointed by President Harding "in just recognition of her very great merits." Fire destroyed the tearoom she opened at Sawokla Farm; the *Muskogee Daily News,* for which she wrote a weekly column, failed; and a cutback in state appropriations at the onset of the Depression in 1929 terminated her job as a research assistant with the Oklahoma Historical Society. Had it not been for the generosity of relatives, friends, and a group of prominent citizens, she would have gone to her grave a pauper.

Although Miss Robertson was impoverished, her spirit was buoyed by the homage bestowed by a grateful state. The University of Tulsa conferred on her an honorary LL.D. degree. The Federation of Business and Professional Women's Clubs named her "Oklahoma's Most Famous Woman." Will Rogers made her the subject of one of his syndicated columns, "Ain't Old People Lovely?" And a formal proposal was submitted to the State Legislature, recommending that a statue of Alice Mary Robertson be placed near that of Sequoyah in the nation's Capitol. (In 1933, Oklahomans changed their minds: Will Rogers, in bronze, now stands in the National Statuary Hall Collection.)

When she died of cancer in 1931, among the messages received by her family was one from President Herbert Hoover, whom she had known when he was Secretary of Commerce. Referring to her as a "leader in education of Indian youth" whose life had been "rich in usefulness," he called attention to the fact that she was "a woman whose ancestry, idealism and outlook linked the pioneer past with the progress of the present."

WINNIFRED MASON HUCK
REPUBLICAN OF ILLINOIS

Having lived most of her early years in the shadow of the Capitol, Winnifred Mason Huck, 40, campaigned rather glibly, saying, "I'll know where to hang my hat in Congress." Not long after answering her first roll call as a GOP representative at large from Illinois in November 1922, she felt compelled to issue a qualifying statement: "But I never mentioned that I would know where I could go to powder my nose."

Although the "Men Only" sign in the House of Representatives had been removed when Jeannette Rankin arrived in 1917, no special amenities had been provided either for the Montanan or for the women who came later. Winnifred Huck was the first to call attention to the fact.

If the election of Mrs. Huck (without the expenditure of a single cent) to the four-month unexpired term of her deceased father, William E. Mason, left a certain segment of the electorate indifferent, it startled no one. As the daughter of "Billy" Mason, the spellbinding pacifist who had indicted the nation in 1917 for waging a "dollar war," she had a readymade following. Moreover, her pledge to devote legislative efforts "chiefly toward a constructive educational plan which will show the folly of war" carried a special appeal to the many newcomers joining the flourishing post-World War I peace movement.

Congresswoman Huck proposed a constitutional amendment that struck at the heart of the President's war-making powers. Its provisions would make a declaration of war impossible except by direct vote of the people. "In a country where the people control their government," she declared in her maiden speech, "there is no opportunity for a war to originate."

Should so iconoclastic an idea be adopted, the militarists argued, it could cripple the nation in an emergency. "An open invitation to any and all aggressors," one member of the House Foreign Affairs Committee labeled it.

"We women have a great deal to do," Senator Rebecca Felton said to Representative Huck when the two were introduced. "I am glad that you are young and strong." She might also have mentioned Mrs. Huck's courage and determination. It required these qualities and more in the early 1920s for a woman—even a congresswoman—to suggest that women merited a "new place in the sun."

Women differ from men only "as to what we believe to be the

more important issues before our country," Winnifred Huck told
her colleages.

> We are anxious . . . that marriage shall not take away the wom-
> an's right to choose her own citizenship; that married women
> shall not be discriminated against in the economic world; and
> that the mother shall have in all States an equal right with the fa-
> ther in the care, custody, and control of the child. We want a
> universal marriage and divorce law of the right sort. . . . Al-
> though we recognize the importance and absolute necessity of
> appropriation and tariff bills, we feel that these other issues are
> equally important and should not be put off year after year.

Music, art, and literature had been the chief interests of Chi-
cago-born (1882) Winnifred Sprague Mason before her marriage in 1904 to former classmate Robert Wardlow Huck, who
had been football captain at Western High School in Washington, D.C. When she became the political pride of Illinois wom-
en—the first wife and mother to sit in Congress—her civil-engineer husband and their four children agreed that she should
pursue a career in politics. Although she lost a special primary
race for the 2d District House seat in 1923, she hit the campaign
trail again (for congressman at large) in 1924. This time
Richard Yates, the incumbent, proved unbeatable. The best she
could do was place third.

From politics Winnifred Huck turned to investigative reporting. For the *Chicago Evening Post* she volunteered to examine
the much maligned correctional system. With the knowledge
and consent of Ohio Governor Vic Donahey and Cleveland District Court Judge Francis L. Stevens, she took an assumed
name, committed a theft, and was sentenced to six months in
the state prison at Marysville. Officially pardoned after serving
30 days, she wandered from city to city, through several states,
sometimes working as a waitress, a cook, or a chambermaid, only
to be discharged when it was discovered that she had a criminal
record. In a series of articles and lectures, she shared with readers and listeners answers to such timely questions as "Do Jails
Reform?" "Are Prisons Humane?" and "Can a Woman Convict
'Come Back'?"

Cancer confined Mrs. Huck to her home from 1931 until 1936,
when she entered Chicago's Presbyterian Hospital. Here, less
than a month before her 54th birthday, she died.

Winnifred Huck had to settle for less than she aspired to in
the political world. Yet, for the very brief time she was in office,
this fourth U.S. congresswoman demonstrated that motherhood

need not be a handicap—and could be an asset—in a profession for which fatherhood had long been a praiseworthy qualification.

MAE E. NOLAN
REPUBLICAN OF CALIFORNIA

When an unlikely coalition of influential San Francisco Republicans representing both business and labor first approached 36-year-old Mae Ella Nolan to run for the congressional seat left vacant by her deceased husband, they knew what kind of woman they were picking. She was quiet, pleasant, businesslike. In view of the fact that these characteristics do not make an ideal candidate, why did the GOP team pressure John Ignatius Nolan's widow to forsake her privacy in order to represent the 5th, or Mission, District? One candid opinion:

> The Nolan name means victory. There are two kinds of congressmen—those who are after pork pie for their own little districts, and those who go after a principle with a view to helping everybody in the long run. There are many of the former kind and few of the latter. Among them was "Johnny" Nolan. Among them, too, the voters know, will be Mae.

Like her late husband, an iron-molder by trade, the former Mae Ella Hunt was an offspring of Irish Catholic immigrants (County Mayo) who had settled in the port city on the Golden Gate. Her early life revolved around the home (a six-room apartment on the corner of Asbury and Frederick Streets), school (St. Vincent's), and church (Star of the Sea). A course at Ayres Business College prepared her for a stenographer's position with Wells Fargo Express, where she was working when she met Johnny Nolan.

The year was 1912, and he had just been elected to Congress on the Bull Moose ticket. They were married the following spring and spent their honeymoon aboard a steamer bound for Washington via the Panama Canal. Congressman Nolan was 39; his petite, auburn-haired, brown-eyed bride, 26.

When Mrs. Nolan went to Capitol Hill on her own in 1923 (to finish John Nolan's unexpired term in the 67th Congress and the subsequent full term to which he had been elected 11 days before his death), she took with her active support from the Labor Party, government employees, and women, as well as from liberal Republicans. To manage the Washington office, she took her only sister, Theresa Hunt Glynn, who had been Nolan's secretary for six years.

Widespread publicity was given to Congresswoman Nolan's selection as the first woman to chair a House committee: Expenditures in the Post Office Department. To the fledgling congresswoman, however, her appointment to the Labor Committee took precedence over everything else. As chairman of this committee, John Nolan had presided over hearings on his bill to provide a minimum wage of $3 a day for 120,000 federal workers. From a front-row seat she had listened as charwomen, janitors, gravediggers from the national cemeteries, papercutters, and a host of others described what it was like to live on $40 a month, the government scale in the early 1920s for eight hours six days a week.

"I want to do what I can to see this great humanitarian measure enacted into law," she told Washington well-wishers. As a freshman member, she would have a small voice, but she counted on being heard as John Nolan's widow. Defending the measure, she said that the day laborers were "totally defenseless: prohibited by law from striking or moonlighting, they are forced to accept sub-human salaries." The House listened—to her and to other proponents—and passed the bill. In the Senate, however, a Southern faction bent on maintaining cheap labor in Dixie defeated it.

"Politics is entirely too masculine to have any attraction for feminine responsibilities," Congresswoman Nolan said in announcing her decision to shake from her heels "the political dust of Washington." Her 10-year-old daughter, Corliss, did not like boarding school. "On the West Coast we can have a normal home life," Congresswoman Nolan said, explaining her desire to return to California, "and I can play golf and bridge and do other things I enjoy."

At the time of Mrs. Nolan's election a political analyst had remarked, "Womankind has taken another step in her slow but steady march to human equality." But had she? Mae Nolan was, in a sense, a political accident—a widow whose claim to office was her late husband's name and reputation.

High Ground

Before the mid-1920s anyone searching for an emerging pattern among U.S. congresswomen had to be disappointed. It would never be fair to judge them as a bloc, but the three elected to the 69th Congress (1925–27) were similar in one respect: They shared a deep commitment to national defense. There were no pacifists among them. And, though there was no way of knowing it at the time, Representatives Florence Prag Kahn, Mary Teresa Norton, and Edith Nourse Rogers were destined to explode the one-term-only stereotype and meet the tenurial men on their own high ground.

FLORENCE P. KAHN
REPUBLICAN OF CALIFORNIA

One question on the University of California entrance examination in 1883 baffled 14-year-old Florence Prag. It referred to Sir Francis Bacon, whose name was unfamiliar to this daughter of Jewish immigrants. Rather than leave the query unanswered, she wrote, "The tenets of my faith prohibit me from knowing anything about bacon." The faculty board agreed that a youngster with that much aplomb could do college work.

This incident reveals why Florence Prag acquired a legendary reputation as a ready wit and later became an overnight hit on the congressional stage.

Her political odyssey was pure American romance: Witty poor girl rises from obscurity to national prominence in a land of goals unlimited. After starting her career as a teacher of high school English and mathematics in San Francisco, a city where it was possible for her widowed mother to take the giant step from classroom to board of education caucus room, Miss Prag became the wife of Julius Kahn, a Broadway actor turned congressman, served as his unsalaried aide from the turn of the century until his death in 1924, and, at age 57, went to Congress herself.

"Old lady Kahn," her critics called her. "She's merely Julius's widow. Robert Dollar [the steamship magnate] and the Fleishhacker brothers [banking tycoons Herbert and Mortimer] own her." Florence Kahn's first election victory probably was a tribute more to her late husband than to herself. But there is no doubt that her subsequent triumphs at the polls were her own. Although many wealthy San Franciscans were her friends, no one owned her. She left the Golden Gate pledged "to no man and to no thing," and from the beginning to the end of her 12-year tenure in the House she demonstrated rare independence.

Mrs. Kahn's first weeks in Congress offered a microcosm of the new approach she brought with her. When committee appointments were parceled out and she was named to Indian Affairs, she broke tradition by refusing to accept the assignment. "The only Indians in my district are in front of cigar stores," she told the Republican caucus, "and I can't do anything for them." She compromised on Education but badgered party leaders until they assigned her to Military Affairs, the committee of which her husband had been chairman. During her third term, as the result of a precedent-shattering move by party chieftains, she became the first woman named to the powerful Appropriations Committee.

Nothing in Mrs. Kahn's personal life dimmed the image of independence that she manifested in public. Her appearance reflected no effort at compromise with the dictates of fashion. She refused to have a permanent wave, preferring to push her gray hair up in a loose, untidy coil inside a net on top of her head. Her hats were often askew. She scorned dieting. Yet she was continually a center of attraction—and not only on the House floor. Gallery spectators came "to hear the latest Kahn quips." Once asked to explain her enormous popularity, she smiled, brown eyes twinkling. "Sex appeal," she replied.

A legend gradually grew around her: "It's possible to predict how she's going to vote, but only God has the slightest ink-

ling of what she's going to say." When New York's reform-minded
Fiorello LaGuardia called her "nothing but a stand-patter following reactionary Senator Moses" (George H. Moses of New
Hampshire), Mrs. Kahn wriggled out of her seat and scored a
perfect put-down: "Why shouldn't I choose Moses as my leader?
Haven't my people been following him for ages?" On another
occasion pious William David Upshaw, Democrat of Georgia,
referred to opponents of a national movie-censorship measure
as unclean. "Don't you dare call *me* unclean," objected opponent Kahn. The virtuous ladies who accused her of having been
influenced by a San Francisco motion picture executive, were,
according to a Capitol Hill onlooker, "left gasping." "Of course
I have been," Florence Kahn told them. "Look at him [he was
young and handsome] and tell me if I'm to blame."

For all her lighthearted banter, she was a no-nonsense legislator. As the *Pictorial Review* pointed out, "Congress treats her
like a man, fears her, admires her and listens to her." In 1929,
for example, it was evident that semi-isolated San Francisco
could expand economically only if it was linked to Oakland by
a bridge. While Mrs. Kahn readied the necessary legislation, the
Navy Department, which feared that the $75 million appropria-
tion might mean less money for shipbuilding, readied its torpe-
does. Because a bridge over any navigable waterway required
the unanimous consent of Congress, Florence Kahn needed a
host of allies. She got them and the city got the Bay Bridge.

Other public works she obtained for the 4th District, a part
of San Francisco that cut across all economic classes, embracing
Chinatown and the Italian North Beach section as well as affluent Pacific Heights and the downtown business and financial
areas, included more port facilities, more federal office buildings, more air and naval stations, more hospitals—even a dirigi-
ble base.

At a time in U.S. history notable for the flowering of a peace
movement, Florence Kahn was a forceful champion of a strong
military force. "Preparedness," she said, "never caused a war,
unpreparedness never prevented one." Guided by granite convictions concerning patriotism, she insisted that those who had
made personal sacrifices for their country be recognized. Part of
the Kahn legislative legacy was a congressional act creating the
Gold Star Mothers.

A mother herself (two sons), Mrs. Kahn believed firmly in
women's rights, though she was not an activist in the same sense
as Jeannette Rankin. "My mother's philosophy," says Julius Kahn,
Jr., a San Francisco attorney, "was that more women should in-

telligently exercise the rights they had been granted." In a prepared speech delivered at the Waldorf Astoria Hotel, the congresswoman told Republican women planning to campaign for public office that they had a responsibility "to obliterate sex in politics." The real strength, she said, "lies in the individual." Paraphrasing a statement by her friend Associate Supreme Court Justice Oliver Wendell Holmes, she declared, "I think the time has come to spread the gospel not what the Government should do for the citizen, but what the citizen should do for the Government." (A generation later Holmes's words would be "borrowed" by another, better-known politician. John Fitzgerald Kennedy, in his 1961 inaugural address, exhorted "fellow Americans" to "ask not what your country can do for you—ask what you can do for your country.")

By plausible coincidence, another Supreme Court Justice—Harlan F. Stone, one of her neighbors at the Mayflower Hotel—was the inspiration for another of her speeches. The year was 1932, and she was a member of the Appropriations Subcommittee on the Judiciary. Kidnaping had grown to something of an epidemic, dramatized most notoriously by the Lindbergh affair. With Stone (who, as Attorney General in 1924 had appointed 29-year-old J. Edgar Hoover Director of the Federal Bureau of Investigation) as her mentor, she drew up legislation to widen the venue of the FBI. To the arguments she presented before the House, columnists and editorial writers responded with more than the usual thunder pro and con. Some of it sounded as if Armageddon lay just over the horizon.

She was accused of laying the foundation for a national police force and taking the first step toward dictatorship. "Ridiculous," Florence Kahn replied. "I'm speaking for the nation's mothers who demand protection for their children." In record time Congress enacted a package of major anticrime bills (including the Lindbergh Act, which made kidnaping a federal crime punishable by death) that struck away many of the legal fetters that had kept the FBI more or less impotent. Her chief contribution —a continuing one—was fiscal. The House went along with subcommittee recommendations that Director Hoover be granted sufficient funds to professionalize law enforcement. Hoover, widely reputed to be a misogynist, astounded everyone by publicly proclaiming Mrs. Kahn "The Mother of the FBI." (In posthumous respect, he paid her another singular tribute by serving as an honorary pallbearer at her funeral in 1948.)

Florence Kahn's first six political years looked like a walk. There was a sheen of inevitability about the way she regularly

won re-election. And in the 1932 Democratic electoral landslide she not only emerged unscathed but rolled up the biggest
plurality of her career—more than 55,000 votes. Press speculation had her on a sure track for the Senate. "No use kidding myself," she said. "I couldn't make it."

Not until the 1934 off-year elections, when a mere 103 Republicans were elected to the 435-member House, did the 4th District begin to reflect the national trend. Her plurality that year
over Chauncey Tramutolo, a perennial Democratic contender,
dwindled to 3,620. With the cresting of the New Deal wave in
1936, she was trapped. Frank R. Havenner, a newspaperman
who ran as both a Democrat and a Progressive, topped her in
the runoff by more than 20,000 votes.

Until a heart attack invalided her in 1942, Florence Kahn remained active in public life. She was women's division chairman
of the 1939 Golden Gate Exposition and cochairman for northern California of the American Women's Voluntary Service (a
World War II citizens' organization).

A few days before her 80th birthday in 1946, she granted a
press interview—her first in a decade. In the living room of her
Nob Hill apartment, against a backdrop of photographs autographed by every President from William McKinley to Franklin
Roosevelt, she appeared very thin. But her eyes were bright, and,
as *San Francisco Chronicle* reporter Tedd Thomey discovered
immediately, age had not dulled her wit. "I know why you're
here," she said. "You want to do my obituary."

MARY T. NORTON
DEMOCRAT OF NEW JERSEY

Mary Teresa Norton, the first Democratic congresswoman and
the first to be elected in the East, was, at 49, a handsome, full-
figured New Jersey matron with flashing dark eyes and energy
to match. She also had the right qualifications for political success. Yet her triumph sprang not so much from her recognized
ability as from Boss Frank Hague's powerful, smooth-running
Democratic machine.

"I had no political background whatsoever when I first entered public life," she told Frank Buckley of the *Washington
Post* after the 1924 elections. "I had not been a suffragist; not
that I did not believe in the cause, but because I was too occupied otherwise. After the death of my only child, a boy, I sought
to assuage my grief in work for children." A series of volunteer
jobs honed and broadened her organizational skills. She ex-

panded day nursery facilities in Hudson County; during World War I she helped administer a Knights of Columbus canteen at Camp Merritt and served as chairman of a large Red Cross unit.

All of her accomplishments were known to Hague when, as president of the Day Nursery Association of Jersey City, she paid him an official visit (he was then mayor of Jersey City) to ask that municipal funds be allocated to the welfare work in which she was involved. The timing of their meeting was fortuitous for both. Tennessee had just cast the ratifying vote for the 19th Amendment. Mary Norton departed with the assurance that financial aid would be forthcoming; the mayor, watching her leave, knew he had found the right person to head his women's organization.

"When Mayor Hague sent for me in 1920 to ask if I would allow my name to go on the Democratic State Committee, I had no thought of a career in politics," she told reporter Buckley. "I accepted only because I felt under obligation for the response to my appeal for the nursery. As a committeewoman I was abruptly cast into a pool of public service and had either to sink or swim."

Swim she did—sometimes through choppy waters, always upstream. The records she established along the way included a host of firsts—first woman elected a New Jersey freeholder (1922); first to chair three House committees: District of Columbia (1931–37), Labor (1937–46), and Administration (1949–51); first to serve as a state party chairman (1932–35 and 1940–44); first to be cochairman of a national party Platform Committee (1944) and chairman of the Credentials Committee (1948).

Had she not declined the honor, she would have been nominated for Vice President of the United States in 1932. "Women deluged me with letters criticizing me for what they regarded as a betrayal of the cause of women," she said, after the Democratic National Convention in Chicago, "but they did not know that a majority had agreed on John Nance Garner [Texas Democrat and Speaker of the House], and, in such circumstances, my nomination would have been just a grand gesture."

Hague never denied the accusation that he had pushed Mrs. Norton's political career "to give respectability to his machine politics." That she became more than a figurehead to attract feminine votes evidently pleased him. They remained lifelong friends. To the end, she insisted that Mayor Hague "never asked me to vote a measure in Congress."

He did not have to. For a number of reasons, some political, more religious, all very human, the two held similar views. Frank Hague always hated Prohibition. Mary Norton introduced the first constitutional amendment to repeal the Volstead Act. Neither the mayor nor the congresswoman, owing to the tenets of their faith, could condone contraception. At the hearings on the Gillett bill favoring liberalized laws on birth-control information, she was one of 17 who spoke in opposition. ("The dissemination of birth control literature would be unnecessary if men and women would practice self-control.") Both Hague and Congresswoman Norton stumped for Alfred E. Smith during the 1932 preconvention Presidential campaign and tried to stop Franklin D. Roosevelt. When Hague later swung to the New Deal, Mary Norton followed.

The Mary Norton–Al Smith friendship was rooted in their shared obsession with social reform. "She fought for the underdog," Eleanor Roosevelt once wrote. "A champion of human rights and an ardent advocate of the cause of welfare" is the way New Jersey Representative Peter W. Rodino, Jr., remembers her. "We nicknamed her 'Battling Mary' out of genuine admiration."

To bring about social reforms, as well as to prosper politically, Mary Norton made use of her own boundless energy and still legendary powers of persuasion and phrasemaking. In reply to a colleague who agreed to "yield to the lady," she snapped, "I'm no lady; I'm a member of Congress, and I'll proceed on that basis." When Representative Frank L. Bowman, Republican of West Virginia, remarked at the opening of the initial meeting of the House District Committee over which she presided, "This is the first time in my life I have been controlled by a woman," her comeback was "It's the first time I've had the privilege of presiding over a body of men, and I rather like the prospect."

Although serving as the unofficial mayor of the nation's capital was, in the 1930s, called the "most thankless job in Washington"—it brought no political reward, no involvement with bills important to constituents—Mary Norton welcomed the assignment as a "high honor and privilege." Characteristically, she referred to the more than 400,000 voteless citizens of the District of Columbia as her "adopted people" and pledged "to seek home rule for democracy's stepchildren."

Her efforts to get the vote for Washingtonians failed, as did a resolution she introduced to stiffen penalties imposed on District prostitutes who solicited from cruising limousines. She suffered another setback when her proposition to legalize gambling, "since experience seems to have demonstrated the impossibility of stamping it out," was turned down. But, by demonstrating a remarkable facility in cutting through red tape, she succeeded in such unglamorous tasks as improving public transportation and cleaning up the capital's slums. She also secured passage of the first old-age pension bill for District of Columbia residents and a $1.5 million appropriation to build Glenn Dale Hospital for tubercular children.

The refreshing affection that District leaders and ordinary citizens held for Mary Norton was not manifested by the local aristocracy. "To snooty Washington society she is a business school graduate, Tammany and Catholic," Duff Gilfond wrote in *American Mercury,* "and hence unacceptable." But social Washington interested Congresswoman Norton not at all. Although friendly and gregarious, she had not come to the national capital to engage in what she called "fripperies." Her congressional life—all 26 years of it—was programed in such a way that relaxation was included only as an afterthought. Unless invited to the White House, she spent her evenings reading—usually congressional reports, but occasionally detective stories. On weekends when she did not return to Jersey City, her favorite pastime was to drive through the countryside of neighboring Maryland and Virginia. Guests at her Washington apartment were restricted to political callers, for whom she sometimes prepared a simple meal featuring chicken or lamb chops.

The brisk tempo Mary Norton maintained on Capitol Hill was merely an extension of the pace set in the middle-class environment in which she grew up. The second of five children born to Thomas and Marie Shea Hopkins, naturalized citizens who had emigrated from County Langford, Mary Teresa was only 17 when her mother died. For the ensuing five years she was the manager of a household that included two younger sisters and a brother. After completing her formal education at the Packard Business School in New York City, she worked as a stenographer in Manhattan until her marriage in 1909 (at age 34) to Robert Francis Norton, a longtime friend associated with a Jersey City wholesale cooperage firm. To the delight of feminists, he raised no objection to his wife's entering politics. He did, however, deplore "losing a good cook."

Widowhood was thrust on Mrs. Norton not long before she became eligible, in accordance with the seniority system, to accede to the Labor Committee chairmanship, a post made vacant by the death of William P. Connery of Massachusetts. In 1925, when, as a freshman in Congress she was assigned to this

committee, it was not particularly active or important. Could
Southern conservative Democrats have then known how powerful it would become later on, they would have blocked the appointment of a woman, particularly one as inflexible and persistent in the pursuit of social reform as Mary Norton.

Even after she announced that she would resign as chairman
of the District Committee in order to move into the labor slot,
Southerners tried to persuade her to reconsider. She agreed to
confer with their spokesman, House Speaker William Bankhead
of Alabama, but her mind was made up. "I represent a labor
district [Jersey City and Bayonne], and I feel the people of
that district have more claim on me than do the people of the
District of Columbia or anyone else," she said. "They have returned me to Congress seven times. I would indeed be ungrate-
ful if I did not take advantage of the opportunity better to
serve them."

With the committee chairmanship, Mary Norton inherited the
most difficult professional assignment of her 62 years: pushing
Roosevelt's stiff wage and hour bill past an unsympathetic Rules
Committee and through a recalcitrant House. To the infighting
she faced, the media added the ingredient of sexual bias. *Newsweek*'s assessment was typical:

> The opposition is determined, numerous and powerful; to over-
> come it, the bill's proponents need canny leadership and an un-
> broken front. They have neither. . . . Mrs. Mary T. Norton is
> charming and able. . . . But she gave nearly all of her time
> to the District; she doesn't know much about organized labor and
> its relations with industry.
>
> A great deal depends on the parliamentary skill, the capacity
> for rough-and-tumble debate, of the person piloting a controversial
> measure. Many of the labor bill's friends doubt that Mrs. Norton
> has that capacity. . . .
>
> "She'll try to shriek at 'em, sure as hell," one Congressman pre-
> dicted.
>
> . . . Her face pales and tightens at any suggestion that she
> can't do the job herself. Proud that she holds the best post any
> Congresswoman has ever had, proud that she and Secretary of
> Labor Frances Perkins share two of the Federal Government's
> key positions in labor relations, she is going to hold the fort for
> womanhood.

It was not womanhood for which she held the fort but blue-
collar workers. Seeking a 25-cent minimum wage and time and
a half for hours over 40 a week, at one point she went on the
air nationwide to urge the electorate to pressure Congress. "All
of those who are working under substandard conditions are pray-

ing for passage of the bill," she told listeners. "The prayers and petitions of 2 million people must not go unanswered."

To force the measure out of committee, she resorted to a rarely used and seldom successful parliamentary device, the discharge petition. Although she was able to convince the prescribed number of colleagues (half the total membership of the House, plus one) to sign the petition, the bill failed to pass. Undaunted, she started anew. Again she collected the 218 signatures and again she campaigned for support. This time she was successful. The Fair Labor Standards Act of 1938, which placed a floor under wages and a ceiling over working hours, has been called a landmark in labor's progress toward maturity and power. (Later she was instrumental in raising the minimum wage to 75 cents an hour.)

Mrs. Norton's interest in labor affairs never waned, but, when the Republicans organized the House in 1947, she resigned from the Labor Committee, brusquely stating that she had "no respect" for its new chairman (Fred H. Hartley of New Jersey, cosponsor of the Taft-Hartley bill). "He has attended only 10 meetings of this committee in 10 years," she said. "I refuse to serve under him. It would be too hard on my blood pressure."

Two years later, from a hospital where she was critically ill with pneumonia, she sent word, scrawled on the back of an envelope, that she would not be a candidate for re-election in 1950. In her 12th term and almost 75, she said her health would not permit another campaign. There was lively speculation that she would be appointed a District commissioner. Instead, she became a consultant on womanpower at the Department of Labor. In 1952 she took leave not only of Washington but also of her native Jersey City and settled in Greenwich, Connecticut, where a sister lived.

On at least one occasion before her retirement Mary Norton said publicly that she planned to write a book—a "volume of memoirs and comments on my experiences." She died in 1959, leaving trunks full of papers but not the promised autobiography. It would have been a book to reveal, in unparalleled detail, the political texture of the twenties, thirties, and forties, and to shatter the myth that a woman's place is not in the House.

EDITH NOURSE ROGERS
REPUBLICAN OF MASSACHUSETTS

Fittingly, the first New England congresswoman was a direct descendant of Priscilla Mullens ("Speak for yourself, John"), a

Pilgrim who arrived in Plymouth aboard the *Mayflower*. Massachusetts Representative Edith Nourse Rogers was a composite of early American virtues. She was also ebullient, a gifted bargainer, and utterly beguiling. Although her political career was enhanced by these attributes, it was not launched because of them. As the widow of a congressman, she was the strongest candidate the politicians could put forward on short notice.

Her husband, John Jacob Rogers, was beginning his seventh term in the House when he died in March 1925. After some urging from political leaders and friends, Mrs. Rogers agreed to be the GOP nominee in the special June election. Her Democratic opponent, former Governor Eugene N. Foss, was a tested politician, but he had little chance of winning in the predominantly Republican 5th District (Middlesex County) against a gallant, sorrowing widow who proved to be an unusually effective campaigner. Whether Edith Rogers won on sentiment or merit, or a combination of both, her victory was impressive. She attracted a larger proportion of the total vote than incumbent John Rogers had in the 1924 general election and defeated Foss by a margin of better than 2-to-1.

If chic Congresswoman Rogers, whose brown hair frosted with white was the only indication she had reached her 44th birthday, fitted the popular image of a materially privileged American, it was because she had been reared in an affluent household, presided over by a Lowell textile manufacturer, and educated at Rogers Hall and Madame Julien's in Paris. But she was by no means preoccupied with wealth or social status.

Childless when the United States declared war in 1917 and her husband absented himself temporarily from Congress to enlist in the field artillery, she went overseas with a contingent of civilian volunteers. While the suffrage movement was attracting its largest following, Edith Rogers could be found either on the early morning shift at the YMCA Eagle Hut in London or in a Red Cross uniform caring for wounded soldiers in France. Back in Washington, she became the first Gray Lady in the nation's capital, where her tireless service to disabled veterans earned her the title "Angel of Walter Reed."

Presidents took note. In succession, Harding, Coolidge, and Hoover named her their personal representative to hospitalized veterans. As a $1-a-year appointee she crisscrossed the nation —often by plane—popping up unexpectedly on wards to ask patients if they had any complaints. Many did, and Mrs. Rogers took them personally to the White House. A generation later, as a member of the Foreign Affairs Committee, she toured U.S.

military hospitals in Europe. In the course of a visit to Italy, German bullets whistled past her. To that extent, she became a veteran herself.

Sooner or later members of Congress stake out legislative territory that they treat with a kind of proprietary instinct. What evolves from the territory in question depends on their motives, the amount of power they acquire, and how they wield that power. It was not happenstance that Congresswoman Rogers selected an area of jurisdiction—the veteran—that was more humanitarian than political. By the time she became chairman of the Veterans' Affairs Committee in 1947, her legislative skill was a legend. The most impressive, though not the best-known, bill bearing her name was for a $15 million appropriation to build a nationwide network of veterans' hospitals, which she guided through the House, over the opposition of the committee chairman, fewer than five years after arriving on Capitol Hill.

Her political stewardship on behalf of servicemen and women reached its zenith with passage of the GI Bill of Rights in 1944. Congress, representing a grateful nation, by appropriating money for tuition and books (up to $500 a year for four years) and for living expenses ($50 and up per month), made it possible for veterans to complete their education. No one contributed more to the drafting of this bill than Edith Nourse Rogers, and, in tribute to the role she played, President Roosevelt gave her the pen with which he signed it into law.

A totally new phenomenon of the war years—women in the service and uniform of the country's fighting forces—was another of Edith Rogers's legislative coups. It represented the culmination of a spirited floor fight. The logic of her argument in favor of creating a volunteer Women's Auxiliary Army Corps (WAAC) was inescapable—thousands of able-bodied GIs were assigned to desk jobs that women could perform at least as well as they—but the idea that young females should be officially introduced into the rough, all-male domain of army camps was intolerable to many legislators. Eventually acceding to the reasoning of Edith Rogers and her allies, however, Congress went on to authorize the navy WAVES, the coast guard SPARS, and the Marine Corps Women's Reserve.

"On the floor, despite her effervescing femininity, she conducts herself like a man," Duff Gilfond reported from the House press gallery. "She doesn't get on her mark, get set, and then recite her speech in schoolgirl fashion. Bouncing out of her seat, she shoots a question in a high-pitched Boston accent and leaps in where other gentlewomen fear to tread." One of the first to protest the persecution of Jews in Nazi Germany, she also opposed American neutrality, on the ground that neutrality could not be legislated. Originally she supported the United Nations, but in 1953 she called for the withdrawal of U.S. support and advocated moving U.N. headquarters from American soil if member nations admitted Red China.

A self-appointed watchdog to protect the welfare of millworkers and other industrial employees in northeastern Massachusetts, Edith Rogers backed cotton along with veterans and quite as sincerely. It seemed to some of her colleagues that she extolled the versatile virtues of cotton morning, noon, and night. On occasion she even forsook her modish ensembles for cotton dresses and urged all congressmen to wear cotton suits.

Representative Rogers unquestionably enjoyed floor fights, though she did not always win them—and at least one brought a threat to her life. At the height of the controversy over whether a Czechoslovakian shoe manufacturer should be allowed to establish schools in the United States, she presented proof that the so-called schools were in reality factories and that the "student" wages could "wreck the higher-paid, unionized domestic shoe industry." A letter she received warned her to "keep your mouth shut or else." Police protection was provided. No attempt to kill her was made; neither was the author of the letter ever taken into custody.

To thousands in the 5th District, Congresswoman Rogers was known as a combination business adviser, mother-confessor, and friend in need. A woman of sturdy independence, with a ready shoulder for a constituent's lament, she won re-election by greater and greater margins. During the New Deal heyday, she received some of her largest pluralities. In 1952, the Democrats tried a new tack and nominated a woman, Helen M. Fitzgerald-Cullen; the ploy did not work.

Edith Rogers's popularity was confined neither to her district nor to the ranks of the GOP. It was national in scope and crossed party lines. When the Democratic-controlled state legislature moved to carve up the 5th District in the late 1950s, it was House Majority Leader John W. McCormack, a south-Boston Democrat, who stepped in and prevented the bill's being read.

Her charm and merry disposition notwithstanding, she could, on those occasions when she violated congressional courtesy by inviting important constituents of other Massachusetts members to lunch, irritate her colleagues. But, as one of them pointed out, "We always forgave her. Who could remain at odds with dear, well-meaning Edith?"

When Mrs. Rogers had first been elected in 1925, professional politicians had predicted that she would not "last long" in Congress. Only a few of these soothsayers were still on the scene in 1960 when she celebrated a double anniversary: her 35th year on the Hill and her 79th birthday. The only concessions she had made to old age were to shorten the long walks she had always enjoyed and to rely somewhat more on the telephone for transacting business.

Two days before the September 1960 primary—in which she was unopposed for a 19th consecutive term—word of her death came as a shock. It was later revealed that she had been admitted to Massachusetts General Hospital three weeks earlier and had asked her doctor not to inform the public that she was ill.

Of Edith Nourse Rogers, who had set a world record for continuous national legislative service by a woman, the *Boston Globe* said in eulogy, "Whoever is chosen to succeed her, it will probably be a long time before the position she occupied will, in the larger sense, be filled."

She would have approved the man who would try. Voters by the thousands extended her a posthumous courtesy by going to the polls and electing Deputy Director of the Veterans Administration, F. Bradford Morse.

In Search of an Image

Measured against the first half of the 1920s, the congressional ground that women gained during the second five years was considerable. Numerically, their strength increased to nine by 1930. Whereas their earlier election cadence had been one step forward, one step back, they now moved straight ahead, re-election being the key. "Gentlewomen of the House of Representatives" was the new designation Speaker Nicholas Longworth gave them, having decided it was "more dignified and less threadbare" than "Ladies of the House."

Some things remained the same. They were still news just because they were women. Thus the nation was informed through the press that Representative Katherine Langley of Kentucky "was gowned in midnight blue trimmed in brilliant red," that Representative Ruth Baker Pratt of New York "wore a dark costume relieved by a white waist," and so on, until news accounts very often appeared to have been lifted from the society pages.

To onlookers in the gallery, the women on the floor continued to be the stellar attraction. Tourists came to listen to the oratory of William Jennings Bryan's daughter or watch Ruth Hanna McCormick "wheeling and dealing." They were also eager to catch a glimpse of Mrs. Pratt, the richest woman in the House. Arkansans asked the Capitol ushers to point out Pearl Oldfield or Effiegene Wingo, and Tennesseans looked for Willa Eslick.

The new congresswomen raised some new questions for Washington hostesses. What protocol should be followed in the seating arrangements at private dinner parties? Were the widows to be ranked according to the seniority their dead husbands had held or according to their own neophyte status? As everyone knows, there is a large gap in distinction between the chair occupied by the widow of a 12-term congressman and that assigned a newcomer. The matter was settled when quasi-official word was passed that the gentlewomen should be ranked in their own right.

KATHERINE LANGLEY
REPUBLICAN OF KENTUCKY

The doors to capital society, as Mary Norton had discovered, did not open automatically for congresswomen. Katherine Langley, a duly elected Republican representative from eastern Kentucky, had close ties with the United Daughters of the Confederacy, the Eastern Star, and the DAR, yet she was *personna non grata*. Because she was the daughter of a late—and respected—congressman from North Carolina, James Madison Gudger, Jr., she obviously would have been welcome had her husband not been a convicted felon.

John Wesley Langley, a veteran of 18 years in the House, was sentenced to 2 years in prison in 1924 for conspiring illegally to transport and sell whisky. While free on bail pending appeal, he won re-election. Either his mountaineer constituents felt that the Prohibition law was a pretty good thing to violate or that being caught was no disgrace—only bad luck. After the appellate court upheld the verdict and he entered the federal penitentiary in Atlanta, Katherine Langley, to "vindicate" the family name, sought—and won—the right to represent the 10th District.

It was not only social Washington that considered the Langley arrangement gauche. Kentucky hill people excepted, hardly anyone approved of awarding a wife (even one with 14 years of Capitol Hill experience as secretary to her husband) the political office lost by a spouse found guilty of a felony. (Forty-six years later, in the only other recorded Langley-like ploy at the congressional level, a sympathy vote failed to materialize. After the 1972 conviction of John Dowdy on counts of bribery, conspiracy, and perjury, his wife sought—but did not win—the east-Texas seat from which he retired after serving 10 terms.)

Mrs. Langley's election by a sizable margin in 1926 was unquestionably due to the inherent loyalty of the Cumberland mountain folk—loyalty to her husband, not to her. "They believe he was the victim of a political conspiracy," explained the *Lexington Leader*. And what God-fearing Republican could have rejected his impassioned plea to "send my wife, the mother of our three children, to Washington" because "she knows better than anyone else my unfinished plans"? Lest his constituents had forgotten, he recalled that he had always been loyal to the District. He listed his successful efforts "to obtain pork" for the people, citing specifically the pensions he had secured and the jobs he had obtained for friends. Only the Democrats and the *Louisville Times* grumbled, "It is interesting to note Mr. Langley mentions not one instance in which he sought to serve the nation."

In her campaign speeches (she delivered over 100 and spent $99 in a two-month period), 39-year-old Katherine Langley glorified her husband's name and promised "to carry forward the principles for which he stands." A speech teacher before her marriage, she had a facility for packaging her words well. During a rally in Prestonsburg one listener was overheard saying, "John Langley wears the breeches, but the lady has the brains."

Although Langley had earned a degree from a night law school, his wife, by virtue of having been graduated from the Woman's College in Richmond and having done postgraduate work at Emerson College of Oratory in Boston, was considered the better educated of the two. Her party credentials were also superior to those of her husband. She was not only the first woman member and first woman vice-chairman of the Republican State Central Committee in Kentucky but also the first chairman of the Women's Republican State Committee.

Her congressional reward for party service was an appointment to the GOP Committee on Committees, the select group that decides who will be appointed to each House committee. It marked another first for a woman.

Between Katherine Langley and her colleagues it was not political love at first sight. "She offends the squeamish by her unstinted display of gypsy colors on the floor and the conspicuousness with which she dresses her bushy blue-black hair," one Capitol Hill correspondent wrote. She also invited unfavorable comments because of her obsession with flowery rhetoric: She came from the "heart of the hills." Coal, "king of energy," was dug by "stalwart and sturdy miners." Sometimes given to verse, she described the Kentucky mountaineer as "a man whose grip is a little tighter, whose smile is a little brighter, whose faith is a little whiter."

She could also be obtrusive. During a crucial debate on taxation, she rose to praise the performance of Kentucky basketball players: "St. Louis has its Lindbergh; the Yankees their Babe Ruth; Ashland has its Tom Cats; last, but not least, the tenth district has its mountain lions, the game little fighters of Carr Creek."

If her performance unsettled Washington, it had quite the reverse effect in Kentucky. This "guardian angel of patronage," who had hired her married daughter as her secretary, was returned to Congress in 1928 by a larger vote than she had received two years earlier. Had a marital spat between the Langleys not made headlines during her second term, she might have served a third.

Largely through Katherine Langley's efforts, President Coolidge consented to grant her husband executive clemency—with the understanding that he would never again seek public office. In 1929, however, denying that he had agreed to such a disclaimer, he announced from the family home in Pikeville that he would try to regain his House seat. From Washington, Congresswoman Langley said she had no intention of stepping aside "for John or anyone else." The brouhaha ended with her name going on the ballot but with a sufficient number of disenchanted Republicans staying away from the polls to put Democrat A. J. May in the winner's column.

After John Langley's death in 1932, his widow became the beneficiary of the type of patronage they had both so adeptly dispensed. The governor appointed her to the Kentucky Railroad Commission.

When she died in 1948, the *New York Times* recalled her "campaign of vindication." As a political gimmick it had worked. She had served a term in Congress while her husband had served a term in the penitentiary. But, as for proving that there had been a miscarriage of justice in the government's case against John Langley, she had failed. About the only thing she had demonstrated was how the House of Representatives can be used to keep a family on the public payroll.

PEARL PEDEN OLDFIELD
DEMOCRAT OF ARKANSAS

When Representative William A. Oldfield of Batesville, Arkansas, died suddenly in mid-November 1928, influential politicians in the 2d Congressional District prevailed on his widow to accept the nomination to fill his unexpired term in the 70th Congress and the succeeding full term. The press labeled the move a "chivalric gesture." In truth, gentlemanly courtesy had little to do with it; the act was pure political strategy. The election of diffident, 52-year-old Fannie Pearl Oldfield was a maneuver to hold the House seat until a suitable male candidate could be found to replace the late popular and politically powerful congressman.

Unlike some congressional widows, Miss Pearl, as she was popularly known, did not covet her deceased husband's place. She had spent 19 years watching from the sidelines as he became Democratic Whip, a member of the Ways and Means Committee, and chairman of his party's Congressional Campaign Committee. Now she was ready to fade from public sight into a "private and inconspicuous existence."

A well-educated woman (Arkansas College in Batesville) from the prominent Peden family (of Cotton Plant in Woodruff County), she, nevertheless, felt "very inadequate" without her husband's advice and guidance. In Congress she limited her activity to what she called "taking care of things." Being a caretaker meant filling requests from constituents for seed packets, answering mail, and maintaining a daily vigil on the floor—from prayer to adjournment.

Long before the 71st Congress was gaveled to a close, Pearl Oldfield told the *New York Times* how much she looked forward to retiring "to the sphere in which I believe women belong— the home." Thirty-one years later, when Wilbur D. Mills, speaking as a representative from the 2d Arkansas District, informed the House that she had died, hardly anyone remembered her. Considering her preoccupation with obscurity, this was, of course, as she herself would have wanted it.

RUTH HANNA McCORMICK
REPUBLICAN OF ILLINOIS

Ruth McCormick's father was Marcus Alonzo Hanna, self-made mining and shipping millionaire, Republican friend of big business, President-maker. He was also a political boss, and in his daughter this heritage showed.

Some said that Ruth Hanna's political education had begun in the nursery. Perhaps it had, for she early admitted that she was fond of "playing politics." Growing up in Cleveland during the golden age of Ohio Republicanism, she not only watched Mark

Hanna groom his amiable friend Governor William McKinley for the White House race against William Jennings Bryan but also made her first political speech in behalf of the President-to-be —from the rear platform of a private railroad car. The year was 1896, and she was 16.

Why Ruth and not her brother or her sister, both much older than she, became Mark Hanna's protégée remains unclear. It may have been, quite simply, that she found the rudiments of politics infinitely more interesting than, say, the history lessons at Dobbs Ferry or the lectures on economics at Miss Porter's. Like her father, she never acquired any real enthusiasm for formal education. And so, in the end, she was tutored by him—in the observation of people, the significance of personal and party loyalty, the intrigue of caucuses, the tedium of conventions, and, above all, the worth of an effective vote-getting organization. "Precincts," he told her, "are as important as policies and principles."

The political schooling continued while Mark Hanna was in the Senate. After McKinley was assassinated, she became her father's confidential secretary, kept regular office hours, and spent time on the Hill to "absorb the language and the routine of the legislative branch."

In the Hanna home diagonally across Lafayette Park from the White House, she presided over the coffee urn at the daily breakfasts—often attended by President Theodore Roosevelt— that her father hosted. "That was partly because mother had a rule of her own that she would not participate in any affair that began so early in the morning," Ruth explained, "and partly because father wanted me to know the public men who were there and to become familiar with politics through their table talk. It certainly was an education."

The aura of politics even followed Ruth Hanna to the altar. Her marriage in 1903 to Medill McCormick, 25-year-old heir to two eminent and contentious Chicago institutions, the McCormick Harvester Company and the daily and Sunday *Tribune,* was both a social event and a political incident. The Cleveland nuptials brought together, in addition to the bride and groom, President Roosevelt, who traveled from Washington to attend, and Senator Hanna, who, if Old Guard Republicans had their way, would replace the White House occupant in the next campaign. (Hanna's death in 1904 made possible Roosevelt's nomination by acclamation.)

During the 1912 Presidential race, when young McCormick removed himself from newspapering to manage Roosevelt's

western headquarters, his wife volunteered to work for the Bull
Moose Party in Chicago. Her husband's election to the Illinois
Legislature the same year gave the couple an opportunity to
labor as a team. While he argued for suffrage on the floor, she
lobbied for it in the halls of the State Capitol. Their efforts
were successful—to a degree. A law passed in 1913 granted Illinois women the right to vote in Presidential and municipal
elections.

"Her face always turned toward the next turn in the road,"
said a friend, Estelline Bennett, "she began to give enthusiastic
attention to national suffrage." Simultaneously she campaigned
for her husband, who was elected a congressman at large in 1916
(he served with Jeannette Rankin) and a U.S. senator two years
later.

Once the 19th Amendment was ratified, Ruth Hanna McCormick sallied forth on her own. As head of the newly established
woman's section of the Republican National Committee, she
launched a drive to educate women in the use of the vote. Be-
lieving, as her father had, that the key to any aspect of politics
is a successful organization at the grassroots level, she honey-
combed Illinois with women's Republican clubs. Later Katharine
Hamill of the *Woman's Journal* would write, "It was due to Mrs.
McCormick's judgment in the selection of county and district
leaders and her untiring devotion to the promotion of these
clubs that they have become a very powerful factor in the political life of the state."

Senator Medill McCormick died in 1925. Had he lived, it is
certain that his wife would never have sought elective office. Her
politics was an adjunct to his, for his advancement. There were
published statements that one of her ambitions was to make him
President. While not denying the credibility of such reports, William Hard, a family intimate and a political analyst, believed that
"she gave to his career, as she gave to their three children,
tenacity of dedication inspired by love rather than by ambition."

Only after Charles S. Deneen defeated her husband for renomination to the Senate in 1924 did she seriously seek political
preferment for herself. At the GOP National Convention in
Cleveland that year, she ran for national committeewoman. She
was offered the post "without a contest" if she would support
Lennington ("Len") Small for governor. Not wanting to be
beholden to anyone, especially a member of the Deneen camp,
she rejected the bargain—and won the office.

As the leader of a statewide network of political clubs, Ruth

McCormick could afford to be independent of the so-called Illinois Republican machine. This independence was very much in evidence from start to finish of her successful campaign for U.S. representative at large in 1928. "No Promises and No Bunk" was her slogan, and just how refreshingly free she was of the doubletalk so prevalent in politics was manifest in the statement she made at the opening of her Chicago headquarters:

> Usually, when a candidate announces his candidacy, we read in the papers that owing to the demand of his constituency and the pressure of his friends, he has reluctantly agreed to make this great sacrifice and run for office. In all candor and honesty I must say that nobody asked me to run. I have had no demand upon me from constituents, friends, enemies, neighbors or family, and as far as I know, nobody wants me to run. But I hope at the end of the campaign that I am going to find a sufficient number of people who think I ought to run.

Her wish was amply fulfilled. Not only did she collect 500,-000 more votes than her nearest competitor; she actually led the state ticket. And curiously enough Len Small supported her; so did Chicago Mayor William Hale ("Big Bill") Thompson, who had been defeated by Medill McCormick in his first campaign for the Senate. "The politicians could not afford to oppose her," as the *New Republic* pointed out. "Backed by the women's clubs, she represented the 'better element.' " Mark Hanna's daughter again demonstrated she had learned her political lessons well. While she took no position for or against Small or Thompson, neither did she disavow their endorsement in counties where they were popular. The caption under her cloche-framed face on the cover of *Time* acknowledged that she had "learned the law of the jungle."

Less than three weeks after her election to the House, *Collier's* reported "Sooner or later she will certainly be U.S. senator from Illinois . . . because she is just about twice as efficient in politics as any man in that state . . . and has demonstrated she need ask no odds of a male opponent in a statewide election. She has an old score to settle with Senator Deneen. Two years from now she may go out and take Deneen's job away from him."

Forty-nine-year-old Ruth McCormick did not wait two years. A month after being sworn in (at the beginning of a special congressional session called by President Herbert Hoover in April 1929), she proclaimed her intention to become the first elected woman senator. "At last—or rather, perhaps, so soon—a woman has become a genuinely formidable candidate for election to the United States Senate, and is entirely recognized so to be," editorialized the *Review of Reviews.*

Out of pique (or paranoia) some in the press and politics did not share this view. Calling the congresswoman "self-seeking," *Christian Century* accused her of wanting "to prove to the country that she knows as thoroughly and can use as effectively all the tricks of the political game in its most cynical and corrupting fashion. She has established no record for public service which would entitle her to seek this highest office in the gift of the state. Her record in Congress is a virtual cipher."

Mrs. Lottie Holman O'Neill, a Deneenite in the Illinois Legislature, declared, "Mrs. McCormick's personal ambition brooks no interference. She is Mark Hanna's daughter, with his desire to boss."

The candidate replied, "I learned from my father that to be in public life one must possess two things: the hide of a rhinoceros and a sense of the ridiculous. Mrs. O'Neill, I find, is misinformed on all points except the accusation that I am Mark Hanna's daughter."

Ruth McCormick, in her drive to unseat Deneen, ran a professional show throughout. It was not in the spirit of boasting that she said, "Don't forget, I was the first woman ward politician. I've got this state laid out like a checkerboard so that I can hit the right towns in about four counties a day."

The months preceding the April 1930 primary, when the temperature dropped below zero, found her climbing in and out of her shiny, chauffeur-driven Marmon touring car to address the crowds that flocked to see and hear her in the state's 102 counties. Blessed with enormous wealth, she could have traveled in a steam-heated special train, as she had once done (at a cost of $12,000) to hurry from New York to a waiting audience in Chicago. Or she could have followed the course chosen by Deneen and used the radio. Instead of motoring through the freezing days and nights, she could have talked from her home in Georgetown, from her country house on the 2,000-acre dairy farm she owned and operated near Rockford, from her ranch in Wyoming, from her apartment in Chicago's Palmer House, or even from her suite of offices on Michigan Avenue (where the presence of Alice Roosevelt Longworth, a longtime friend, would have made the photographs twice as distinguished). But, as she told a syndicated columnist, "That would have been make-believe politics." Make-believe politics was the one thing that Mark Hanna's daughter knew the least about. Scorning comfort, she covered the 17,000 carefully charted miles and finished the tour as peppy as her hulky chauffeur was bedraggled.

Ruth McCormick's physical appearance contrasted sharply with her energy and stamina. She was tall and very thin, with birdlike legs and almost transparent wrists. Her unrouged face was always pale, her thin lips devoid of color. But, when she started to talk politics, a glow from her brown eyes would light up her delicate features. And her low, crisply accented voice would rise to an animated pitch. "My God!" exclaimed a newspaperman assigned to her winter trip, "I never saw a woman who had more sex appeal on the platform and less off."

While Mrs. McCormick, with her early, prompt advocacy of suffrage and of legislation for the protection of labor, for farm relief, and for outlawing war, had shown herself to be more of a progressive Republican than her opponent, Charles Deneen, the candidates shared the same opinion on the two most volatile national issues: They favored Prohibition and opposed the World Court. Therefore, the contest between them was essentially personality-oriented.

Deneen, once characterized as "not unlike Dear Old Charlie of *Strange Interlude*: full of desire, but impotent," had been forced to cooperate, in the course of the pitiless struggle for survival in Cook County politics, with various corrupt members of rival machines. It was in his favor, on the other hand, that he was a genius in the mastery of the political maneuver—and had a long record of wins to prove it. In 1892 (when his future rival was a girl of 12), he reached the Illinois Legislature. Five years later he became state's attorney, then served as governor for two terms, and, finally, in 1925, went to the Senate.

But Deneen's blend of "practical" political skills was no match for a statewide grassroots campaign organization that was without parallel. Thus the first man in history to battle a woman for his seat in the Senate failed to retain it. Ruth Hanna McCormick, who emerged in command of the largest organized following put together by any woman in American politics, won decisively. Her 170,000-vote margin was not only a political victory but a personal one as well. She avenged herself for Deneen's 1924 defeat of her husband by only 6,000 votes. The *Tribune*, bursting with family pride, called her nomination the "first conspicuous and unequivocal acknowledgment of the full implication of the 19th Amendment." It was indeed a triumph for feminine leadership, but it had many other significances. One of them was that Illinois had made up its mind to crash through the sex barrier surrounding the Senate.

Because winning a GOP primary in Illinois was tantamount to election, it would have been easy to prophesy (and most political pundits did) that former Senator J. Hamilton Lewis, the Democratic nominee, whom Medill McCormick had defeated in the 1918 Senate race, could not win in November. But 1930 events were unpredictable.

Prohibition was very much on everybody's mind. Mrs. McCormick favored retaining the Volstead Act; Lewis wanted it repealed. Who could say that Illinois was Republican enough to vote for a "dry" Republican in preference to a "wet" Democrat? Another issue was the worsening Depression, for which the Hoover Administration was being blamed.

The biggest imponderable of all was the potential effect of Mrs. McCormick's voluntary disclosure before a special Senate Campaign Expenditures Committee that she had spent $252,-572 to capture the nomination for a job that paid $10,000 a year. (Deneen's outlay had been $24,495.) Over 1 million people had voted, and there were twice that many eligible Republicans; so she had actually allotted less than 25 cents to each voter. Still, the total amount matched her salary as a senator for 25 years! The *New Republic* insisted that her nomination had been "a case of 'May the best dollar win!' " Some senators, taking note of allegations that the well-kept McCormick records did not include "contributions by Mayor Thompson's notorious machine," declared that, in the event she was elected, they intended to keep her waiting on the threshold while they looked into the matter. "She could become a senator-eject," said one who would not allow his name to be used.

Her veracity questioned, Mrs. McCormick struck back. Claiming that the chairman of the Senate investigating committee, Republican Gerald P. Nye of North Dakota, had ordered her phones tapped and had sent agents "to rifle my files," she hired private detectives to shadow Nye and his staff.

The verdict rendered by the electorate on November 4 was a resounding victory for J. Hamilton Lewis. He rolled up a plurality of nearly 750,000.

Ruth McCormick's defeat was partially attributable to Prohibition and the Depression, issues that gave the Democrats the dynamite to blow Republicans off the Illinois map. But there were other factors. Her huge (for the time) campaign expenditure, while not illegal, was deeply resented ("How can democracy survive if only the rich may run for office?"). And she had outsmarted herself by playing counterspy during the Nye inquiry. This uncharacteristic role had been instantly headlined: SHE SNOOPS TO CONQUER.

By using one elective office as a steppingstone to another, Congresswoman McCormick took a calculated gamble: all or nothing. But even as a loser she remained a towering figure in the Republican Party. And, had she not been adamant about not wanting "to be *appointed* to anything—ever," there need not have been a last hurrah. This was deliberate. Now there was time for the farm, for the *Rockford Republican,* the newspaper she had bought, and, eventually, for a new husband, Albert Gallatin Simms, a former House colleague and GOP national committeeman from New Mexico.

If at some point in the prolonged popularity of Franklin Roosevelt's New Deal the GOP had regained a political foothold, the odds were that Ruth Hanna McCormick Simms would have reappeared on the national political scene. Death in 1944, however, ended speculation.

RUTH BRYAN OWEN
DEMOCRAT OF FLORIDA

During the 1930 House showdown vote on the Smoot-Hawley tariff bill, there were no murmurings from the gallery as Ruth Hanna McCormick, an unshakable partisan of the Hoover Administration, cast a distinctly audible "Yes." But when Florida's Democratic congresswoman, Ruth Bryan Owen, also voted in favor of the most restrictive piece of trade legislation in U.S. history, expressions of incredulity were exchanged. One Democrat, recalling the extreme differences in political ideology between Mark Hanna and William Jennings Bryan, said to another, "The 'Great Commoner' must be turning over in his grave."

Asked about the unyielding free-trade posture of her late father, Congresswoman Owen was noncommittal. She meant no familial disrespect, but as an intensely loyal representative of the 4th District, which included the Eastern industrialists living in Miami, she considered political history irrelevant. "To vote 'No' when I know without a doubt that my constituents want me to say 'Yes,' " she said, "would be a form of political treason."

That kind of sentiment was typical of Ruth Bryan Owen, who had obviously been helped in politics by her family name yet had painstakingly avoided exploiting it. She was a woman referred to as "rich," not in terms of dollars but in the no less tangible assets of courage, charm, and charisma. Tall and stately, with a fine figure, she moved in a lithe and graceful manner. Her prematurely gray hair, cut short, fell back in soft waves to frame high cheekbones, hazel eyes, and a finely chiseled nose.

"In a very short time she has captivated Washington completely," journalist Duff Gilfond said in assessing her impact on the nation's capital. "Her male colleagues are daft about her. Handsome elderly men of the Senate come over to the House floor to sit by her side, and when she swings over to the higher chamber to listen to a debate dozens of Senators leave their seats to shake hands with her." The one committee on which she expressed a desire to serve—Foreign Affairs—increased its membership to make room for her.

The path Ruth Bryan Owen took to Congress was a circuitous one. Born in her parents' native Illinois in 1885, she was two when her mother joined William Jennings Bryan in Lincoln, Nebraska, where he had opened a law office As profound an influence as he exerted on young Ruth's life, the imprint her mother made was barely less significant. Mary Baird Bryan was also a law graduate who had been admitted to the bar. "I would like to emulate her," Ruth once said. "She is a thoroughly feminine woman with the mind of a thoroughly masculine man."

The year that Bryan made his first bid for the Presidency (1896, against McKinley) Ruth was only 11, but she already had acquired a sense of the dual aspects of political fame: the exhilaration and the humiliation. The story is told that, not long after mingling with neighbors and friends celebrating her father's nomination, she was handed a caricature of him as a devil with horns and a tail. "She must have wanted to yield to tears," an acquaintance recalls, "but instead she looked at the libel briefly, then became engrossed in something else—as if nothing had happened."

Although she served as Bryan's campaign secretary during his third and final try for the White House in 1908, she was less interested in politics than in the dissolution of her unhappy marriage. At 18, after spending two years at the University of Nebraska, she had married William Homer Leavitt, a young artist. In 1909, when divorce became inevitable, she was left with the responsibility for a small daughter and son. Before remarrying a year later, she assumed a breadwinner's role by lecturing for the Nebraska Extension Service and writing for a newspaper syndicate.

As the wife of Ceylon-born Reginald Altham Owen, a British officer in the Royal Engineers whom she had met during a trip abroad with her parents, she led a peripatetic existence that took her to Kingston, London, Cairo, Port Said, and, eventually, Coral Gables by way of India, China, Japan, Russia, and Canada. During World War I she assisted Mrs. Herbert Hoover with the American Women's War Relief Fund in England, studied nursing and practiced it with the British Volunteer Aid Detachment in Egypt, and sang with an entertainment unit dispatched to military hospitals and rest camps in Palestine.

In Florida, where the family had grown to include two Owen children, Reginald Bryan and Helen Rudd, Ruth found it necessary to supplement her husband's pension (he was a victim of nephritis) by spending part of each year on the Chautauqua circuit. That she became one of the highest-paid women lecturers testifies not only to her eloquent oratory but also to the public's fascination with "Modern Arabian Nights," a major topic in her repertoire.

Her character, talent, and energy became as well known in southern Florida as elsewhere. Soon she was chairman, director, or president of a host of civic, church, and educational endeavors, including the Miami Woman's Club, the DAR, the Miami Theatre Guild, a Bible school, the PTA, the Council for Child Welfare, and the University of Miami Public Speaking Department. When this circle of interests widened to include politics, the die was cast.

She lost the Democratic nomination for Congress in 1926 by just 776 votes. "It must be remembered that I was running in a state that failed to ratify the Suffrage Amendment," she said afterward. (In a bow to the 30th anniversary of the Florida League of Women Voters in 1969, the State Legislature voted 167 to 0 to grant women the right to vote.) "There was not the friendliest feeling toward any woman taking her place in political life."

In the Bryan tradition of "If at first you don't succeed," Ruth Owen announced she would "try again." Then Major Owen died, and she wavered. Counsel from her mother, widowed but two years earlier, helped the would-be congresswoman place her personal tragedy in perspective. In the spring she bought the best attention-getter her budget would allow, a 1928 green Ford coupe, christened it "The Spirit of Florida," and set out "to meet the voters personally" from Jacksonville to Key West. The 4th District was the longest in the nation, stretching 500 miles along Florida's east coast. When the campaign ended, the speedometer showed nearly 10,000 miles traveled and the official election records showed a plurality of more than 30,000 votes for the first woman to seek a House seat from the Deep South.

Her speeches were unorthodox in that she did not dwell on the shortcomings of her opponents, preferring to explain how, if elected, she would fulfill her obligations on Capitol Hill. She made no mention whatsoever of the national ticket and was not present at the one Al Smith rally in Florida. "This desertion of the party that had nominated her put her in wrong with many of its leaders," wrote one political analyst, "but it also put her into Congress from a violently anti-Catholic State."

The same dedicated concern for grassroots problems that convinced the 4th District electorate to send her to the House went into the performance Ruth Owen gave there. Within three weeks after the Mediterranean fruit fly appeared in the state, Congress, largely through her efforts, appropriated more than $4 million to eradicate it. She was one of the first in either legislative branch to give constituents a voice in government through direct mail polls. At least once a year, usually in the company of her younger daughter, Helen Rudd, she toured the entire district. Driving an auto trailer equipped for both work and rest, she went to listen and also, in her words, "to give an accounting of my stewardship."

Another of Ruth Owen's innovations was a program involving young people. "You hear a lot of talk about the worthlessness of modern youth," she said. "Nonsense! The modern youth is all right; if you give him the right ideals, he will keep America the glorious nation it is." Annually she led 36 high school students (a boy and a girl from each of the 18 counties in her district) on a tour through Washington that began at the Library of Congress "to examine the Declaration of Independence" and ended in the White House Oval Office. She called her experiment "a laboratory course in civil government for potential public leaders" and said, "The young are the ones to whom we must throw the torch."

At a time when championing the preservation of wildlife was not yet the fashion, Ruth Owen voiced her concern about the possible extinction of the white ibis and the alligator. After returning from an extended trip by car, houseboat, Goodyear blimp, and seaplane through the sawgrass and swamp of the waterplain that covers most of the southern tip of Florida, she challenged Congress to allocate funds to protect this wilderness wonderland. The bill she introduced set in motion a movement that later culminated in the creation of Everglades National Park.

Though not a reformer to the degree her father had been, she never hesitated to call for change whenever she felt it was in the public interest. Early in her second term (she was unopposed for re-election in 1930), she proposed a Federal Department of Home and Child. And, as daring as it seemed in 1931, she found it "not at all difficult to envision a woman Secretary in the President's Cabinet."

Explaining the need for a clearinghouse to dispense information concerning children, she said, "The crux of the matter is that government activities dealing with the child are disconnected and scattered among a dozen different boards, bureaus, and departments." As a congresswoman, she pointed out, "I have to play a game of hide-and-seek with these government agencies, who themselves appear to be playing pussy-wants-a-corner, whenever I seek answers to questions asked by the wives and mothers of my district. Consider," she said, "how confusing the labyrinth must be to the laywoman."

While no one quarreled with the fact that government reorganization would effect economy of effort and expenditure, opponents objected to Congresswoman Owen's proposal to unify existing services on the ground that it represented "infringement of states' rights." Such a department, they said, would "*thrust* advice on state and family."

When she made her bid for renomination in 1932, the "wet" forces were gathering strength for modification or repeal of Prohibition. Everyone in Florida knew her "dry" position. She had sometimes joked about it. While speaking in a downpour on one occasion, she said, "I know it must be very uncomfortable for you all to stand there in the rain, but think of my position, in the face of family traditions [her father was a lifelong Prohibitionist], to come out on a wet platform."

Her defeat in the Democratic primary was due, as she said later, to the fact that "I did not turn 'wet' fast enough to suit my constituents." But in the lame-duck session she accepted the mandate of the electorate and answered "Aye" to repeal the 18th Amendment.

Under Franklin Roosevelt's new deal for women, Ruth Bryan Owen became the first of her sex to head a U.S. diplomatic mission abroad. She went to Denmark in 1933 as envoy extraordinary and minister plenipotentiary. Romance triumphed over professional diplomacy three years later, however, and she re-

signed to marry Captain Borge Rohde of the Danish Royal
Guards. Back in the United States, the new Mrs. Rohde resumed lecturing and writing. President Harry S. Truman returned her to the public spotlight in 1945 by appointing her a
special assistant with the State Department to assist in the creation of the United Nations in San Francisco, and in 1949 he
named her an alternate delegate to the U.N. General Assembly.

In a magazine article Mrs. Owen wrote after leaving Congress, she discussed the subject of her daughter and politics.
"I took Helen Rudd into the House with me—just as I was
taken there by my father when I was only five," she explained.
"She has already given evidence both of natural equipment for
a political life and of marked predisposition toward it. Yes, I
am looking forward to such a future for her."

Ruth Owen Rohde did not live to see her hope fulfilled (she
died in 1954 while on a visit to Copenhagen), but her daughter
did go into politics. Rudd Brown (she had dropped her first
name), the slim, striking brunette wife of prize-winning geo-
chemist Harrison Brown, ran for Congress twice (1958 and
1960) from California's 21st District, a sprawling area embracing
half of Los Angeles and several suburban valleys. Despite her
political momentum as a Democratic Party leader and the fact
that her leadership had been tested at both the state and federal levels of government, she failed to wrest this conservative
stronghold from the Republican male incumbent. "Nevertheless," the Associated Press pointed out, "she made her mark as
a progressive force—in the best public service tradition of a
distinguished family."

RUTH BAKER PRATT
REPUBLICAN OF NEW YORK

New York's first female member of Congress, Ruth Baker
Pratt, who had cut her political teeth in 1925 as a Republican
on the Tammany-controlled Manhattan Board of Aldermen,
loathed being called "Gentlewoman." In the manner of yet-to-
come feminists, whose movement in the 1960s she would live
to witness, Mrs. Pratt had the courage to proclaim that "sex has
no place whatever in politics."

She reserved her most aristocratic scorn and sardonic style
for the press, which she contended "perpetuates the myth that
women have a different role to play in public life than have
men." She resented reporters' singling her out, "like the first
English Channel swimmer, the first female bandit, or the first

woman police officer," to ask, "What is the woman's view-point?" "I always avoided answering if I could," she once said, "for I really have no idea what the 'woman's viewpoint' is."

With disquieting vigor, in an article written exclusively for the *Ladies' Home Journal,* she challenged society to end discrimination in the political arena:

> A man enters public life and not the slightest attention is paid to the fact that he is a man. A woman runs for office and there is more interest in the fact that she is a woman than in her qualifications for the job she seeks. She is completely shackled by her sex. At every turn she is confronted with the fact that the activities of the world have been cut from a he pattern.
>
> She is a woman candidate, not merely a candidate, as a man is. If elected, she becomes the woman this or that, not simply the title. Where the masculinity of her confreres is taken for granted, her femininity always causes mild surprise and is good for an old-fashioned debate on whether women generally are not miscast when assuming roles which have heretofore been reserved for the other sex. . . . Men and women should be put on a parity, the sole issue being which candidate is best qualified to perform the duties of the office concerned.

That candidate for the House of Representatives from New York's 17th District in 1928 was 50-year-old Ruth Baker Pratt, who won against the power of a solidly built Democratic machine, carrying her opponent's home assembly district by four votes and her own by a 3-to-1 margin. She ran on her record as the only female alderman New York City had ever had, the record of a fearless minority member confronting 64 men who had proved powerless to deter her, in her ardor for good city housekeeping and economy, from mercilessly twisting the tail of the Tammany Tiger.

That a woman of her genteel background, with money beyond imagining, had condescended to sit with an uncouth gang of Tammany politicans was considered remarkable. She discerned no paradox. "It was a great opportunity for service," she said, which also explained her well-known philanthropic role in prewidowhood days.

Massachusetts-born (1877) Ruth Sears Baker, daughter of a cotton manufacturer, was educated in mathematics at Wellesley and in the violin in Europe. In 1903 she was married to John Teele Pratt, thereby becoming the wife of a Standard Oil Company heir and the daughter-in-law of the founder of Pratt Institute. Automatically her name was added to the Manhattan Social Register, to the Junior League, and to the rosters of such elite clubs as the Colony and Piping Rock. There were servants, of course, to manage the family townhouse and the Long Island estate, but Mrs. Pratt was not the kind of mother to leave the rearing of the couple's five children to tutors and governesses.

Tall, dark-eyed Ruth Pratt, a quiet, earnest persuader, little disposed to fireworks but endowed with a bafflling power to persevere, was good at almost everything she tried—except re-forming Tammany Hall. She spent years climbing up the GOP hierarchy: vice-chairman of the Ways and Means Committee of the Republican National Committee in 1919, a Presidential elec-tor in 1920, a delegate to the Republican State Convention in 1922 (through 1938) and to the National Convention in 1924 (through 1944), and associate leader of the New York City 15th ("silk-stocking") Assembly District in 1923.

National elective office was not on her mind during the two terms she spent in the smoke-filled aldermanic committee rooms, sometimes smoking a cigarette herself. "Since I was fa-miliar with the history of Tammany graft and corruption, it was my duty to protest the extravagance and waste," she said. And protest she did. Calling the aldermen "rubber stamps for the Board of Estimate," she said they were not worth the chairs they sat in. Mayor and municipal idol James J. Walker was singled out for many of her indictments. "It's the worst administration in history," she declared, "thanks to his carelessness, indiffer-ence, bungling, and inefficiency." The municipal budget was scandalous, she said, citing page after page of figures to show how Tammany was robbing the taxpayers.

While knocking on doors as a political candidate, Mrs. Pratt experienced the shock of poverty as only an affluent American with a bothersome conscience can. Surely nothing less than fed-eral low-income housing could abolish the tenements she called "unfit for animals, much less human beings." This realization, plus the fact she was unable to convince the Board of Alder-men to "mend its ways," caused her to accept the GOP nomina-tion for Congress.

Almost immediately, volunteers started flowing into her ho-tel headquarters. She was referred to as the "young men's can-didate," because 45 men under 30 volunteered to divide the 17th District among them and work it. Her paid staff totaled only four—all amateurs who needed the money—but a com-mittee of 1,200 unpaid workers did everything from address-ing circulars to running down floaters.

Following   her   election,   Alderman   Peter   McGuinness sounded a sour note: "Them cold babies down there in Congress won't let her talk two hours like she has done here. There won't be no chance there like here in the Board of Aldermen, where men are men."

Asked by a newsman if she intended to be as critical of her colleagues in Washington as she had been of those in Manhattan, Mrs. Pratt replied, "If members of Congress behave as the Board of Aldermen did, surely." Then she paused. "But they won't."

Chivalry in the House exceeded her expectations. Those in power, remembering the shrewd eye she had kept on New York City's budget, appointed her to the prestigious Banking and Currency Committee. During debate on the Smoot-Hawley tariff bill, she was accorded the privilege of reading the American Federation of Labor's protest against the increase in sugar rates, though it was addressed to James A. Frear of Wisconsin. Socially, too, the congressional men in her life were complimentary. She was known among them as a "deft and heartening hostess," and invitations were coveted to her Georgetown home, where on occasion she delighted guests by joining them in a game of poker.

As Broadway's Congressman (because her mid-Manhattan District included a section of this thoroughfare), she represented both the Four Hundred and O. Henry's Four Million. To the latter she gave unstinting service, becoming extremely adept at cutting through immigration red tape.

A typical case involved a young Italian who wrote to ask if she could help him bring his wife and children to the United States, though the quota barred them. He had been advised to go over and "fetch his brood," but if he did he would lose the job he needed to support them. Mrs. Pratt wrote on his behalf to the State Department, to the Labor Department, to the Bureau of Immigration, to the American consul in Naples, and to the authorities on Ellis Island. The Italian got a passport for his family.

"I want every man, woman and child in my constituency to feel that he has a friend in Washington," she was fond of saying. If a request was legitimate, she felt dutybound to do whatever she could to satisfy it. When a wealthy man sought vouchers to admit him to the royal enclosure at Ascot, she arranged for him to pick them up at the American Embassy in London. There were times, of course, when she had to disappoint constituents. "A surprising number of visitors," she said, "simply

do not understand why I cannot arrange for them 'to peep into
the White House dining room when the President and his family are having dinner.' "

Ruth Pratt was re-elected in 1930 over formidable opposition from City Magistrate Louis B. Brodsky, a Democrat, and
the popular columnist, Heywood Broun, a Socialist. Broun aimed
his salvos at her floor record: "She has made only two speeches,"
he said, "one advocating a two-cent reduction in the sugar tariff
and another in which she read an address given by President
Hoover to the Boy Scouts." He conveniently overlooked the
one she gave advocating more liberal provisions for World War
veterans and their dependents.

Whatever her House record, it would have been a near mir-
acle if she had won again in 1932, the year that voters in New
York and in 41 other states replaced a host of Republicans in
Congress with followers of Franklin Roosevelt's New Deal.
Hoover's defeat was more of a blow to Ruth Pratt than her own.
After seconding his renomination at the Chicago convention,
she had campaigned as vigorously for him as for herself.

Practicing the politics she had always preached ("There is no
limit to the influence one can exert by working through
party machinery"), Ruth Pratt gamely joined the Republican
Builders, a group of professionals determined to bring the GOP
back to life. She also served as national committeeman and in the
1940s was elected president of the Woman's National Republican Club. By the time the party re-emerged with a semblance
of its former glory with the inauguration in 1953 of Dwight D.
Eisenhower, she had reached her declining years. Periodically,
until her death in 1965, she was asked to comment on the future of women in politics. Her reply that she was optimistic
brought the inevitable "Why?" "Because," she said, "the modern
woman runs for office as I did—as a citizen."

EFFIEGENE L. WINGO
DEMOCRAT OF ARKANSAS

"Widows' Row" in the House of Representatives was lengthened following the November 1930 elections to include a place
for a second Arkansas congresswoman, Effiegene Locke Wingo.
She joined, for the lame-duck session, fellow Democrat Pearl
Oldfield and, by decree of the voters, served in the 72d Congress (1931–33).

The political commentators who dismissed Congresswoman

Wingo as a "seat-warmer" either did not know or had forgotten that, in Arkansas and Washington at least, she had the reputation of being a doer. True, she was succeeding her late husband, Otis Theodore Wingo, but, during the four years preceding his death, while he recuperated from severe injuries suffered in an automobile accident, she had become his eyes and ears in the 4th Congressional District. As an unpaid staffer she impressed constituents with her friendliness and ombudsman-like concern.

It was not happenstance that, once nominated by the Democratic State Central Committee, Effiegene Wingo received the wholehearted endorsement of the Arkansas GOP hierarchy. A woman of crisp wit and well-nurtured tolerance, there was nothing doctrinaire about either her social or her political philosophy. Moreover, her commitment to her native state ran deep.

Her roots did also. Lockesburg, the small town where she was born in 1883, the eldest of seven children of Irish Protestant pioneers, had been founded by descendants of Matthew Locke, an 18th-century congressman from North Carolina. It was a matter of pride to Effiegene Locke that he had refused to vote for ratification of the Federal Constitution in 1789 because it did not contain a bill of rights.

Considering the restrictive educational mores applied to young ladies at the turn of the century, Effiegene's academic accomplishments were rather remarkable: a diploma in music from Union Female College in Oxford, Mississippi, and a B.A. degree (at age 18) from Maddox Seminary in Little Rock. Pretty (a tall brunette with large, deep-set eyes) and talented, she might have been a concert pianist or organist had she not, at 19, caught the eye of Otis Wingo.

When they met at a Confederate veterans' reunion in De-Queen, he noted that she was wearing two Presidential campaign buttons—one depicting Theodore Roosevelt, the other William Jennings Bryan. "What are your politics?" he asked.

Holding up a flower she had picked from her mother's garden, she answered facetiously, "Tuberoses."

"That was my inning," she later wrote in her diary.

It was also the beginning of her association with politics, for, soon after their marriage, her husband was elected to the State Senate. Seventeen years as a congressional wife and a mother active in the Washington PTA followed.

Effiegene Wingo took office in the wake of one of the most searing droughts ever to plague Arkansas. It had turned her district—11 counties strung along the Oklahoma border—into a dustbowl and the hungry farmers into angry beggars. Complicating the natural catastrophe was the Great Depression.

The crisis called for innovation and boldness. When federal relief and Red Cross aid were exhausted, Mrs. Wingo herself went "begging," asking the more affluent citizen groups in the capital for donations of food, clothing, medicine—anything they could spare. Rain in 1931 revived the Arkansas peach orchards and the corn and cotton fields, but it took New Deal legislation to cope with the unemployment.

During Roosevelt's first Administration, the Arkansas congresswoman removed herself from the social scene and delegated to her daughter Blanche Sawyer the duties of official hostess in order to concentrate on improving the lot of her constituents. Aided by the staff hired by her husband, she maneuvered into the foothills of the Ozarks a veterans' hospital, a federal building (at Texarkana), railroad bridges, highways, levees, loans for home and school construction, and public welfare grants. During this same period she sat with Ruth Bryan Owen on the Foreign Affairs Committee.

If, as some detractors said, her record was more notable for its harvest than for its seed-planting, the same stricture could be broadly applied. In the prevailing climate of chaos and crisis, few legislative leaders emerged during the 1930s.

On the advice of her physician, Congresswoman Wingo had to forgo seeking re-election. Still committed to public service, however, she became associated with a project sensibly geared to the pace of a woman in less than robust health. With friends in and out of Congress, she cofounded the National Institute of Public Affairs, a privately financed, nonpartisan organization designed to provide college-age youths "with an interest in and an aptitude for civil service" an opportunity to receive on-the-job training in various federal agencies. Prior to her death in 1962, Effiegene Wingo was a full partner in a variety of other educational and research projects, but this one marked the high point of her postcongressional career. It was the prototype of the enormously successful ongoing federal intern program.

WILLA B. ESLICK

DEMOCRAT OF TENNESSEE

Willa Eslick, Tennessee's first congresswoman, literally lost her husband to politics. Compounding the tragedy for her, she was a witness (from the gallery) to his sudden death on the floor of the House. "I want to go from the sordid side" were the last words Edward E. Eslick uttered in an impassioned plea for passage of the soldiers' bonus bill before succumbing to a heart attack on June 14, 1932.

Because Congress was in recess when Mrs. Eslick was elected in August, she was not sworn in until the lame-duck session opened early in December. In the interim, a spot check of her 7th District, an 11-county agricultural section of western Tennessee, confirmed what she already knew: The Depression had a stranglehold on the farmer.

During her brief term, it distressed Willa Eslick that she could give "few comforting words" to her constituents. Although she joined an *ad hoc* forum that met at night to exchange ideas on easing the agricultural crisis, the only cheerful report she could send to Tennessee was that she would back a plan to deal with "farm-mortgage foreclosures." It was "only a stopgap effort to save homes," she explained, "until something can be done to improve general conditions." That "something" might have been the Muscle Shoals project to develop cheap electric power generated by dams on the Tennessee River—a project she supported and Congress authorized. But Hoover vetoed the bill.

It is not surprising that Tennessee-born Willa Blake Eslick, who left the state only to study music in New York City and to accompany her husband to Washington, was little known outside of Giles County, where she spent most of her life and where she died in 1961 at the age of 82. What is unusual, however, is that her election to Congress is so vaguely remembered there. "All of us living then and now," says Maxwell MacMaster of the Giles County Library Board of Trustees, "are certain she was *appointed.*" Statistics from the State Coordinator of Elections in Nashville are the only documentary evidence that she won a special election against three male opponents in the dog days of 1932.

A Matter of Duty

HATTIE W. CARAWAY
DEMOCRAT OF ARKANSAS

"Another election, and no woman in the Senate."

In any number of variations, this was a common complaint among feminists during the years following Senator Rebecca Felton's very brief stay on Capitol Hill. Some blamed the men for impeding women's progress; others held their own sex accountable—criticizing women for being too diffident, too trusting, too modest, too polite, and too pacifistic. The most substantial reason was that the prejudice against a woman's holding high office was difficult to overcome.

Quite a few mustered sufficient courage to storm the gates. But, with the exception of Illinois Representative Ruth Hanna McCormick, none built the kind of following that could overcome the handicaps of gender, inexperience, and, in some cases, insufficient funds. Even in defeat, however, each female senatorial candidate brought a resurgence of hope. Mrs. Jack Hooper, a Wisconsin Independent who tried to unseat "Fighting Bob" La Follette; Miss Thelma Parkinson, Democrat of New Jersey, who challenged diplomat Dwight W. Morrow; and Mrs. McCormick—all served as visible reminders that someday a woman would be elected to the Senate.

That day came in 1932 with the election of Hattie Caraway. But, because she had no opposition, her victory was viewed by traditionalists as something less than a political landmark.

The senatorial commission that Mrs. Caraway took with her

to Washington and presented at the opening of the lame-duck session of the 72d Congress in December 1931 bore the signature of Governor Harvey Parnell. It entitled her to occupy the seat of her husband, Thaddeus Horatius Caraway, who had died during his second term in office. Because his death had occurred more than a year before the general election, Arkansas law decreed that his successor must be chosen at a special election. The governor called for one to be held on January 12, 1932. While Hattie Caraway, still in mourning, sat as an interim appointee on Capitol Hill, a power struggle erupted back in Arkansas over which man should fall heir to "Thad's" political mantle. Days of haggling produced no consensus; so the Democratic State Central Committee agreed to let his widow be the nominee to fill the vacancy. Governor Parnell himself supported the move, pointing out that she "could use the money" (meaning the $10,000-a-year salary). Nomination by the Democratic hierarchy, according to the peculiarities of Deep South one-party politics, was tantamount to election. Thus Hattie Caraway, without making a single appearance as a candidate before the Arkansas electorate, became the first woman to be elected to the Senate.

She did not have to read the newspapers to learn that what had transpired was "a gracious nod on the part of state politicos, nothing more." She knew that the honor was purely a "polite gesture." What tipped the scales in favor of her accepting the post were personal and family responsibilities. One son was still in school, and she had to meet mortgage payments on a house in Jonesboro. A sense of duty was also involved. She felt an obligation to continue her husband's work.

For Mrs. Caraway, the ethic of standing up to life's challenges was inbred. On the farm of her strict Methodist parents near Bakersville, Tennessee, where she was born in 1878, the worth of an individual as a morally upright person was what counted. Learning and working went hand in hand. By the time she was five years old—before being enrolled in the nearest one-room schoolhouse—Hattie Ophelia Wyatt had memorized the alphabet. And before entering not too distant Dickson Normal College when she was only 14, she was waiting on customers in her father's country store, taking her turn at harvesting the vegetables, and milking three cows a day.

She was graduated from Dickson in 1896 with a B.A. degree and an engagement ring from a fellow senior, 24-year-old Thad Caraway. In 1902 they were married. As the wife of a fledgling lawyer, first in Lake City, Arkansas, then in Jonesboro, she simply went on doing the things she had learned how to do in rural Humphreys County. Like any other manager of a low-income household, she had to cut a corner here, scrimp a bit there. Even so, there was always the frustration of not having enough cash to pay all the bills.

Never a feminist, Hattie Caraway made no apologies. "It's not that I was against women getting the vote," she explained, "but looking after a husband and raising a family [three sons] left me mighty little time for anything else, especially as there were many years when I did all my own work. After suffrage, I just added voting to cooking and sewing."

The "woman's place is in the home" adage became almost a fetish with Mrs. Caraway. Living in the nation's capital off and on while her husband was in Congress, she rarely made an appearance at a social event. Nor did she join a single club. It was not that she was antisocial or unfriendly; rather, the wife-mother role sufficed. The transition from self-imposed obscurity to the center stage of the Senate was effected only slowly and not without a certain amount of awkwardness. She never did adjust to the curiosity of the tourists. "I'm really afraid they are going to poke me with their umbrellas," she once confessed. Furthermore, she seemed unable to cloak herself with the dignity the men expected of anyone admitted to their exclusive club. She carried her lunch to work, had milk delivered to her mahogany-paneled office suite, and left the empty bottles outside the door in the marble corridor.

The antithesis of her loquacious husband, she sat quietly in the Upper Chamber, sometimes reading, sometimes knitting—but always listening. At the conclusion of an overly long debate on the Federal Land Bank bill, she said, "It's funny how they talk on after we [women] have all made up our minds." Her mind was always made up. She was in the Senate, as everyone knew, "to carry on Thad's work." That meant voting as he would have voted.

Whether in the spotlight of the Senate or the dimmer lights of her apartment, Hattie Caraway's mode of dress never changed. Over her dumpling-like figure, she wore full-skirted, dark-colored Victorian dresses and, when spring arrived, simply added a white collar. Feminine chic rated low on her list of priorities. "Do the men think we ladies need a beauty shop?" she asked when the subject of installing one on Capitol Hill was broached.

"Conspicuously inconspicuous" was a phrase writers often used in referring to her. Nevertheless, in no time at all her name became known nationwide. The presence of a woman in the Senate was what editors called a "first-time story," always thrilling to readers who in their own way identified with feats or achievements performed for the first time. That she was there through the "widow's succession" they considered irrelevant.

In Arkansas in the spring of 1932 the political barometer forecast the build-up of a hotly contested Senate race. One by one, six prominent men, representing a cross section of experience and leadership, announced their "availability" for the junior senator's job. Among the earliest to file was World War Governor Charles Hillman Brough, an activist who had gone into Louisiana in 1929 to impeach Governor Huey P. Long. Another was former Senator William F. Kirby. Representing the business community was O. L. Bodenhamer, an oil magnate from El Dorado. The remainder of the list included Democratic National Committeeman Vincent M. Miles, former National Commander of the American Legion Melbourne M. Martin, and former Pulaski County Sheriff and Democratic State Committee Secretary William G. Hutton.

As the May 10 filing deadline approached, two other likely candidates—Hattie Caraway and Governor Parnell—remained to be heard from. The ambitions of the governor were inextricably linked to those of the woman he had helped place in the Senate. At the time of her nomination she had agreed to serve "only until the expiration of Thad's term." But now there were rumors from the Federal City that she might change her mind.

She did, declaring at the eleventh hour that she would seek re-election. The news was received with incredulity by Parnell and others who remembered her solemn promise "to retire" to permit the governor to run. Whether because of chivalry, out of respect for the memory of Thaddeus Caraway, or both, this breach of promise was not made public at the time. Resentment, however, surfaced. Wide publicity was given to "Hattie's slim chances." Out of an estimated 300,000 votes, "she might receive 3,000," one opponent said. They would come mainly from a few die-hard feminists "who would vote for a woman as a matter of principle," from personal friends, and from those who had been the beneficiaries of her husband's favors.

Before Hattie Caraway left Washington early in July to begin her canvass of the state, she asked Louisiana Senator Huey Long, who occupied an adjacent Senate desk, to read her departing statement to assembled colleagues:

> I have stayed at my post in the United States Senate as long as I thought I could be of any service to this country. . . . I have stayed here supporting every effort to secure relief for my peo-

ple. . . . I am now going back to Arkansas to campaign for re-election to the Senate on my record. I believe my people will approve of the record I have made.

Senator Long added a personal political postscript:

To my surprise, Mrs. Caraway has voted contrary to her Party Leader [Senator Joseph T. Robinson] on many important issues. We know her votes were far more worthy and necessary to the people. Her rejection of the influence of Senator Robinson has stamped her as a courageous person, such as this body needs.

Left unsaid was the fact that the Arkansas junior senator had voted *with* her male counterpart from the Bayou State on almost all issues brought before the assembly, particularly on the radical ones dearest to his heart: redistribution of the wealth and tax reform.

Mrs. Caraway launched her campaign on July 15 in Hot Springs. Her platform in this darkening Depression year was simple, and according to the press, "immensely appealing":

I stand for economy in government, state and federal; legislation that is going to work toward relief of the people who really need relief—the man who is losing his home and the man who has lost his job, and the farmer who cannot get the cost of production for his products.

Other than the necessity that something be done to bring back prosperity, there were really no overriding campaign issues. The race would be based on personalities and records of accomplishment. Routine. Or, as the *New York Times* said, "just another biennial scourge."

It would have been, too, except for an announcement from Louisiana. On July 20 Huey Long, an adroit manipulator of crowds, sent word that beginning August 1—one week before Primary Day—he would tour Arkansas in behalf of his colleague. With Senator Caraway's reply that she "wanted him to come and give firsthand information" about her record, the campaign took on a different complexion. Immediately her name was transferred from the list of also-rans to the roster of candidates entitled to serious consideration.

Huey Long, like Hattie Caraway, was a junior senator. But he had taken a different route and used different means to get to Washington. He had stepped out of the Statehouse, using ruthless demagoguery as a springboard to Congress. His famous or infamous, depending on one's political persuasion, "Share Our Wealth" plan was a thinly disguised stratagem to land him in the White House.

Long's convoy, headlined A LOUISIANA MEDICINE SHOW, arrived on schedule, with the Kingfish's blue Cadillac crossing the state line at 9 A.M. on the designated day. The imaginative and somewhat bizarre week-long tour of the state marked the beginning of the end of the slow-moving, lackluster, frock-coat school of political campaigning for high office. What Huey Long introduced to Arkansas was part circus, part revival meeting. The hoopla and evangelizing were geared to converting voters to whom it had never occurred that a woman should represent them in the Senate and also to measure his political influence outside his home state. It was a politician's dream machine. Music blared from sound trucks to attract the crowds; posters lured the people from farms and road forks. Meticulous planning schedules put the Cadillac at just the place where the turnout would be the largest (more than 30,000 assembled in Little Rock). The press was kept happy with a steady diet of handouts. Once Hattie and Huey were on the platform, very often a portable one atop one of the trucks, the men who had passed out pamphlets would assume the role of watchdogs: ejecting drunks, breaking up fights, stroking a howling pup, quieting babies. While the local master of ceremonies, recruited by the advance men, introduced the speakers, one of the sound trucks and one of the vans loaded with flyers, windshield stickers, and other printed matter heralding the candidate would leapfrog to the next stop.

Huey Long, very much the star, succeeded in creating a stellar role for Hattie Caraway as well. This 54-year-old woman dressed in black, with graying hair parted in the middle and drawn back into a plain knot, who had never before addressed a public gathering, spoke before 39 mass meetings in almost as many county seats scattered over the entire state. Together, the duo covered 2,103 highway miles and transmitted their message to approximately 200,000 people—all within the brief time of seven days and seven nights.

Taking a cue from her director, Hattie Caraway acquired a knack for leading up to a climax and waiting for the burst of applause. She refused to attack any of her rivals by name and would not permit Senator Long to do so, but she did take witty cognizance of them:

> I see that one of my opponents claims to have the ear of the President, while another says he has the ear of the Democratic nominee. I am making no collection of ears myself, but I have two good ones of my own, and if you return me to the Senate, I promise you they will always be attuned to your needs.

To convince skeptics and scoffers that their road to salvation lay in the re-election of Hattie Caraway, Huey shouted one refrain over and over: "She voted with you people and your interests in spite of all the pressure Wall Street could bring to bear." Or, if the case warranted—the retail sales tax, for example—"She voted against it." Again and again he alluded to her courage:

> Word came to me that the bankers were going to have her voting their way yet, because of financial difficulties. But she didn't swerve. While she was there in the Senate, a-standing by you, the sheriff sold her home for a mortgage she couldn't pay because she didn't have the money. That was the test, my friends. With all the big-bellied politicans in America campaigning against this one little woman, she stood by you in spite of the fact that the sheriff was selling her home. And don't you ever forget that she wouldn't have to have this home sold. There was an easy road for her to take. Wall Street takes care of its own. But this brave little woman senator stood by you in spite of it and in spite of the fact that the big men politicians of her own state had their feet on her throat.

Only one of Mrs. Caraway's opponents mentioned Long. Four days before the election, former Governor Brough said that she had made the mistake of her life by bringing the self-styled Kingfish to Arkansas. He called Long's methods "crude, cruel and obscene" and said that the large crowds were attracted by mere curiosity "to see a showman in action." The crowds may have come out of curiosity, but the curious went to the polls and voted for Hattie Caraway. The balloting on August 9 gave her 128,426 votes, a total that nearly equaled the combined tally of the six men. Her election in November was a mere formality.

The favorable verdict in Arkansas prompted criticism in Washington. "Just Huey's echo" is what press, public, and even some senators promptly dubbed Hattie Caraway. "Untrue," she replied.

> Right up to the day he made his offer, I hardly knew him. To tell the honest truth, I was a good deal embarrassed when he said he wanted to help me in my fight for re-election. While the proposition had assets, it was not without its liabilities. And when I did decide to accept, I made up my mind to leave no room for future misunderstandings. I told him straight out that it must be *my* campaign, not his.
>
> On top of everything, I let him know that he was barking up the wrong tree if he thought he was going to give orders in the

event of my election. Looking him square in the eye, I said, "Mr. Long, I wouldn't give a dime for my seat in the Senate if I couldn't vote according to my convictions and conscience."

A time came when Huey Long did ask her to vote with him —against the proposal that the United States join the World Court. She told him she was sorry but "couldn't oblige." Hattie Caraway had "no great hopes for the Court" but felt that "at least it was a move in the direction of world peace."

Being the first woman elected to the Senate by popular vote did not alter Hattie Caraway's voting pattern. Her strong interests continued to be legacies from her husband: farm relief, flood control, legislation against lobbies ("Thad hated lobbyists"), and safety in commercial aviation. Repeatedly, but without success, she introduced a favorite bill: a parachute for every airline passenger. Party regular that she was, nearly the whole catalogue of New Deal reforms elicited her unqualified, although barely audible, "Aye."

Membership on the Agriculture and Forestry Committee and on Commerce put her in an advantageous position to assist constituents. "These are matters I know something about," she said. "You can tell by looking at me that I'm a farm woman." But Depression problems, though fairly easy to comprehend, were difficult to solve. She received as many as 5,000 letters a month, most of which began, "Being a woman, I know you will understand." Sometimes the best she could do was to forward a government "how-to" booklet with greetings from "Miss Hattie."

In 1938, without help from Long (he had been assassinated in 1935), she won a second six-year term by defeating Representative John L. McClellan. Her principal campaign asset was her manager, Garrett Whiteside, who was also her office secretary. He was rounding out his 31st year in the service of Arkansas legislators. Referred to on Capitol Hill as the "97th Senator," he used his finely tuned political senses to deliver the votes for Hattie Caraway—a comfortable plurality of 11,650.

Despite re-election, despite her status as a senior senator (Joseph Robinson had died in 1937), and despite being chairman of an essential committee (Enrolled Bills, of which Harry Truman was a member), Senator Caraway still did not emerge as anything other than the deputy of her deceased husband. "The way he voted," she insisted, "was always good enough for Arkansas." So she introduced the kind of legislation he would have advocated—the kind that boosted and bolstered Arkansas industry and education, the kind that supported the farm bloc and real estate and highway interests. He had backed President

Wilson's peace policies. She was a champion of neutrality. When she voted reluctantly in favor of Roosevelt's lend-lease bill, it was with the hope that if America sent supplies it would not have to send men. Once Congress had declared war on the Berlin-Tokyo Axis, she accepted the war as a reality of life, and, like so many other Americans, joined the effort to win it. Throughout World War II, she included in her conscientious correspondence the relatives of constituents killed in battle. Each one received a letter of sympathy, with a neighborly postscript: "If there is anything I can do, please let me know."

To the everlasting gratitude of feminists, she endorsed the Lucretia Mott Equal Rights Amendment. Before 1943, when she spoke out, this piece of legislation had been introduced in the Senate 11 times, each time to die aborning. She had long been convinced, she said, that there was too much prejudice against women, especially in politics. "There is no sound reason why women, if they have the time and the ability, shouldn't sit with men on city councils, in state legislatures, and on Capitol Hill. Particularly if they have *ability!*"

Although Mrs. Caraway defended the rights of women, unshakable racial attitudes prevented her from doing the same for Negroes. In a rare defiance of the Administration, she argued against the antilynching bill. She once told a *Collier's* reporter that she disliked "mean and narrow sectionalism," yet she answered "Nay" to ending the poll tax.

By the time Hattie Caraway decided to campaign for a third full term, she had won acceptance of a sort from many male colleagues, mostly those who were both Southern and Democratic. "She's endowed with common sense," said one. "When she talks, it is briefly and sensibly, every word going to the heart of the matter." "Our woman senator is blazing a new trail and a glowing one," wrote publisher Roberta Fulbright in the *Fayetteville Daily Journal.* "Long enough has this old world done without the contribution women are able to make to [solving] its problems." Ironically, Mrs. Fulbright's congressman son, J. William, would be the one to terminate Hattie Caraway's senatorial career. Handsome, well-to-do, Oxford-educated, he announced his candidacy early—on January 31, 1944. "So you're trying to unseat the sitting hen," Winston Churchill commented during a visit the 39-year-old Fulbright made to London two months later. If the Prime Minister had understood the intricacies of Arkansas politics, Representative Fulbright would have explained that Hattie Caraway had not prompted him to enter the race. He was after the scalp of another contender, Governor Homer Adkins, the man who had earlier fired him from the presidency of the University of Arkansas.

Hattie Caraway, convinced that she was entitled to retain the seat, donned a new straw hat and headed home to Jonesboro to do battle with a male quartet. Besides Fulbright and Adkins, she would face millionaire T. H. Barton, head of the Lion Oil Refining Company and the state's number one industrialist, and J. Rosser Venable, a World War I veteran from Little Rock.

During the scorching summer she crisscrossed the state, speaking competently and pleasantly. Now 66, she managed to radiate confidence. But no one could match the luster, the earnestness, and the reputation of Fulbright. President Roosevelt and Secretary of State Cordell Hull had praised his "statesmanlike qualities." And few would disagree with *Time*'s appraisal that he was "as friendly as an Arkansas hound pup."

Her defeat was foretold by United Press columnist Allen Drury, who wrote caustically and not quite accurately, "It may well be—in fact the press and the Hill in general are sure it will be—that the days of the quiet little grandmother . . . who wanders in, reads a newspaper or sits solemnly in the presiding chair, and then wanders out again, having won nothing, lost nothing, and done nothing, are numbered."

More than 185,000 votes were cast in the July primary. Fulbright led his nearest rival, Governor Adkins, by 16,352 ballots. The political life of Hattie Wyatt Caraway, who placed a poor fourth, was over.

Walking away from power and privilege is never easy. Hattie Caraway delayed leaving the capital, hoping for a prestigious position, preferably with the Department of Agriculture, where she could put to use her 13 years of Senate committee experience. But, when President Truman offered her an appointment to the three-member Employees' Compensation Commission, she accepted. In 1946 she was elevated to a $9,000-a-year job on the Employees' Compensation Appeals Board, a post she held until her death in suburban Falls Church, Virginia, in 1950.

Partly by chance, partly by choice, Hattie Caraway would always have a secure niche in political history. The first woman elected (and re-elected) to the Senate, she would be remembered for that accomplishment alone—and by some for the promise she did not keep.

Winds of Change

The 1932 national election was described by columnist Arthur
Krock of the *New York Times* as "a political cataclysm unprecedented in the nation's history." His interpretation was valid. The electorate, by an outsized margin, terminated the White
House lease Republicans had held for 12 years and granted the
Democrats a generous majority in Congress. This same plebiscite
also launched the New Deal, a radical economic recovery plan
that was to change drastically much in American life.

For Democratic women, recently stirred to unprecedented
political activity, the year 1932 was marked by a flourish of hope.
Their gain of two new seats in the House represented something of a milestone. Furthermore, it touched off a winning
streak that would give them a total of seven places before the
decade ended. The erosion of Republicans was so thorough by
1938 that the lone GOP woman to survive in the 75th Congress
was Representative Edith Nourse Rogers of Massachusetts.

The Democratic congresswomen were of a liberal mien, but
individually they reflected different shades of the political spectrum. Their diverse viewpoints added color and motion to the
era that ushered in Franklin D. Roosevelt's Presidency.

What they said—and did—was reported in a more serious vein
than heretofore. Their couture received only infrequent attention from the press. In the austere times spawned by the Great

Depression, things frivolous were irrelevant. Purposeful work had priority.

VIRGINIA E. JENCKES
DEMOCRAT OF INDIANA

In congressional politics, a candidate occasionally gains office because of an abrupt shift in opinion on a national issue. A case in point: the 1932 election of Virginia Ellis Jenckes in Indiana's newly reshaped 6th Congressional District.

Before the spring primary, practically the only place that 49-year-old Mrs. Jenckes was known and admired was Vigo County, where she had been born and schooled, where she owned 1,300 acres of productive farmland near Terre Haute, and where she had won her public service stripes as founder and secretary of the Wabash and Maumee Valley Improvement Association. As a candidate for Congress, she first jolted pundits by collecting enough primary votes to defeat fellow Democrat Courtland C. Gillen, a one-term incumbent from Greencastle. In the second and decisive round in November she retired Fred S. Purnell of Attica, who had been a Republican representative for 16 years (beginning in the 65th Congress as a colleague of Jeannette Rankin's).

Both campaigns were won largely because of Mrs. Jenckes's logical and convincing case against Prohibition. Her 10-county district was a microcosm of American economic troubles in 1932. Its distilleries and breweries had been shuttered and padlocked since 1919; locally grown corn, worth as much as $1.84 a bushel in 1920, had skidded downward to an intolerable low of 15 cents.

Both Gillen and Purnell vigorously supported the Volstead Act. Virginia Jenckes, emphasizing the rise in grain prices and the reduction in unemployment that Repeal would bring, produced an unanswerable argument that swept her to victory.

An enthusiastic and outspoken campaigner, Mrs. Jenckes, chauffeured by her daughter, covered more than 15,000 miles in her quest for votes. High on her list of local concerns, she told audiences, was control of the wandering and sometimes vicious Wabash River. She reminded listeners that for the previous 10 years she had badgered the federal government to construct floodwalls and drainage canals to prevent the $2 million annual loss suffered in this very large fertile valley. And she did not let them forget that she had had firsthand experience with controlling the Wabash: Once, when the river had threatened to burst its banks and flood a $15,000 crop, she had labored with neighboring farmers through an entire night, helping them pile 3,000 sandbags atop a recently completed dike.

Except for her pince-nez, town-bred Mrs. Jenckes looked and talked like a farmer's wife, which she had been from the time of her 1912 marriage to Ray Greene Jenckes until his death in 1921. She wore her long, wavy gray hair parted in the middle, combed back, and circled around her head in a wide braid. Her complexion was ruddy; her figure, firm. She could define "parity index" in terms as practical as those she employed in describing either new uses for cornhusks or ways to stretch the food dollar.

The high hopes Virginia Jenckes took to Washington for her Hoosier constituents, whether farmers or flood victims, seemed justified. Indeed, Roosevelt's promise of "action—and action now" was fulfilled with unheard-of alacrity. During the fabled "Hundred Days," she voted on an amazing array of measures designed to rescue the plummeting economy. And, before the first session of the 73d Congress ended, repeal of Prohibition was ensured.

But on another level—finding an outlet for her personal powers of persuasion—she discovered that her optimism had been premature. Her request to serve on either the Rivers and Harbors or Agriculture Committee was turned aside. Only one of the three committees on which the Democratic leadership placed her—Civil Service, the District of Columbia, and Mines and Mining—was relevant to her constituency. The largest coal mine in Indiana was in the area she represented, and there had been a mine on her property—before flood waters inundated it.

Looking ahead pragmatically, Congresswoman Jenckes announced that she intended "to take her District Committee assignment seriously." Guided by Chairman Mary Norton's voice of experience, she quickly demonstrated a sharp social conscience. She became the self-appointed guardian of overworked and underpaid D.C. police, firemen, and jail guards and worked with the zeal of a reformer to shorten their hours, raise their wages, and provide for their financial security in old age.

The farmers back home questioned her allegiance. So did the jobless—particularly after funds for Roosevelt's Civil Works Administration began to run out in the spring of 1934. Restive Hoosiers talked of ousting New Dealers in the November election. And Representative Jenckes was very nearly a victim of their discontent and dissatisfaction. With Purnell again the challenger, she watched her 1932 plurality of more than 10,000 shrink to a precarious 383.

The 74th Congress (1935–37) did somewhat better by the electorate. The farmer's lot began to improve. New bridges were due to span the Wabash, levees were earmarked under the Works Progress Administration (WPA) for critical spots along its banks, and a federal building would rise in Indianapolis. The good showing she made in the 1936 election was not so much a personal victory as a reflection of the fact it was a watershed year for the New Deal.

The death of her daughter (from tuberculosis) the same year was an emotional shock from which she recovered very slowly and only by immersing herself in work. During her third term, she moved on many different legislative fronts—all praiseworthy but not necessarily germane to Indiana—and her name appeared on a veritable blizzard of bills and amendments.

Though consumerism was not then a potent political issue, she became an implacable foe of dishonest merchandising. The bill she introduced "to thoroughly revise the Food and Drugs Act" would have extended consumer protection to cosmetics, therapeutic devices, obesity remedies, and a host of other over-the-counter items, some of which remained outside of government control in 1972.

She attacked all manner of subversives. "I appeal to every mother in the District of Columbia and throughout the nation," she said on one occasion, "to become informed concerning the indoctrination of Communism in the public schools of our Nation's Capital as well as schools throughout America."

Adversaries accused her of wearing the flag on her sleeve. She did not deny the allegation. "I'm a patriot," she declared, and she promptly sent a letter to the Federal Communications Commission suggesting that American shortwave broadcasters sign off with "The Star-spangled Banner."

Like her colleague Florence Kahn, she was a champion of the Federal Bureau of Investigation (FBI). Whenever Director J. Edgar Hoover's budget requests were debated on the floor, she was among the first to urge approval. "If this House of Representatives refuses to appropriate the amount of money Mr. Hoover deems necessary," she said more than once, "then this House of Representatives and the Congress must stand responsible for any increase in kidnaping, white slavery, extortion, and other crimes." As a rule her remarks were followed by applause and Hoover's monetary requests were granted.

Virginia Jenckes's defeat by former Representative Noble J.

Johnson in 1938 was primarily due to her strained relations with the Statehouse. When she told the Indiana Women's Democratic Club that Governor Paul V. McNutt "failed to cooperate with the congressional delegation on work relief," Pleas Greenlee, McNutt's patronage secretary, branded her a traitor and marked her for "elimination at the next election."

Her postcongressional life took on some of the aspects of a cloak-and-dagger affair when she helped five Hungarian priests who had escaped from a Budapest prison enter the United States. An advocate of U.S. intervention on the side of the anti-Communists during the ill-fated 1956 uprisings in Hungary, she accused the Eisenhower Administration of treating the Hungarians "like the devil."

After moving from her farmhouse to an efficiency apartment in Indianapolis in 1969, Mrs. Jenckes announced she "had retired." Although in her early 90s and handicapped by a hearing impairment, she is as outspoken and peppery as ever. Inflation is one of her current worries, and she blames the high cost of government. "Congressmen are paid too much and have too big an office force," she said in an interview with Susan Lennis of the *Indianapolis Star*. "They don't pay much attention to giving—it's more getting."

KATHRYN O'LOUGHLIN McCARTHY
DEMOCRAT OF KANSAS

Ranchers on the Kansas prairies, like Indiana farmers, threw political tradition to the winds in 1932 and entrusted their legislative hopes to a woman who was also a Democrat. To replace the Republican 6th District incumbent and former judge, Charles I. Sparks of Goodland, they selected Kathryn Ellen O'Loughlin, a 38-year-old lawyer whose life began on a ranch near Hays.

In contrast to her colleague Virginia Jenckes, Miss O'Loughlin was well prepared to serve as a U.S. representative. She had been not only a delegate to three state Democratic conventions but a successful candidate for the State Legislature as well. "The new 'Lady from Kansas,' whose slender figure gives no hint of a youth spent tramping wheat stacks, driving teams of wild horses, trudging frozen miles to country schools, is the legislator the suffrage fighters promised us" is the way the *Ladies' Home Journal* heralded the arrival in Washington of John O'Loughlin's Kate.

Kathryn O'Loughlin, product of Irish heritage and prairie environment, was a woman of courage and conviction who possessed an agile, alert, and above-average mind. Over her father's objections, she had gone east—to the University of Chicago—to earn a law degree. And almost from the moment she was admitted to the bar she began to watch for the right moment to enter the national political mainstream. When it actually came, she was the only one who thought it was right—and proved it by defeating eight men in the primary.

During a thorough canvassing of her huge district (26 counties comprising the northwestern quarter of the state), she was applauded by the farmers for her blunt appraisal of what should be done about the mountains of wheat and corn rotting in the fields and on the ground along railroad sidings. She proposed, in one-two-three order, reduction of the tariff, liquidation of the Farm Board, and a dollar based on commodity prices instead of the gold standard. Other boosts to the economy she said she would ask for in Washington were collection of war debts and lower taxes. The latter, she declared, could be effected through a more effiicient government. "It's as urgent as ploughing and harvesting."

In Mankato a listener who had always been opposed to women holding public office became so overwhelmingly enamored of Miss McLoughlin's assets that he not only joined her campaign but proposed marriage. In the political wedding of the year, celebrated on February 4, 1933, in a small Catholic church on the O'Loughlin ranch, Kathryn Ellen became the bride of newly elected State Senator Daniel M. McCarthy.

Kathryn O'Loughlin McCarthy fared no better than Virginia Jenckes with regard to committee assignments, but she took the rare step (for a freshman) of challenging the system. Her letter of resignation from the Committee on Insular Affairs did not ask, "Where, pray tell, are the islands of Kansas?"; yet the question was implicit. She was rebuffed in her bid for Agriculture but did land a place on Education.

As the Depression continued to silence school bells all across the land (in the spring of 1934, 316 schools had been closed in Kansas alone) and a high percentage of the nation's teachers were subsisting on between $450 and $750 a year, Rrepresentative McCarthy sought to convince her more conservative colleagues that government grants to education "would not surrender the educational system to Federal control." Her particular concern was aid to vocational training—home economics, agriculture, and industrial arts. Because she was familiar with the public education process (she had graduated from Hays State Teachers College before attending law school), she made a persuasive spokeswoman for the emergency legislation proposed by the Education Committee and enacted by Congress.

Kathryn McCarthy kept her finger on the pulse of the Kansas farmer by calling periodic meetings of county representatives in her district and inviting their reaction to measures proposed in Washington. She came away from one of these polling sessions with the announcement that the Agricultural Adjustment Act (AAA) was "saving the farmer." In 1933 there was validity to such a statement.

By 1934, however, when this New Deal legislation faced its first electoral test, farmers' attitudes had changed. In Kansas there arose crystallized opposition to the AAA, and Kathryn McCarthy was caught in the middle. As the *New York Times* explained:

> Mrs. McCarthy has called attention to the cooperation of the farmers in the recovery plan as proof of its popularity. Now come the farmers and voice disapproval of the corn-hog and grain sections.
>
> When the AAA adventure began, the Kansas farmer was hard up. He was without experience with governmental red tape. He was caught in the psychology of the quick relief the New Deal was supposed to bring.

More than a year of government control had worn down the farmer's enthusiasm for regimented agriculture. Independent to the core, he refused to go on trying to fit his crops into a production strait jacket. Having become disgusted with the entire business, he refused support to anyone who claimed that the AAA was beneficial to agriculture.

If Kathryn McCarthy's conquest of the Kansas farmer did not long endure, she had the satisfaction of giving her 1934 opponent, Republican Frank Carlson, a spirited race. His plurality was only slightly more than 7,500 votes.

"Kansas never broods over things," William Allen White once editorialized in the *Emporia Gazette*. Neither did Mrs. McCarthy. As long as her health permitted (she died at age 58 in 1952), she remained active on the periphery of politics, giving advice, campaigning, and casting her vote at Democratic state and national conventions. She also resumed her law practice.

When the Agricultural Adjustment Act was struck down by the Supreme Court, she could say, as did others who had been willing to follow Roosevelt's new and untrod path, that "the nation's farm economy had made an impressive recovery from the depression trough of 1932 and 1933."

MARIAN W. CLARKE
REPUBLICAN OF NEW YORK

The only GOP addition to the feminine congressional contingent during the first seven years of the New Deal was Marian Williams Clarke of New York. The widow of six-term Representative John D. Clarke, who had been killed in an automobile accident, she served during the second session of the 73d Congress (1934) and did not seek re-election. Attesting to their die-hard Republicanism, voters from the four-county area (Broome, Chanango, Delaware, and Otsego) comprising the 34th Congressional District struggled in from their farms during one of the worst blizzards in memory to give Mrs. Clarke a majority in a special election held on December 28, 1933.

Although born in the East (Standing Stone, Pennsylvania, in 1880), Marian Williams grew up in Wyoming. She and Clarke met on the campus of Colorado College, where he was doing postgraduate work and where she earned her B.A. degree in 1902. Before marrying and moving to New York three years later, she was a newspaperwoman in Colorado Springs.

Regardless of how much legislative skill Marian Clarke might have possessed (she boasted about having been a "gallery member" and a "general factotum" in her husband's office), the chance of any non-New Deal measures' being considered by the top-heavy Democratic Congress simply did not exist. Other than speaking briefly on the need for a tariff to protect a shoe industry in her constituency "from cheap labor and unfair competition" and urging restoration of a cut in equipment allowances for rural mail carriers "whose lives are already so hard," she was a member of the silent minority.

Until 1939, when her only son lost his life (also in an automobile accident), she remained active in Republican circles and served as an alternate delegate to the 1936 GOP National Convention in Cleveland. Prior to her own death in Cooperstown in 1953, she lived in seclusion on the Clarke farm, Arbor Hill, near Delhi, New York.

ISABELLA GREENWAY
DEMOCRAT OF ARIZONA

When Arizona's only House seat was vacated in 1933 by Lewis
W. Douglas, newly chosen Director of the Budget, the landslide
choice of the electorate to fill the vacancy was Isabella Greenway, well-to-do rancher and businesswoman. As congresswoman
at large, she was responsible to a statewide constituency of
nearly 450,000 people.

Under ordinary circumstances, the challenge of responding to
citizen confidence would have been enormous. But the circumstances were not ordinary. More than 140,000 men and women
were on relief. The Depression had shut down the copper
mines, the state's primary revenue source, and no one knew
when they would reopen.

Congress was not in session, but the stricken state was entitled to its fair share from the Public Works Administration till.
Ten days after being elected, Isabella Greenway was in the office of Secretary of Interior Harold L. Ickes, who was also PWA
administrator. Their encounter, as related by Emily Newell Blair,
a New Deal appointee, illustrates the charming and uniquely
persuasive manner that was synonymous with the Greenway
name:

> The interview was set for one o'clock. Entering on the stroke, she
> found Ickes weary and worn-looking. "I hate to talk to a man
> just before he has lunch," she said.
>
> "I never eat lunch," returned Ickes.
>
> "Oh but you should," protested Mrs. Greenway and, diving
> into her capacious bag, produced a big red apple.
>
> "This isn't the Garden of Eden, you know," remonstrated the
> Secretary.
>
> "That makes it perfectly safe," retorted Mrs. Greenway, and
> disappeared into the outer office. She sent a messenger to the
> corner to buy a bottle of milk. Shortly she was back in the office
> pouring the milk into a glass for the Secretary. "Now we can
> talk," she said.
>
> "Mrs. Greenway, my time is very valuable. Can you compress
> all that Arizona wants onto one page?"
>
> "Mr. Secretary," she replied, "Arizona would never forgive me
> if I could get all it wanted onto one page."
>
> Again she dove into her bag, retrieved a much-scribbled-over
> envelope, and outlined the projects one by one. When she left
> the Secretary, he knew what Arizona wanted.

What the congresswoman came away with was the assurance

of an immediate appropriation of $14 million for a Verde River irrigation project. It would put 3,000 men to work for three years. Flood control construction at Nogales and a post office building in Phoenix would remove another 6,000 from the dole. An auspicious beginning.

Isabella Greenway's PWA initiative made her highly news-worthy. Asked by a member of the Washington press corps if her success with Ickes had been abetted by her close friendship with the First Family, she paraphrased a statement she had made to political adversaries during her campaign: "A great deal has been said about my being a friend of the Roosevelts. I did not ask for votes on the basis of friendship but on the basis I was qualified to do the work. And it is on that basis I am getting the job done."

Whether or not she "had a latchkey to the White House," as one magazine writer reported, Isabella Greenway enjoyed a very special relationship with its occupants. Democrats, particularly in Arizona, had been aware of the bond even before she sec-onded FDR's nomination at the Chicago Convention. During the ensuing Presidential campaign, Roosevelt was a guest at her Quarter Circle Double-X Ranch near Williams, and the speech he made at the rodeo-style rally she hosted there was widely publicized. But only after the First Lady was seen arriving, on foot, at the Willard Hotel to escort Isabella to the White House for lunch did Washington begin to take the measure of the re-lationship.

It had begun with Eleanor's uncle, Theodore Roosevelt, whom Kentucky-born Isabella Selmes had known intimately as a child. She and the First Lady-to-be had been school chums at Miss Chapin's in Manhattan, and in 1905, at the age of 19, she was a bridesmaid at Eleanor and Franklin's wedding. To the Roosevelt children she was "Aunt Isabella."

For drama and theatricality, the Arizona congresswoman's life surpassed anything in fiction. After her New York City debut, she was introduced to two young men who had fought with the Rough Riders, Robert H. Monroe Ferguson and John Campbell Greenway. She married the first in 1905 and the second in 1923. When Ferguson contracted tuberculosis, they homesteaded, with two young children, in the New Mexico desert, living in tents until their house was finished. He died in 1921. Green-way, who had distinguished himself as an officer with the Ameri-can Expeditionary Force in France, was a copper magnate and one of Arizona's favorite sons. Their ranch at Ajo was a center of memorable hospitality.

Widowed again in 1926, Isabella Greenway moved with her infant son, John Selmes Greenway, and two older children to Tucson, where she launched a program to aid veterans (in New Mexico she had laid the foundation for a public service career by serving as state director of the Women's Land Army). The Arizona Hut, which she opened and managed, was a woodcraft factory employing convalescent soldiers from two wars. As the furniture piled up in a warehouse, she sold her copper stock and with the proceeds built the Arizona Inn, equipping it with furniture and handicrafts manufactured at the Hut.

Mrs. Greenway was introduced to politics in 1928 when she toured the state for Presidential hopeful Al Smith. That same year she was elected to the Democratic National Committee. No one expected her to take the position seriously, but she did, making an 8-hour-a-day job of it.

A blend of Scotch-Irish exuberance, Southern cordiality, and Western independence, Congresswoman Greenway was, at 47, arrestingly pretty. Some said she looked like Lillie Langtry, the English actress noted for her beauty; to others, she suggested a full-blown rose—comparisons prompted by her rosy complexion (she used no cosmetics) and misty-blonde hair, worn casually, bobbed and bouffant.

What surprised everyone on Capitol Hill was that in her maiden speech she took issue with FDR. He had announced his opposition to the soldiers' bonus, claiming that the more than $2 billion demanded by World War veterans was needed for his recovery program. Representative Greenway, by choosing to inject herself into the explosive battle brewing in the House, said she was as concerned with "satisfying ex-servicemen" as with removing the bill from its "political football status." The measure passed in the House but was rejected in the Senate. Not until her second term (she was re-elected by better than a 2-to-1 margin) did the bonus bill—a thorny issue that during four administrations had cost numerous members, including Alice Robertson, their congressional seats—become law.

Isabella Greenway's second legislative disagreement with the President came during the protracted House labors on the omnibus social security bill. Roosevelt had said he would insist on passage of the entire package. But the subject was so extraordinarily complex that it invited a great deal of hair-splitting, even among the bill's adherents. Representative Greenway, fearing that agreement could not be reached on so unwieldy and ambitious a scheme, moved to force separate consideration of the old-age pension provisions, over which there was the least controversy. "I am determined to save something from this wreck," she said.

Such a display of ostentatious independence by a woman who occupied, in the view of the *New York Times,* "a position reserved for her as a well-meaning social and sentimental vassal of the Administration" puzzled New Deal stalwarts. What they failed to recognize was that the West in Arizona's congresswoman would more or less inevitably find deep personal loyalty compatible with political differences.

The arguments she used to save the old-age pension feature were that it was not only an urgent social necessity but an economic stimulant as well, because regular pensions would remove older workers from the labor market, thus easing the crunch of unemployment. Moreover, the spending of those pensions would vitalize the channels of commerce.

Those who believed she would remain hitched to the Roosevelt policies no matter what political heavens fell drew all sorts of inferences from her independent course. "In a single day in the Capitol's whispering galleries," wrote Duncan Airman in the *New York Times Magazine,* "it is possible to hear that Mrs. Greenway is 'breaking with the White House,' that she is a 'hopeless' politician about to be returned to ranch life in Arizona by outraged Republican majorities, that she will join the House 'mavericks,' and that she secretly yearns to be Vice President."

Although political dissent over social security legislation was never stilled, the bill passed both the House and the Senate by large majorities. It became law with the President's signature in August 1935.

The following March, Isabella Greenway announced that she would not seek re-election. Citing a desire to devote more time to "family activities," she said, "Our interests are widely scattered and right exacting." Reminded that she had been mentioned as a candidate for governor of Arizona, she said, "I don't intend to be a candidate."

Indications that her disagreement with certain policies of the Roosevelt Administration was the root cause of her decision to leave Washington were apparently borne out in 1940 when she joined Democrats-for-Willkie (Wendell L. Willkie, the Republican Presidential nominee), a movement opposing a third term for FDR. After the advent of World War II, she headed the American Women's Voluntary Service. She also remarried, becoming the wife of Harry O. King, a New York and Bridgeport industrialist whom she had met during the early New Deal days when he was NRA (National Recovery Administration) administrator for the copper industry. In 1953, after a long illness, she died in Tucson at 67.

As a congresswoman-elect, Isabella Greenway had speculated about her future. "Whatever happens," she told a friend, "I must succeed for Arizona." To the extent that she went to Congress with a full-fledged political philosophy and with the courage to follow it, she did not fail.

CAROLINE O'DAY
DEMOCRAT OF NEW YORK

Coincidental with Congresswoman Marion Clarke's predictable entrance-exit routine on the national political stage, the Republican Party chose New York as the show place for an attempted comeback from the 1932 debacle. As one of its two representative-at-large nominees, the GOP leadership selected an able lawyer, Natalie F. Couch. She was given a better-than-even chance to collect more votes than the only female Democratic candidate, Caroline O'Day, a social worker.

In contrast to the rather spiritless congressional campaigns nationwide, the contest in the Empire State was lively. Both women took strong, divergent stands on national issues, turning the foray into a virtual minireferendum on the Roosevelt Administration. Miss Couch, a party leader who had broadened her law experience by working in the State Appellate Division, hammered away at a long list of grievances against the New Deal, accusing it of everything from "undermining the capitalist system" to "programming the farmer to death." Mrs. O'Day, as expected, voiced 100 per cent approval of FDR's recovery plan.

The surprise of the campaign was the personal appearance of Eleanor Roosevelt. Never before had a First Lady left the White House to campaign. It was reported that she had asked for—and received—permission from the President "to endorse her friend and former co-worker." Whether she had or not was not important. The crowds responded with a massive outpouring of support for Mrs. O'Day. And, even though she did not capture her home county of Westchester, and in fact carried only 9 of the state's 62 counties, she became the first woman to be elected at large from New York. Her backing came almost exclusively from Manhattan, where Mrs. Roosevelt had spoken, and the four other boroughs.

Although Caroline O'Day retained the seat for three successive terms (the Republicans entered a woman candidate in each race: Miss Couch again in 1936, Helen Zimmerman M. Rodgers of Buffalo in 1938, and Mary Honor Donlon in 1940), the margin of her subsequent victories never topped the 1934 figure. Furthermore, Republican-oriented Westchester County voted against her in ever increasing numbers. The political significance of this election pattern is that it closely paralleled the national voting trend (outside the South) during the 1930s.

Somewhat ironically, Caroline O'Day got her party's nod for representative at large because of her reputation for getting out the Democratic vote, particularly in upstate Republican strongholds. At one point she had toured this area by car with Mrs. Roosevelt. Together they had traveled 8,000 miles and achieved, according to the *New York Times,* "marked success in organizing women Democrats into a potent political force."

Mrs. O'Day's saga of political involvement had actually begun with the suffrage movement (in 1917 she had lobbied beside Jeannette Rankin in Albany to obtain the vote for New York women). Later, joining the Westchester League of Women Voters, she taught the rudiments of politics to other women. As early as 1923 she was elected associate chairman of the Democratic State Committee, and in 1932 James A. Farley, Roosevelt's political tactician, pushed aside well-known John Fitzgibbon of Oswego to make room for her on the National Committee.

Although Caroline O'Day and Ruth Baker Pratt, a former New York congresswoman still active in GOP circles, were never within shouting distance of one another and on political ideology were instinctive opposites, there were parallels, if not actual similarities, between them. Each was the widow of a Standard Oil executive; both owned large suburban estates; and both had turned to social-welfare service after World War I because they believed wealth imposed an obligation to those less fortunate. Of the two, Caroline O'Day was of a far more progressive political persuasion; yet they both displayed a similar passion for improving the lot of the poor. Whereas Ruth Pratt had zeroed in on slums and graft, Mrs. O'Day's special concern was for aliens and blue-collar workers.

A transplanted Southerner (by way of Europe, where she became a painter and etcher of distinction), she had been born Caroline Love Goodwin on a plantation in Perry, Georgia (near Macon) in 1875 and educated at Lucy Cobb Institute, a fashionable private boarding school for young ladies located in Athens. Her physical appearance was often likened to the *Portrait of a Lady* by Velásquez—slender, with a narrow face, high cheekbones, clear blue eyes, and hair arranged in an elegant French knot. She married Daniel T. O'Day in 1902, and when he died in 1916 was left with the responsibility of rearing their two sons and a daughter. Solicitude for their education prompted her to seek—and obtain—the top post on the Rye School Board.

Volunteer social work at the Henry Street Settlement led to her first professional appointment. In 1921 Governor Alfred E. Smith named her to the State Board of Social Welfare, the agency charged with supervision of public institutions caring for dependent juveniles. With the advent of the National Recovery Administration (NRA), she served as state director. As a member of the Consumers League, she exposed exploitation of workers by the candy industry. Employers hired beginners for $2–3 a week, then, as soon as they became experienced, fired them in order to take on more beginners at the same low wages. Mrs. O'Day also helped obtain the first minimum-wage scale for New York laundry workers.

A survey she made of conditions on Ellis Island for Frances Perkins, chairman of the State Industrial Commission, was responsible for her appointment to the House Immigration and Naturalization Committee. She won her first major legislative victory when members adopted her resolution (by a vote of 200 to 118) to permit 2,600 aliens to remain in the United States pending further investigation. Based on personal observation, her report disclosed that the people involved were "deserving human beings" whose deportation would mean "unusual hardship for their 7,000 dependents." An outspoken critic of the Dies (Martin Dies of Texas) bill to deport "undesirable" aliens, she signed the minority report stating that the measure was "founded on the fallacy that ideas and beliefs may be effectively changed or suppressed by legislation."

Her zealous defense of minorities did not, curiously, include the equal rights amendment. "I fear it would wipe out the protective laws for women in industry for which I worked so hard in New York," she said. "There's too much legislation needed for poor mothers, undernourished children and overworked factory girls to consider seriously the blind insistence of equal rights."

Ever a doer, she was a mixture of idealism and pragmatic realism. When Mary Norton, as chairman of the Labor Committee, led the fight for Roosevelt's federal labor standards bill, Representative O'Day was in the forefront. Although she decried its limited scope, she knew it would at least guarantee the principle of wage-hour regulation in the statute books. Furthermore, she wanted the substitute amendment offered by rebellious Southerners exposed for what it was: "petty protectionism for slave wages."

This antipathy toward racial discrimination was a legacy not from her native South but from the integrated Paris of her student days. In 1939 she joined Secretary of the Interior Harold Ickes in publicly protesting the refusal by the DAR to permit Marian Anderson, the eminent Negro contralto, to sing in Constitution Hall.* Going further, she sent to prominent people invitations asking them to support the concert, rescheduled for the Mall at the base of the Lincoln Memorial.

Caroline O'Day's friendship with the Roosevelts led to frequent accusations by the Republicans that she was a "New Deal rubber stamp." The GOP claim was only moderately extravagant. She consistently supported all major New Deal measures that came before Congress, with few notable exceptions: She voted against repeal of the arms embargo in 1939 and against the 1940 selective service bill, both of which the Administration favored.

A resolute peace worker for many years, she was vice-chairman of the Women's International League for Peace and Freedom, and in 1936 flew to Buenos Aires to present to the Inter-American Conference for the Maintenance of Peace an anti-war petition containing more than 1 million signatures. "Women will no longer consent to war," she told the delegates. "There is no problem affecting humanity that cannot be settled without recourse to the battlefield." If another war should occur, she declared on another occasion, "I would just kiss my children good-bye and start off for Leavenworth."

As the days of peace ran out in 1939, Caroline O'Day stepped up her efforts to prevent "our country from walking blindly into the Death Valley of the jungle." She assailed the U.S. Army and Navy as the "strongest and most powerful lobby in the nation." She even offered to endorse any Republican who backed peace legislation, and she deliberately alienated some members of the Immigration Committee by insisting that "the willingness to bear arms is not the truest way of showing patriotism."

* The Daughters of the American Revolution has repeatedly refuted allegations that the organization was guilty of such an insult to Marian Anderson. The facts are these: Constitution Hall had been reserved by the National Symphony Orchestra, six months in advance, for the evening of April 9, 1939, the date requested by Miss Anderson's manager; moreover, eight years earlier, when Negroes were barred from every public stage in the segregated capital, the DAR had rented the Hall to Roland Hayes.

Pacificism fell out of favor after the Pearl Harbor attack on December 7, 1941, and Caroline O'Day, with other antiwar militants, fell silent—partly because nobody was listening, partly because she was ill. An invalid throughout the 1940 campaign, she relied on her daughter Elia as a stand-in. To still rumors that she would be too ill to serve if elected, her physician issued a statement in late October that she had recovered sufficiently to resume her activities "in the near future." She took the oath of office for the 77th Congress (1941–43) at her home in Rye and resumed her congressional duties on a limited scale until injured by a fall in 1942. On December 31 she retired from office, having announced earlier that she would not seek re-election. On January 4, 1943, the day after the expiration of her fourth term, she died.

Early in her political career, Mrs. O'Day had mentioned that she would like a chance to prove, "as other women in Congress have proved, that women can be as good and useful as the men." That she convinced New York voters was evident during her lifetime. They chose another woman (a Republican) as representative at large in 1942.

NAN WOOD HONEYMAN
DEMOCRAT OF OREGON

Oregon's shift away from rock-ribbed Republicanism, to which the electorate had been wedded since Civil War days, suggested to Democrat Nan Wood Honeyman in 1935 that she could move from the State House of Representatives to Congress. On announcing her candidacy, she was asked if her family had agreed with her decision to run. "Yes," she said. "If I'm elected, my son will stay in Portland with his father [David T. Honeyman] and our daughter Judith will go East with me."

In the 3d District (Multnomah County) race, she made support of the Roosevelt program a major plank in her platform and defeated the Republican incumbent, William A. Ekwall, by a comfortable margin. That Oregon, which had granted suffrage to women in 1912, would one day send a woman to Washington had long been a realistic possibility, but to the elders in the Grand Old Party it came as a mild shock that the first one would be a Democrat.

Mrs. Honeyman, 55, who had been an active worker for other politicians over the years, acquired a political reputation of her own in 1933, when she was president of the Oregon Constitutional Convention that ratified the 21st Amendment. A teetotaler herself, she led the drive to repeal Prohibition because she "didn't believe that any law governing people's personal conduct should be a part of the Constitution."

Like Isabella Greenway and Caroline O'Day, Nan Honeyman was a friend of the Roosevelts. While a student at the Finch School in Manhattan at the turn of the century, she was an attendant, with Harvard undergraduate Franklin Roosevelt, at the Hyde Park wedding of his niece and a member of the Oyster Bay branch of the family. At the 1936 Democratic Convention in Philadelphia she seconded FDR's nomination.

During the years when Eleanor Roosevelt made periodic visits to her daughter Anna Boettiger in Seattle, she sometimes stopped at the large Honeyman home on the heights above Portland. Once she set up a temporary office there to write her syndicated "My Day" column.

Mrs. Honeyman, though born in West Point, New York, considered herself a native Oregonian because she was only two when her parents moved to Portland. To the extent that everyone is a product of his heritage, it is not unusual that Nan Wood Honeyman cast her lot with political liberals. Her paternal forebears had won religious liberty by founding the Free Church of Scotland. And her father, Charles Erskine Scott Wood, who resigned his West Point commission because he "couldn't stand blind authority on one side and blind response on the other," was a "New Dealer" long before the term was coined. For 60 years on the Pacific Coast he voiced his protest against economic injustice.

Of the 95 new faces at the convening of the 75th Congress, the only feminine one belonged to Nan Honeyman, a matronly-looking woman with graying hair. It was of more interest to Oregonians that she was named to the Rivers and Harbors Committee (also to Indian Affairs and to Irrigation and Reclamation). She had told constituents that her chief activity in Washington "will be for the port," and she was assured of a prestigious place from which to function.

Representative Honeyman spoke in committee, but only infrequently and never as a proponent of the Portland port. From the floor she suggested that her nation's defenses be strengthened. She also asked the District of Columbia Committee to designate a street as Oregon Avenue. And she proposed that the federal government sponsor a national poetry award. For all of her intelligence, when presented with an ideal opportunity to address herself to campaign promises, she did not do so. During hearings on legislation crucial to the operation of Bonneville Dam, then nearing completion on the Columbia River, she said that she had no opinion of her own but wanted only what President Roosevelt wanted. This was more than the pro-Republican Portland *Oregonian* could tolerate. "It is true," the paper editorialized, "that Representative Honeyman voted to override Mr. Roosevelt's veto of the farm interest bill; otherwise she has confined her endeavors to singing whatever tune the President indicates."

When massive citizen opposition arose over FDR's attempt to alter the complexion of the Supreme Court (his enemies called it "packing the Court"), she committed the unpardonable sin of answering protest mail from constituents with a letter duplicated on a multigraph machine. In essence, her reply said that she could not be dissuaded from backing the President in his plan "to liberalize the judiciary." For this caper she was tagged by critics—including many Democrats—a "stencil for the White House duplicating machine."

Asked during one of her home visits about future plans, Representative Honeyman said that she would run for re-election "if the populace sufficiently admires my maiden record." Despite growing criticism that she had not accomplished anything for Oregon and complaints from persons having business with her in Washington that she was "mercurially elusive," she entered the 1938 race—against State Senator Homer D. Angell, a moderate-to-liberal Republican who practiced law in Portland.

Campaign tactics ran along predictable partisan lines. Representative Honeyman contended that "for the best interests of the state, it is imperative that Oregon have a New Deal delegation in Washington." Angell raised some questions: "Why imperative? How imperative? Are we to understand that Oregon will be deprived of its just share of federal funds unless we obey the mandate of the New Deal to elect its slate of candidates?"

Less than a week before the November 8 election, Secretary of the Interior Harold Ickes, on a trip along the Pacific Coast to publicize Roosevelt's record, tarried long enough in Oregon to accompany Nan Honeyman to the Bonneville Dam and say a few words about hydroelectric power. Recording the incident in his diary, he wrote, "Mrs. Honeyman admitted that she was having a hard fight, and I am doubtful whether she will be able to muster enough votes to win since she has a strong candidate against her." The balloting confirmed Ickes's doubts: Nan Honeyman was defeated. If it was any consolation to her, only one Democrat in the state was elected to a major office in 1938.

Attempting to make a comeback in 1940, Mrs. Honeyman had

the active support of Eleanor Roosevelt, who delivered a major speech in Portland on her behalf. But continuing Republican resurgence in the state plus Congressman Angell's achievements in the 76th Congress (1939–41) combined to thwart her aspirations. Her loyalty to the New Deal paid off handsomely in 1942 when President Roosevelt named her collector of customs for the Portland District, a position she held until the Republicans reclaimed the White House in 1953.

Toward the end of her life—she died in 1970—it became clear that Nan Wood Honeyman's most interesting achievement was herself: a woman shamelessly opportunistic yet politically naïve. Because she broke promises and failed to communicate with constituents, she wrote her own congressional obituary.

ELIZABETH H. GASQUE
DEMOCRAT OF SOUTH CAROLINA

The first woman to represent South Carolina in the U.S. House of Representatives, Elizabeth Hawley Gasque (pronounced "gasky") had no chance to display her ability on the Hill. She was not even a seat-warmer in the traditional sense, for the 75th Congress was not in session during the three and one-half months (mid-September 1938 to January 3, 1939) when she filled the vacancy caused by the death of her husband, Allard H. Gasque. She won the right to succeed the 15-year congressional veteran from the 6th District in a perfunctory one-party special election in which she received 5,255 votes versus a combined total of 225 for two male Democratic opponents.

Coming as she did from the Southern aristocracy of Rice Creek Plantation in Blythewood, Elizabeth Marguerite Hawley ("Bessie" to her friends) had been thoroughly indoctrinated in matters literary, religious, and social and had earned a degree in "expression" at Greenville Female College (now Furman University) in 1907. As a wife and mother (two sons and two daughters), she managed a household in Florence before moving to Washington in 1923.

Representative Gasque used the time that a member of Congress normally spends scoring legislative points pursuing social prestige. She traveled on the same dinner-party circuit with a host of prominent men and women and made her own political-society splash as a hostess for one of the annual balls given in honor of President Roosevelt's birthday. Her case of Potomac fever has never been cured. She still calls Washington her "natural home," though her official residence is Cedar Tree Plantation in Ridgeway, the estate of her second husband, the late A. J. Van Exem, whom she married in 1942.

Eightyish—she refuses to give her exact age—Mrs. Van Exem devotes her days to a variety of activities, including the promotion of native arts and crafts. An early exponent of South Carolina as a vacation paradise, hospitable "Miss Bessie" can still find exactly the right words to set a tempting tourist trap. She is flattered by invitations to speak. "And why not?" asks a friend. "Should an old congresswoman just fade away?"

A Question of Equality

Despite the well-known reputation of senators for courtesy and chivalry, 15 years after ratification of the 19th Amendment, most of them had not changed their attitude concerning women's political place: It was *not* in the U.S. Senate. Rebecca Felton had been tolerated—but only briefly. And Hattie Caraway, even after testing her popularity in the political market place, had discovered that she did not, in the figurative sense, enjoy full membership in the most exclusive gentlemen's club in the world.

Curiously enough, the domestic rather than the political arrangements of the Senate accounted for the prevailing bias. The basement bar had been dismantled and the snuff boxes on the side walls were rarely filled, but the anteroom and corridors still served as clubrooms and taverns. Racy stories were recounted there, and now and then during a night session a flask made its appearance. "The Senate's objections to women may have a chivalrous basis after all," rationalized *Outlook*. "Perhaps it is simply that the Senators want to keep the ladies from coming into too close association with bad influences."

Whatever the root causes of their discrimination, the question in the mid-1930s was no longer whether more women would be admitted but how soon. The answer came earlier than expected. A series of unforeseen political developments in Louisiana, Alabama, and South Dakota altered, if only temporarily, the complexion of the august body. Only later did women activists real-

ize that through the seating of Rose McConnell Long, Dixie Bibb
Graves, and Gladys Pyle they had won merely a battle, not the
war.

ROSE McCONNELL LONG
DEMOCRAT OF LOUISIANA

Rose McConnell Long was not the first choice of the Louisiana
Democratic machine to inherit the Senate seat of her assassinated
husband, Huey Pierce Long. Governor O. K. Allen got the nod
but died before he could be sworn in. His successor, Governor
James A. Noe, acted quickly to prevent a fractious struggle among
power-starved followers of the self-styled Kingfish. On January
31, 1936, he named Mrs. Long. He also promised that the State
Central Committee would promptly nominate her. It did—unanimously—within a week, and she was elected without opposition in April.

Opinions regarding what the cabal had wrought in selecting
Rose Long to be the third woman senator in U.S. history varied
with the political prejudices and personalities of those who expressed them.

Said Governor Noe, "This is the proudest moment of my life."

Hattie Caraway of Arkansas, who owed her re-election in part
to the sound trucks that Huey Long had brought upriver, said,
"It will be nice to have a woman's company in the Senate."

The founder and longtime leader of Louisiana's anti-Long
women, Hilda Phelps Hammond of New Orleans, declared, "It
no longer is an honor to go to the U.S. Senate. . . . It is com-
posed of an aggregation of the cheapest politicians who have
neither courage nor honesty."

The esteemed *Christian Century* commented, "Allotting Senator Long's seat to his widow is the height of something very different from a democratic form of government."

The Lady from Louisiana herself remarked, "That's fine. That's
very fine."

Huey Long had once boasted that his wife possessed the best
political judgment of anyone he knew. With his proclivity for
sweeping statements, he may have believed this. More likely,
however, he was placing a public assessment on the practical
assistance she had rendered as he laid the steppingstones to the
governorship. Because he had always been a one-man show, all
that most people knew about her was that she had been a loyal,
patient wife and a devoted mother to a daughter and two sons.

Emerging from the shadows of domesticity at 43, Rose Long,

Bettmann Archive

JEANNETTE RANKIN, Republican of Montana, the first woman in the U.S. House of Representatives. "I had been *thinking peace* until I had built up a peace-thinking habit."

Georgia's "Grand Old Lady," REBECCA LATIMER FELTON, first woman to serve in the U.S. Senate. With her successor, Senator-elect Walter F. George (left), and Georgia's senior senator, William J. Harris, she posed for news photographers before taking the oath of office on November 21, 1922.

French Collection, Library of Congress

The first wife and mother elected to the House of Representatives, WINNIFRED MASON HUCK of Illinois filled a vacancy created by the death of her father, William E. Mason, in 1922. Shy about applying makeup in the presence of gentlemen, she literally had to search for a place in which to use her powder puff in private.

Among the letters on the desk of ALICE M. ROBERTSON, Republican of Oklahoma, are many from veterans of the Spanish-American War and World War I whom she befriended.

Democratic Representative MARY T. NORTON of New Jersey was one of two congresswomen recruited by Representative John Philip Hill of Maryland to draft legislation repealing the Volstead Act.

The first woman elected to the Senate, HATTIE W. CARAWAY of Arkansas (left) was joined during her 14 years on Capitol Hill (1931–45) by ROSE McCONNELL LONG (right) of Louisiana, who succeeded her assassinated husband, Huey Long, in 1936.

Not until 1927 were congresswomen provided with a cloakroom for their exclusive use. Enjoying the privacy are FLORENCE P. KAHN of California, about to receive a message from a House page, and EDITH NOURSE ROGERS of Massachusetts.

Two-term Florida representative RUTH BRYAN OWEN with her daughter Helen Rudd in the garden of "Chota Khoti," the Owen home in Coconut Grove (1931). As her mother predicted, Rudd Brown has followed the family tradition of public service. Twice a candidate for Congress, she also served as a local and state leader in the Democratic Party.

G. W. Romer

French Collection, Library of Congress

To such a degree was RUTH HANNA McCORMICK, Illinois representative at large, the accepted leader of a truly organized element of the Republican Party that in the course of factional disputes she was sometimes denounced as a boss. The secret of her success was that she had mastered the intricacies of practical politics.

Margaret Chase Smith, Republican of Maine, the only woman to serve in both the House and the Senate, also has the distinction of having been the first woman to seek the Presidency on a major-party ticket.

Participating in Washington's social life—often an extension of the day's business—are Representative Frances P. Bolton of Ohio and Senate Minority Leader Everett Dirksen of Illinois.

By radio in their Connecticut home, CLARE BOOTHE LUCE and her husband, publisher Henry R. Luce, learn of her re-election to the House in 1944.

Representative VERA D. BUCHANAN of Pennsylvania introduces President Harry S. Truman during a whistle-stop appearance in October, 1952.

Brooklyn's first congresswoman, Representative EDNA F. KELLY.

Washington Democratic Representative
JULIA BUTLER HANSEN addresses a lun-
cheon meeting after the 1970 dedication
of the Bonneville Power Administration
steel-storage yard.

As the "heeded and acknowledged voice
of education in the Congress of the
United States," Oregon's EDITH GREEN is
presented a Distinguished Service Award
by Oregon State University president
Robert MacVicar in 1972.

MARTHA W. GRIFFITHS, Michigan congresswoman, greets President Lyndon B.
Johnson at Detroit airport during the 1964
campaign.

Oregon's Democratic Senator Maurine B. Neuberger, who served in
Congress from 1960 to 1967.

First black congresswoman Shirley
Chisholm of Brooklyn came to
Congress in 1969.

Otto Storch

Representative Margaret M. Heckler, Republican of Massachusetts, with
a child at the Taunton day-care center.

nervous at first, turned out to be not a shrinking violet but a pleasant contrast to her bombastic, arrogant, egotistical predecessor. Referring to her as a "diminutive liquid-eyed lady," *Time* described the reaction to her presence in the Capitol:

> For years dowdy Hattie Caraway had sat alone relatively neglected in the Senate. Now Senators, leaving the floor, frequently pause to pass the time of day with Mrs. Long. Senators on the Democratic side have taken noticeably more care of their personal appearance since she arrived. Bachelor Senators—Rush Holt of West Virginia and Richard Russell of Georgia—have been seen hovering near her desk. As the best-looking Senator her colleagues have ever seen, she is shown special consideration on all sides.
>
> In the press gallery some ill-bred wag suggested that the parliamentary inquiry most frequently in Senators' minds is "Will the Senator from Louisiana yield?"

Rumors that she was engaged to remarry popped up from time to time in the Hearst papers but were always vehemently denied by her secretary, Earle J. Christenberry. Rose Long issued her own refutation when she told one reporter, "The senator was the greatest man who ever lived. After knowing him, who could be interested in other men?"

Rose Long's feelings for her husband had not always run so deep. Their marriage, for her, had been mostly a series of frustrating experiences, each directly attributable to Huey's being wedded to politics. Even their courtship had been marred by his ardent pursuit of the political trade. There were times when she was not sure whether he loved her for what she was or for what she could contribute as a politician's wife.

Rose McConnell, a farmer's daughter born near Greensburg, Indiana, in 1892, was descended on her mother's side from a distinguished line of planters, physicians, and lawyers. Only nine years old when her parents relocated in Louisiana, she was educated in Shreveport public schools, then employed as a stenographer for a local insurance office.

In his autobiography Long wrote that he met his future wife in high school. The story was probably apocryphal, but it took on a certain truth from constant retelling—and from the fact that in the same account of his life he paid very little attention to his early days as a traveling salesman.

What is a matter of record is that their romance began in 1910 when her bride loaf cake won a baking contest he judged as a salesman peddling a lard substitute manufactured from cottonseed oil. He was still "on the road" (selling starch) when they were married in Memphis in 1913. Borrowing money, they moved to furnished rooms in New Orleans, and, with secretarial help from Rose, Huey studied law at Tulane University. In 1918, when he ran for a place on the Railroad Commission, she managed his Shreveport campaign office, keeping track of rural voters while keeping an eye on one-year-old Rose Lolita.

This same daughter smiled down from the Senate gallery with classmates from Louisiana State University on February 10, 1936, as her mother took the oath of office, administered by Vice President John Nance Garner. Afterward, Senator Long sidestepped reporters' questions concerning where she stood on the President's program (Huey Long had ended his days damning the New Deal). She said only that she would work for the "cause of the farmer and of labor."

Rose Long made no attempt to scale any legislative heights. However, she found her niche, and it was committee work. Of the five Senate committees to which she was appointed, she devoted the most time to Public Lands and Surveys. In the privacy of its hearing room she delivered her maiden speech—a mild plea for passage of a bill to enlarge Chalmette National Historial Park on the site of the Battle of New Orleans. "Had we not won that battle," she said of the great victory that Andrew Jackson won fifteen days after the War of 1812 had ended, "we would today have a British colony west of the Mississippi."

A definite if not dynamic personality, the lady senator took pride in proving that the Long voice, to be effective, did not have to be either loud or long-winded. Whereas citations referring to Huey Long in the *Congressional Record* for the first session of the 74th Congress filled two and one-half pages, the space required to list Rose Long's utterances was little more than one-quarter of a column. She understood enough about politics and politicking to view her role for precisely what it was: the legatee of her husband's political estate. Appropriately enough, when the 74th Congress ended in January 1937, she unobtrusively left Washington—bound for Shreveport and the seclusion afforded by home.

The Senate was informed of Rose Long's death in 1970 by Allen J. Ellender, one of the last survivors of the Long machine and the gentleman from Louisiana who succeeded her. In the brief eulogy he delivered in the chamber, he pointed out that "Huey Long, Rose Long, and Russell Long form the only father-mother-son combination in the history of the U.S. Senate." He mentioned that Chalmette Battlefield "for which she gathered testimony," had been given international recognition during the sesquicentennial of New Orleans. Then he spoke about Rose Long's background. "While she was a schoolteacher," he said, "she met the late Huey P. Long and they were married."

Maybe such wishful thinking would have amused her; maybe it would have simply annoyed her. Whether she would have liked it or not, one thing Rose McConnell Long did not need was a fictionalized record.

DIXIE BIBB GRAVES
DEMOCRAT OF ALABAMA

Alabama's Constitution was destined to be amended, but in 1937 it prohibited the governor from being appointed or elected to *any* office until at least one year after the expiration of his term. Such a restriction created a crisis of conscience for Democratic Governor Bibb Graves when Senator Hugo La Fayette Black resigned to accept an appointment to the Supreme Court.

Out of the running himself, Governor Graves followed a course of action he felt could be fully justified: A special election would be held April 26, 1938; in the interim, his 55-year-old wife, Dixie, would occupy the seat vacated by Black. "She has as good a heart and head as anybody!" he boomed to reporters gathered in the corridor outside of Hugo Black's Senate suite on the afternoon of August 19.

After the fact, a peculiar, multiple-edged, political-economic logic became evident in his choice. The appointment of Mrs. Graves would not endanger the chances of any aspirant to the post. The way was opened for Alabama congressmen to seek to fill the Senate vacancy without resigning from the House. Moreover, the governor was spared the embarrassment of having to choose any one of several close friends who were highly qualified for the job, who believed they were entitled to it—and who wanted it. Time had been bought to update the poll books (nearly 100,000 voters had not paid their poll tax). Finally, but by no means an inconsequential matter, the Graves family income would be supplemented by a salary of $10,000 a year (the governor earned little more than half this amount). An additional $12,000 would be available for clerk hire.

Predictably, the governor's nomination was challenged. His motives were questioned, as were his wife's qualifications for the office. Minnesota Republican Representative Harold Knutson spoke many a congressional mind when he said, sarcastically, "I hope it will not be necessary for Mrs. Graves to go outside her family for office help." A letter to one of the Birmingham papers from Mary Harrison Fisher of Gadsen expressed a cross section of feminine anger:

> In the Senate of the United States, where matters of such grave importance arise as to try the ability (and the souls) of veterans of many years, there is no place for a woman appointee unless her past experience would justify such action.
>
> Distinguished charm of person, of manner and mind may well grace the Governor's mansion. At a time like this in the affairs of the nation, these attributes would hardly suffice upon the floor of the Senate, where the logic and constructive statesmanship of a hard-headed fighting man are needed. To those who have called the appointment of a woman "sentiment," I call it just what it is: plain foolishness!

Sidewalk comment in Montgomery and elsewhere in Alabama was highly critical. The kindliest construction that detractors placed upon the governor's choice was that he showed "very bad taste." "Outrageous" was a frequently heard adjective, and other remarks were to the effect that, aside from any sentimental reasons, Governor Graves was not indifferent to the political advantage or the financial considerations. An editorial in the *Birmingham News*, labeled by the author as a "frank and honest opinion," summed up the opposition:

> The appointment of Mrs. Graves is much more to be deplored than the appointment of the widow of a senator to succeed him. . . . She is not the person to succeed Hugo Black in the U.S. Senate. . . . Her appointment does not meet the needs of the standing and prestige of Alabama in Congress, or give to this state's interests the representation to which its citizens are entitled on the floor of the Senate.
>
> . . . Furthermore, it is out of line with the spirit of the constitutional provision that forbids the governor himself to receive this appointment.

Apparently oblivious of the skepticism and anger, Dixie Bibb Graves, with senior Senator John H. Bankhead, II (who had declined to comment on the affair) as her escort, was sworn in and took her seat in the 75th Congress on August 20, one day before the first session ended. Among the onlookers was Senator Hattie Caraway of Arkansas, occupying Hugo Black's old seat in the center of the Democratic side of the chamber.

Some weeks later *Time* reported, "After a good look, shocked Washingtonians decided that Governor Graves could have made a worse appointment." If Dixie Bibb Graves did not possess the experience usually demanded of a senator, she was intelligent, had a keen memory, and in certain respects was her husband's equal in political sophistication.

The name Bibb is synonymous with Alabama history. Brothers William and Thomas Bibb, the first and second governors of the state, were among the forebears of Miss Dixie, as Alabamians called her, and also of David Bibb Graves. Dixie Bibb and Bibb Graves were first cousins, had grown up together on a farm in Hope Hull (he was orphaned in infancy), attended school in nearby Montgomery, and were married in 1900. She was 18, a young woman of beauty and a fine elocutionist; Bibb Graves, 27, was serving his second term in the State Legislature.

While her husband commanded an artillery regiment overseas during World War I, she made surgical dressings and presided over the state chapter of the Daughters of the Confederacy. Later she was one of a small group who helped pioneer the "Votes for Women" movement in Alabama, rallying support with her own slogan: "All citizens should be permitted to take part in government."

Before Bibb Graves reached the Statehouse the first time (in 1926, the same year that he and Hugo Black, a candidate for the Senate, joined the politically omnipotent Ku Klux Klan), Miss Dixie immersed herself in club work. She belonged to almost every organization in town, including the No-Name Literary Society. She also taught Bible classes at the Central Christian Church, served as a trustee of the Alabama Boys' Industrial School, and was a moving force in the WCTU and in Alabama's campaign to wipe out illiteracy.

When her husband ran again for governor in 1934, those following his campaign were not unmindful that she sometimes filled in for him at the rostrum and even wrote some of his speeches. Asked about her participation, she told Dolly Dalrymple of the *Birmingham News* that she was "just an ordinary woman—the wife of an extraordinary man." In this context, it was not surprising that after his election she was frequently mentioned as a possible gubernatorial candidate to succeed him in 1938.

As a freshman senator, Dixie Bibb Graves was given a seat at the rear of the chamber—in a section known as the "Cherokee Strip" because it was on the Republican side and accommodated the Democratic overflow (75 Democrats were members in 1937). "I'm supposed to be seen, perhaps," she told a radio audience on one occasion, "but certainly not heard."

She did speak, however—and was heard. On November 16, the day after the second session was gaveled to order, she offered a counterthrust to the Ludlow amendment that would take from Congress the power to declare a foreign war. Her measure advocated the immediate drafting during a national emergency "of any or all men, women, money, material and any or all other national resources for unlimited use and service, and without profit." An ardent New Dealer, she was heeding the President's warning—in the face of alarming war news from Europe—that the United States "must adopt such measures as will minimize our risk of involvement."

It was on the issue of law and order, however, that Senator Graves made the most passionate plea of her brief senatorial career. "It was a hit," said the *Washington Herald* of her emotional attack against the Wagner-Van Nuys antilynching bill. Some watchers in the gallery thought they saw tears in her eyes when she told the Senate that some advocates of the measure had been misinformed about conditions in Alabama: "The South, by efficient law enforcement, aided by aroused opinion, has reduced lynchings two-thirds in the past ten years, and in another five years it will be wiped out entirely. Isn't that an amazing record? I abhor lynchings. But only a compelling emergency should cause this body to strike down the sovereignty of indestructible States."

Her remarks drew applause on the Senate floor and a paean from the *Montgomery Advertiser* entitled, "SHE SPOKE AS A DAUGHTER OF THE DEEP SOUTH." Governor Graves ordered 10,000 reprints and told reporters that he was "the chestiest man in Alabama—prouder than ever of my appointment and appointee. She's won her spurs by herself without help from anyone. She didn't need any."

Not unexpectedly, there were some angry cries of dismay, mainly from the North. The humanitarian questions raised by a Brooklyn man, published in the letters-to-the-editor column of the *New York Times,* tapped a known underground stream of resentment concerning elected officials who condoned lawlessness and gnawed away at freedom and equality:

> She intimates that we need have no fear . . . that within the next five years, who knows but what lynching will be entirely eliminated.
>
> And during the next five years would we citizens deprive those wholesome Southerners of the ecstatic joy of listening to a Negro skull crumple under the heavy blow of a leaden bludgeon? Or the pleasure of painstakingly painting the nude body of an as-yet innocent victim with viscous tar? Or the delicious odor of burnt flesh as her constituents laughingly light the fire that sears the

sufferer to a crisper brown? Or the delightful sight of the dangling Negro as ambitious hawkers peddle their peanuts and popcorn to a moronic mob?

And our mighty guardians of liberty stood in awe as the weeping Senator Graves pleaded for no remedy rather than any.

Down in Alabama, where her popularity was gaining strength, a write-in campaign was launched to place Senator Graves's name before the voters at the upcoming special election, rescheduled for January 4, 1938. Capital correspondent Ralph Hurst of the *Birmingham News* said the effort was designed not to elect her to the Senate but "to advertise and build her up and to measure her strength . . . with a view of having her become a candidate for the regular six-year Senate term in the May primary." Others hinted that the scheme was to promote her candidacy for the governorship. All speculation halted, however, when Lister Hill, a popular figure in state politics and a veteran congressman, won the special election.

With an almost perfect attendance record to her credit, Senator Graves ended her five months in office. Alabamians generally agreed that their lady senator had turned in a better performance than expected. Patronage alone accounted for thousands of dollars in bridges and roads.

Widowed in 1942, Miss Dixie almost immediately reactivated all of her club memberships—and added some new ones. She worked for the USO and the American Red Cross; she spearheaded a statewide recruitment drive for the Women's Army Auxiliary Corps (WAAC), and, as state adviser to the National Foundation for Infantile Paralysis, she traveled often to Washington, sometimes as the guest of President and Mrs. Harry Truman. Time did not run out for Mrs. Graves until 1965. She died six months before her 84th birthday—still as active in club work as old age would allow.

GLADYS PYLE

REPUBLICAN OF SOUTH DAKOTA

The chronology of political events in 1938 included a first for a Republican woman. Gladys Pyle, the GOP choice in South Dakota to oppose a former Democratic state legislator, John T. McCullen, was elected to the U.S. Senate on November 8—with the distinction of receiving the largest number of votes given any major candidate.

Because Senator Pyle's term would expire on January 3, 1939, and Congress would not be in session, her triumph was alluded to in some circles as a hollow victory. She would never know what it was like to fidget through a filibuster or confront a witness at a committee hearing, but she had no intention of passing up the opportunity to work for her constituents from a power base in the nation's capital.

With her mother, a stenographer, and a clerk, this gray-haired, bustling 48-year-old interim senator drove from South Dakota to Washington at her own expense "because I wouldn't feel like a senator unless I did."

Social responsibility was characteristic of Huron-born Gladys Pyle, whose personal motto was "Citizenship Is Service." Like her two sisters and brother, she was not unmindful of a family tradition that scorned apathy. Her mother, Mamie Shields Pyle, had led the Universal Franchise League, which won suffrage for South Dakota women in 1918, and two years later was chosen to be a member of the Electoral College. After the death of State Attorney General John L. Pyle, it was but a matter of time before his place on the Huron College Board of Trustees was passed to his daughter Gladys, class of 1911.

By any measure, Miss Pyle's public career was achievement-oriented. At 22, after postgraduate work at the American Conservatory of Music and the University of Chicago, she began eight years of high school teaching that took her into the Latin, music, and mathematics classrooms in Miller and Huron and to the principal's office in Wessington. At 32, she was elected to the State Legislature, where she served two terms; at 37, she was secretary of state, and at 40, winner of the primary for governor.

Although the top vote-getter in a field of five, including a former governor, Miss Pyle did not receive the 35 per cent required for nomination. At the GOP State Convention called to choose a nominee, she lost on the 12th ballot—a victim of the bankers' lobby. Her main campaign had been "to clean up the state banking department." When the state superintendent of banks was subsequently sent to prison for embezzling more than $1 million, the new governor appointed her to the State Securities Commission. Not only did she demand closer supervision of state funds; she also helped write the budget law, credited with giving South Dakota a "greatly improved fiscal policy." By the time she went into business for herself (life insurance and farm management), she possessed the essential prerequisite needed by either a man or a woman: financial expertise.

The first thing Senator Pyle did in Washington was to affix

her nameplate on the door of her suite in the Senate Office Building. Next she called on top government officials who might have forgotten that South Dakotans were still trying to pull themselves out of the Depression. Invited to address the National Republican Committee, meeting in Washington to lay plans for the 1940 Presidential campaign, she joined Michigan's Senator Arthur H. Vandenberg, Senator-elect Alexander Wiley of Wisconsin, and Ohio Representative George Bender in turning GOP policy toward a more liberal course.

At the 1940 GOP National Convention in Philadelphia ex-Senator Pyle was selected to deliver the nominating speech when the South Dakota delegation, in a surprise move, placed in nomination for President Governor Harlan J. Bushfield. It marked still another political first—for her and for women.

Gladys Pyle's public service continued. She served for 14 years on the South Dakota State Board of Charities and Corrections. In 1968, shortly before her 79th birthday, asked what political advice she would give younger women, she said, "The Greek word for idiot, literally translated, means one who does not participate in politics. That sums up my conviction on the subject."

Under No Illusions

FRANCES P. BOLTON

REPUBLICAN OF OHIO

About midway in her long congressional career (1940–69) Ohio Republican Frances Bolton was asked by a colleague where she got her even temper, her calm disposition. "Where few want to go," she said. "In hell!"

If the listener was startled, it was probably because he had been conditioned to accept at face value the many glowing word portraits that painted Mrs. Bolton as being free from life's devilish problems. She was ever the "richest woman in Congress." No one mentioned the poor little rich girl.

The world in which Frances Payne Bingham grew up appeared to glitter. It was one of vast liquid assets flowing from oil, coal, iron, and shipping; of distinguished heritage (Robert Treat Paine, signer of the Declaration of Independence, and John Howard Payne, author of "Home Sweet Home"); of society pedigrees and debutante parties. There were winters at an estate in Palm Beach, summers at a country house near Lake Erie, leisurely trips to Europe, education at the best private schools at home and abroad.

Miss Bingham never knew financial hardship, but neither did she know the familial reassurance that a plain-looking, shy young girl needs. Before she reached her 14th birthday the two people who might have bestowed such reassurance—her mother and her oldest brother—died. Her sister Betty, whose outgrown dresses Frances had to wear, enjoyed playing the role of a sibling who is prettier and older. "Oh, Francie, you can't do anything right!" was a favorite remark of hers, repeated just often enough to instill in an impressionable child feelings of incompetence and insecurity.

Frances's father, Charles William Bingham, for all his admirable qualities, was not the kind of man who could manifest warmth or affection or break with Victorian tradition—even as a new century dawned. His firm principles and brusque, authoritarian discipline ruled life in the family's spacious, well-staffed house on Cleveland's fashionable Euclid Avenue.

Particularly vivid in Frances's memory is the fear that welled up in her one morning during her 19th year when he said, "I want to talk to you in my study after breakfast."

Once they were in that room he asked, "Francie, have you been going about with the visiting nurse?"

"Yes, sir."

"Why did you do it without asking me?"

"Because I knew you would say 'no.' "

"Yes," he said, "I would. But, since you have done it, tell me about it."

As a member of the Brownies (a Cleveland debutante club), she explained, she had joined a group effort to aid the public health nurses. She worked five half-days a week, reporting at 8 o'clock in the morning to make the tenement rounds. She did what she was told, mainly removing tattered clothing from small children and bathing them with soap and Lysol.

Father Bingham did not give permission for her to continue the work, nor did he flatly say that she must end something she obviously found satisfying. His concluding remark, however, eased somewhat the guilt stemming from having led a double life without telling him. "Now that you have seen how most people in this world have to live, I hope you will never forget it," he said.

She would not. This initiation into the manifold problems of nursing and public health education was to remain a major preoccupation for life.

The marriage of Frances Payne Bingham to Chester Castle Bolton in 1907, when she was 22 and he 25, followed an engagement of the socially prescribed length. It was not in the old-fashioned sense either a prearranged union or a marriage of convenience, but simply a wedding of peers. He was a neighbor, Harvard-educated, the industrialist son of Mark Hanna's business partner, and someone she had known as long as she could remember. Tragedy was to test their union; so was the monetary imbalance resulting from a wife's having more money than her husband (she inherited millions from her uncle Oliver Hazard Payne). Meanwhile a world war intervened.

Before Frances Bolton moved with three young sons to Washington, where Captain Bolton's talent had been drafted by the War Industries Board, she had begun in earnest to channel her abundant energy toward upgrading the nursing profession. Her first public speeches were delivered when she was a member of the board of Cleveland's Lakeside Hospital. She spared no details in describing why "our custodians of health should not be treated as domestic servants," and she invited listeners to tour the attic rooms where nurses were required to live. "All I hope is you go up and see for yourselves," she said, "and I defy you to sleep well afterwards."

In the national interest she was instrumental in convincing the Secretary of War and fellow Clevelander, Newton D. Baker, to establish the Army School of Nursing. This master stroke—accomplished despite persuasive arguments by Red Cross officials that volunteers had already been trained to care for the wounded and were only waiting for permission to sail to France—required all the patience, grit, and articulation that Frances Bolton could command. At one point she thwarted bureaucratic delaying tactics by announcing in Baker's outer office that she would not leave until he signed the activation order.

Influenzal pneumonia, after the birth of her only daughter (who lived but one day), nearly snuffed out Mrs. Bolton's life in 1919. She credits the discipline of yoga with restoring her health and enabling her to cope later, when her oldest son, 18-year-old Charles, broke his neck in a diving accident and in the agonizing years immediately afterward when she helped him regain the use of one set of paralyzed muscles, then another.

Attention to Charles's progress did not permit Mrs. Bolton actively to join her husband's campaign for Congress in 1928, but, once the transition had been made to a new home on Wyoming Avenue in Northwest Washington, she did not neglect the formal social duties then required of a congressman's wife. And from a desk in the Bolton library she continued to supervise the Payne Fund, which she had established with her uncle Oliver's gift. This philanthropy enabled her to attack at the grassroots some of the problems that cried out for remedy, not relief. Foremost was education for nurses. Toward its improvement she gave $1.5 million in stock certificates to Western Reserve University to establish a school of nursing. Systematic contributions also launched the National Committee for the Study of Juvenile Reading; an observation post in Switzerland (she called it her "window to the world") where, among other things, a perspective on narcotics traffic could be obtained; and research centers to appraise such diverse phenomena as radio communication (at Ohio State University) and parapsychology (at Duke University).

In 1936, when the GOP carried only Maine and Vermont, Chester Bolton lost the 22d District. While he laid the groundwork for his comeback, his wife tended to the party's renaissance as a member of the Ohio State Republican Committee and as vice-chairman of the national GOP assembly making a comprehensive survey of party policies.

From outside the range of political floodlights, she was suddenly and dramatically placed in front of them the day in October 1939 when Chester Bolton died. Not all local party leaders wanted a widow as their representative in Congress, and some accepted her candidacy only when her supporters suggested that she probably would get tired of the job in a few months and go on to other things. Those same protestors were undoubtedly swayed by being reminded that it had been a Bolton check for $125,000 that had assured Cleveland the Republican National Convention in 1936.

If the backing she received from the party hierarchy was less than unanimous, Frances Bolton was to have the satisfaction of a sweeping popular victory. In the special February 1940 election she easily won the right to succeed her husband, defeating by an almost 2-to-1 margin Democrat Anthony A. Fleger, a lawyer and former mayor of Parma. It did not hurt her popularity when she announced that she would return to the U.S. Treasury the $10,000 pension that Congress had voted to grant all widows of congressmen. "Under the circumstances," she wrote, "this would be excessive."

The freshman representative from Ohio enlarged the House female contingent in the 76th Congress to six—two of whom, Mary Norton and Edith Rogers, were in their 15th year of continuous service. What they and the male assemblage saw in 54-year-old Frances Bolton was a youngish-looking, rather short, sprightly woman with a trim, very erect figure. A Florida tan set off the brilliant blue of her eyes. There was determination in the set of her firm chin, and the promise of affability in her quick smile. The mature Mrs. Bolton bore no resemblance to the not very pretty, insecure Miss Bingham.

The district Frances Bolton represented was, in a way, a political family heirloom, won in 1874 by her maternal grandfather, Henry B. Payne, a Democrat who later went to the Senate. Rated according to population it was the largest in the country: over 700,000 (and to grow to nearly 1 million before reapportionment based on the 1950 census reduced it to a more manageable 350,-000). Primarily metropolitan, it had a sizable proportion of shipping and factory workers, a high percentage of foreign-born, some farmers, and all of the wealthy residents of several posh Cleveland suburbs.

As war clouds darkened over Europe and debates over U.S. neutrality lengthened in Congress, the way she cast her votes reflected the vaguely isolationist mood characterizing both her own frame of mind and that of most of her constituents. She reluctantly supported the controversial draft bill (peacetime conscription had never before been tried in the United States), having succumbed to the argument that a show of U.S. strength would discourage an aggressor. But later she said "No" to Roosevelt's "billion dollars for defense" and to the lend-lease plan that would entitle Russia, as well as the Western European allies, to receive war materiel from the United States.

Not long before the Japanese attack on Pearl Harbor in December 1941, she gradually moved toward a preparedness stand, while not forsaking her hope that an alternative to war could be found. This shift in ideology was due partly to the conclusions she reached after "seeking out and facing the facts" as a member of the Foreign Affairs Committee and partly to the insight she gained from two longtime GOP members, John Vorys of Ohio and Charles Eaton of New Jersey, staunch proponents of armed might. Then, too, her two youngest sons, Kenyon and Oliver, were in the army. She spoke for them, she said at a later date, when she told House members to "stop their bickering [over parities, subsidies, and crop penalties] and get on with defeating the Axis."

The first building blocks in Frances Bolton's legislative career were measures to advance the nursing profession. Nowhere in Congress did nurses have a more determined and effective tribune. The focus of her wartime activity was recruitment—an extension of the battle she had fought a quarter of a century earlier in Newton Baker's anteroom. The $5 million Bolton Act creating a U.S. Cadet Nurse Corps gave the country more than 124,000 women trained through grants covering their tuition, fees, uniforms, maintenance, and pocket money in return for a pledge to serve in the armed forces or essential civilian posts until at least six months after the end of hostilities. From this departure point she secured passage of a bill giving nurses in uniform a pay scale identical to that of male officers.

At a time when segregation was practiced by the U.S. military, Frances Bolton insisted that Negro nurses "be given full opportunity to prove themselves." Her concern for this minority led her to accept a place on the advisory councils of Alabama's Tuskegee Institute and Meharry Medical College in Tennessee.

As a champion of equal rights, she did not believe in distinctions between the sexes "either in their privileges and opportunities or in their duties." During the cold war she openly advocated that women be drafted: "I am afraid that gallantry is sorely out of date, and as a woman I find it rather stupid. . . . Women's place includes defending the home." In the sixties she sponsored an equal-rights-for-men bill: It authorized the U.S. Army and the U.S. Navy to commission male nurses.

Curious by nature, she was never altogether satisfied with her performance in Congress until she had collected facts firsthand. She became a peripatetic congressman (the title "congresswoman" was anathema to her), traveling hundreds of thousands of miles during World War II and afterward on all sorts of missions and sometimes under frustrating circumstances.

To inspect American hospitals in England in 1944 she had to coax British authorities to let her board a BOAC plane, because the U.S. Army Air Force was forbidden to carry civilians. For her tour in France she borrowed a nurse's uniform to comply with the military ban against civilian clothes. After the Iron Curtain was lowered and Secretary of State Dean Acheson told her it would be impossible to obtain a visa from the Soviet Union, she called on Russian Ambassador Andrei Gromyko—and became the first member of the Foreign Affairs Committee ever to set foot on Russian soil.

The African survey she proposed at age 71 turned into a solo fact-finding mission. Members of the Subcommittee on Africa said they could not remain away from their offices for three months. Taxpayers could not be expected to pay for a trip by a committee of one—even if it was the chairman. Out came her checkbook. She assembled a team consisting of a Defense Department transportation officer, a Signal Corps photographer, and a physician from the Mayo Clinic. Aboard commercial planes, trains, boats, and various other types of carriers she traveled 20,000 miles to study schools, hospitals, and mission stations in 24 countries south and east of the Sahara. On her return in 1955 she said:

We Westerners have gone over there somewhat ruthlessly to get rather than to give. Now we must turn in a different direction. We must make it come from our hearts. . . . Nor shall we be doing all the giving, for Africa has much to give. There is a quality in the African that the world needs: there is rare adaptability, a capacity of quick comprehension, an eagerness and a hunger to learn, to know, to do, that is both stimulating and challenging.

Taking up the challenge, she gave a young girl from Kenya the wherewithal to graduate from a U.S. medical school, funded a Nigerian boy's education, and became a founding member of the Women's Committee of the African-American Institute. Her public support of independence for African nations—both as a delegate to the United Nations and as a member of Congress—is replete with empathetic advice about schools and health facilities. Her personal and political commitment did not go without recognition from Africans. President Diroi Hamani of Niger called her the "godmother of Africa."

Washington critics of Representative Bolton's foreign affairs work, while giving her high grades for effort and effervescence, claimed that many of her impromptu utterances were flawed by sweeping partisan overstatements ("The President [Truman] is to blame for failing to keep our agreements and for turning to vacillation and appeasement in Europe") and that her more formal pronouncements were marred by equally sweeping generalities ("Africa is the land of the future where 200 million people can move, if we and they will it so, from the oxcart to the atomic age in one splendid leap").

This was one side of the story. There was another. It was on Frances Bolton's recommendation that the Committee on Foreign Affairs consented to streamline some of its antiquated machinery. Five permanent subcommittees were established, each specializing in geographical areas of which there were counterparts in the State Department. The information she gathered in Russia and its satellite countries provided the basis for three scholarly reports focusing on the dangers the United States could expect from worldwide Communist expansion. Among the things she spelled out was the need for American leadership in the Republic of Korea: "This country will fall into hands that will make the world a very unsafe place for us." On June 27, 1950, the North Koreans invaded the South, and President Truman ordered U.S. military forces to return their fire.

If by paying so much attention to international affairs Frances Bolton gave her constituents a clear and vulnerable target at which to shoot, she also gave them a performance easier to admire than to fault. Clevelanders were intrigued by a woman who could escape an elephant charge in the Congo, dine with Saudi Arabia's King Ibn Saud and his harem, convince Russian U.N. Ambassador Andrei Vishinsky to use his influence to bring to the United States the teenage sons of a Romanian couple in exile, exchange gifts with the Queen Mother of Ruanda-Urundi, host the American visit of the Angel of Dienbienphu, and ease taut tempers in the course of an angry committee dispute with the improbable question "Mr. Chairman, wouldn't it be a good idea if we all got up and sang?"

There were other reasons Ohioans repeatedly sent Frances Bolton back to Washington while sometimes putting a Democrat in the State Capitol or in the Senate. She faithfully apprised them of important congressional goings-on through a regular newsletter, she answered all mail promptly, and she planned her office schedule in such a way as to permit time for conversation with constituents. That she had the money to increase her staff in Washington and in Cleveland and suburban Mayfield beyond the number paid for by Congress was more of a boon to the folks at home than to their representative. The efficiency of her well-paid aides could be counted on for anything from tickets to the Cherry Blossom Festival to letters of recommendation for a job.

Frances Bolton's campaign philosophy and routine also helped cement constituency support. She never spent more than the law allowed. She drove her own moderately priced sedan whenever she made the rounds in Cleveland, almost never turned down a bid to speak, and reveled in an opportunity to shake hands or dance the polka. In 1952, when her bid for a seventh term received more than usual national attention because her 36-year-old son, Oliver, was running in the 11th Ohio District, her hectic schedule that began at 6 A.M. and ended after 10 P.M. exhausted many cameramen and reporters.

As the only mother-son team ever to serve concurrently in Congress, the Boltons frequently captured headlines, especially when they proved her pre-election statement that Oliver was "no carbon copy" and split their first House vote, or when perennial rumors of a Bolton dynasty surfaced and had to be denied—even as Oliver, recovering from a heart attack in 1956, announced he would not seek re-election.

"I'll miss having my grandchildren nearby," she said of the news. There may also have been a small sigh of relief, for this was the son who, when she asked him if there was anything he would like her to do during his campaign, replied, "Sure there is—just keep the hell out of my district!"

Redistricting posed some serious problems for Frances Bolton in the 1960s, and she worried about them—just as she did about each election. Not one to prolong tension, however, she consoled herself with the fact that she was in a better position than ever to exercise power and influence. The "Dean of Congresswomen" title had passed to her from Edith Nourse Rogers. She was the ranking minority member of the Foreign Affairs Committee and chairman of the Republican side of the Ohio delegation. At her handsome Wyoming Avenue home she entertained the great and near great. There, amid antique furnishings and oil paintings of Yankee ancestors, an evening would begin with cocktails and end with the hostess's saying to departing guests, "Thank you. You've given me a lovely time, asking me to talk about myself all evening."

It had always been Mrs. Bolton's contention that all women—especially those in Congress—had to work twice as hard as men for everything they accomplished. "The Lord, after creating the world, put a man in charge of it," she told the Women's National Press Club in 1965. "He messed everything up, so the Lord turned everything over to a woman, and He gave her everything He had given man, plus two more things: pain, so she would understand what creation is, and laughter, so that she could stand that and the man."

In the course of the marathon civil rights debate in the 1960s she fought to include women in the federal ban against discrimination. Directing her remarks to the males in the House, she said, "Your bones harden long before our bones do. We live longer, have more endurance." It was one argument no congressman dared refute: The debater was a still-sprightly octogenarian.

Under no illusions that her age would not be an issue in the 1968 congressional contest, Representative Bolton, nevertheless, entered the race with optimism. To her opponent, 55-year-old Charles A. Vanik, a seven-term Democratic congressman, she addressed the warning that he would not "have an easy time of it running against what he likes to call 'a nice old lady.'"

She was right, but even the till-death-do-us-part loyalty of thousands of her constituents could not overcome what gerrymandering had done. The 22d District had been turned largely into an extension of the city of Cleveland, with all the city's problems.

After a redrawing of the boundaries of the 22d, Vanik chose to leave his old (and also altered) adjacent district to challenge Representative Bolton, bringing with him a band of devoted helpers—including many young people who had been in the cheering section of Presidential-hopeful Eugene McCarthy. Vanik never referred to Frances Bolton's age but it became an issue when a *Cleveland Press* endorsement pointed out that he was "in the prime of life."

Frances Bolton, looking 20 years younger than her 83 years, gave the fight everything she had. The stakes were high: If the GOP gained control of Congress, she could become chairman of the House Foreign Affairs Committee.

When a reporter asked her how much she was counting on a sweep of Ohio by Richard Nixon, she replied crisply, "Not much." Of third party candidate George Wallace, she said, "What on earth is Wallace going to do to us? That's the thing that terrifies both Democrats and Republicans."

Her campaign manager, Don Gropp, figured that some Wallace voters would go for Frances Bolton because "she's more conservative than Vanik." That comparison was clearly true, but, owing to a shift in population and some gerrymandering, the district had become overwhelmingly Democratic. Liberal Vanik won the 22d.

"No, I don't want to be named an ambassador," she said after losing her bid for a 15th consecutive term. "I'm retired. Now I can do what I please."

Voice of Reason

MARGARET CHASE SMITH
REPUBLICAN OF MAINE

Chronic absenteeism, though not a new phenomenon in the U.S. Senate, became something of a way of life in 1972, as a result of extensive junketing, moonlighting on the lucrative lecture circuit, and campaigning for the Presidency. On any given day an average of 22, or almost one-quarter, of the 100 senators failed to appear in the chamber.

The poor record led Majority Leader Mike Mansfield of Montana to accuse absent members of "doing a distinct disservice to the Senate and to the people whom you have the honor to represent." If we were an industry, he continued, "we would pay a price for not being here, and if we did not produce we would be fired." Then he threw up his hands in disgust.

"Why," asked Senator Margaret Chase Smith, holder of the all-time consecutive roll call voting record (2,941), "doesn't the Senate do something about absenteeism instead of piously wringing hands?" She not only answered her own question ("Because the Senate is a club of prima donnas—99 Kings and one Queen—dedicated to their own personal accommodation") but also did something. The constitutional amendment she introduced would expel any senator who missed more than 60 per cent of the yea and nay votes.

This action-oriented response to forestall a crisis is typical Margaret Chase Smith—bold, forthright, with a respectable sprinkling of outrage. While no one needed to call attention to probable Senate resistance to her self-disciplinary measure, she did precisely that: "The Senate is simply incapable of disciplining its members, whether it be violation of Senate rules of order and conduct, breach of national security, improper use or abuse of authority—or absenteeism. . . . No wonder the American public is so fed up with Congress."

Throughout her 32 years on Capitol Hill, the welfare of the nation, more than that of the Republican Party or even of the State of Maine, molded the logic of her legislative behavior. Independent and recalcitrant, she has sometimes been labeled a maverick. "I'm a moderate Republican," she says, "and once I've carefully completed my homework and arrived at a decision, it's done. I don't worry afterward."

The first time she reproached the Senate has since been called her "finest hour." Speaking, she said, "as a Republican . . . as a woman . . . as a United States Senator . . . as an American," Margaret Smith, on June 1, 1950, accused a GOP colleague, Joseph R. McCarthy of Wisconsin (without ever mentioning him by name), of turning the Senate into a "forum of hate." Hers was the initial outcry by an elected official against "McCarthyism," a word that would make its way into the American language as a definition of "inquisitorial investigative methods, ostensibly in the suppression of communism."

"The American people," she said, "are sick and tired of being afraid to speak their minds lest they be politically smeared as 'Communists' or 'Fascists' by their opponents. Freedom of speech is not what it used to be in America. It has been so abused by some that it is not exercised by others."

She concluded with a "Declaration of Conscience," signed also by six other senators, in which she charged that "certain elements of the Republican Party" were "materially" adding to the confusion "in the hopes of riding . . . to victory through the selfish political exploitation of fear, bigotry, ignorance and intolerance."

How much influence did her speech have on the Senate censure of McCarthy four years later? "Quite a bit," she says. The candidate that the Wisconsin senator hand-picked to replace her in the Senate in the 1954 primary lost by a 5-to-1 margin—despite the fact that McCarthy spent a great deal of time and money campaigning for him in Maine. "If a woman could win against *his* candidate," she has said, "the other senators must have thought he wasn't as powerful as he claimed to be—or seemed to be."

McCarthy's vindictiveness in the wake of the Maine senator's remarks also led to his being struck down for institutional contempt. Against Senate regulations, he removed Senator Smith from the key investigating subcommittee of the Expenditures Committee. When she confronted McCarthy about the matter, he told her that she was not being "bumped," that he merely preferred having Senator Richard M. Nixon serve with him because "he did a tremendous job on the House Un-American Activities Committee."

"Joe," she said, "I was making investigations in the House three years before you and Nixon got to Washington!"

Margaret Chase Smith's congressional career began on June 10, 1940, in the pattern set by many women who had preceded her: She was the widow of a congressman. But her talent as a promising politician had been established long before she became Mrs. Clyde H. Smith.

Her parents, George Emery and Carrie Murray Chase, were a hardworking middle-class couple of Irish, English, and Scottish descent. Their modest home on North Avenue in Skowhegan, a small mill town on the Kennebec River, was built by family labor, and when the income from George Chase's one-chair barber shop had to be supplemented, Carrie Chase would take a part-time job as a pieceworker in the local shoe factory, as a store clerk, or as a waitress. Margaret, the eldest of six (two boys died at an early age), clerked on Saturdays for 10 cents an hour at Green Brothers' five-and-dime store as soon as she was tall enough to reach the shelves. While in high school, where she took a commercial course, she sometimes worked nights at the telephone-company switchboard. Among the calls she answered were those from Skowhegan's first selectman, Clyde Smith. Usually he wanted to know the correct time, and she remembers that "he had a fascinating voice."

After her 1916 graduation from high school she held a series of jobs: teacher in the one-room schoolhouse in nearby Pitt (for $8.50 a week), girl Friday (circulation, advertising, editorial) for the weekly *Independent Reporter* ($28 a week), and office manager of the woolen company owned by Daniel E. Cummins ($50 a week).

Of her four-year courtship with Smith, Margaret says, "Mostly we went campaigning." Whatever free time she had was devoted to various civic projects, including those sponsored by the local Sorosis Club. At 28 she was elected president of the parent group, the State Federation of Business and Professional Women's Clubs, and two years later she became Somerset County Committeewoman on the Republican State Committee.

The campaigning went right on after the May 1930 wedding that joined Margaret Madeline Chase, 32, and Clyde Harold Smith, 53. No political amateur (in his lifetime he won all of the 48 offices he sought), Smith turned down a bid to run for governor in 1936 (a year when only Maine and Vermont remained in the Republican column) to accept his party's nomination for the U.S. House of Representatives.

Eagerly, Margaret Smith went on her husband's Washington payroll as his secretary. "I'm a real product of nepotism" she said after her election to the Senate in 1948. "I wouldn't be in Congress if I hadn't been a member of my husband's staff."

She might have added that Congressman Smith's favoritism bought for the 2d Maine District a hardworking 15-hour-a-day Jill-of-all-trades. She not only handled his correspondence and helped with speech-writing but also traveled through the South to collect employment data for his work on the Labor Committee (under the chairmanship of Mary Norton) and returned to the state periodically to brief constituents on legislative progress.

Shortly before Clyde Smith succumbed to a heart attack in April 1940, his wife entered her name in the primary. His concern at the time, she says, was to preserve for the 2d District the social gains he had helped achieve.

Anything but an unknown, Margaret Smith could call on all sorts of people she had worked with, especially women, to support her candidacy in the special June election (to fill her husband's unexpired term) and again in the September general election for the 77th Congress. She campaigned "like a pro," a friend recalls, and in the fall race won by a plurality of 31,304 votes. In the intervening years before 1972 no contest was even close, though she faced some strong opponents.

Her request for a place on the Labor Committee denied, Congresswoman Smith applied her business acumen to the job at hand and early earned the respect of colleagues on the minor committees to which she was appointed. Concurrently her doggedness came to the fore. Every year she asked for a seat on the Naval Affairs Committee—later redesignated the Armed Services Committee. In 1943 her request was granted. From this vantage point she could watch over shipbuilding and related interests vital to the economic life of a state with 3,478 miles of tidal shore line.

Margaret Smith's solid commitment to military preparedness, which she attributes to "the normal inclination of a majority of American citizens," became apparent to the public in

1940 when, unlike most Republicans in the House, she voted in favor of both selective service to draft men for one year and the bill to arm U.S. merchant ships. She also supported lend-lease, the lone member of the Maine delegation to do so.

After Pearl Harbor Representative Smith introduced legislation creating the WAVES (Women Accepted for Volunteer Emergency Service). When a colleague opposed her proposal to send WAVES overseas, with the argument "There will be hardships that no American woman should have to endure," she won her case with one sentence: "Then we'd better bring all the nurses home." Subsequently, WAVES took over jobs in Alaska, Hawaii, and the Caribbean that released men for combat duty.

Although Margaret Smith shared her late husband's liberal views on labor, her voting pattern also mirrored her own disenchantment with the low wages then prevalent in Maine. She voted with the Democrats against the Smith-Connally antistrike bill and to broaden Social Security coverage and raise federal salaries. Her "No" against the Republican-sponsored cut in President Truman's budget evoked from the conservative *Chicago Tribune* a hope that she "would be read out of the party." In defense of her refusal over the years to toe the GOP line, she has said, "The people have clearly shown that they don't want a 'Big Business' Republican Party or a 'Labor' Democratic Party."

Clearly, Margaret Smith's congressional performance was to Maine's liking: sound, not spectacular. The feeling among her constituents was that if she wanted to stay in the House for life they would keep her there. But in 1947, when aging Senator Wallace H. White said he would retire at the end of his term, she announced her candidacy for the Senate.

However popular she was in the 2d District, her decision did not fit into plans that state Republican leaders had for White's successor. One who intended to seek the office but asked not to be identified said, "The little lady has simply stepped out of her class. The Senate is big-league stuff. Nobody in Maine can get into the Senate without a political machine, fat campaign funds, the right business connections, and the help of the powers-that-be. Margaret hasn't got any of these things."

Once Margaret Chase Smith makes up her mind, however, she will not be budged. The governorship was suggested to her. "No, thank you," she said, and took on not only the GOP hierarchy but, in the primary, three well-known, well-liked men. One was Governor Horace A. Hildreth, who had the monetary backing of the regular Republican organization. Another was a man who had never lost an election, former Governor Sumner Sewall. The third was a Congregational minister, Albion P. Beverage, whose spellbinding oratory compensated for his lack of political experience.

In addition to formidable opposition, lack of party endorsement, and inadequate funds, candidate Smith had another handicap. Because of a conviction that she owed it to her constituents to observe personally the critical international scene, she had spent the 1947 congressional winter recess touring Europe and the Middle East; consequently, she got a late start on the campaign trail.

Not until January 1948 was she able to get away from Washington to make the rounds of the state. On days when the natives allowed that "it wuz cold enough to freeze two dry rags together," she often made as many as five public appearances. She slipped on the ice in Bangor and broke her right arm but, after the bones were set, kept a speaking date that same afternoon in Rockland, 60 miles away, and made another speech in a Portland suburb that night.

Campaign funds were raised chiefly through contributions of $10 or less. Not atypical was the dollar bill sent by an 18-year-old girl who wrote, "I regret only two things—that this must be merely a token gift to your senatorial campaign, and that I am not yet old enough to vote."

Critics dismissed Margaret Smith with some curious accusations. Maine's junior senator, Owen Brewster, spread the word that she had been "a New Dealer right from the start." Another Republican said, "She has followed the Communist line." She carefully set the record straight but did not bother to reply to allegations that were totally without foundation. The most unsavory rumor charged her with alienation of affection—with taking Clyde Smith away from his first wife, Edna Page Smith. The truth was that the first Mrs. Smith had obtained an uncontested divorce in January 1914, a year and a half before Miss Chase and Smith met.

The focus of Margaret Chase Smith's campaign speeches was her slogan: "Don't Trade a Record for a Promise." She destroyed the myth that she had strayed too often from Republican ideology by inviting skeptics to examine the tally: Her vote had been with the party 95 per cent of the time. "I've gotten the reputation of being a liberal," she said, "because I cast those votes on some very dramatic issues." Summing up the way she handled herself, a constituent remarked, "That Margaret is straight as a yard of pump water."

On June 21 women went to the polls in unprecedented numbers. All 61 voters on the tiny fishing island Matinicus cast their ballots—for Margaret Chase Smith. To the astonishment of political experts, she won by a landslide. The 63,786 votes she collected exceeded the combined total of her three opponents!

Any supporter uncertain about the outcome of the September 13 runoff could have taken heart from glancing at the table of contents in the September 11 issue of the *Saturday Evening Post.* "Senator from the Five-and-Ten," a lead article, carried the unmistakable, if slightly premature, message of victory. "A new star," wrote author Beverly Smith, "perhaps of steadier glow than any on view since enactment of the Woman's Suffrage Amendment 28 years ago has risen over the national political horizon." Citing her remarkable campaign prowess, he stated:

> She has something money can't buy: friends. . . . She has friends everywhere from back in the 1920's when she was the youthful president of the Maine Federation of Business and Professional Women's Clubs; housewives who have written her in Washington about some personal problem and received a thoughtful answer, and telephone operators. . . . She knows all the plays of the big game and has invented some of her own, [including] the most neglected play in the book—keeping her promises.

The true strength of her political personality was revealed by the election statistics. She captured over 70 per cent of the total vote and smothered her Democratic opponent, Dr. Adrian H. Scolten, a Portland dermatologist. "The voting in Maine [a Republican sweep of major offices] offers no comfort for the Democrats in November" editorialized *U.S. News & World Report.* As it turned out, the "As Maine goes, . . ." adage was not a reliable barometer in 1948. In one of the biggest upsets of the century, Thomas E. Dewey lost the Presidency to the incumbent Democrat, Harry S. Truman.

The soft-voiced, 5-foot 4-inch woman of cheerful mien whom 95 male senators found in their midst in January 1949 was, according to columnist Doris Fleeson, "attractive but not glossy." "She has the kind of beauty," a male reporter said, "which wins the admiration of men without arousing the antagonism of women." Her eyes, a striking feature, could be blue, gray, or green, depending on the light. The strands of white in her softly waved hair were the only indication that she had recently observed her 52d birthday.

Congress respects a runner who's willing to force the pace. That Margaret Chase Smith had fought hard to gain admission to the Senate impressed her colleagues—especially those who had themselves previously served in the House. Even Democrats conceded that the "Dame Yankee," with her meticulous attention to detail, retentive mind, willingness to work long hours, and fetish about keeping her word, could be an asset to the Senate.

Following her own advice to women eying the political system ("Work your way up instead of expecting to start at the top"), she labored five years in order to gain admittance to the committee of her choice, Armed Services. Would Senator Smith, the public wondered, be as determined a fact-finder as Representative Smith had been?

She obliged. When Defense Secretary Charles Wilson for nearly an hour sidestepped her sharp queries about who had ordered a cutback in the number of Air Force wings, she laid aside a list of 32 questions and asked for written answers from "someone capable of supplying them."

One of the most publicized exchanges between Margaret Smith and a congressional witness took place in 1957 after President Dwight D. Eisenhower had nominated Colonel James Maitland Stewart of the Air Force Reserve for promotion to brigadier general. This was the Jimmy Stewart of Hollywood who had risen from private to colonel during World War II, had commanded a B-17 wing in the Eighth Air Force, had flown 20 bombing missions over Germany, and had been decorated for heroism. The witness, Lieutenant General Emmett ("Rosie") O'Donnell, Air Force chief of personnel and himself a distinguished combat flier, was asked why Stewart should be promoted over 1,900 eligible colonels when he had spent only nine days on active reserve duty in 11 years and was not qualified to pilot a single military plane then being flown.

"Stewart has made a great contribution to the Air Force," O'Donnell replied. "We don't think we should promote people to general officer merely on the basis of a good attendance record."

This star of such movies as *The Spirit of St. Louis* and *Strategic Air Command*, if promoted and in the event of an enemy attack, would become deputy director of operations at SAC headquarters. Senator Smith recommended that Stewart's promotion (and those of some others) be turned down. It was. After he had complied with regulations concerning required flying time and the Air Force had given assurance that in case of war he would be assigned to public relations duty, she raised no objection to his being advanced in rank.

If Senator Smith's frontal probing in the Stewart affair rocked the White House, her unexpected vote against Eisenhower nominee Lewis L. Strauss to be Secretary of Commerce almost blew it apart. "Strauss," she said, "had been evasive, nonresponsive, and not too careful about his facts." "The President is more burned up about Mrs. Smith's action than about anything that has happened during his second term" an Eisenhower aide said. "Neither he nor the [GOP] National Committee will forget the disservice she has rendered the party."

Only twice in the previous 100 years had a Presidential Cabinet appointment been rejected by the Senate. Margaret Smith cared nothing at all about historical precedent. "I like integrity and I like others to be honest" she said. "I could not vote for Mr. Strauss."

The lesson should have been clear. Senator Smith was giving fair warning: She would brook no interference with her senatorial independence. Yet, little more than a decade later, when Richard Nixon sought support for his Supreme Court nominee G. Harrold Carswell, White House aide Bryce N. Harlow used what he *presumed* to be her favorable disposition toward Carswell to lobby Republican waverers. "It was an old con game, grown hoary with age," wrote columnist Max Lerner, "but Mrs. Smith stopped it dead." Her distinctly audible "No" was crucial to the Senate's rejection of Carswell.

She was, as *Time* reported, "seething, but outwardly as serene as the fresh rose she wears each day." She did not, however, as Richard Harris charged in the *New Yorker,* "curse" Presidential counselor Harlow and "slam down the receiver" when he evaded her telephone query about his maneuver. Whatever her shortcomings, neither profanity nor an unleashed temper is among them. To correct the record, she asked for a "point of privilege," rose on the Senate floor, and accused Harlow of "impugning the integrity and veracity" of her office. "I am shocked at the repeated irresponsibility of Mr. Harlow both before and after the vote," she said, adding that "he has a serious obligation" to substantiate his declaration that she "had been won over—or retract his statement and apologize."

Although Harlow declared in a letter to the *New Yorker* that he "never discussed the subject with [Harris] or . . . with anyone he may have interviewed" and that "even despite her anger she did not curse," Harris permitted the false allegations to be published in *Decision,* a book based on his *New Yorker* account of the Senate infighting over the Carswell nomination. Senator Smith's persistence eventually wrested a public retraction from Harris, who may have remembered that in 1956 she won a $15,000 libel suit against the authors and publisher of *U.S.A. Confidential* for "mistaken statements" concerning her character.

"What a sad commentary it is," she says, "that a public official has to take so much time to refute lies and to go into such detail to document that refutation. No wonder many fine people avoid public service."

Another irony of politics is that odd trivia attract more attention than genuinely important but undramatic legislative activity. When Senator Smith joined Representative Frances Bolton of Ohio in sponsoring a bill to adopt the rose as the national flower, the verbal play on this new "War of the Roses" proved irresistible to the press. Yet Senator Smith's subsequent warning that reduction in military spending could make "the United States a second-rate power incapable of assuring the future security and freedom of its people" was relegated to the back pages, if reported at all.

The Lady from Maine has never asked any privileges because of her sex; neither has she hesitated to rebuke men who try to restrict women to the home. "You never hear the comment that 'Men are all right in their place,'" she says. "I definitely resent being called a feminist," she wrote in her book *Declaration of Conscience* (1972); yet she feels that the proper place of women is "everywhere."

As if to prove it, in January 1964 she announced her candidacy for the highest office in the land and entered her name in the New Hampshire and Illinois Presidential primaries. When Vermont senator George D. Aiken nominated her at the Republican National Convention in San Francisco that summer, he was proposing not only the first woman to serve in both houses of Congress but the first to seek the Presidency of the United States on a major party ticket. She received 27 delegate votes, more than anyone else except the GOP nominee, Senator Barry Goldwater of Arizona.

"What will Margaret do next?" many wanted to know. They did not have to wait long to find out. In 1966, after winning her fourth term (with a typically frugal outlay of $4,500), she became chairman of the prestigious Senate Republican Conference, replacing retiring Leverett Saltonsall of Massachusetts. Senator Aiken, dean of Republican senators, could have had the coveted post for the asking; instead, he nominated his "distinguished New England colleague," thereby ensuring her election. Re-elected, Mrs. Smith presided at party caucuses and helped mastermind committee assignments. No other woman has ever been accorded such a high position of outright political leadership.

Throughout this century, Democratic Presidential and congressional winners in Maine have been a novelty. Not once was Franklin D. Roosevelt able to collect Maine's electoral votes. And until 1958, when down-easters sent Governor Edmund S. Muskie of Waterville to the Senate, no Democratic senator had every been popularly elected. That the majority over the years sought no alternative to granitic Republicanism did not, however, prevent the Democratic Party from fielding candidates against Margaret Chase Smith.

Colby College professor Paul A. Fullam, by challenging Senator Smith with a series of "Are you proud?" questions concerning the state of Maine's economy in 1954, made some headway. That year she received only 58 per cent of the votes, compared to 70 per cent in 1948.

Much more widely publicized (a *Time* cover story) but not as bitter was the 1960 contest. It marked the first time that two women with major party backing competed for a Senate seat. The Democratic nominee was Lucia Marie Cormier, 48, a former schoolteacher, a Roman Catholic, and the proprietor of a gift shop in Rumford—with an impressive political record. In 12 years she had risen to the post of minority leader in the State Legislature.

Richard Nixon, battling to overcome John F. Kennedy in the Presidential race, visited the state—at Senator Smith's invitation—and aroused local pride by saying in Bangor, "You've heard of people riding in on a candidate's coattails. Here in Maine we're hanging on as hard as we can to Margaret's skirts." However, at one point during the campaign Margaret Smith confided to a friend that she might be defeated. Maine's nascent Democrats were displaying increasing confidence. And Lucia Cormier's folksy ways—especially along the Canadian border where she could converse fluently in the French patois of the residents—had a particular appeal to voters who for one reason or another had become disenchanted with the Republican Party.

The two women pursued the electorate down to the deadline (Maine had finally joined the other 49 states by moving its congressional election from September to November), Miss Cormier bustling all over the state and Senator Smith, with only weekends to spare, relying on a well-organized network of volunteers to get out the vote. In the end, the incumbent not only defeated her challenger but received 15,000 more Maine votes than Nixon did.

Sixty-three and silver-haired when sworn in for her third term, she showed no visible signs of slowing down. Gradually, almost unobtrusively, she moved into the position of leading spokesman for the opposition.

After the Cuban missile crisis, she found fault with President Kennedy because, she said, he had not backed his strong words with action. "We have the nuclear capability," she declared in a speech on the Senate floor late in 1961, "and he [Nikita Khrushchev] knows and fears it. But we have practically told him we do not have the will to use that one power with which we can stop him. Yes, we have the nuclear capability—but not the nuclear credibility."

President Kennedy answered in a word. She is "ignorant," he told a *Look* reporter. The Soviet Premier, on the other hand, asked, "Who can remain calm and indifferent to such provocative statements?" She was, in Krushchev's words, "the devil in disguise of a woman [who] in her hatred of everything new and progressive has decided to best all records of savagery."

By 1972 Margaret Chase Smith was no longer merely the senior senator from Maine. She had acquired a national and even international political reputation. Whether at 74 she would seek a fifth term was a source of considerable speculation. Complicating the conjecture was the fact that her administrative assistant for 23 years, William C. Lewis, Jr., had suffered a heart attack. More than an aide, Lewis has been described by Donald R. Larrabee of the *Maine Sunday Telegram* as "the master strategist behind every campaign . . . and the moving force behind Mrs. Smith's remarkable career."

With Lewis's recovery ensured, she announced her decision "to seek re-election and to offer a continuity of past-approved service and representation." Her own good health was also taken into consideration. Ahead lay not only a primary contest—her first in 18 years—but also opposition from an incumbent Democratic congressman in the general election.

The GOP contender who risked a challenge against the greatest votegetter in Maine's history was a newcomer to the state: Robert A. G. Monks, an under-40 Harvard- and Cambridge-educated millionaire lawyer-industrialist. He conducted a full-scale, personal campaign, traveling throughout the state and investing heavily in expensive radio and television time. Senator

Smith, on the other hand, continued her practice of campaigning only when Congress was not in session and spent less than $10,000 to win the primary by better than 2 to 1.

To dull the impact of age, an issue Monks introduced, she talked about it herself, sometimes greeting audiences with "Meet the frail and feeble old lady." She also "pleaded guilty" to Monks's charge that she was running a pinch-penny campaign: "I don't believe a seat in the Senate ought to be up for auction to the highest bidder."

From Peace to War

"Yesterday, December 7, 1941—a date which will live in in-famy . . ." No one who heard President Roosevelt's address to the joint session of Congress can forget its blazoning effect. The Japanese bombing of Pearl Harbor was the detonator that forced the United States into World War II, the "greatest crisis [the] country has faced in this century," according to historian Arthur Schlesinger, Jr.

In the years immediately preceding the surprise attack by Japan, Congress, as it dealt with foreign affairs, had been pre-occupied with totalitarian aggression in Europe. Influenced by a popular opinion preponderantly against American involve-ment in a foreign war, both the House and the Senate attempted to legislate isolation.

A turning point came with German attacks on American ship-ping in the fall of 1941, and the Administration called for repeal of the Neutrality Act "to permit arming of American merchant vessels." Although congressional support appeared in doubt, the measure eventually passed, but just barely. The tal-ly in the House was 212-to-194, a margin of 18.

It is worth noting that the eight congresswomen split their votes. Republicans Edith Nourse Rogers of Massachusetts and Margaret Chase Smith of Maine and Democrats Mary Norton of New Jersey and Katharine Byron of Maryland favored the amendment, while Republicans Frances Bolton of Ohio, Jessie

Sumner of Illinois, and Jeannette Rankin of Montana opposed it. Democrat Caroline O'Day of New York, absent because of ill health, was paired against the resolution.

Even the infamous day did not produce a unanimous declaration of war. Representative Rankin, who consistently maintained she had "no regrets" about voting against U.S. entry into World War I, clung to her conviction that "armed conflict should be avoided at all costs" and cast the only dissenting vote.

JESSIE SUMNER
REPUBLICAN OF ILLINOIS

Isolationism cut across party lines and geographical boundaries. Republicans, however, had a more pronounced isolationist coloration than the Democrats, and the heartland of opposition to international alliances was the Midwest.

There, with a head-over-heels assist from Robert R. McCormick's "Save Our Republic" *Chicago Tribune,* the GOP elected to the House in 1938 the most implacable and outspoken antiwar, anti–New Deal candidate it could find. She was Jessie Sumner, a chubby, blonde, fast-talking county judge from the 18th District (six counties strung along the Indiana border), whose castigation of interventionists was matched only by her unbridled invective against the Roosevelt Administration.

In the House the Grand Old Party had its male coterie of spellbinding "America First" protagonists. Now, to join their strident chorus and to counterbalance pacifist Caroline O'Day on the Democratic side came a woman who shared the *Tribune's* view that FDR and Anglophiles were deliberately leading the nation into a second world war.

A forceful speaker who juggled legislative jargon with skill and wit, she quickly established herself, on and off the House floor, as the epithet queen of politics. Her characterization of the President, whom she always called "Papa Roosevelt," as a "political Lorelei" drew thunderous applause from partisan audiences. His foreign policy, she said, was a closed book to the rest of the country. "What do you know about that foreign policy?" she asked a Detroit gathering. "The secrets of that foreign policy and what we have been doing in our transactions with other nations . . . have been locked in a closet, like the corpses of Bluebeard's wives." One week after England and France declared war on Germany, she warned the public not to be intimidated by the "beaters of the tom-toms," who, she said, "treat Americans as if they have no more control over their destinies than turkeys at Thanksgiving time."

Jessie Sumner's lawyer-*cum*-politician style had been shaped by heritage and education. Born in Milford, a small town 80 miles south of Chicago, of English-Irish-Scottish lineage, she belonged to a family that had produced General ("Old Rough and Ready") Zachary Taylor, later the 12th President, and controversial Reconstructionist Charles Sumner of Massachusetts. After earning a degree in economics at Smith College, she studied law at the University of Chicago, at Columbia, and at Oxford. Postgraduate work in commerce followed at New York University and the University of Wisconsin. She was admitted to the bar in 1923, worked briefly for the Chase National Bank in Manhattan, then returned to Illinois to practice law. She lost her first try for political office when she was defeated in the primary for state's attorney but won her second, defeating two male opponents for the Iroquois County judgeship left vacant by the death of her uncle.

Pursuit of knowledge and a career left little time for romance, and Jessie Sumner wound up at 40 with impeccable credentials for Congress but without anyone to keep house for. Far from being bitter about her spinsterhood, she liked to point out that "a woman who has neither husband nor children" is in an enviable position to do anything she pleases. "Lots of women could succeed in politics," she said, "if they didn't prefer the so-called A-1 career, marriage."

The first woman in the Illinois congressional delegation since the departure of Ruth Hanna McCormick in 1931, Jessie Sumner encountered no objections when she asked to be appointed to the Banking and Currency Committee. The conflict-of-interest issue could have been raised inasmuch as she was a director of the Sumner National Bank, founded by her father in Sheldon, but, as one would-be political reformer asked, "On the eve of war, who would listen?"

For combined physical and emotional energy, Congresswoman Sumner had few equals on the Hill. Remarked one colleague, "She's both exhilarating and exhausting." She walked at least six miles a day to and from her Mayflower Hotel apartment and her office, which she boasted "is in the building named for one of my predecessors" ("Uncle Joe" Cannon, an Old Guard Republican who had represented the 18th Illinois District for almost 50 years). She typed her own speeches. "I think better on the typewriter," she explained. "Besides, after retyping my first draft about three times, I know the text by heart."

In committee or on the floor, whenever she made a statement based on law, no one questioned its validity. She was listened to with deference. But her special perception of the war and U.S. foreign policy was with justification ridiculed by Democrats and even by some liberal Republicans. For some unfathomed reason, she insisted that "if a committee had been sent to see Hitler at the right time, all of the trouble might have been avoided." One of her most absurd proposals, presented in the form of an amendment in the spring of 1944, demanded that D-Day be postponed. "The invasion," she said "will be costly and stupid." She condemned the 54-word Fulbright resolution pledging Congress to postwar international collaboration in maintaining peace as a "Machiavellian scheme to make permanent the policy of handouts across the sea." Denouncing the U.N. Charter as leading to a "world superstate," she called the United Nations itself the "new plunderbird." After Congress agreed that the United States should be a member nation (she was one of 15 casting dissenting votes in the House), she said, "We have joined the dance of death on the European and Asiatic battlefields."

That she reflected the majority viewpoint of her constituents was evident in the fact they re-elected her, over younger Democratic opponents, for three more terms. Had she not decided in 1946 to resume her law practice and manage the family farm and banking interests, her tenure probably would have continued.

"Being a congressman in wartime is a heartbreaking job," she said. "This is the place where you see or foresee most of the trouble and sorrow suffered by our people, but all you seem to achieve is a growing feeling of frustration."

The history of Jessie Sumner is the history of the rise and fall of isolationism in the Midwest and in Congress. Now in her 70s, she sometimes reminisces about her crusade "for peace and neutrality." As the record shows, she did not lose every battle. During the debate on a $20 billion naval appropriations bill, she offered an amendment "to ban the use of funds for extravagant christening services at battleship launchings." With military costs rising, she urged the navy to discontinue its long traditions of having a bottle of champagne smacked against a bow and of presenting the feminine sponsor with an orchid and a gift (usually an expensive piece of jewelry or a wristwatch). "If Helen of Troy could launch a thousand ships without a diamond bracelet," she told the House, "our women can do the same." Her colleagues, grinning broadly, agreed—unanimously.

CLARA G. McMILLAN
DEMOCRAT OF SOUTH CAROLINA

Jessie Sumner excepted, all women serving in the House during the 76th Congress (1939–41) were widows. In this regard, nothing had changed very much in 20 years.

When Representative Thomas S. McMillan, Democrat of South Carolina, died midway in his eighth term, party leaders in the 1st District decided to perpetuate the McMillan name by nominating his widow, Clara, 45, to succeed him. Against token opposition (Shep Hutto of Dorchester and James DeTreville of Walterboro), in a special fall election in 1939, she was elected to represent nine counties in the piney, moss-hung low country around Charleston.

Clara McMillan hoped the United States could stay out of the war, but she shared the opinion of most Southerners that neutrality was not the answer. Moreover, to provide for the eventuality that America might join the battle to defeat Hitler, she favored an immediate acceleration of military preparedness—and said as much during the 1940 debate over the Burke-Wadsworth selective service bill.

Speaking "with a heavy heart but with honest conviction," she recommended conscription to ensure "peace and freedom." The citizenry, she said, "must sacrifice for it." Dispassionately, she explained her willingness:

> I have five sons. The oldest will come immediately under the operation of the bill and be subject to its provisions, as he is past 21 years. My second son is almost 19 years old and is now taking military training in a school organized for that purpose. If and when my sons are needed for the defense of their country, I do not want them to go up against experienced soldiers, untrained and unskilled.

On September 7, 1940, the first peacetime draft in the nation's history became law.

Before ending her 14 months in the House, Representative McMillan announced that she would not seek re-election. The decision did not reflect personal preference but, rather, the self-proclaimed ambition of a lawyer from North Charleston. His name was L. Mendel Rivers, and he was elected. From her information liaison job in the State Department, she watched him rise to head the House Armed Services Committee, and, later, from her home in Ulmers, South Carolina, she had a close-up view of the magical Rivers touch as it turned the 1st District into one of the most fortified patches of geography in the nation.

FLORENCE REVILLE GIBBS
DEMOCRAT OF GEORGIA

It was pure coincidence, but the first female representative from Georgia, 50-year-old Florence Gibbs, was born and spent her youth in Thomson, the red-clay hamlet that produced Thomas E. Watson, the senator whose seat Rebecca Felton won by appointment in 1922.

As the nominee selected by local Democratic chieftains to complete the 3-month unexpired term of her late husband, Mrs. Gibbs was a soft-spoken, unassertive person who had no professional experience to recommend her. The daughter of Thomas Porter Reville, a country doctor, she had grown up in the characteristic sheltered ambience of the turn-of-the-century South. Her personal record at the time of her nomination consisted of being a graduate of Brenau College in Gainesville, the widow of Willis Benjamin Gibbs, and the mother of two children, a daughter and a son.

That the special election called on October 1, 1940, by Governor E. D. Rivers failed to excite the electorate became evident when the votes were counted. From the 20-county area in the southeastern corner of the state that she would represent in Congress, a mere 2,469 went to the polls.

"She was good for political patronage—mainly post office appointments," one constituent remembers. "The job wasn't really to her liking."

Florence Gibbs retired with the adjournment of the 76th Congress to live out her life quietly in Jesup, where her son had opened a law office. She died there in 1964 at the age of 74.

KATHARINE E. BYRON
DEMOCRAT OF MARYLAND

Less than two months after Congressman William D. Byron was sworn in for his second term in 1941, he was killed in an airplane crash. In order that western Marylanders not be deprived of representation in the House any longer than was absolutely necessary, a special election was authorized. In the running were former Alleghany County Commissioner A. Charles Stewart of Frostburg, a Republican, and Katharine Edgar Byron, of Williamsport, who had been persuaded by Democratic leaders in the 6th District to enter the contest for her late husband's congressional seat.

On the basis of party registration alone—84,000 Democrats to 67,000 Republicans—she was the odds-on favorite to become the state's first congresswoman. Widowhood was bound to attract the sympathy vote. As one Democratic official said, "Who knows, with her instinctive knack for commanding respect, we could pick up feminine support in the opposition camp."

Both sides poured major support into the campaign. The Democrats sent Eleanor Roosevelt, who spoke and posed for pictures with Mrs. Byron at the Fort Cumberland Hotel; James Domengeaux of Louisiana, a member of the House Mines Committee; and Estes Kefauver, veteran Tennessee congressman. The GOP countered with high-ranking officials from national party headquarters in Washington.

Stewart, appealing to the antiwar faction, said her election would mean one more vote in Congress for an Administration "whose present inclination is to spill the blood of our boys in the squabbles of Europe." Denying his allegation that she would be a rubber stamp for Roosevelt, Mrs. Byron declared that "going to war will not be too large a price to pay to rescue Europe from the Nazis."

It was a nip-and-tuck race that ended with Katharine Byron's carrying three of the five counties and winning by the slender margin of 1,115 votes. In all probability, women gave Mrs. Byron her slight edge. "I am mindful of the double responsibility of not only representing the district with as much energy and distinction as possible," she said from Hagerstown after her victory was ensured, "just as I feel that I must so act as to justify the people's confidence in women in public life."

The international balance in 1941 was full of imponderables and uncertainties. The 37-year-old brunette mother of five sons ranging in age from 3 to 16 years had no illusions about war. She was the daughter of a brigadier general in the Michigan National Guard and the widow of a World War I aerial gunnery officer. On the House floor in mid-November, she spoke in favor of amending the Neutrality Act. "I asked my oldest son, who is of military age, how he thought I should

vote," she said. "'Vote for it and I'll be proud of you,' he told
me." In the debate preceding the declaration of war on December 8, she dedicated the lives of her sons, if necessary, to defeat the enemy.

The news about Pearl Harbor reached Katharine Byron, as it
did millions of others, by radio at home, but, unlike some, she
did not permit the dire announcement to change her social
plans. That Sunday she dined at Friendship, the palatial estate
of Hope-diamond owner Evelyn Walsh McLean. "There were
many vacant places at the table," she recalls, "and some grim
talk. I had seen smoke curling skyward as I passed the Japanese Embassy on Massachusetts Avenue. Only later did I learn
that official documents were being burned."

Detroit-born Katharine Edgar got her social start in the fashionable setting of Springfield Farm, the Maryland estate of her
maternal grandfather, Judge Louis Emory McComas, a friend
of Republican Presidents and an esteemed member of both
the House and the Senate during the 1880s and early 1900s.
At the Byron house on Woodley Road in Washington, her
guest list tended to be eclectic, politically liberal, and occasionally surprising: American Indians in tribal dress, for instance.

When Goodloe Edgar Byron, her third-eldest son, ran successfully for Congress in 1970, his 68-year-old mother turned
trouper for his campaign and clearly was one of his political assets. She rallied friends, raised money, gave speeches, passed
out literature, and shared in his satisfying moment of victory.

Afterward, she reminisced about her own political career,
which, owing to a tangle of circumstances, ended sooner than
she had expected. "I filed for re-election and made my first
speech—in William D. Byron Park, a memorial to my husband in Williamsport," she recalled.

> Citizen morale was low. The military picture was bleak. The
> country still reeled from the crippling blow dealt by the Japanese
> to . . . the Pacific fleet. A call had gone out for women to pitch
> in. The governess who cared for my boys was also a registered
> nurse and she wanted to volunteer for army duty. I knew I
> couldn't replace her. But what could I say?

The 6th District went Republican that year, J. Glenn Beall,
Sr., winning the seat. Mrs. Byron spent the war years on two
fronts: at home looking after her boys and at the Red Cross
doing anything that needed to be done.

In the years since, four of the Byron sons have donned
uniforms (one was rejected because of a hearing impairment).

She is demonstrably proud of them and she also dotes on her 17 grandchildren.

Katharine Byron today spends much of her time on luxury cruises, but Washington still has a special electricity for her. In the elegant Georgetown house she designed after the war, the paintings and portraits are touchstones to a past at once tragic and happy—interwoven now with congressional history.

VERONICA B. BOLAND

DEMOCRAT OF PENNSYLVANIA

Passing almost unnoticed amid the postmortems on the results of the first congressional elections during World War II was the outcome of an uncontested race in the 11th Pennsylvania District (Lackawanna County). Veronica Grace Boland of Scranton, the winner, went to Washington as the Commonwealth's first congresswoman.

Asked to comment on the significance of Mrs. Boland's victory, Postmaster General Frank C. Walker, fellow Democrat and family friend, told the *Scranton Tribune* that her election to fill the unexpired term of her late husband, Patrick J. Boland, majority whip of the House, "came as a deserved recognition of Mr. Boland's long public service."

The attractive 43-year-old widow agreed. "I really can't get excited about it," she told reporters. "I would rather have Mr. Boland there, of course. I've always preferred the background."

Sworn in on November 19, 1942, Veronica Boland stayed on the job until December 16, when weary members of the 77th Congress adjourned to enjoy the holidays with the rest of the nation. In 28 days not even the most experienced lawmaker in the land could be expected to accomplish anything on Capitol Hill. Accordingly, she did not serve on a committee, made no speeches, and went back to Scranton, where she had been born (the daughter of Irish immigrants, Patrick and Winifred Barrett) and educated (Technical High School, class of 1918), to rear her sons, Patrick, Jr., and Eugene. Before undergoing eye surgery in 1957, she held the position of executive secretary with the Dutch Manufacturing Company in Scranton.

WINIFRED C. STANLEY

REPUBLICAN OF NEW YORK

On the basis of the 1940 census, New York State faced the unhappy task of trimming its congressional delegation from 45 to 43. The Republicans, hoping to expedite reapportionment, incorporated in their party platform a plank advocating that the two at-large seats be eliminated. Simultaneously, they began casting about for a candidate who not only could win but would be willing to lose—in the sense that there might not be an opportunity for re-election.

The brightest star on the political horizon at the 1942 GOP Convention in Saratoga Springs turned out to be Winifred C. Stanley of Buffalo. She was not only a successful assistant district attorney in Erie County but also a vivacious, undeniably female, blue-eyed young lady who would later be described by *Newsweek* as "pretty enough to 'twitterpate' some of her colleagues."

Whether campaigning alone or crisscrossing the state aboard Thomas E. Dewey's gubernatorial campaign train, Miss Stanley added a welcome touch of glamour to the male-dominated scene. Moreover, her oratorical approach was refreshing. Instead of raking the New Deal, she emphasized the "renewed sense of purpose" the Republican Party could bring to the nation.

In a field of eight candidates for representative at large, including two other women (Democrat Flora D. Johnson of Syracuse, mother of two teen-age daughters and her husband's partner in a machine-tool business, and Communist Elizabeth Gurley Flynn), Winifred Stanley was the top vote-getter. She swept the state, losing only Greater New York, perennially Democratic territory, and Albany County. Ballots cast for her, including those cast by members of the armed forces, totaled nearly 2 million. At 33, she was the youngest woman yet elected to Congress.

Winning the war *and* the peace was the overriding issue before the confident 78th Congress. Winifred Stanley was concerned less with what she called the "poetry" of victory than with the "prose" of postwar readjustment. "Maintaining the peace," she said, "is like maintaining democracy. It's a lifetime job."

Early in the session she addressed herself to the question of "carrying over into peacetime the drive and energy which women have contributed to the war effort." As long as women remain "secondary wage earners," she declared, "we shall be paying only lip service to those glorious and fundamental guarantees of our nation's heritage."

The amendment to the National Labor Relations Act that she introduced would have made it unlawful "to discriminate against any employee, in the rate of compensation paid, on account of sex." The proposition that jobs should be filled by those best qualified by ability, training, and experience had been introduced before in the House. So had arguments against it (some Southerners delighted in labeling such bills "much ado about little"). In 1943, as previously, the measure died for lack of support. (Twenty years would elapse before Congress passed the Equal Pay Act.)

Miss Stanley traces her equal-rights philosophy to an incident that occurred during her years as a trial lawyer in Buffalo. "Going to court one morning," she recalls, "I found the courtroom door closed to women—because of the criminal nature of the case being tried. Juries had always been closed to them." Because she considered the right to serve on a jury "second in importance only to the right to vote," she used the forums afforded by women's clubs, church societies, and political organizations to argue that "justice could be served only by extending to women—whose rights, property, and very lives are often vitally affected by law suits (both civil and criminal) —the opportunity of jury service." Not coincidentally, jury panels were opened to women in New York at about the same time she was named to the DA's staff, the first woman assistant prosecutor in the history of Erie County.

The eldest of six children, Winifred Claire Stanley was born in the Bronx, but she thinks of Buffalo (where she went to school) as her hometown. Had she elected to pursue a career in architecture or teaching, she would have been following in the footsteps of either her father, John Francis Stanley, who designed Mount Olivet Chapel in Erie County, or her mother, who had taught English and music in her native New England. "It is a source of disappointment that I inherited neither my father's talent for painting and sketching nor my mother's musical gifts," she says.

What she did inherit was a brilliant mind. After being graduated from the University of Buffalo and its law school (scholarship student, *magna cum laude*), she began her professional career with a firm specializing in corporation law. It was her trial work in the district attorney's office, however, that convinced her the government needed a personal touch. By the time she traded a $3,100-a-year salary to represent 13.5 million constituents in a job that paid $10,000, the direction she would take in Washington was already firmly fixed.

What Miss Stanley had not foreseen was that she would be denied an appointment to the House Judiciary Committee. Her efforts to persuade the gentleman in charge of committee assignments, New York representative James W. Wadsworth, Jr., 66-year-old adherent to the maxim that "a woman's place is in the home," to consider her were in vain. "He based his decision," she recalls, "on the grounds that first-year members of Congress are rarely assigned to such an important committee, and since the at-large post was being abolished, there would be no continuity of service. Unfortunately, his decision could not be appealed."

Although her appointment to the Patents and Copyrights Committee did not represent her legal specialty, she impressed oldtimers with her ready acceptance of tedious research. She also served on the Civil Service Committee.

Following up her campaign promise "to accomplish as much as possible in the two years allotted," Representative Stanley functioned as a studious and pragmatic postwar planner. On her priority list were "well-equipped and well-staffed veterans' hospitals" and a long-range plan to ensure jobs once the war effort ended. Toward these ends, she enlisted the aid of influential colleagues and organized citizen lobbies. "My constituents were always my priority," she remembers, and she turned down a congressional trip to Europe because "it would have been of no benefit to them."

A victim of the housing shortage that plagued the nation's capital, Winifred Stanley spent months moving from hotel to hotel before discovering a vacant apartment at Dorchester House on 16th Street, N.W. It had everything, she remembers: a view of the Washington Monument, spaciousness, convenient transportation, a roof garden—even the copper tubing to be used to air-condition the building. The contract to install the cooling system was canceled, however, after a local newspaper printed a letter from an irate taxpayer who questioned the propriety of "using anything as vital to the war effort as copper to air-condition an apartment house occupied by Secretary of Labor Frances Perkins." Considering the conglomerate of problems confronting the War Production Board, it is hardly surprising that the copper was not removed from Dorchester House and that non-airconditioned buildings with less prestigious tenants were supplied with the rationed metal.

Despite the sweltering humidity of Washington summers, could Miss Stanley be lured back to the federal city? Her response: "The privilege of serving in Congress would be well worth a 'repeat performance,' especially at this point in time. Reforms which, as freshmen members of the '78th' we worked hard to attain—changes in the seniority system, for example —may well be accomplished within the foreseeable future."

Of the 435 representatives in the 78th Congress, only 15 were still in the House in the 92d. One, Lyndon B. Johnson, had gone on to the White House. Twenty-four others had moved to the Senate, including Margaret Chase Smith.

As for Miss Stanley, she accepted an appointment in Governor Dewey's administration as chief counsel to the New York State Employees' Retirement System. Appointed an assistant attorney general in 1955, she has established a legal reputation in Albany not unlike the one she earned in Buffalo. A recognized authority in administrative and constitutional law and habeas corpus, she has been singled out for praise by colleagues and judges alike for her clarity of expression in the preparation of briefs and for her eloquence in arguing cases before appellate courts. A photograph of a judge of the Court of Appeals (New York's highest court) that hangs in her office is inscribed "To Winifred C. Stanley, a superb lawyer."

WILLA L. FULMER
DEMOCRAT OF SOUTH CAROLINA

For one new representative in the lame-duck session of the 78th Congress, the duties were both sad and frustrating. Democrat Willa Fulmer of the South Carolina 2d District, elected on November 7, 1944, to fill the unexpired term of her deceased husband, spent the better part of the two months she served sifting through what she called the "papers of a lifetime."

Hampton Pitts Fulmer, like other Southerners who represented uncontested districts, had remained in the House term after term: 23 years. A successful Orangeburg cotton farmer, he had built his national reputation as chairman of the House Agriculture Committee. While her husband had been becoming politically powerful and the couple's three daughters had been emerging as personages in their own right, Mrs. Fulmer, who as Willa Essie Lybrand had left Greenville Female College at age 17 to marry, had allowed herself the old-fashioned privilege of being simply mistress of the manor.

Because Congressman Fulmer's death had reduced the Democratic House majority to a politically perilous two seats, the State Executive Committee lost no time seeking a successor. The day after her husband's funeral Willa Fulmer had been approached by phone about taking the job. Thinking that the caller was playing a practical joke, she had hung up. When she later accepted the nomination, she said she did so "with a deep sense of improbability." Had she received a mandate from the people (she was unopposed), Mrs. Fulmer would have responded with at least a modicum of enthusiasm for the task ahead. But the election had offered no encouragement: Out of a total population of 361,933, fewer than 8,000 had gone to the polls.

Sixty years old and a grandmother when her brief term ended in January 1945, Mrs. Fulmer severed all property connections in South Carolina (where she had been born in 1884) and added a new dimension to her life—travel. While aboard a luxury liner bound for Europe in May 1968, she suffered a heart attack and died.

Star Billing

CLARE BOOTHE LUCE

REPUBLICAN OF CONNECTICUT

Clare Boothe Luce brought assets to Congress that other office-holders may not have envied but that must have reduced quite a few officeseekers to a state of green-eyed jealousy. She possessed a singular combination of beauty and brains, fame and fortune.

Only the physical and mental attributes were inherited. The birthplace of Ann Clare Boothe in 1903 was a run-down apartment on New York City's Riverside Drive. Because her father, William F. Boothe, could not earn a steady income as a professional violinist, Clare and her older brother David spent their childhood in what she describes as "genteel poverty." Sometimes the family went on the road with Will Boothe, which meant that her formal schooling was erratic.

When Clare was nine, her father deserted his wife. Anna Snyder Boothe, whose work experience had been limited to clerking in a department store and dancing and singing in a chorus line, took the children to her parents' home in Hoboken, New Jersey. After Anna's father, William Snyder, died, the trio moved back to Manhattan—this time to a small, dimly lit flat on Columbus Avenue.

Until Mrs. Boothe obtained a job selling jewelry, blonde, curly-haired Clare accounted for the only weekly paycheck. David Belasco had been persuaded to hire her as Mary Pickford's understudy in *The Good Little Devil*. Miss Pickford never missed a performance; thus Miss Boothe was never seen by the play-goers. Her first public appearance, with Ernest Truex in *The Dummy,* was followed by a walk-on role in the Biograph Studio film ironically entitled *Over the Hill to the Poorhouse.* By her own admission, she was "not very good," and, published accounts to the contrary, Clare Boothe Luce has never considered herself an actress.

Anna Boothe, with earnings derived from stock purchased on the advice of a Wall Street acquaintance, took her daughter to London and on to Paris in 1913. Plans for Clare to spend a year studying French and acquiring an appreciation of European art and architecture were interrupted by the outbreak of war.

Not until her 12th birthday was she exposed to any continuous classroom instruction. Enrolled on a scholarship at the Cathedral School of St. Mary in Garden City, Long Island, she subsequently was graduated, first in her class, from the Castle School in Tarrytown-on-the-Hudson. The yearbook predicted she would become a "famous author." Credit for her scholastic success, she says, belongs to her father. "He encouraged David and me to explore the secondhand books he brought home from time to time."

Having been taught by Miss Cassity Mason, Castle headmistress, that "You can do anything a man can do, and probably do it a lot better," Clare, at 16, went to work—making paper party decorations for the Dennison Company. When an appendicitis attack forced her to leave after three months, she was relieved. "The job was depressing," she remembers.

Mrs. Boothe's marriage to Albert E. Austin, a prosperous Greenwich, Connecticut, physician, not only saved the family from further financial crises but also gave Clare the first emotional security she had ever known. She actually had time to reflect on her future. Still practical, she studied typing and shorthand at a business school. At night she wrote poetry, some of which was published, and short stories, all of which were rejected.

Indirectly, her stepfather, who would later be elected to Congress, was responsible for Clare Boothe's involvement in politics. In 1922 she accompanied the Austins to Berlin, Germany, where the doctor observed new plastic-surgery techniques designed to treat disfigured World War I veterans. On the return trip aboard the *Olympic* she met and impressed Mrs. Oliver H. P. Belmont, then searching for young, talented crusaders to work for the National Woman's Party. Clare joined the rank and file.

Her assignment, according to biographer Stephen Shadegg, "was to attract public attention, enlist new converts, and help destroy the notion that feminine activists had to be rich, chesty old matrons or disgruntled, plain spinsters—in short, to radiate youth and sex appeal." Not the least of her contributions was the publicity she garnered for the women's movement by donning a leather helmet and goggles and, from the open cockpit of a World War I Jenny circling above Syracuse, New York, dropping leaflets advertising the 75th anniversary of the Seneca Falls Equal Rights Convention.

The social whirl of New York City and Newport, Rhode Island, replaced politics during her six-year marriage to multimillionaire George Tuttle Brokaw, 23 years her senior. But, after a 1929 Reno divorce—a step she took when her husband's alcoholism made life for her and their young daughter unbearable—she became intrigued by a clique of actors, producers, and writers who believed that plays, films, and books should be used to impart a political message.

Clare, then on the staff of the magazine *Vanity Fair,* was recruited by columnist Jay Franklin to be the unpaid executive secretary of the budding National Party. With Donald Freeman (managing editor of *Vanity Fair*), wealthy socialite Mrs. Harrison Williams, and James Forrestal (later the first Secretary of Defense), she helped draft a platform. The liberal planks were designed to wrest the country from the "disastrous economic policies" advocated by both major parties.

On her way to the 1932 Democratic National Convention, where she was to lure dissident Democrats to the new party, she met Frank R. Kent, well-known political reporter, to whom she described her latest venture. "I have here," said Mr. Kent, "a little book that I carry for just such young women as you," and he gave her a copy of *The Great Game of Politics.* She read it that night and never again mentioned the National Party. All that remains of it is its slogan, which Jay Franklin later incorporated in the publicity campaign he masterminded for Franklin D. Roosevelt. The slogan was "A New Deal for America."

At the convention that nominated Roosevelt, Clare met Bernard M. Baruch, the financier destined to become a legend as an unofficial adviser to Presidents. A friendship developed, and she was admitted to the select group of FDR intimates. "The lowly kitchen maid of the New Deal cabinet," she called herself.

What eventually caused her clear-cut break with Roosevelt

was his economic and social philosophy. In an unpublished script entitled *Oh Pyramids!* she satirized the National Recovery Administration (NRA), a federal agency established to control the nation's business activities. A planned economy is anathema to a free America, she told NRA czar Hugh Johnson.

When Roosevelt ran for a third term in 1940, Clare, then the wife of Henry Robinson Luce, founder-publisher of *Time, Life,* and *Fortune,* became the most telling feminine voice on the side of Wendell L. Willkie, the big businessman turned liberal Republican crusader who had won the Presidential nomination in a stunning upset over Ohio senator Robert Taft and New York governor Thomas Dewey. For the first time the masses discovered her flair for wit and hyperbole. Her low, precise voice and the intensity and zeal of her delivery infected the 22,000 at Madison Square Garden who heard her address the largest Willkie rally in New York City. It was the climax of three weeks of campaigning that from the start revealed her as a political counterpoise to Dorothy Thompson, the widely read, influential *New York Herald Tribune* columnist, who had switched her support from Willkie to Roosevelt.

Once Clare Boothe Luce burst into the political sky like a comet, GOP leaders in Connecticut (one of the Luce homes was in Greenwich) decided she was the answer to pro–New Deal Representative Le Roy D. Downs, a newspaper publisher from South Norwalk who had captured his House seat from her stepfather in 1940. At the 1942 Republican state nominating convention she was given an 84-to-2 vote over six other hopefuls, including industrialist Vivien Kellems, to represent the 4th Congressional District.

The possibility of defeat was never out of the nominee's thoughts—or far from those of success-oriented Henry Luce. In private she had confessed to Albert P. Morano, who had been on Dr. Austin's Washington staff, what she considered to be the political drawbacks of her candidacy. At the top of the list was the fact that she was not well known in Fairfield County. She had spent most of the past fifteen years as a successful author (*Stuffed Shirts*) and playwright (*The Women, Kiss the Boys Goodbye*) in New York City or traveling the world, sometimes as a *Life* correspondent. A long apprenticeship in neighborliness was, she said, an important asset for a member of Congress. Yet, as she wrote Morano, "[it] is one I do not seem to possess today."

To overcome the obvious political disadvantages, she waged

an energetic, professionally organized campaign. Plying between Bridgeport, Danbury, and Greenwich, she made 116 speeches. At factory gates she displayed her union card showing membership in the Dramatists' Guild. Polish voters, icy at the outset, were warmed on being reminded that she had been the last American woman to leave Warsaw before the Nazi invasion. She made Roosevelt her chief target, accusing him of inefficiency on the home front and of "talking a tough war but waging a soft one." Willkie returned past favors by coming into the 4th District to speak for her; Dorothy Thompson, refusing to permit ideological differences to interfere with friendship, endorsed her in paid advertisements. Out of the more than 120,000 votes cast, Clare Luce's victory margin was 6,858. (Socialist David Mansell siphoned off 15,573.)

Because the first Connecticut congresswoman was also a celebrated public figure, newsmen in the capital sharpened their pencils in anticipation of her arrival. Their speculation about the kind of lawmaker she would make was mixed. One oldtimer commented that she had four strikes against her: She was rich, intelligent, pretty, and Republican.

But she muffed her entrance. She arrived in Washington from Hollywood, where she was under contract to Warner Brothers as technical adviser on a film about China. Although the train was two hours late, reporters were waiting at Union Station when it pulled in. Clare Luce, unaware of their presence, hurriedly debarked and taxied to the Wardman Park Hotel. The repercussions were not pleasant. At a press conference in her office the next day, she went through trial by fury. The confrontation itself ended in a draw, but not the competition to score points. Here Clare Luce, with her gift for crystalline expression, usually had the edge.

Criticized by Amy Porter of *Collier's* for having the effrontery, as a freshman, to ask for a place on the House Foreign Affairs Committee, Clare, through her administrative assistant Al Morano, left Miss Porter apologetic in full view of the facts. Four first-term Democrats (including Mike Mansfield of Montana, J. William Fulbright of Arkansas, and Will Rogers, Jr., of California) had been named to this committee. Yet not one had as much personal knowledge of overseas operations as the former correspondent.

Like a Venus in armor, Congresswoman Luce seemed personally invulnerable to attack. She did not lose her temper under fire or become maladroit or confused. Sometimes she sent a critical writer a note defending her position. More often she sent a note of thanks to a reporter whose objectivity she appreciated. If she had an Achilles' heel, she kept it secret.

Although she did not envision that her maiden speech would be historic, it was. Entitled "America in the Postwar Air World," it left neither her critics nor her admirers speechless. Vice President Henry Wallace's call for an international postwar freedom of the airways was her central theme. "Until this hour," she said, "the sovereignty of the skies policy has stood us in excellent stead, both commercially and militarily, and I hope diplomatically." Suggesting that members read Wallace's article on the subject in *American* magazine, she went on: "Much of what Mr. Wallace calls his global thinking is, no matter how you slice it, still globaloney. Mr. Wallace's warp of sense and his woof of nonsense is a very tricky cloth out of which to cut the pattern of a postwar world." She had proved again that she was quick to seize the psychological moment for the most crushing verbal effect.

"Globaloney" would never appear in Webster's dictionary, but it made front-page headlines across the country the next day and was called a "cheap wisecrack" by editorial writers who considered it brazen for a congressional neophyte to attack the Vice President of the United States. Roosevelt delegated the task of refuting Clare Luce's reasoning to Congressman Fulbright. A former Rhodes scholar, he made a grammatical error in his rebuttal, stating that she had inferred that Wallace's proposal would endanger U.S. security. "I inferred nothing," Clare said. "I implied, and the gentleman from Arkansas did the inferring." The man who would one day chair the Senate Foreign Relations Committee admitted years later that he had never forgotten his embarrassment.

Such repartee tended to obscure her substantial record in the 78th Congress: a proposal for a nonaggression pact or military alliance with England, France, and other European countries (an objective later achieved with the formation of the North Atlantic Treaty Organization); a demand for repeal of the Chinese Exclusion Act; a resolution calling for racial equality in the Armed Services; condemnation of the DAR for refusing to let Marian Anderson perform in Constitution Hall; and a plea that Britain grant independence to India (which elicited an angry six-page cablegram from Prime Minister Winston Churchill).

Clare's flair for phrasemaking reached its political zenith in her famous "GI Jim and GI Joe" speech, delivered at the 1944 GOP National Convention. Quoting a 1940 promise by FDR that

American boys would not be sent to fight a foreign war, she suggested that Democratic bungling was responsible for excessive battle casualties:

> Who is GI Jim? Ask rather, who *was* GI Jim. He was Joe's pal, his buddy, his brother. Jim was the fellow who lived next door to you. . . . Jim did not complain too much about his government. . . . Jim figured that anybody can make mistakes. . . . If Jim could stand here and talk to you he might say, "Listen folks, the past wasn't perfect. But skip it. Get on with the business of making this old world better." . . . And this we will do, for Jim's sake.

"The Republicans have found their ablest campaign orator next to Wendell Willkie," editorialized the *Salem Capital Journal,* an influential Oregon paper, "and she is perhaps more subtle than the latter, a better master of satired invective and phrase-coiner—using the rapier rather than the broadsword." Quentin Reynolds, on the other hand, saw her as an assassin. "It is not the first time," he wrote, "that a citizen named Booth treacherously assaulted a President of the United States."

Representative Luce had a prodigious capacity for hard work, for working under pressure, and for being able to juggle many tasks with serenity. "Congress," she once said, "is no place for a sluggard. Some of the members work harder than ditchdiggers." About those who did not, she also had a comment: "If all the Congressmen who dozed on the floor during [debates] were laid end to end, they would [be] much more comfortable." Representative Michael Bradley of Pennsylvania called this "flippant and wisecracking . . . irresponsible and unreliable"—but his was almost a lone voice crying amid the laughter.

By the slim margin of 2,008 votes, Clare Luce was re-elected in 1944, defeating a young Bridgeport lawyer, Margaret E. Connors. "Actually," said an observer, "Mrs. Luce didn't win; Miss Connors lost by switching her campaign tactics in the last weeks from hammering away at winning the war to slinging mud at the congresswoman."

The incumbent could be proud that the Democrats had poured much money and talent into Fairfield County in an effort to topple her—and had failed. Vice President Wallace, Secretary of the Interior Harold Ickes, former Under Secretary of State Sumner Welles, and members of what she called the "Broadway-Browder axis of carpetbagging New Deal celebrities" were all guest stars in the anti-Luce show. The President himself, an arm around Miss Connors, denounced Clare Luce from the platform of his campaign train when it stopped in Bridgeport, and on election night, as early returns seemed to augur her downfall, he said in Hyde Park, "Her defeat would be a good thing for this country, and it's a rough thing to say about a lady."

Clare Luce fought back in this bitterest of campaigns. She dismissed Ickes as "that prodigious bureaucrat with the soul of a meat ax and the mind of a commissar." Reviewing FDR's statements about the danger of war from 1937 to Pearl Harbor, she charged, "He is the only American President who ever lied us into a war because he did not have the political courage to lead us into it. . . . The shame of Pearl Harbor is Mr. Roosevelt's shame."

The ambivalence of American foreign policy was sharply criticized by Clare Luce during her second term. She was a principled and consistent anti-Communist at a time when many politicians were infatuated with "Uncle Joe" Stalin. In the wake of the historic Yalta Conference (attended by Roosevelt, Churchill, and Stalin), she issued a blunt warning against a "soft policy toward Communism." On the House floor she spoke often and at length about the consequences of relying on an "enduring Soviet-U.S. friendship." Her predictions concerning the Communists' being a threat to the free world were borne out in the cold war, which haunted the United States from V-J Day until the early 1960s.

The domestic scene did not escape Representative Luce's attention during the crucial postwar period. Included in the well-thought-out legislation she introduced were bills to make it easier for veterans to get jobs, to eliminate discrimination by industry against minorities (particularly Negroes), to grant an income-tax deduction to members of the medical profession for the amount of time they devoted to charity patients, to create a department of science for the specific purpose of upgrading scientific research and instruction, and to establish civilian control over atomic power.

One of the oddest rumors that surfaced during her congressional years was that she did not write her own speeches. Perhaps the reason for this rumor was that there was no obvious driving of herself; the capacity for working at peak achievement seemed to come as naturally to her, out of boundless health, as her beauty. The sum total of what she looked like was as breathtaking as what she did. "There's nothing Clare Boothe Luce can't do," Frank Gervasi wrote in *Collier's*. "She might even get to be President or Vice President."

Close associates said that she cherished the thought of being not the President but the wife of the President. Meanwhile it was reported that her next political step would be into the Senate. Had the 42-year-old congresswoman wanted to become a senator, the political situation in Connecticut in 1946 was such that she could undoubtedly have had the GOP nomination.

Instead, she made an announcement in January that marked her retirement, temporarily at least, from elective office. She had decided not to seek re-election to the House, she said, for "good and sufficient reasons which will become obvious in time." Still in mourning for her daughter Ann Brokaw, who, while a student at Stanford University in 1944, had been killed in an automobile accident, Clare Luce was also on the threshold of converting to Roman Catholicism. Because the 4th District included many Catholics, she felt that her spiritual decision might be branded a politically motivated act. After all, certain detractors had been able to create the impression that a cold and calculating mind had directed her climb to prestige and power.

The ex-congresswoman returned to writing (mainly about religion) and lecturing (on foreign policy) but at strategic moments found politics irresistible. Her description of Democratic Presidential nominee Harry Truman as a "man of phlegm, not fire," touched off the first convention demonstration when Republicans convened in Philadelphia in 1948. Two years later she kept a pledge to Al Morano and helped him win the GOP congressional nomination in Fairfield County. In 1952 she liked Ike and made more than 100 speeches in his behalf. A week after Dwight D. Eisenhower's election, they met to discuss the role she would play in the first GOP Administration in 20 years. She rejected his suggestion that she serve as Secretary of Labor, on the ground that she did not feel qualified. What she did accept—but only after Henry Luce had urged her to "keep your rendezvous with history" and agreed to spend at least six months of each year abroad—was the post of ambassador to Italy.

This tour of duty was not entirely free of diplomatic blunders, but, when ill health (caused by exposure to arsenate of lead present in dust falling from old paint on the ceiling of her bedroom-study in Rome) forced her to resign in 1957, only the Communists cheered. One of her achievements was the peaceful settlement in 1954 of a nine-year dispute between Italy and Yugoslavia, on one side, and the Allied powers, on the other, over the territorial division of Trieste.

The Italian experience predisposed Clare Luce to accept a second ambassadorial nomination—to Brazil in 1959. However, a vindictive filibuster by Senator Wayne Morse finally led her to reject the post, even though the Senate confirmed her appointment 79 to 11. It was later established that Morse, who resurrected some of her campaign oratory ("Roosevelt lied us into war") in an attempt to prove she was "unfit" for the assignment, was actually lashing out at Henry Luce's *Time,* which had severely criticized the Oregon maverick when he switched from the Republican to the Democratic Party. "The irony of this comedy of errors," James Reston wrote in the *New York Times,* "is that Mrs. Luce is precisely the kind of intelligent, world-minded appointee Senator Fulbright [chairman of the Foreign Relations Committee] is trying to encourage."

Bypassing the 1960 Presidential campaign, Clare enthusiastically cochaired Citizens for (Barry) Goldwater four years later and subsequently backed Richard Nixon. On his 1972 visit to Honolulu, she was hostess at her Kahala Avenue home, where she has lived since Henry Luce's death in 1967, to a large gathering of Island Republicans.

When her play *Slam the Door Softly* premiered in Los Angeles in 1971, her political life had come full circle. This production, originally entitled *A Doll's House 1970* and obviously inspired by Henrik Ibsen's 1897 drama about a woman who rebelled against her role as a subservient housewife, reactivated the early Clare Boothe Luce crusade for the feminine cause, which eventually widened to include the larger arena of partisan politics.

On Merit

Women particularly concerned about obtaining qualified representatives in Congress were pleased with the results of the 1944 elections. Without exception, the three female newcomers elected in November and the two chosen later in special elections—all Democrats—were of high professional caliber. Moreover, the males in charge of parceling out committee assignments acknowledged this fact and placed the neophytes in slots commensurate with their individual expertise. Emily Taft Douglas of Illinois and Helen Gahagan Douglas of California were assigned to the Foreign Affairs Committee; Chase Going Woodhouse of Connecticut was named to Banking and Currency; Helen Douglas Mankin of Georgia to the Revision of the Laws Committee, and Jane Pratt of North Carolina to Flood Control and to the Committee on Territories.

Among the seven incumbents, the only casualty was Senator Hattie Caraway, defeated in the Arkansas primary. Her absence from the 79th Congress (1945–47) left the Senate an all-male institution for the first time since she arrived there in 1931. In geographical terms, a precedent was set: Connecticut and Illinois became the first states to be represented by two women serving concurrently.

The significance of what had transpired was duly noted in the media. Cabell Phillips of the *New York Times* pointed out that, "while the impact of women in Congress continues to be questioned by traditionalists, it is apparent that the majority does not go along with their ungallant view."

EMILY TAFT DOUGLAS
DEMOCRAT OF ILLINOIS

In 1944 Emily Taft Douglas sharply reversed what had been a tradition among women in national politics since 1916. She *preceded* her husband in Congress. Paul Douglas, professor of economics at the University of Chicago, had run as an independent Democrat for the Senate in 1942 and lost. While waiting to try again, he enlisted, at age 50, in the U.S. Marine Corps; he was subsequently commissioned and ordered to the South Pacific combat zone. Meanwhile, his wife, Emily, was elected a representative at large from Illinois.

This twist of events growing out of the exigencies of World War II was one of the reasons Mrs. Douglas consented to be a candidate. When Democratic leaders had asked her to be on the ticket, she declined but agreed to search for a woman who could qualify as a nominee. After the first one she approached said, "Sorry, I have a husband to look after," Emily Douglas decided to reconsider. Although she had a 10-year-old daughter and a full-time job, she had no husband at home.

Methodically, she ticked off her qualifications. As organizing secretary of the Illinois League of Women Voters, she had traveled often throughout the state and was therefore more than casually acquainted with its citizens—and they with her. Serving as chairman of the League's Department of Government and Foreign Policy had broadened and deepened her knowledge of international matters, as had her work with the Carnegie-endowed International Relations Center in Chicago. Furthermore, with her husband she had campaigned in Cook County for a variety of liberal candidates and causes. Selling war bonds and volunteering for Red Cross duty should count for something. And being the wife of a serviceman overseas would obviously be an asset.

With characteristic thoroughness, she also evaluated her chances of winning. As a candidate for the at-large seat, she would have to attract support from the entire state, a feat only one other woman, Republican Ruth Hanna McCormick, had accomplished. The incumbency of her GOP opponent, Stephen A. Day, an isolationist, would be worth between 4 and 6 per cent of the total vote. He would also have the backing of the influential, anti-Roosevelt *Chicago Tribune*.

It was a gamble, but her overwhelming desire to work within the system to build a lasting world peace tipped the scales in favor of her accepting the challenge. "Fortunately, Jean [her daughter] was happy about my decision," Emily Douglas recalls. "Moving to Washington excited her not at all, but the anticipation of sleeping aboard a train did!"

The campaign was long and arduous, with the Democratic candidates making group appearances during the week and speaking solo on weekends. At the time America was confronted with a fateful choice: In the chaos of the postwar world, should it return to the familiar isolationism that would insulate it from dangers abroad? Or should it continue to intervene in world affairs with the awesome power at its disposal? She favored the activist path.

Nearly 4 million voters cast ballots. Although Day carried 80 of the 112 counties, Mrs. Douglas's plurality of 191,235 was larger than that received by Franklin Roosevelt in Illinois. Her impressive strength was partly due to the confidence she inspired, but it owed something, as well, to the small groups downstate (an area normally unfriendly to Democrats) whose members campaigned vigorously on her behalf, calling attention to her keen grasp of world affairs.

"Building a permanent, workable peace is the big job of this generation," Mrs. Douglas told a United Press reporter after her victory. "It is evident that the electorate made a definite decision to get rid of extreme isolationists and obstructionists. The people have decided that this country is not going to lose the peace our men are fighting for."

Emily Douglas's conviction that a balance must be struck among contending world powers sprang from two diverse sources. In 1935, while on a European trip with her husband, she had witnessed the ruthlessness of Nazism and Fascism. The day on which Benito Mussolini announced he had sent his Italian legions into Ethiopia the Douglases were in Rome. "I think out of all that wild and delirious multitude we probably were the only ones who froze with fear and foreboding of what that meant," she said afterward. "Suddenly, all the things we had seen and suspected that summer fell into place. It came crystal clear to us then and there that if Hitler and Mussolini and the forces they represented were not stopped, the whole world would be engulfed."

Much earlier she had been influenced by two Republicans—
a distant cousin, President William Howard Taft, and her father,
Lorado Taft, the noted sculptor, himself an internationalist. But
Woodrow Wilson also was one of her heroes, and it was his effort on behalf of the League of Nations that caused her to become a registered Democrat.

At first glance, the aims and goals of the Emily Taft who grew
up in her native Chicago might seem at odds with those of the
Emily Douglas who went to Congress. As far back as she can
remember, she was stage struck. Her parents said they would
give their consent to a theatrical career only if she finished college. She graduated with honors in three years (class of 1920)
from the University of Chicago, studied at the American Academy of Dramatic Art in New York, then toured in a succession
of plays. After being an understudy in the Greenwich Village
production of *The Return of Peter Grimm,* she wound up playing the lead in the 1926 Broadway hit *The Cat and the Canary.*
But even as she was enjoying the applause, she became acutely
aware of a growing identification with the unscripted world beyond the footlights. Returning to the Midwest, she transferred
her talent to the civic stage. It was there she met Paul Douglas,
and in 1931 they were married.

The poise, mental discipline, and fine articulation manifested
in Washington by Congresswoman Douglas, an attractive, blue-
eyed brunette who looked much younger than 45, were readily
appreciated. On her third day in the House she was asked to
preside briefly in the Speaker's chair. Afterward she admitted
that the experience left her "a little trembly," but, compared to
some of her other ordeals—finding a place to live in the over-
crowded capital, for example—she considered it hardly worth
mentioning.

While wartime employees continued to pour into the federal city and its environs, Emily Douglas, like any other newcomer, had to take potluck. For several months she shared a
house with three WAVES and a cat; in the Shoreham Hotel
she did her congressional homework seated in an empty bath-
tub so that Jean could sleep undisturbed in the only other
room.

She threw herself into the job she had promised to do—
promoting a peaceful world—and accepted numerous speaking engagements to espouse the Dumbarton Oaks plan for es-
tablishing the United Nations. "I am going to proceed on the
thesis that the will to get along with other nations is of greater
importance than the machinery," she said. "We must be pre-

pared to make whatever compromises and sacrifices that security demands—then persuade the other nations of our sincerity."

Confessing that there were points she would like to change in the Dumbarton Oaks proposals, she emphasized that "continued teamwork among the great powers is more important than a flawless blueprint." In an extension of her campaign oratory, she underscored the role of women in peacemaking. "If they understood and exercised their power they could remake the world," she said on several occasions.

Once the war with Japan was over, she introduced (with Democratic Representative Jerry Voorhis of California) legislation to empower the United Nations to control armaments and outlaw the atomic bomb—thorny issues partially resolved 18 years later when the Nuclear Test-Ban Treaty was signed by 106 nations, including Great Britain, Russia, and the United States.

Congresswoman Douglas visited Europe in 1945 with members of a Foreign Affairs subcommittee to study the progress being made by UNRRA (the U.N. Relief and Rehabilitation Administration) in refugee resettlement. On her return she proposed a program "to regenerate the youngsters reared under the tyranny of Naziism and Fascism" and also suggested that more American youth—particularly the poor—be exposed to the world of books. She drafted a measure (cosponsored in the Senate by Lister Hill of Alabama) to fund bookmobiles that would operate in impoverished sections of the country. Although the Hill-Douglas bill was not enacted into law during her term in the House, her husband reintroduced it when he became a senator, and the Library Services Act was signed in 1956.

Emily Douglas was defeated in her try for re-election in 1946 by William G. Stratton, a former member of the House and a World War II naval veteran. Democrats—particularly those in the progressive wing—experienced setbacks across the entire nation that year. Republicans gained control of Congress with a program calling for lower taxes and reduced federal expenditures.

Barely two years later she was campaigning again, this time for her husband in his successful bid for a Senate seat. The same year was marked by the publication of her first book, *Appleseed Farm*, a story for juveniles. Subsequently she wrote *Remember the Ladies: The Story of Great Women Who Helped Shape America* (1966) and *Margaret Sanger: Pioneer of the Future* (1970), a biography that received wide critical acclaim.

In 1946 Emily Taft Douglas told a national meeting of the Business and Professional Women's Clubs that "women have come a long way, and in a hurry." She pointed out, however, that they were still far from being as effective in public affairs as they should be. Has her evaluation changed in the intervening 26 years? "No," she says. The warning she issued a generation ago is still valid: "We are living in one of the great and terrible moments of history. Whether its greatness or its terror is to be uppermost in the days to come is largely in women's hands."

HELEN GAHAGAN DOUGLAS
DEMOCRAT OF CALIFORNIA

Arriving in Washington to represent California's 14th District, Helen Gahagan Douglas, a tall, graceful, auburn-haired beauty with bright blue eyes, was billed as "the Democrat's answer to Clare Boothe Luce." Although neither congresswoman appreciated the comparison, it was inevitable. Not only was Representative Douglas as glamorous as her Republican counterpart (Heywood Broun once wrote, "Helen Gahagan is the ten most beautiful women in the world"), she also possessed the same kind of intellect—quick, lively, probing. The life of each was a kind of epic drama of achievement.

Congress, anticipating a superior performance from Helen Douglas, as it had from Clare Luce, was not disappointed. Speculation that these two highly articulate women would sooner or later indulge in verbal hair-pulling was totally without foundation. At a dinner hosted by Washington's press women, the Gentlewoman from California said she had not come to Congress "to feud with Clare but to try to serve constructively." Mrs. Luce, sitting nearby, stretched out her hand, and the two shook on a pact they were to keep.

That matter settled, the *New York Times* explored the fascinating similarities between Helen Douglas and her namesake Emily Douglas. "It is more than the accident of name that links the identities of the Douglas girls," wrote *Times*man Phillips. Curiously, there were many parallels. The congresswoman from California, like the congresswoman from Illinois, was a convert from Republicanism who had started in politics by speaking out forcefully for social change at the precinct level. Having been a witness to the sinister, expanding influence of Adolf Hitler, she too had been moved to deplore Nazi tyranny publicly. About the same age as Emily, she had been reared in the same kind of cultured, well-to-do environment (born in Boonton, New Jersey, in 1900, she grew up in Brooklyn). Her resolve "to become a great actress" was made before she celebrated her 10th birthday.

Unlike Emily Douglas, she left college (Barnard) for the stage—despite parental opposition, especially from her well-to-do civil-engineer father. She conquered Broadway in a series of successes (*Dreams for Sale, Fashions for Men, Chains, The Enchanted Cottage,* and *Young Woodley,* among others), then at the height of her fame cut herself off from the public for two years to study voice in preparation for operatic roles. During the long run of David Belasco's *Tonight or Never,* she and her costar from Hollywood, Melvyn Douglas, had been married.

It was while on a concert tour of Central Europe in 1937 that Helen Gahagan Douglas came to grips with the implications of the Nazi threat to the free world. In Prague she was asked to eliminate all German songs from her program. Before leaving Salzburg, where she signed a contract to sing at the Vienna Opera the following year, she realized that even the musicians had been mesmerized by Hitler's Germanic dream. "They had rationalized the Nazi philosophy—all of it— especially the anti-Semitism," she recalls. Her long training in make-believe had not deadened her concern for realities. Back in the States, she cabled that she would not return to Austria. Had she fulfilled her contract, she would have been in Vienna when the Nazis occupied it in 1938.

Helen Douglas attributes much of her solicitude for social justice to earlier incidents in her life. Her paternal grandmother, Hannah M. Gahagan, whose family had operated an underground railway before the Civil War and who as a young matron in 1870 had scandalized Troy, Ohio, by demanding that women be allowed to use the public library, instilled in her granddaughter a healthy respect for human rights.

When the first Depression-driven caravans of destitute farm families from the Midwest Dust Bowl began to arrive in California in the late 1930s, Mrs. Douglas was shocked by public reaction. A heated debate erupted, she remembers, "not over what was to be done for the migrants, but over whether they were in the state in the numbers 'some' said they were and whether they lived under the conditions 'some' said they did." She went to see for herself. "And there they were," she says. "*Pitiable.* There's no way to describe their plight. One had to see it."

The combination of the threat of world domination by the
Nazis and the plight of the Okies turned her into a politican:

> I did not decide that I wanted a political career. I already had
> a stage career, a husband, and children [Peter, Mary Helen, and
> stepson Gregory from Melvyn Douglas's first marriage]. I might
> have stuck happily to my own affairs. But I realized that public
> affairs were also *my* affairs. I became active in politics because
> I saw the possibility, if we all sat back and did nothing, of a
> world in which there would no longer be any stages for actors
> to act on.

She joined the Farm Security Administration to help allevi-
ate the misery of migratory workers. In 1939 President Roosevelt appointed her to the National Advisory Committee of the
Works Progress Administration (WPA). Her work with the National Youth Administration (NYA), the California Housing
and Planning Association task force, and other New Deal agencies eventually led to friendship with Eleanor Roosevelt and
guest privileges at the White House.

Helen Douglas made over 150 speeches in California and
elsewhere for the Roosevelt-Wallace ticket in 1940. That same
year she was elected a Democratic National Committeewoman
and a delegate to the national convention in Chicago. But what
really brought her to the attention of party leaders was the 1942
drive she led to round up pro-Roosevelt congressional candidates and get out the vote for them. In a year when Democrats lost heavily elsewhere in the country, they picked up
four House seats in California.

With Representative Thomas Ford's voluntary retirement in
1944, Helen Gahagan Douglas was the logical choice to succeed
him. It did not upset her that she was tagged a carpetbagger
because the Douglas home was in Outpost, an exclusive section of Hollywood, and not in the 14th District. She had already demonstrated her loyalty to the exploited she sought to
represent in downtown Los Angeles: Mexicans, Negroes, Russian Jews, Italians, Chinese, Japanese, Poles, and Irish.

Campaign help came not only from such movie luminaries
as Virginia Bruce, Walter Huston, and Eddie Cantor but from
migrant laborers and organized labor as well. She also had the
support of servicemen's wives, for her husband (a World War
I veteran and overage), who had enlisted as a private in the
army, was in 1944 a major in the China-Burma-India Theater.

The strategy she used to defeat Republican William D. Campbell by almost 4,000 votes set the style she would follow in her
successful bids for re-election in 1946 (against Frederick M.

Roberts, a Negro) and in 1948 (against well-financed W. Wallace Braden). She met the people in apartment-house foyers, on front porches, in the railroad yards, at the corner grocery, outside factory gates, in the produce markets. Wherever she was, she wore the air of a woman enjoying herself. She fired audiences with the intensity of her own emotion. And she was optimistic: The Democrats had met the threat of war; they could meet the challenge of peace.

To those with raised eyebrows who asked, "Hey, Helen, why aren't you home with the kids?" she had a sincere answer: "Politics is a job that needs doing—by anyone who is interested enough to train for it and work at it. It's like housekeeping; somebody has to do it. Whether the job is done by men or women is not important—only whether the job is done well or badly."

From experience she knew that it was possible to edit a political speech with one hand and serve breakfast to her children with the other. Often her speeches were not finished until far into the night. Many times in Washington the police, seeing her house ablaze with light at 4 A.M., stopped to inquire if everything was all right. She would explain that she was "just working." Following one such encounter, she heard a patrolman mutter, "If a congressman has to get up before daylight, I don't ever want to be one."

It was not unusual for Representative Douglas to work to the point of exhaustion. If she drooped during a meeting of the Foreign Affairs Committee, she could expect a penciled note from Frances Bolton: "How about sitting up straight and giving your heart a bit more room?"

The House seldom heard the fine Gahagan stage voice, but she used it often in the committee room—where it got results. A staunch supporter of the United Nations, she fought for adequate appropriations to fund it. While the Marshall Plan was being debated, she helped defeat crippling amendments. When a bill giving control of atomic energy to the military was secretly making its way, without title or number, through the Military Affairs Committee, she exposed the fact. With Senator Brien McMahon of Connecticut, she prepared legislation placing atomic patents under civilian control. "If we permit the military to determine our policy on atomic energy," she said, "we serve notice in unmistakable terms that we believe this new power is a better sword than plow, and that we intend to live by the sword." The Federation of Atomic Scientists called the McMahon-Douglas bill the most important piece of legislation ever passed by Congress.

On the troubled domestic front (beset by inflation, housing shortages, labor discontent) she put on her activist hat and lined up support to ease economic distress and allay mounting frustration, particularly among returning veterans. Her name became synonymous with the fight for decent housing as she moved on one front and then another to force Congress to deal with the crisis. Her farm bankruptcy bill was designed to save the small farmer during times of temporary hardship. She wrote and introduced the first legislation to protect the rights of citizens appearing before congressional committees.

"The most courageous fighter for Liberalism in Congress" is the way the *New Republic* described her. Like any champion of liberal causes during a period in American history marked by spy-hunting and Red-chasing, she made enemies, some of whom turned on her. The allegedly Communist-controlled Independent Progressives, exploiting a confused public, denounced her as a "social fascist" and demanded that she be "destroyed" for placing herself in the forefront of the congressional struggle to launch the Marshall Plan. The wealthy called her a traitor to her class. The DAR (of which Grandmother Gahagan had been a regent) labeled her a "nigger lover" because she had aggressively defended the conduct of Negro soldiers during the war.

Clouding Helen Douglas's political future, pro and con, were California's peculiar election laws under which Republicans and Democrats were permitted to run in each other's primaries and candidates could be—and were—nominated by both parties. The system was originally intended to frustrate would-be party bosses, and it accomplished that, but it also turned California into a political never-never land. "One of the results of cross-filing [abolished in 1959], according to a Western politician, was that "some of California's leading Republicans became undistinguishable from Democrats and vice versa. Issues had a way of simply disappearing when candidates ran in both primaries."

The 1950 senatorial race, however, presented voters with a clear-cut choice: Representative Richard Milhous Nixon, an archetypal Republican, versus Representative Helen Gahagan Douglas, a down-the-line Fair Dealer. The issue, thus, was less federal intervention opposed to more. "There are few contests this year," wrote syndicated columnist Raymond Moley, "for either the Senate or the House where the distinction between candidates is so clear."

Then suddenly, without warning, the so-called real issue was pushed aside. In midsummer, South Korea was invaded by the North Koreans and President Truman ordered U.S. military forces to aid the non-Communists. "The Korean war," Ernest Havemann reported in *Life,* "has sliced the political picture into a jigsaw puzzle, and the pieces keep changing shape even as the experts try to fit them together."

The speed with which this event affected politics was remarkable. After the shooting started, the major political focus shifted from domestic to foreign policy; battlefield reverses in August further narrowed the focus—to the war itself. In the California senatorial race, as elsewhere, the big issues were President Truman, Secretary of State Dean Acheson, and Secretary of Defense Louis Johnson, who, in the opinion of the people really concerned about the world situation, were responsible for a "tragic record of indecision, lost opportunities, and inept leadership."

Both Helen Douglas and Richard Nixon ranged the state tirelessly, circling each other warily. Because the congresswoman had voted against funding the House Un-American Activities Committee, on which Nixon served, he accused her of being "soft on communism." He also repeatedly reminded the electorate that she had once said, "Communism is no real threat to the democratic institutions of our country."

She *had* made this statement—at the beginning of a lengthy speech entitled "My Democratic Credo," delivered on the House floor in 1946. In the same speech she also discussed democracy and said, "Communism has no place in our society. We have something better." The import of her remarks was that the fear of Communism in the United States was "not rational"—that "irrational fear of communism" was being deliberately used in many quarters "to blind us to our real problems" (an indirect reference to the tactics of Senator Joseph McCarthy, the leading Republican Red-hunter).

By taking her opening sentence out of context, Nixon, with an assist from the right-wing press, was able to create the illusion that Helen Gahagan Douglas was a crypto-Communist. This kind of "red smear," as it came to be labeled, was augmented by Nixon in his charge that Helen Douglas had sided with the left-wing clique in Congress. Again and again he cited the fact that she had voted some 354 times with the pro-Communist Congressman Vito Marcantonio, a member of the American Labor Party. Helen Douglas had indeed voted with Marcantonio—on domestic issues: for slum clearance, for middle-class housing, to increase and expand Social Security, to raise the minimum wage, and for a number of other New Deal and Fair Deal measures. But on foreign affairs—which Nixon and his supporters did not mention—Nixon had voted with Marcantonio against aid to Korea, to reduce Marshall Plan funds, against extension of the Reciprocal Trade Agreement Act, to cut Atlantic Charter funds in half, and to reduce aid to China.

"This does not make Mr. Nixon a Communist," Helen Douglas said. "It only proves that he and Mr. Marcantonio and the majority in the Republican Party see eye to eye in voting against measures of vital importance to our program to stem the tide of communist aggression around the world." The best way to keep communism out of the United States, she declared, "is to keep democracy in it."

In California, where politics had picked up the old silent-film bromide that "anything can happen and usually does," nobody was sure what effect this bitter campaign rhetoric would have. On October 30, political analyst Ralph de Toledano reported, "Both sides recognize that even a small shift of opinion on November 7 will decide the election."

When the tally was in, the size of the Nixon victory was the big surprise. His plurality was 680,947 out of a total of slightly more than 3.5 million votes cast.

Those who had campaigned for Helen Gahagan Douglas (some of whom had been the recipients of telephone calls and unsigned letters alleging, "Mrs. Douglas has consistently followed the Communist line") pointed out that the defensive is no place to be—in war, politics, or anything. "She was put in the position of having to spend what time and money she had at her disposal trying to explain," Harry W. Flannery, a writer who had delivered speeches on her behalf, stated in a post-mortem published by *Commonweal.* "Mrs. Douglas had a broom trying to sweep back the sea."

The Douglas-Nixon contest attracted national attention in 1950 mainly because California had recently become the nation's second state in population. But, as an example of a political campaign rife with innuendo, rumor-mongering, and scare tactics, it has become a classic. When Nixon became President in 1969, he rewarded the man who had masterminded the strategy, Murray Chotiner, with the position of special counsel. He also added some footnotes to political history when Kenneth Harris, a correspondent for the *London Observer,* raised the point during an interview that "the main criticism of you in the past was . . . your election campaign for the Senate in 1950."

The President responded with a long explanation, the gist of which was that he

> . . . really ran on one issue, which was simply the choice be-
> tween freedom and state socialism. . . . With the Russians and
> the Chinese being involved in Korea, it wasn't unnatural that
> Communism should have become an issue. . . . The Democrats
> attacked my voting record in the House of Representatives; I
> naturally attacked hers. My supporters were accused of calling
> up influential voters and making innuendos against Mrs. Douglas
> of Communist sympathies. . . . We did not do this. My lieutenants
> knew nothing about this. . . . The fact is, I am not at all sure
> any such calls were made.

Helen Douglas, who had once said, "I'm in politics to stay as long as I'm useful," left the political stage as abruptly as she had terminated her European concert tour 13 years earlier. The time had come, she declared, "for the children not to have to see their mother by appointment."

Returning to the theater, she starred in the Broadway production of *First Lady* (1952), played Agatha in *Family Reunion* (1954), and costarred with Basil Rathbone in *One Plus One* (1956). A serious student of Emily Dickinson, she later added poetry reading to her repertoire.

Helen Douglas's ability to turn a warm impulse into cold resolution has resulted in a book, *The Eleanor Roosevelt We Remember* (1963), in study trips to the Middle East, South America, and Russia, and in hundreds of lectures in which she has imparted a highly personal message: "Our national policies are not serving our interests; they are perilous."

One topic that she has intentionally excluded from her public statements over the years since she exited from Washington is the 1950 senatorial race. She voluntarily broke her silence on the subject in 1972 only after realizing that President Nixon was "trying to do to Senator George McGovern [the Democratic challenger] what he did to me." With an intensity described by Joyce Purnick of the *New York Post* as "belying her 71 years," Helen Gahagan Douglas "took off the gloves and took on Richard Nixon." Although still recuperating from breast surgery performed early in 1972, she roved the Northeast seeking support for McGovern. She said:

> There is no new Nixon. . . . It is part of [his] technique to
> falsely represent his opponent. Of course he can't charge Mc-

Govern with being a Communist—after all it isn't McGovern who just returned from Russia and mainland China. . . . so he says McGovern wants to disarm us when all he wants to do is trim the fat. Nixon will cut anything—he'll cut schools, he'll cut drug programs, he'll play with the nation's health. He doesn't care what he cuts as long as it isn't defense. His whole record shows that he has no compassion for people.

The handsome, white-haired former congresswoman is not bitter about Richard Nixon. Rather, "I'm frightened," she told reporter Purnick, "about what's happening to us as people. Something is eroding us at the very core."

CHASE GOING WOODHOUSE
DEMOCRAT OF CONNECTICUT

Above the din of election-night hoopla in New London on November 7, 1944, a young matron was heard to say, "Connecticut has come a long way since 1920!" Considering that the state had been one of the last to ratify the Woman Suffrage Amendment and was now sending two women (out of a delegation of six) to the U.S. House of Representatives, there was ample cause for a burst of pride.

Of the three Democratic newcomers to the 79th Congress, Chase Going Woodhouse was unquestionably the best qualified in terms of legislative and political preparation. She not only had ably filled the office of secretary of state in Connecticut but was also a longtime active campaigner who enjoyed seniority in party circles.

Chase Woodhouse, the political antithesis of her Republican colleague Clare Boothe Luce, carried among her credentials a special experience that established her dedication to social purposes, an experience unexpected in a woman reared in the small towns of turn-of-the century Canada and the United States. At Montreal's McGill University, where she was the first woman to be graduated (with honors) in economics, she had been exposed to the inspired teaching and counseling of Stephen Leacock, chairman of the Department of Political Science and Economics. Under his tutelage she developed a liberal attitude toward popular democracy and an allegiance to the doctrine that there should be a full measure of government responsibility for human welfare.

When her postgraduate study at the University of Berlin was interrupted by the outbreak of World War I, she returned home, enrolled at the University of Chicago, and subsequently married Edward James Woodhouse, who taught government at Yale. Except for time out to have two children (a son and a daughter), she lectured on economics at Smith College from 1918 to 1925. One of her students—in a very large class—was Jessie Sumner of Milford, Illinois, who, like her mentor, would go to Congress. (Reminiscing about the coincidence, Chase Woodhouse confesses that she made little impression on Miss Sumner's economic philosophy. "This was very evident," she says, "when we were both members of the Banking and Currency Committee.")

The views that liberal-minded Chase Going Woodhouse held concerning government finance were entirely consonant with those of both the Roosevelt and Truman administrations. She had been delineating them at Connecticut College since 1934 and on various other campuses—from North Carolina to Oregon—where she had been invited to teach during summer sessions. They came under public scrutiny during her spirited congressional campaign against incumbent John D. Williams, a World War I veteran, Norwich selectman, and builder.

"Full employment during peacetime is possible," she declared, "if we convert from a wartime economy rapidly enough and keep wages up." Moreover, she argued, the tax laws should be revised and a more equitable system of federal-state responsibility, fiscal and otherwise, should be established. Admittedly, the seeming incompatibility of economic laws and social ends troubled her.

Her election—by the modest plurality of 3,040 out of 122,-986 votes cast—was an upset. Until all the ballots had been counted, the general consensus was that the 2d District—the four-county area making up the eastern third of the state—would not deviate from its usual Republican pattern.

Trim and articulate, Mrs. Woodhouse, at the time she took the oath of office, was already white-haired, although only 54 years old. Pince-nez glasses enhanced her professorial image. She had an enormous capacity for intellectual output and was a tireless debater. Said one admirer, "Chase discovered perpetual motion."

"I'm going to evaluate every piece of legislation in terms of how many jobs there will be after the war," she told Washington reporters. On one issue, however, she had already made up her mind: "Caution should be exercised in [not] bringing our troops home too quickly." Pointing out that her own son had been serving with the Air Force in the Pacific for more than 40 months, she said, "I'm willing that he stay as long as necessary, rather than have his son sent there to fight 25 years from now."

After touring occupied Germany to study the effects of inflation, Representative Woodhouse warned, "Only the fighting is over; we still must win the war, and that means working out a system of economic cooperation between nations." Toward this end, she worked doggedly for congressional sanction of the Bretton Woods plan to create an International Monetary Fund and an International Bank for Reconstruction and Development. Because of her support—in the Banking and Currency Committee, on the House floor, and before public forums—she is given a proportionate share of credit for the fact that these financial institutions became specialized agencies of the United Nations.

Domestically, she channeled her energy into two areas: postwar housing and retention of wartime price controls. Decrying the shortage of low- and middle-income houses that had been "accumulating for over 20 years," she pushed legislation that would provide for the unification of government housing agencies, "long needed," she said, "in the interest of efficiency and economy," and promoted the idea of more federal aid to encourage private building, slum clearance, and improved financing of rural homes.

Although she had been supported in her political campaign by organized labor, Representative Woodhouse did not hesitate to criticize the building industry. "It is technologically backward," she declared. "It is still too largely a handicraft industry in a machine and power age. Technology will win; therefore, it is only a question of how long those fighting a delaying action will hold out."

The test of government in the early postwar years was its ability to meet hard, practical problems in hard, practical ways. The most nettlesome problem was inflation. When price increases failed to taper off in 1946, the public in general and housewives in particular showed their displeasure at the polls. It was "the year of the Republican congressional landslide." Ironically, a factor contributing to Mrs. Woodhouse's defeat was that her own party's Administration, failing to heed her warning, had terminated price and rent controls.

She was able to make a political comeback in 1948 (only one other woman, Jeannette Rankin, successfully re-entered Congress after being defeated), but in 1950, the year the Korean War began, Mrs. Woodhouse was caught up in the vicissitudes of 2d District partisan politics. Horace Seely-Brown,

Jr., the World War II veteran who had taken the House seat away from her in 1946 (and whom she had defeated in 1948) reclaimed it for the Republicans.

Recognition of her very long party service came in the form of a Presidential appointment as special assistant to the director of the Office of Price Stabilization. In this post she was able to continue to work as a consumer advocate. Had a GOP Administration not moved into Washington, she would have stayed on.

At 81, Mrs. Woodhouse lives in a restored farmhouse (*circa* 1726) situated on 390 acres in Baltic, Connecticut. From there she commutes daily to Hartford, where she directs the Service Bureau for Connecticut Organizations, a unique educational resource funded by the Beatrice Fox Auerbach Foundation. Despite her advanced years, even the thought of retirement is anathema to her. She clings to the tenet of self-renewal. "Work," she says, "is the thing I do best." If she could so something else better, she would. But she can't.

HELEN DOUGLAS MANKIN
DEMOCRAT OF GEORGIA

Coming from a white Southern politician—who also happened to be a woman—the words were astonishingly forthright: "I say to you quite frankly, the time has come for simple justice, and that means abolishing the poll tax." The speaker was Helen Mankin, a successful Atlanta attorney who defeated 17 men to win the right to represent Georgia's 5th District in a special election early in 1946.

She had spoken the words a year earlier when, as a veteran member of the State Assembly, she had supported Governor Ellis Arnall's appeal to remove the poll tax. Now, in the first congressional race since its removal, she became one of the beneficiaries of its abolition.

On the night of the election, with the ballots from only one precinct yet to be counted, Thomas L. Camp, for 15 years secretary to Representative Robert Ramspeck, appeared to have won the seat vacated by his former boss, who had resigned to accept an executive post with the Air Transport Association. After the results from Atlanta's Ward 3, Precinct B, where all but 10 registered voters were Negroes, disclosed that Mrs. Mankin had received 956 votes versus 35 for her opponents, she was declared the winner.

What helped Helen Mankin win, in addition to the Negro vote

and a heavy turnout at the polls, was her imaginative campaign. She brought the vital issues—equalization of railroad freight rates and federal aid to education—home to the people. With support from women's and church groups, organized labor, progressive organizations, and influential individuals (including Governor Arnall and her husband, Guy), she demonstrated that liberal sentiments could elicit political backing in the South.

"I'm a liberal but not a radical," she told a *New York Herald Tribune* reporter in Washington, and she proved it by her roll-call record. She supported the federal housing program and price controls, rejected the antilabor Case bill and the Hobbs bill directed against the Teamsters' Union. As a member of the Civil Service Committee, she continued to work on a program her predecessor had initiated: a merit system for the hiring and promotion of federal employees.

Georgians visiting the House gallery could count on finding their congresswoman on the floor following the proceedings closely. "I'll bet Helen will get impatient here," a constituent remarked one day. "Back home the legislature doesn't take so long to get a bill—particularly a good one—passed."

Forty-nine-year-old Helen Mankin—a brunette with a strong, handsome face; a deep, throaty voice; and a tall (5 feet 9 inches), rangy figure—had a cosmopolitan background. Her schoolteacher parents, Hamilton and Corinne Williams Douglas, had studied law together at the University of Michigan before moving to Atlanta. "There were five good reasons why my mother did not practice," Helen Mankin liked to say. "I was one of them."

Before studying law herself (at the Atlanta Law School her father had founded), Helen Douglas earned a B.A. degree at Rockford (Illinois) College in 1917, then left for France to drive an ambulance for an American hospital unit attached to the French Army. During her 13 months overseas, she earned two citations. A stint as a free-lance reporter followed. She filed copy from Europe, Mexico, Canada, Alaska, and the United States, always traveling by automobile. One of her articles was entitled "Thirteen Thousand Manless Miles."

Mrs. Mankin's political career was born out of frustration. Having led an unsuccessful drive for a state child labor law, she decided that she might accomplish her objective from within the system. She took $150 she had saved for painting the family farmhouse, paid the filing fee, and declared herself Fulton County candidate for the 205-member Georgia Assembly.

"Nobody thought she had a chance," recalls her son Guy, Jr. "But she got an 800-vote plurality." During the nearly 10 years she served (1937–46), she earned the esteem of all save diehard reactionaries for her courageous and able support of a host of progressive and liberal measures.

When she sought re-election to the 80th Congress, voters in the 5th District (a tricounty area surrounding Atlanta) gave her a primary vote of 53,882 against 43,162 for Judge James C. Davis, but, under Georgia's unit rule, Judge Davis was declared the nominee (he carried DeKalb and Rockdale counties, for a total of eight units, whereas she was entitled to only six, the number allotted to Fulton County). She filed a suit claiming the unit rule was "weighted in favor of rural areas," but she lost in the federal district court. An intraparty internecine fight ensued. The state Democratic Central Committee certified her nomination; the state convention, upholding the unit rule, declared Judge Davis the party nominee. Unruffled, Mrs. Mankin conducted a serious campaign and received 19,527 write-in votes at the general election in November. All things considered, the number was impressive—but not impressive enough to defeat Davis.

Again she contested Georgia's election procedures; again she was unsuccessful. Was she bitter? "Not really," Mrs. Mankin said. She believed the county unit-rule system would one day be declared unconstitutional by the Supreme Court. And it was. In the meantime, however, she was killed in an automobile accident (1956).

"Helen was dedicated to the proposition that championing change in the South was not necessarily a man's job," a male colleague once said. That proposition stood up under a series of telling tests.

JANE PRATT
DEMOCRAT OF NORTH CAROLINA

Jane Pratt of North Carolina believes implicitly that the rewards of being a congressional administrative assistant (AA) "can be great." She should know. After 22 years as an AA, she went to Congress herself.

She did not always have politics in mind. But in 1924 when 8th District Representative William C. Hammer asked her to be his aide, she willingly gave up the editorship of the weekly *Troy Montgomerian* to move to Washington. After Hammer's death in 1930, she worked successively for Congressmen Hinton James of Laurinburg, J. Walter Lambeth of Thomasville, and William O. Burgin of Lexington.

Jane Pratt's success story suggests that loyalty is what congressmen prize first in their staffers. From her they got it. So did their constituents. Eventually she became as well known in the 8th District as any of her bosses. It required only 30 minutes for the State Democratic Executive Committee to nominate her to fill the vacancy created by Burgin's death in April 1946.

Campaigning in politically safe territory, she ran away with the special May election, defeating Republican Frank Hulin, a Lexington lumberman, by more than 20,000 votes. The only surprise was that she carried Wilkes County, a Republican stronghold for as long as anyone could remember.

A fourth-generation North Carolinian, Miss Pratt was born in 1902 in Morven, a small town near the South Carolina border named for the Morven in Scotland and settled by Scottish and English emigrants. One of seven children (five girls, two boys) of James and Lena Little Pratt, she was christened Eliza Jane. Her father, a merchant and a farmer, had two "loves," Miss Pratt recalls: the "good earth" and "good schools." His tall, brown-eyed, auburn-haired daughter, who admits she learned about the boll weevil before she learned to read, has never lost her enthusiasm for gardens and gardening.

She enrolled at Queens College in Charlotte to study music, but, when her father's health failed in 1920, she had to leave the campus and go to work. The course she began at Kings Business College in Charlotte she completed at Temple Secretarial School in downtown Washington.

If congressional aides are expected to remain in the background, they nevertheless are entitled to ringside seats at all historic dramas unfolding on the Hill. Among the visual memories Miss Pratt treasures is Charles Lindbergh's appearance before a joint session of Congress after his solo flight to Paris. She also looked down from the House gallery on the December day in 1941 when President Roosevelt faced Congress, opened a black notebook, and asked for a declaration of war against Japan.

For her, however, the most dramatic event in the House chamber, she says, was being sworn in by Speaker Sam Rayburn. As North Carolina's first congresswoman, she rated escorts from both the House and the Senate: Representative Alfred L. Bulwinkle and Senator Clyde R. Hoey. Half a hundred friends from home looked on and barely two hours later heard her answer her first roll call.

Moving from the so-called shadows to the limelight was relatively easy for Jane Pratt. Not only had she mastered the legislative system, but she knew the background, the purpose, and the prospects of almost every bill in the hopper. Committee work posed no unfamiliar problems, nor did constituent mail. She had dealt with every conceivable aspect of the 12-county district, from reforestation in Scotland County to dam construction in Wilkes County.

"With her background and training," declared Washington correspondent Red Buck Bryant in the *Charlotte Observer,* "Miss Pratt would make a worthy Congressman for years instead of for a few months." Not immodestly, she agreed. So did her constituents. The fact of political life, however, was that campaign costs were enormously high, and she had no personal fortune. She bowed out as a congresswoman at the end of her term in 1947.

During the 38 years she spent in Washington, she never really left Capitol Hill, although she did serve 10 of those years with three federal agencies (the Office of Alien Property, the Department of Agriculture, and the Library of Congress). Former Representative A. Paul Kitchin of Wadesboro, whose AA Jane Pratt was from 1957 until his defeat in 1962, gives her credit for guiding him "through many hard areas" and singles out her "procedural expertise" for special praise.

Jane Pratt retired in 1967 at age 65. What that means is that she no longer commutes between North Carolina and Washington, D.C. But her continuing interest in politics has an outlet through membership on the state Democratic Executive Committee. She is cautiously optimistic about the future of women in elective political life—in North Carolina, at least:

> The men here were slow to accept suffrage, and the majority have not yet fully recognized women as equal political partners. But, looking back, I can remember the time when only a handful of women would turn out for a rally. Now they sometimes outnumber the men. And they work as regular members of a campaign organization. Unfortunately, when a campaign ends, they are all too often relegated to their former roles as second-class politicians.

Paper Triumph

VERA C. BUSHFIELD
REPUBLICAN OF SOUTH DAKOTA

"Honored, that's how I feel," said South Dakota's Vera C. Bushfield, 59, when Republican Governor George T. Mickelson informed her she was his appointee to a short term in the U.S. Senate. Given the note of condescension struck by the governor, it was a generous statement.

"My action," Mickelson said on October 6, 1948, "will permit the late Harlan J. Bushfield's office to function normally and without interruption." (By law, the office would have been closed within 60 days had no successor been named. Franking privileges and other services would have been terminated sooner.) "The appointment is being made," he explained, "with the understanding that shortly before the 80th Congress [1947–49] reconvenes she will resign and thus enable me to give seniority rights to the new senator-elect [to be chosen at the general election on November 2]. South Dakota's best interests . . . will be taken care of under these arrangements."

The winner in November, as expected, was Congressman Karl E. Mundt. Had he been given the interim appointment, South Dakota would have temporarily been without full congressional representation—a serious matter to a geographically large, sparsely populated state entitled to only two U.S. representatives.

Because Congress was in recess at the time of Mrs. Bush-

field's appointment, she was confronted with the same dilemma that the state's first elected female senator, Gladys Pyle,
had faced 10 years earlier: to go or not to go to Washington.
In announcing that Harry Westphal would continue in charge
of the Capitol Hill office, Senator Vera Bushfield said she would
"carry on with the help of a small staff in Pierre. Since I will
have the responsibility for only three months, I can serve the
constituency best by making myself as accessible as possible."
Spared the floor debates and committee meetings that con-
sume so much of a senator's time when Congress is in session, she was able to devote her full attention to constituents,
some of whom had problems they could not solve alone.

With many residents, Vera Bushfield was on a first-name basis. As first lady of South Dakota during the two terms of her
husband's governorship (1939–43), she had traveled to all parts
of the state. Once the couple's children (one daughter, two
sons) were grown, the Bushfields functioned as a team. A
GOP leader who recalls those years said, "She could have been
a mere ornament, but that wasn't her style. Harlan was the energetic oratorical espouser of conservative Republicanism; Vera
doubled as a capable sounding board and effective supporter
of issues important to women and children." Earlier she had
been an active member of the Hand County Child Welfare
Commission.

The Bushfields were unknown nationally before Harlan's
name was placed in nomination as a favorite-son candidate for
the Presidency at the 1940 GOP National Convention (ex-Senator Gladys Pyle of Huron delivered the nominating speech).
In both the Statehouse and the U.S. Capitol he earned a deserved reputation as an adversary of big government and an
advocate of isolationism. The sensible and plain-spoken people
of South Dakota had traditionally favored political leaders who
stood for a diminished (as opposed to an expanded) role for
the federal government and for withdrawal from (as opposed
to increased involvement in) the affairs of other nations.

The omens for Vera Bushfield's successful continuation of
her husband's senatorial service were good from the outset. She
shared his political ideology. Furthermore, her background had
given her an appreciation of the problems peculiar to a provincial, somewhat isolated state largely dependent on agriculture.

A farmer's daughter, Vera Sarah Cahalan was born in 1889,
the year South Dakota was admitted to the Union. Her parents
had arrived in Dakota Territory from Iowa only a few years
earlier to settle in Miller, a tiny dot on the map approximate-

ly 75 miles east and slightly north of Pierre. One of her most vivid memories of those pioneer days is of the resourcefulness of her mother. "My father [Maurice Francis Cahalan], traveling by horse and buggy, was gone from home for a week or more at a time, buying and shipping cattle to markets in Sioux City and Chicago. There were few doctors and no nurses in our immediate vicinity, so mother [Mary Ellen Connors Cahalan] was always available to give a helping hand when an emergency arose."

Growing up in the long, cold winters and shimmering summer heat of mid-America, where the frontier spirit lingered and distance, paradoxically, drew people toegether, Vera, her brother, and two sisters had an uneventful childhood. "We were average, ordinary people," she says, "imbued, like our neighbors, with a real sense of social responsibility." She knew the hard-penny economics of a kitchen garden and the joy of a store-bought dress, as well as the benefits of a good education. At Dakota Wesleyan University in Mitchell she took a commercial course, and in 1912 she graduated with a degree in domestic science from Stout Institute in Menominee, Wisconsin. That same year she married Harlan J. Bushfield, a 29-year-old lawyer who had lived in Miller from infancy. She was a pretty young woman: brown hair, blue eyes; not tall, but trim of figure.

By the time Vera Bushfield left the governor's mansion to accompany her husband to the nation's capital, she knew more about the inner workings of government than some men and incomparably more than most women. The economic aspects were her specialty. Governor Bushfield had abolished the state property tax, cut the budget by 25 per cent, and placed South Dakota on a pay-as-you-go basis.

Senator Bushfield's death in 1948 was not entirely unexpected. He had announced at the beginning of the year that he would not seek re-election, because of failing health. The fatal cerebral hemorrhage he suffered on September 27 followed 10 days of hospitalization. "His demise," said Governor Mickelson, "was undoubtedly hastened by his many years in public office."

For Mrs. Bushfield, the Senate appointment had a therapeutic effect, helping her through the first months of widowhood. It was a Presidential election year, and, despite the introspective nature of South Dakota, the state reflected the national mood. The GOP challenger, New York governor Thomas E. Dewey, was favored over incumbent Harry S. Truman. Dewey's defeat (he carried South Dakota) spread gloom across the Great Plains. It meant four more years of Secretary of Agriculture Charles F. Brannan, whose farm program wheat and corn growers blamed for falling grain prices. Senator Bushfield did not need to be told that more storage bins were needed for the surplus crops. But how does a lawmaker deal with an Administration that refuses to admit that the Brannan Plan, the Democratic answer to the farm crisis, has been a failure? In a rare display of defensiveness, she placed the matter in the hands of the elected members of the South Dakota delegation: Senator J. Chandler Gurney and Representatives Mundt and Francis H. Case.

When the Senate reconvened on December 21, it was Senator Gurney who presented Senator Bushfield's letter of resignation, "effective at 12:01 A.M. December 27," and the certificate of appointment of Senator-elect Mundt. Joining Mundt at the swearing-in ritual was a Louisianian who would also be able to take advantage of seniority over other new senators taking seats in the 81st Congress: Russell B. Long, son of ex-Senator Rose McConnell Long.

Vera Bushfield, a woman of considerable natural reserve, neither sought nor desired another government position, political or otherwise. She turned her full attention to an obligation she had been forced to slight during the decade of public life she had shared with her husband: getting to know her grandchildren. "For me," she said at the time, "a voice, long-distance, on a Sunday afternoon has never sufficed."

Asked in 1971 to assess the progress, if any, women had made in the mainstream of politics since she served in the Senate, Mrs. Bushfield, 80 and a great-grandmother, offered this view:

> A congressional wife who has followed her husband's career can be more helpful to constituents than someone who has not been in so privileged a position.
>
> As for a woman making a career of politics, we have had proof that congresswomen have done much to demonstrate they are as capable of holding office as most men. On many occasions a woman is more conscious of the pulse of the people than a man. She has a better understanding of what life in the home is like. She is closer to the youth. With intelligence and effort, she can easily learn the fundamentals of government, especially nowadays when education is available to anyone who has the ambition to pursue it. More than ever the political odds are in a woman's favor.

Postwar Pattern

World War II had given women influence in the major political parties hitherto denied them. With millions of men in the armed forces, it was imperative to use women workers, not only for campaign leg work but in local and state committee positions as well. In addition, the fact that women for the first time constituted a majority of the electorate made an impression on male party leaders. They realized that, to win the feminine vote, they must grant women more responsibility in formulating party policies.

Yet the profound social and economic changes, accelerated by World War II, which altered women's relationships with their fellow human beings did not carry with them the tacit acknowledgment that women were expected to assume responsibility for governing proportionate to their numbers. Of the 15 women who ran for Congress in 1946, 7 were elected to the House, and 1, Vera Bushfield of South Dakota, served briefly in the Senate. The total in the 81st Congress (1949–51) was 9, the same as it had been 20 years earlier, with Margaret Chase Smith the lone female senator. On the basis of new geographical territory conquered by women in 1946 and 1948, the statistical realities were somewhat encouraging. Added to the list were New Mexico (represented by Georgia L. Lusk); a four-county area extending northward from Manhattan (by Katharine St. George); Utah (by Reva Beck Bosone), and

Brooklyn (by Edna F. Kelly). Cecil M. Harden was the first Republican congresswoman from Indiana.

GEORGIA L. LUSK
DEMOCRAT OF NEW MEXICO

Nine men and two women vied to serve as one of New Mexico's two representatives at large in 1946. In the June primary 53-year-old Georgia L. Lusk, a lifelong Democrat, came in second; in the general election she was the top vote-getter.

Her course was marked out for her as it is for all first-term members of Congress. She was expected to make no speeches, vote right, answer her mail, and attend committee meetings (in her case, Veterans' Affairs). She answered her mail; she did not miss committee sessions; she confined her oratory to a maiden speech. Usually she voted with her party; occasionally she did not. She voted to override President Truman's veto of the controversial Taft-Hartley bill, for example, and said "No" to reducing taxes. On foreign policy, she generally supported the Administration. She favored economic and military aid to Greece and Turkey, as well as the European Recovery Program.

Her professional specialty—education—was the chief reason she was in politics. A former teacher and school superintendent who also owned a large ranch, she campaigned on a platform that supported federal aid to education—but not federal "meddling" in the state school system. "If it's important for the government to give financial assistance to transportation, why not to education?" she asked. She was also in favor of creating a new Cabinet post: Secretary of Education.

Though a small woman, gray-haired and motherly-looking, she was a sleeves-rolled-up worker. "Totally without pretense" is the way one constituent described her. From the Carlsbad ranch of her pioneer parents, she had ridden horseback to and from a one-room rural school before going off to college. An accomplished teacher when she married cattleman Dolph Lusk in 1915, she returned to the schoolroom four years later, after his death. There was a hired man to run the ranch but no one to care for her three small boys; so she took them with her on the daily trip by car to and from the Levington schoolhouse fives miles away.

Her first elective post (1924) was school superintendent in Lea County in the southeastern corner of the state. To reach the widely scattered voters, she often had to drive over roads that were little better than trails. Two years later she was re-elected. After winning in 1931 a four-year term as state super-intendent of public instruction, she moved her family to Sante Fe and went on the road again—this time to visit schools. Her tour revealed some shocking deficiencies but none worse than the widespread textbook shortage. In classes conducted in one-room adobe huts, as many as 25 pupils shared a single reader.

Finding the money for books during the Depression was particularly difficult, but Georgia Lusk discovered that the state treasury held $28,000 in nonallocated funds. This "find" repre-sented federal payments for mineral leases on state lands. She convinced the legislature that it should be spent for free text-books. A deft administrator who was willing to explain un-glamorous specifics of education, she managed to gain the sup-port of both liberals and conservatives. Nothing better illus-trates her persuasive power than the fact that, during the eight years she was in office, New Mexico rose from near the bot-tom to the top of the list of states in financing of public schools.

In 1944 she served as a delegate to the first White House Conference on Rural Education. Her proposed remedy for re-ducing the low attendance rate at country schools: "Pay the teachers higher salaries." A $1 million expenditure was recom-mended by the conferees, mainly for salaries but also for im-proved facilities.

Mrs. Lusk's flaw, if it can be called that, was a record of such quiet accomplishment that her real mettle seemed untested. Some said her defeat for renomination in 1948 was due to il-legal maneuvers by the machine backing one of her opponents. Because she lost by a narrow margin—2,451 votes—it was sug-gested that she demand a recount. "I didn't have the money," she said, "and anyway I thought they'd only say 'a woman can't take a lickin'.'"

Appointed by President Truman to the War Claims Commis-sion, she served in her usual reserved fashion—until Presi-dent Eisenhower replaced her with a Republican. Her overt criticism of the patronage system as "blatantly unfair" surprised Lusk-watchers, as did her appeal in court (which she lost).

Back in New Mexico, she was elected to still another four-year term as state superintendent of public instruction and served until 1960, when she retired to live in Santa Fe. Before her death in 1971 at the age of 77, she was asked to comment on the significance of campus riots. "The obvious and legitimate concerns of students with subject mátter and the quality of teaching," she said, "ought to be taken very seriously indeed."

Earlier, Georgia Lusk had summed up for Eleanor Roosevelt the way she felt about the political future of women in general: "They could get ahead faster if they didn't go off on tangents, expect too much, and get discouraged too easily. They'd be better off, too, if they would go into some other line first and demonstrate that they have ability. That's the way the men do it."

KATHARINE ST. GEORGE
REPUBLICAN OF NEW YORK

In Katharine St. George the 80th Congress had a newcomer who, like Georgia Lusk, was of proved competence. However, except for their professionalism and similar attitudes about party loyalty (intense and constant), the two might have come from different worlds.

Mrs. St. George, in politics a conservative Republican, was accustomed to a life of polished elegance. The wife of well-to-do business executive George Baker St. George and the mother of a debutante daughter, she presided with courturiered cool over a mansion in fashionable Tuxedo Park, New York. Her avocations included riding and raising prize-winning pointers and setters. If an antidote for boredom was needed, there were friends and relatives to visit in England.

The challenge of unanswered social and economic questions during the Depression convinced her, she says, that she had talents going to waste, and, by the time she ran for Congress in 1946, she was merely taking another step, albeit a giant one, along a political path on which she had set out 20 years earlier with election to the local board of education as her goal. That accomplished, she was elected to the Tuxedo Park Town Board. Partisan politics followed. The Republicans chose her as treasurer of the Orange County Committee and eventually advanced her to the chairmanship—a first in New York State for a woman. In 1942 she suffered her first defeat, losing the nomination for the State Assembly to Wilson Van Duzer. "My failure to get the nomination was a good thing," she told a reporter. "A politician ought to know how it feels to be licked."

The 29th Congressional District (later redesignated the 28th and, after the 1960 census, the 27th) that Katharine St. George

represented is a four-county, sparsely populated patch of geography extending from Rockland County in the south, through
Orange and Sullivan counties, to Delaware County in the north.
Its predominantly provincial constituents range from resort
owners in the Catskills to truck farmers along the "black belt,"
from laborers in small factories to the wealthy descendants of
Dutch and English settlers. Republicanism had flourished there
for generations. A political dynasty was easy to preserve. The
Hamilton Fish family of Orange County, for example, had
perpetuated itself in Congress for 100 years.

The 1944 ouster of Representative Hamilton Fish, Jr., a vociferous isolationist, was being urged not only by Democratic leaders but also by the internationalists in his own party. A stepped-
up campaign by Mrs. St. George and others pulled him through
the primary. But in November he lost to Orange County lawyer
August W. Bennet, a quasi-Republican who had switched labels
to run on the Good-Government coalition ticket. On the night
Bennet's victory was announced, a friend recalls, Mrs. St. George
made up her mind to try to unseat him two years hence. With
the aid of an efficient secretary, Frances Brown, she launched
her own campaign on April 1, 1945—14 months before the Republican primary.

One advantage she had over her opponent was that she was
on the home front, and she made the most of it. To win support from the four county committees, she entertained the
members in small groups at intimate at-home dinners. At each
affair, by her own account, at least one informal speaker "was
primed" to mention that she was a candidate.

Katharine St. George—"Cassie" to her friends—turned in a
stunning performance on the hustings. Every day she covered
200 miles; every other night she addressed a rally. Her platform promised jobs and homes for veterans, hope for farmers,
and preservation of labor's hard-won gains. There was one
promise she could not keep—yet, in her stirring, convincing
style, "The ultimate goal is to have every union member a
capitalist" sounded believable.

When she appeared with Bennet at Tuxedo Park's Masonic
Temple, he extolled the value of public debate, citing the
Lincoln-Douglas verbal encounters. Said Mrs. St. George, "One
good thing about women in politics is that they are not continually comparing themselves to the Great Emancipator."
About her opponent's record, she said, "It's mediocre—the sort
of record that makes the average citizen disgusted with politics."

She carried all but one of the counties in the primary, and

in November she polled a 17,000-vote majority against a field
of three male contenders. For the ensuing 18 years, the district was indisputably hers. The Democrats ran seven different men and one woman (Marion K. Sanders of Nyack, a
onetime State Department editor) against her—to no avail. Her
plurality was never fewer than 27,000 votes, and in 1952 (the
year Mrs. Sanders was her opponent) it exceeded 53,000.

Fifty years old when she took the oath of office, Cassie St.
George, a petite brunette with a trim figure, did not look old
enough to be a grandmother, but she was. Her reputation as
an energetic, tireless campaigner had preceded her; also the
fact she was a first cousin of the late Franklin D. Roosevelt's.
Family ties notwithstanding, there had never been any political
affinity between Mrs. St. George and FDR.

From her father, Price Collier, she had acquired a gift for
descriptive phrases, a quality that set her speeches apart from
those of the average politician. He was a longtime European
editor of *Forum* magazine, and it was because he was based in
England in 1896 that she was born there. Her education was
more than varied: private schools on both sides of the Atlantic.
By the time she and her mother, the former Katharine Del-
ano, were presented at the court of Kaiser Wilhelm of Germany and his empress, Augusta Victoria, in 1912, she spoke
French and German as fluently as English.

"There are those among House Republican very-high-ups
who hold that Mrs. St. George is one of the smartest politicians
and ablest legislators," Washington correspondent Edward B.
Lockett commented shortly after her arrival in the capital.
House Republican leader Joseph W. Martin, Jr., of Massachusetts introduced her at the 1948 GOP National Convention as
a congresswoman "of great ability and distinction . . . with a
profound knowledge of national affairs."

If she expected the men to back their words with deeds,
she was disappointed. While they asked her to help plot 1950
campaign strategy in the farm belt, they denied her a seat on
the Agriculture Committee, which she had requested (she belonged to both the New York State Agricultural Society and
the Orange County Home Bureau). They also sent her to the
Pacific Northwest to stump for the national ticket but ruled
she could not be a member of the Armed Services Committee, which she had also requested (West Point was in her district).

Forced to play the legislative game by the rules of the hierarchy, she did just that. Hard work on the Post Office and the

Civil Service Committee was rewarded about midway in her congressional career with a place on Government Operations. Then, in 1962, she made history, becoming the first woman to be named to the all-powerful Rules Committee, which determines whether or not a bill reaches the floor for debate.

Of all of her measurable record of accomplishment in the House, it was the campaign she waged to abolish all forms of discrimination against women that attracted the most publicity. At one point her crusade moved *Collier's* to prophesy, "If and when Congress finally does approve an Equal Rights Amendment, it may well bear the name of Representative Katharine Price Collier St. George." As history has recorded, the 1950s did not produce an amendment to ensure equal rights under the law for women. But it was because of Mrs. St. George that such an amendment made more progress than it had in the years since 1923 when it was first introduced.

If it seemed paradoxical that a conservative would do battle for so liberal a cause as equal rights, it must be remembered that the Lady from New York held somewhat unorthodox views about women in general and their place in life in particular. "Women fritter away too much time on things that amount to nothing—the PTAs, etc.," she once told Betty Beale of the *Washington Star*. "A good mother at home is twice as effective as one at a meeting." In her view there were far too many women teachers: "It's ridiculous to have these great big husky boys of 15 and 16 handled by a girl just out of school." But, concerning equal rights, she pushed the legislation because she firmly believed in world peace and felt that women offered the best hope to achieve it. To enhance their effectiveness, she favored removing the stigma of second-class citizenship.

She did not succeed in collecting the 218 signatures needed to bring the legislation to the floor, but hearings were held in both the House and the Senate, and the Senate Judiciary Committee passed the measure. Attached to it, however, was the so-called Hayden rider, which provided that the equal rights amendment "shall not be construed to impair any rights, benefits or exemptions now or hereafter conferred by law, upon persons of the female sex." The rider sounded its death knell, for such a qualification, as the Judiciary Committee noted, "was not acceptable to women who want equal rights under the law."

Never one to mince words, whether advocating atomic-bomb secrecy (the topic of her maiden speech) or castigat-

ing the Democratic Administration ("Truman is trying to so-
cialize these United States under a top-heavy and power-drunk
bureaucracy"), Mrs. St. George always made her position per-
fectly clear. President John F. Kennedy's move to establish an
Urban Affairs Department she called "a very dangerous step
. . . one more blow to state government, and another big grab
on the part of the executive." Of the Peace Corps she said,
"Whatever one may think of it, it was created by executive
order and is completely unconstitutional."

For a veteran congresswoman who had so much equity with
the regulars in the Republican Party and who represented,
as she did, a congressional district that had been a one-party
fastness since the Civil War, the 1964 race should have posed
no threat to re-election. In retrospect, however, Katharine St.
George's defeat might have been predicted. More than a few
doctrinaire Republicans paid the price of the national revolt
against the standard-bearer of the GOP right, Barry M. Goldwater of Arizona, who carried only six states. New York was
not one of them. Sixty-eight-year-old Katharine St. George's
opponent, Democratic-Liberal John G. Dow, 54, of Grand View,
a systems analyst who had made several previous unsuccessful bids for public office, won, though his plurality was slight
—only 6,165 votes.

Mrs. St. George is not as sure as she once was that women
can, and should, play a greater role in politics. "At the federal level, I feel that politics is not an ideal task for a woman," she says. "It interferes with her private and family life,
and should certainly not be undertaken until her children are
grown. Even then it is questionable whether it is worth giving up so much of intimate and family ties."

REVA BECK BOSONE
DEMOCRAT OF UTAH

Reva Beck Bosone, Utah's first congresswoman, might be
called a prime example of that American phenomenon the "reformer"—in the judicial, not the evangelical, sense of the word.
She has been an evolutionary working within the system, a
doer combining pragmatism, idealism, and creativity.

In 1948, Democrats in Salt Lake City and the three adjacent
counties to the north, south, and west that make up the 2d Congressional District found her a refreshing change from the amiable yet somewhat inept Republican contender, William A.

Dawson. She defeated him 92,731-to-68,574 to win one of the two House seats allotted to the state.

Her lifetime record of public service suggests that she has been not only a self-starter but also constantly in motion. She was the first member of her sex in Utah to be elected to the State Legislature (1933), the first to head a major committee, the first to become floor leader (1935), and the first to be elected a municipal judge (1936). During her 12 years on the bench in Salt Lake City, the courtroom became a rapid-fire news center. Cases were handled informally (defendants were often addressed by their first names). Wayward girls were sent to psychiatrists and drunks to physicians or to Alcoholics Anonymous; employers were asked to give petty culprits another chance; traffic violators were read the riot act and fined heavily ($300 for drunken driving, $200 for reckless driving).

Teaching was the profession her father, a pioneer of Danish descent, suggested. For seven years following graduation in 1920 from the University of California at Berkeley, she taught public speaking in high schools in her hometown, American Fork, and in Delta and Ogden. The lure of the law was never far away, however. The advice of her mother, Zilpha Chipman Beck, a descendant of Pilgrims and Mormons, had been "A country is no better than its laws; if you want to serve all of the people, go where the laws are made."

Reva was in law school at the University of Utah when she met Joseph P. Bosone. They were married in 1929 and a year later opened an office together in Helper, a small mining town in Carbon County. "It was a mistake to think we could earn a living practicing law in this poor community during the Depression," she recalls. But she could afford to run for the legislature. Carrying her baby daughter, Zilpha Theresa, she went from door to door to introduce herself and her platform to the voters. During her first term in the Statehouse, the Bosones moved to Salt Lake City, and it was from this metropolitan area that she was re-elected.

In the state legislature she addressed herself to humanitarian issues: a minimum wage-and-hour law for women and children, unemployment insurance, and ratification of the federal constitutional amendment on child labor. Passage of these measures evoked public commendation from Secretary of Labor Frances Perkins and the First Lady, Eleanor Roosevelt.

Representative Bosone gave the impression of being reserved, cautious, methodical—in life style the lawyer still. A tall woman with red hair cut short and combed back in soft waves, she wore rimless glasses and sensible low-cut shoes and looked as if she would be right at home in the kitchen (in Utah she always made preserves and did her own canning).

House colleagues soon learned that reformer though she was, she had an absolutely open mind on any of a dozen issues and readily said so. Only on humanitarian questions was her thinking inflexible. Laws must be passed to outlaw the poll tax and lynching, she insisted; also to guarantee fair employment practices. Moreover, she wanted legislation to promote peace, ensure good housing, control inflation, and conserve natural resources.

As a member of the Public Lands Committee, she said she was where she "belonged" because reclamation, flood control, and soil conservation "are important to the West. Remember," she declared, "we were once a desert and we don't want to go back to it."

The 1950 congressional contest between Reva Beck Bosone and Ivy Baker Priest, the Republican candidate, attracted nationwide interest because it was the sole instance of two women competing for a House seat that year. Mrs. Priest, later appointed Treasurer of the United States, admitted that the odds were heavily against her. "No man wanted to take on Reva," she said, "so I did." Philosophical about losing, Ivy Priest said afterward, "At least we proved that two women can run against each other without tearing each other apart."

The solid, respectable place that Reva Bosone built for herself in the House could not be sustained against the 1952 Eisenhower landslide. She was defeated again in 1954, but returned to Washington in 1957 to serve as legal counsel to the Subcommittee on Safety and Compensation of the House Committee on Education and Labor. In 1961 she was appointed a judicial officer with the Post Office Department.

The tough, moralistic stand toward office holders that she advocated while running for Congress is, she feels, still applicable: "They should do the job that should be done, whether the required course of action is popular or not. The biggest need in politics and government today is for people of integrity and courage, who will do what they believe is right and not worry about the political consequences to themselves."

CECIL M. HARDEN
REPUBLICAN OF INDIANA

Indiana's 6th District (captured and held during the New Deal heyday of the 1930s by Democrat Virginia Jenckes) provided a vivid case study of the nation's cantankerous mood at election time, 1948. Weary of the nettlesome burdens of post-war readjustment, people yearned for tranquility and economic stability.

In normal times this largely rural area—10 counties fanning out westward from Indianapolis—was GOP country. But these were not normal times. The disenchantment of farmers with the Republican Congress raised the very real possibility of wholesale political defection in the Corn Belt.

It was this near-crisis situation that Cecil Harden, 53, faced as the nominee to replace GOP Representative Noble J. Johnson, who dropped out of the running to accept a federal judgeship. By the time she entered the race, her Democratic opponent, Jack J. O'Grady, had been campaigning for three months. Although she was not a political unknown, her previous activity had been more or less behind the scenes within the Republican Party structure. Thus her number one problem was to get her name before the electorate—fast.

Behind the wheel of her station wagon, she drove long and hard, maintained a 7-day-a-week speaking schedule, and visited every town at least once, jamming her mind and her notebook with firsthand impressions from farmers and city dwellers alike. In addition, she contracted for billboard space. How many voters were won over by the sight of a smiling face, compared by some to that of the Duchess of Windsor, will never be known. But it was later agreed that the then novel approach to vote-getting had been worth the price tag.

The Hoosier vote split in a predictable pattern, O'Grady scoring heavily in and around his home territory, Terre Haute. The overall outcome was so close, however, that for a while it looked as if a recount would be required. When the formal tally was in, Mrs. Harden had won by an eyelash: 483 votes. No matter how close, winner takes all. Thus there was a special savor to the Covington gala where nearly the entire population of 2,000 rallied to the mayor's proclamation and celebrated "Cecil Harden Day."

Before her election, Mrs. Harden had scrupulously followed the admonition handed down by Carrie Chapman Catt, the tactician of the suffrage movement: "The only way to get things done is to get them done inside of a political party." Cecil Harden began as a GOP precinct vice-chairman in 1932; in 1938 she moved up to become vice-chairman of both Fountain County and the 6th Congressional District, and in 1944 she was

elected Republican National Committeewoman and a delegate
to the GOP National Convention in Chicago, where Thomas
E. Dewey was nominated for President. Throughout much of
this period she was an active member of her party's state
and national speakers bureau, writing her own speeches and
delivering them with an aura of confident pleasure.

The daughter of Timothy J. Murray, a longtime Democratic
leader in Covington, the town where she was born and reared,
she attended Indiana University and taught school before her
marriage in 1914 to Frost Revere Harden, an automobile dealer
who also served as the postmaster of Covington during part
of the Hoover Administration. Rearing one son did not take all
of her time; thus, even before going into politics, she volunteered for all sorts of local activities: religious, patriotic, professional. Once she had a toe-hold on a rung of politicking
she worked hard and in an orderly fashion. Nothing was done
haphazardly, in a hurry, or catch-as-catch-can. She was as precise about time—no untidy days, hours, or minutes. Each was
meticulously packed with constructive enterprise. Even when
she attended social functions, she was making political contacts
or gleaning politically useful information.

These assets she took to Washington, where in 1949 she began what turned out to be five successive terms in the House
of Representatives. Each re-election campaign was carefully
planned, carefully executed. Although she was never able to
wrest from her male opponents the two Democratic strongholds, Vermillion and Vigo counties, her margin of victory each
election year through 1956 was substantial. In 1958 she was
handicapped by factors she could not alter: a shift in voter
sentiment away from the Eisenhower Administration, mainly due
to its failure to act vigorously in the face of a deep recession
that had spawned more than 5 million jobless. Under an ava-
lanche of Democratic ballots, GOP congressional candidates all
across the country disappeared from political view. The margin of Representative Harden's defeat was not as large as it
might have been, considering the tide of the electorate; nevertheless, it was a defeat. She lost to a Terre Haute high school
football coach, Fred Wampler, by exactly 4,120 votes.

Cecil Harden's congressional record was in the tradition of
midwestern Republicanism: an adamant stand against the "spend-
ers," charges leveled at "socialism" and "left-wing extremists," a
temperate plea to hold the government budget near balance.
In essence, she followed Administration policy, labeled by the

New York Times as "exploding harmlessly and meaninglessly in the political air."

This is not to imply that she was not innovative or that she failed to pay close attention to her constituents. In consort with veteran Charles Halleck and other members of the Indiana delegation, she helped increased appropriations for the soil-bank acreage reserve, sorely needed by Hoosier farmers. And no one. delivered a more cogent floor argument "to end for all time the tragic losses the people of the Wabash Valley suffer from floods almost every year." Improbable as it may seem, the tragedy she called to the attention of Congress in 1958 ("Thousands of acres of rich valley farmland have been flooded and farmers in many cases may be unable to make any kind of crop this season") was precisely the kind of catastrophe for which Congresswoman Virginia Jenckes had requested federal aid 20 years earlier.

President Eisenhower's appointment of former Congresswoman Harden to the newly created post of special assistant for women's affairs in the Post Office Department was in keeping with the chief executive's personal commitment to fill more federal executive jobs with able women. It was also his way of paying a political debt. Cecil Harden, as both a delegate and a member of the credentials committee at the 1952 National Convention, had been caught up in the dramatic fight between Taftmen (backers of Ohio senator Robert A. Taft) and Ikemen. As a member of the Indiana delegation committed to Taft, she had cast her ballot for the Ohio senator. However, as a member of the credentials committee, she had fought for the right of the pro-Eisenhower delegates to be seated. Thus her role in the subsequent nomination of General Eisenhower, however indirect, had been influential.

In 1970 President Richard Nixon named 76-year-old Mrs. Harden to the Advisory Committee of the White House Conference on Aging and subsequently to the 15-member executive committee responsible for implementing the conference. As she approaches the silver anniversary of her induction as a Republican national committeewoman (the Hatch Act required that she resign while holding a federal position), Cecil Murray Harden seems the ageless personification of the strength and highmindedness that have often been brought out by the political freedom won for women by Mrs. Catt and her loyal band of followers.

EDNA F. KELLY
DEMOCRAT OF NEW YORK

For more than 150 years cartoonists accurately portrayed Brooklyn politics as a smoke-filled room crowded with beefy gents who removed cigar stubs from their mouths only long enough to bark commands. On a chilly November morning in 1949 they awoke to find this interpretation passé. Brooklynites had elected a woman to fill the vacancy in the House created by the death of Andrew L. Somers, the 10th District representative for 25 years.

Why a woman? There are few absolutes in politics, but the most likely explanation is that local party leaders of the all-male Kings County machine had agreed to help the Democratic National Committee implement its revolutionary "New Deal for Women" policy. In selecting Edna Kelly, one seasoned observer said, "they may have reasoned that her feminine charm and good looks, as well as her political *savoir-faire,* would be no handicap to the Brooklyn delegation."

Politics was a game that the handsome Mrs. Kelly knew only from the sidelines. Until her husband's death in an automobile accident in 1942, her life had not been very different from that of any other homemaker in the 1200 block of Carroll Street. Her focus had been on her husband, City Court Justice Edward Leo Kelly; their children, William Edward and Maura Patricia; and her parish church, St. Gregory's.

The former Edna Patricia Flannery originally planned to teach school, but marriage changed her plans. The year (1928) she graduated from Hunter College with majors in government and economics was also the year she married Kelly. Her own family background (she was born in Easthampton, Long Island, the youngest of five girls) was wholly apolitical. Public affairs were sometimes discussed at the dinner table, Mrs. Kelly remembers, but "in a roundabout way." Patrick Joseph Flannery, whose special genius was creating topiary gardens for affluent Long Islanders, was civic-minded but did not count himself among those ambitious Irish immigrants who coveted power through politics.

Widowhood dramatically changed Mrs. Kelly's life. Irwin Steingut, minority leader of the State Assembly and longtime ruler of the 18th Assembly District, spotted her while she was working to revitalize the lethargic women's auxiliary of the Madison Democratic Club. He chose her as his coleader and in due time pushed her election to the County Democratic Executive Committee. From the party hierarchy it was but a short step to the party payroll.

"Albany's loss," said Steingut after her election to Congress, "will be Washington's gain." He was referring to her six years of legislative work in the Statehouse. As chief research director, she analyzed the bills that Democratic Assembly members introduced, compared them with similar legislation in other states, then turned her findings over to committee chairmen. It was a job requiring both knowledge of and patience with corridor politics.

The bills that aroused Edna Kelly's partisan interest in Albany dealt with public housing, government aid to education, child-care centers, and revenue sharing. She incorporated these in her congressional campaign platform, along with other humanitarian issues that in her opinion should concern the national legislature: higher Social Security benefits, admission of more displaced persons from Europe, and increased financial support of Israel.

"I must have delivered over a hundred speeches," she recalls, "on and off street corners," zigzagging from Eastern Parkway through Crown Heights, Upper Flatbush, and into Stuyvesant. That she polled twice as many votes as her Republican opponent is not surprising. The constituency—mainly first- and second-generation Italians, Irish, and Jews—was overwhelmingly Democratic.

What the 81st Congress saw in Edna Kelly was a statuesque brunette whose personal trademark was her sleek hair, worn in a becoming chignon. At 43, she was the youngest member of the feminine House contingent, burning with ambition and energy, swift to speak and vehement in argument (as in her high school debating days). She also listened, though sometimes grudgingly.

Appointed to the Foreign Affairs Committee, then generally known as more like a branch of the State Department than an independent body of the Congress, she was an amateur ringed by professionals. But, by the time she acquired sufficient seniority to chair the Subcommittee on Europe in 1955, she had demonstrated that she had acquired more than a speaking acquaintance with the role of the United States in world affairs.

Within two months after the memorable July 1955 Geneva Summit Conference of the Big Four chiefs of state (Eisenhower, Prime Minister Anthony Eden of Great Britain, French Premier Edgar Faure, and the Soviet Union's Nikolai Bulganin), Representative Kelly led a study mission to Europe and Israel. It was the first of five overseas investigations she would head during her 19 years in Congress. All were well intentioned, with goals well defined. It was predictable, however, that, because they resulted from a bipartisan effort to accomplish multiple objectives, the main one being "to evaluate the effectiveness of U.S. foreign policy . . . and appraise further U.S. action," the legislative value of the reports submitted to the House Foreign Affairs Committee would come into dispute. The first mission raised more questions than it answered. In its favor, it may be said that the report articulated what the high-level conferences only signaled: an acceptance by European nations of the common necessity to shun recourse to nuclear war. It spelled out, too, a cautionary note: in view of the progress made by Russia on both its political and military fronts (in the wake of Stalin's death), "there should be no relaxation toward the threat of Soviet Communism."

The subcommittee's conclusions, which mirrored those of its chairman, were negative. "The Russian leopard has not changed its spots," the text warned. "Bold, new, dynamic programs must be devised on a crash basis to overcome the gains made by the Soviets." It was the view of Congresswoman Kelly, a principled and consistent anticommunist, that one had only to examine the depth of Russia's probings into the Middle East to realize that the Soviet world design "might well possess new force and vigor." She was so convinced of her assessment, in fact, that during the subcommittee's stopover in Geneva she personally urged Secretary of State John Foster Dulles "to leave and to show to the world that while we are at the Conference, we, the free world, particularly the United States, are being stabbed in the back by the U.S.S.R."

Edna Kelly's detractors charged that she had blind spots concerning the various Middle East crises, which, like slumbering volcanoes, erupted periodically from the mid-fifties onward. Not surprisingly, congressional opinion was divided—not on the need for a solution but on the kind of action, if any, the United States should take. Representative Kelly sought, with persistence, "positive and comprehensive measures for dealing with the fundamental problems" and allied herself with those who wanted to involve the United Nations. In a letter to President Eisenhower in 1957, she recommended that he "instruct the representative of the U.N., Ambassador Henry Cabot Lodge, to . . . press vigorously for a peace conference without which there can be no moral, just, and lasting solution to the problems of the Arab States and Israel."

This was the line of argument she always pressed, almost without exception. Although the United States did strongly support the United Nations in the 1956 Suez crisis, Soviet influence continued to expand throughout the Middle East. For Edna Kelly, time and history played a cruel trick. Only after she had left Congress did the Administration, once again in Republican hands, take the bold step she had recommended from the beginning and advocate U.N. mediation to settle the critical question of Israeli-Arab relations.

In other matters, particularly economy in foreign aid, Edna Kelly's perseverance paid regular—and sometimes instant—dividends. When it was discovered that the federal government, in direct competition with private enterprise, was acting in behalf of foreign nations as the purchasing agent for items ranging from nylon stockings to jet aircraft, she pushed through a bill that terminated the practice. She was also instrumental in cutting off foreign assistance to countries delinquent in settling their accounts with American business concerns. Her amendment to the 1959 Mutual Security Act brought an annual flow of $1 billion in foreign orders to the United States, a large portion of which was used to pay for the American foreign aid program.

On the matter of religious persecution in the Soviet Union and in other Eastern European countries—well documented and well publicized throughout the post–World War II years—the Senate Foreign Relations Committee, the House Foreign Affairs Committee, and the State Department remained almost mute until 1965. "Unfortunately," said Rabbi Joachim Prinz, speaking on behalf of the American Jewish Conference on Soviet Jewry, "the voice that could have proven the most telling has been absent from the chorus of condemnation—the official voice of the Government of the United States." However, as the full story of the harsh treatment—not just of Jews but of Christians and Muslims too—unfolded at open hearings before the Subcommittee on Europe, hope was kindled that the testimony from influential witnesses would have a forceful impact on the discrimination in Russia and other nations behind the Iron Curtain. "World opinion offers partial protection to those being subjected to harsh treatment," said chairwoman Kelly, "and our action was a first step to evoke an expression of concern about the travesty being perpetrated on the fundamental rights of humanity."

The Brooklyn congresswoman's intense sense of duty in matters affecting relations between the United States and the European nations culminated in President Kennedy's appointing her as a delegate to the 18th General Assembly of the United Nations. From her front-row seat she sent a mixed report to Brooklyn. "The new Soviet Communist 'peace' offensive is in no way substantive," she said. "Rather, it is the result of White House action during the Cuban missile crisis when it became clear that the Administration would fight to maintain our way of life, even in a nuclear age."

Like any member of Congress, Edna Kelly had her areas of strength and of weakness, in terms of accomplishment on both the domestic and the foreign level. Her friend and sometime mentor, Speaker of the House John W. McCormack of Massachusetts, often remarked, "Edna has breadth of vision," and a dispassionate assessment of her political record must give her high marks in foreign affairs. On domestic matters she also deserves a creditable score. She can claim a commendable civil rights record and has helped bring about amendments to the Social Security laws to ensure more adequate coverage for disabled workers, as well as a tax-law revision allowing working widows and widowers to deduct specific expenses for child care. At the end of her 12-year campaign to establish the principle of equal pay for equal work, she was rewarded with one of the pens President Kennedy used to sign the bill into law in June 1963.

Through 1966, re-election posed no problems whatsoever for the Brooklyn congresswoman. Even the men who in 1949 had been reluctant to have a female represent them in the House campaigned for her regularly. From 1950 on she had the additional backing of the Liberal Party, and her plurality, except during the election years of 1952 and 1956, soared with each succeeding election. She weathered redistricting in 1962 (the 10th became the 12th) to poll 92,000 votes, the highest number up to that time and nearly three times as many as her Republican opponent, London Goldberg, received.

It was not Brooklyn but the U.S. Supreme Court and the congressional seniority system that ended her political career. The ruling that districts had to be of equal size and "compact and contiguous" forced the redrawing of lines in 1968. That part of the 12th not ceded to a largely black constituency was incorporated into the 10th District, represented by 80-year-old Emanuel Celler, ranking representative in the seven-member Brooklyn delegation.

Representative Kelly, third in seniority, had two choices: she could run against a black in the newly carved 12th or against Celler. She opted for the latter. Considering that he was rounding out his 45th consecutive year in Congress and was chairman of the House Judiciary Committee, she did surprisingly well, collecting enough votes to reduce Celler's plurality to 8,518 votes. The political fact of the ballot, however, was that her days in Congress were over.

In what direction does a 61-year-old woman unceremoniously dislodged from elective office, yet still very able and dedicated, turn? If that woman is Edna F. Kelly, not to the past. Even before finishing the sorting of her own papers, she began coordinating a project under the aegis of Former Members of Congress, Inc., whereby legislative history is being recorded on tape by the distinguished men and women who lived it.

"Lawmakers-to-come," says Edna Kelly, "will find that their predecessors were never as bad or wholly as good as their mixed notices. But if they want to profit from what has gone before, the record will be here for the listening."

Maintaining Momentum

Labeled a "vintage year for the GOP," 1950 was but a fore-taste of 1952, when Dwight D. Eisenhower would win the Presidency in a ballot-box revolution and Republicans would gain control of Congress for only the second time in nearly a generation. New GOP winners of House seats in 1950 included Marguerite Stitt Church of Illinois and Ruth Thompson of Michigan. The following year two widows of Democratic congressmen, Elizabeth Kee of West Virginia and Vera D. Buchanan of Pennsylvania, won special elections. Missing from the 82d Congress, however, was a long-familiar Democratic face: the handsome Irish countenance of New Jersey Representative Mary Norton. After a quarter of a century on Capitol Hill, she had retired for health reasons.

Throughout the 1952 Presidential campaign, Eisenhower pleaded especially for the women's vote to sweep away "bad government." "I know what can be done with a good broom in the hands of a morally indignant woman," he said in Buffalo. Women, reacting against the Korean deadlock, swarmed to the GOP candidate. And, while the female contingent in the 83d Congress (1953–55) was enlarged to 12, both newcomers—Gracie Pfost of Idaho and Leonor K. Sullivan of Missouri—were Democrats. In the Senate Margaret Chase Smith had the company briefly of two fellow Republicans from Nebraska, Eva Bowring and Hazel H. Abel.

These congresswomen came to Washington during a period marked by an almost obsessive legislative concern with internal security—led by Senator Joseph McCarthy, whose attacks on subversives in government destroyed the reputations of the innocent as well as the guilty. As the national mood of anxiety was further fanned by the cold war and the Korean War, the debates in Congress reflected the complex struggle to align the United States with the responsibilities, opportunities, and dangers of the newest phase of its history—world leadership.

MARGUERITE STITT CHURCH
REPUBLICAN OF ILLINOIS

Representative Marguerite Stitt Church of Illinois liked to tell visitors that her high-backed, leather desk chair was "good for the congressional spine." She was referring of course to the physical support it afforded such an indefatigable worker as herself. For the 12 years (1951–63) she was on the Hill, "Congress," she says, "was my life." Quite literally, she made of the job a day-into-night, year-round affair.

Anyone seeking to unravel the dynamics of this lady from the 13th Illinois District (northern Cook County and adjoining Lake County) has only to examine the record—*Congressional* and personal. In her forceful defense of sound fiscal and foreign policy, there was a hint of a new American vision. In her stand on problems of social welfare, she demonstrated an amazing capacity for fresh thought.

Marguerite Church's instincts have always flowed more from the head than from the heart. A political scientist by education and the widow of Ralph E. Church, longtime member of the Illinois legislature who served in the U.S. House for 13 years before his death in 1950, she possesses the attributes she once said were necessary for after-30 popularity: intelligence, good taste, poise, a sense of humor. (Without the last, she would not have been able to laugh about the time during her first campaign when she moved through Lake County at such a rapid pace that she found herself speaking in Lawrence Smith's district in southern Wisconsin.)

Not the least of her political assets was her campaign strategy. On the basis of "Why advertise the opposition?" she never referred to any of her opponents by name or answered any of their criticisms. Moreover, through her office services to all 13th District voters, she actually campaigned 12 months a year.

Running for office in pro-Republican territory, she was perennially the favorite. Still, the impressive size of the vote she received can only be explained in terms of the widespread appeal she had among Independents, and even Democrats. In her initial election, in 1950, the 140,750-vote tally (versus 49,187 for Democrat Thomas F. Dolan) was the highest ever recorded for a House candidate in the 13th District. The number grew with each successive election. In 1956 (against Helen Benson Leys) and again in 1960 (against Tyler Thompson) she collected the largest number of votes nationwide among candidates entered in a district contest for the House of Representatives.

For five of her six terms in the House she served on the Foreign Affairs Committee, joining two other women, Frances Bolton and Edna Kelly. As a member of subcommittees on Foreign Economic Policy and the Far East and Pacific, she visited almost half of the nations in the world. Armed with investigative skill and a keen intuition, she questioned scores of economic and political leaders about the effectiveness of U.S. aid. Of these trips, she says, "I like to think that my district and my country are safer because I went."

Marguerite Church's interest in overseas affairs first developed for New York–born Marguerite Stitt when she was taken abroad every summer by her parents. Later, at Wellesley College in the period 1910–14, she majored in psychology, completed minors in economics and sociology, joined the debating society, and graduated with a Phi Beta Kappa key. Before enrolling at Columbia University to earn a master's degree in political science, she taught Wellesley sophomores for a year; after receiving her M.A., she was a consulting psychologist with the State Charities Aid Association in Manhattan.

Although marriage in 1918 (followed by the rearing of a family of three children in Evanston, Illinois) terminated her wage-earning, it marked the beginning of her active participation in local and national affairs. Admittedly a vocal crusader "for betterment of almost everything," she emerged over the years as the kind of exponent of change who could win friends and influence people.

In Congress Marguerite Church consistently fought for efficiency and economy in government, including lower taxes. One of her most important pieces of legislation was a measure she introduced while serving on the Government Operations Committee. It advocated implementation of the plans for government reorganization proposed by the Second Hoover Commission. She was also instrumental in passage of the bill to place the federal budget system on an accrued annual expenditure basis. In a totally unrelated field—child welfare—the national law prohibiting bootleg fireworks bears her name.

Presidents from both parties singled her out for special notice. Dwight Eisenhower sent her as one of his personal representatives to the inauguration of Mexico's President Gustavo Lopez Mateos and also asked her to participate in the White House Conference on Children and Youth. In 1962, John F. Kennedy named her a delegate to the 16th General Assembly of the United Nations.

The hallowed rule of seniority did not come under scrutiny during the years Marguerite Church was in Congress. Had the archaic tradition been examined and had she been asked for an opinion, her response would have been that she "thought kindly" of mandatory retirement at 70. "We would lose some who have much still to give," she says, "but the danger as regards many who stay in beyond that age is that they stay too long. Finally, they reach the stage when it is difficult, if not impossible, for them to face life any place else." Adhering to her proposed timetable, she retired at the end of 1962, precisely at age 70. Since then, in her own words, she has "avidly seized and filled new responsibilities"—on a schedule that permits her to enjoy home and family (10 grandchildren and three great-grandchildren).

At the time she left Congress, the 13th Congressional District was carved into a new shape. Ever since, her many loyal friends —with only a slight distortion of the political truth—have been able to say, in as apt a description of the kind of congresswoman she was as is likely to be devised, "It took three men to fill the place Marguerite left!"

RUTH THOMPSON
REPUBLICAN OF MICHIGAN

The process that eventually yielded Ruth Thompson as Michigan's first congresswoman began with the 1950 announcement by 9th District representative Albert J. Engel that he would seek the GOP gubernatorial nomination. Engel, 62, had held the western-Michigan congressional seat for 16 consecutive years.

The first political test for Miss Thompson, a 63-year-old attorney and former county probate judge, was the Republican primary. By waging a highly personal campaign, she defeated a former Michigan lieutenant governor and the Muskegon County GOP chairman. "I started out in my car and stopped all over, ringing doorbells, visiting business places, talking with the people on the streets, and addressing countless gatherings," she said when it was over. "Many of those whom I met were people I had known when I was probate judge—I'd handled their estates, helped them when they wanted to adopt children, or placed young wards of the court in their homes for boarding."

In the 1950 general election race, which matched the vigorous, politically conservative Ruth Thompson against Democrat Noel P. Fox, chairman of the state Labor Mediation Board, the mostly rural Republican 9th District voters gave her a plurality of 7,688 votes out of the 80,132 cast.

From stenographer to congresswoman is a long, steep climb, but tall, angular Ruth Thompson, a spinster of plain habits and unadorned speech, took it in her stride. An only child, she was born and reared in Whitehall on the eastern shore of Lake Michigan. After graduating from Muskegon Business College, she worked as a legal secretary and court registrar while studying law at night for six years. Out of a class of 12 tutored by local lawyers, only Miss Thompson and one other student passed the bar examination.

As Muskegon County's first woman lawyer (1924), she was elected Michigan's first female judge and served three successive four-year terms (1925–37). In 1939 she became the state's first female legislator, serving one term in the Michigan House of Representatives.

Going to Washington, D.C., in 1951 constituted a return engagement for Ruth Thompson. During World War II she had solved legal problems for the Social Security Board and the Labor Department before transferring to the Pentagon, where her legal expertise had been put to use by the War Department in its civilian personnel branch. In 1945 she went to Germany as a member of the Adjutant General's staff attached to U.S. occupation forces.

Although there were grave masculine misgivings on Capitol Hill, members of the House Judiciary Committee admitted the Michigan congresswoman to their previously all-male clique. Her longtime service as a judge and as an active member and chairman of the Michigan Prison Commission for Women was deemed a satisfactory qualification.

The image of Ruth Thompson as a hardworking lawyer, judge, and politician was widely accepted by her colleagues and constituents alike. Small and modest triumphs in the 82d and 83d congresses enabled her not only to run successfully for reelection in 1952 and 1954 but to command pluralities in excess of 20,000 votes each time. The years of her third term, however, were darkly clouded when she became the innocent victim of rivalry among bureaucrats.

The whole affair began with the Air Force asking Congress for seven new jet interceptor bases "urgently needed" to protect the nation's borders. One should be built near Traverse City in northern Michigan, the Air Force recommended, to connect with the important radar center already located 25 miles to the west, at Empire on Lake Michigan. Congress promptly approved the project and voted appropriations, and Ruth Thompson proudly issued an announcement that the 9th District, which includes Traverse City, would get the base. The first two sites selected by the Air Force—Long Lake and Homestead—were rejected by the citizenry who did not want jet planes disrupting the National Music Camp at nearby Interlochen. A third site, Cadillac, was chosen.

Representative Thompson some time later made public the charge that during the selection process she was offered a bribe in the form of a $1,000 campaign contribution if she would promote the Cadillac location. She claimed that she had privately informed Air Force Secretary Harold E. Talbott of the bribe offer and that he had assured her the base would "never, never go to Cadillac." Evidently Talbott changed his mind. Without explanation, his office informed Miss Thompson the base *would* go to Cadillac. Soon afterward he appealed to Clarence Cannon, chairman of the House Appropriations Committee, to approve his choice.

He reckoned without Congresswoman Thompson. In a stormy private session with Talbott, Carl Vinson, chairman of the House Armed Services Committee, and George H. Mahon, chairman of the House Military Appropriations Committee, she reiterated the story of the attempted bribe. The Appropriations Committee formally voted to bar funds for Cadillac and directed the Air Force to choose another site.

Ruth Thompson, insisting that the Air Force had promised the base to her district, recommended that Manistee be chosen. Vinson concurred, and Manistee got the jet base—but not before the voters learned that the bypassing of Cadillac would cost the taxpayers more than $5 million in additional appropriations and would delay construction for at least a year.

The whole affair proved politically embarrassing to Miss Thompson. There was speculation that she would not seek re-election, because of the "unfortunate circumstances beyond her control." Nevertheless, she did—and lost by the narrow margin of 4,505 votes to young (32), politically ambitious Robert P. Griffin, a Traverse City attorney (since 1966, a U.S. senator).

Ruth Thompson died in 1970 at the age of 82. She is remembered by oldtimers on the Hill, and so is the story of the wandering air base.

ELIZABETH KEE
DEMOCRAT OF WEST VIRGINIA

In southern West Virginia the name Kee has been synonymous with Democratic politics longer than anyone can remember. But it is in the 20th century and in the U.S. House of Representatives that the dynastic heritage of the Kee family has been preserved in its purest form, with the 5th District represented successively by father, mother, and son since 1933.

When Representative John Kee died of a heart attack in 1951, his widow, Elizabeth, won a special election to succeed him. Thirteen years and six congresses later, she announced her voluntary retirement. The "Kee seat" went to son James in 1965.

"Elizabeth took to politics as a duck takes to water," a friend once observed. The ease with which she switched from court reporting to campaigning Mrs. Kee credits to her outgoing, gregarious nature. Another asset, particularly for the job of administrative assistant to John Kee, was her business-college education and secretarial experience with the *Roanoke Times* in her native state of Virginia.

"Keenotes," the weekly column she wrote for newspapers in her husband's constituency—and later her own—reflected the political philosophy of a progressive Democrat, which she is.

Because West Virginians have never looked with any enthusiasm on women holding political office, Mrs. Kee's announced candidacy in 1951 could have had an unsettling effect on the coal-mine workers and creek-bed farmers who for generations have eked out an uncertain living within the hidden hollows and tight little valleys of the Appalachians. But there was no grumbling, and there were few second thoughts as voters marked their ballots in the seven-county area dotted with villages bearing such picturesque names as Pipestem and Cucumber. Her victory was clearly a family one. The voters reasoned that Congressman Kee had "looked after" them and his widow would "do the same."

The countless hours Elizabeth Kee had devoted to the physically handicapped, a volunteer effort sparked by her only daughter's lifelong bout with cerebral palsy and polio, were known regionally. Congresswoman Kee pursued her interest in the handicapped as chairman of the Veterans' Affairs Subcommittee on Hospitals. Her active part in the investigation of veterans' facilities during the Korean conflict resulted in improved treatment at all installations.

But it was on economically depressed southern West Virginia that she focused major attention. Hers was the largest bituminous coal–producing district in the nation, but the coal market was shrinking. Working with the United Mine Workers, the National Coal Association, and the Appalachian Electric Power Company, she obtained federal support for a project known as "coal by wire" for the relatively inexpensive production of electricity. In addition to being the prime mover in securing federally financed public works projects (flood control, new post offices, highways), she took the initiative in a movement to attract new industry (aviation and wood products) and to establish centers for the retraining of idle miners. Eventually the 5th District became a "model" for the Area Redevelopment Act.

Through all of her years in office it was vastly reassuring for her to be told publicly that she was living up to her own definition. Before each election she could expect endorsements like this one that appeared, in the *Hinton Daily News*: "So far as the Fifth Congressional District is concerned, it is absolutely unthinkable at this particular time for the voters to even consider anyone else to represent them other than Mrs. Kee." If the editor had had his way, Elizabeth Kee would have been spared the time and cost of a campaign: "We don't want her to have to waste valuable time in campaigning, when she could be devoting her energy and 'know how' in furthering legislation and certain projects for the benefit of southern West Virginia."

Family *doyenne* Elizabeth Kee, now 72, once Mother of the Year from the state where Mother's Day originated, often defined her congressional job as "being all things to all constituents." The folks back home, she said, expect you to be "a psychiatrist, lawyer, clergyman—everything."

VERA D. BUCHANAN
DEMOCRAT OF PENNSYLVANIA

Physical size usually has nothing to do with a candidate's qualifications for Congress. But Vera Buchanan worried that because she was only five feet two inches (110 pounds) the steelworkers who dominated the 33d Pennsylvania District would dismiss her, or, worse, not even see her. She need not have fretted. Although she sometimes had to stand on a milk crate in order to reach the microphone, her rhetoric had the right amount of toughness ("Anti-Truman sentiment is the howling of those in our midst who are bloodthirsty enough to invite world conflict") to make a crowd of union members rise to cheer her.

In a campaign that took her to the mill gates before dawn and into labor halls after dark, liberal-minded Mrs. Buchanan, 49, easily won the right to succeed her late husband as U.S. representative from Allegheny County. Her 1951 triumph over Republican Clifford W. Flegal, 30-year-old McKeesport city controller, duplicated the 2-to-1 victories Frank Buchanan had won at the polls in 1948 and 1950.

A *Pittsburgh Post-Gazette* editorial statement that "Mrs. Buchanan's foremost attribute was that she was the widow of Frank Buchanan," though true, was not the whole truth. The second time around she proved it. Despite the fact that a knee fracture suffered in an auto crash on the Pennsylvania Turnpike hospitalized her during the crucial period preceding the primary, she was the unanimous choice of the Democratic Party over three male hopefuls, including State Senator Elmer J. Holland. And, even though the GOP candidate, Peter F. Bender, was a member of the CIO, it was Vera Buchanan who received the CIO endorsement.

As the first lady of McKeesport while her husband was mayor in the early 1940s, Mrs. Buchanan had carried on a listening campaign, telling townspeople, "We want to know what you have to say." She had served a political apprenticeship of sorts from 1945 until 1951 as a volunteer in Buchanan's Capitol Hill office. Born Vera Daerr, she had worked before her marriage in 1929 as a secretary in Duquesne, a Steel Valley community in her native Allegheny County.

Called the "prettiest femme in Congress" by Walter Winchell, Vera Buchanan was a vivacious, brown-eyed, brown-haired mother of 21-year-old twin daughters (Jane and Joan) when she was sworn in by House Speaker Sam Rayburn. Among the guests at the ceremony was her three-month-old granddaughter, Kristie Lynn Cavalcante, Joan's child.

Publicly, Vera Buchanan said that she had been persuaded by Pittsburgh mayor David L. Lawrence to make the race. "We both wanted to see the things 'Buck' believed in carried on," she said. Her record in Congress is a testament to her success. "She has proved herself a friend of the working people and a foe of vested interests in the same fine manner as her late husband," editorialized a labor journal after she had voted against using the Taft-Hartley Act to end a 1952 wage-contract steel strike and force the men back to work on the companies' terms. "Thank God for the Congressman," said a Braddock steelworker's Czechoslovakian wife who had been reunited with her husband through Vera Buchanan's intercession. "I would have crawled on my stomach to get to the United States."

Mrs. Buchanan's private reason for deciding to succeed her deceased husband was "to set the record straight." While Frank Buchanan served as chairman of the House lobby-investigating subcommittee in 1950, he was singled out for invective by Westbrook Pegler, writer of a syndicated column entitled "Fair Enough." In the neat, figure-skating phrases that distinguished Pegler's journalese (he was proud of the tag "Red-baiter"), Buchanan was accused of, among other things, "ignoring all religious groups." His 38-page reply to the charges—a point-by-point refutation that he hoped to deliver on the House floor—was found in the drawer of the table beside his hospital bed the night he died. His widow wanted to insert the remarks in the *Congressional Record*—"to reach the doubting Thomases," she told her daughters.

"She had a promise in her heart to keep," says Jane (Mrs. John E. Thomas, Jr.). "The ironic twist," Jane explains, "is that although Majority Leader John McCormack and Speaker Rayburn agreed with Mom, they advised her to forget the malicious attacks. If she were to resurrect the past, they felt, Pegler might aim his vituperation at her."

Midway in her third term, on June 29, 1955, Vera Buchanan was admitted to the Navy Medical Center in suburban Bethesda, Maryland, suffering from what was diagnosed at the time as bronchial pneumonia. Even after the diagnosis was changed to cancer, she carried on the congressional work for which she had such unquenchable zest.

Shortly before her death on November 26, Congressman McCormack, in Pittsburgh to deliver an address, stopped by McKeesport Hospital to see her. As he rose to leave, she said, "Good-by, my friend," and blew him a kiss.

"I won't say 'good-by,'" McCormack replied, "just 'so long.'" I'll see you up in the Gallery."

GRACIE PFOST

DEMOCRAT OF IDAHO

Had Hollywood producers followed the political career of Gracie Pfost, they would have found the makings of a thrilling drama—a Western with a woman's angle. Even without Indian war dances or the waylaying of stagecoaches, the script would have been exciting: a reputed plot by selfish interests against a pretty and spirited heroine battling for the common people.

The scene for conflict was set, according to Mrs. Pfost, when she "dared to be a vigorous defender of the people's right" by advocating federal instead of private construction of the high dam at Hell's Canyon on the Snake River. Arrayed against her were Republican opponents who, she claimed, urged the "gimme-and-get boys in the private electric utilities" to "get Gracie Pfost."

The first time they succeeded. The year was 1950, and in a near photofinish she lost the 1st Congressional District by 783 votes to John T. Wood, a 72-year-old Coeur d'Alene physician. In a return match two years later, the Nampa redhead, by then nicknamed "Hell's Belle," carried the Idaho panhandle, but just barely. The outcome was in doubt for nearly a week before she was officially declared the winner by a margin of 591 votes.

Congress was a star to which Gracie Pfost hitched her wagon early in life. "I would not have gotten there," she once said, "if I had not been more persistent than a hound dog worrying a bone." The first public office she aspired to—Canyon County Treasurer—she lost by 1,500 votes. While waiting to try again, she continued in her position as deputy county clerk, auditor, and recorder. "I took advantage of every opportunity that presented itself to give service to the people," she explained. "I worked hours and hours of overtime. The second time I ran, I was elected, and I was re-elected four more times."

Throughout her 10 years in the U.S. House of Representatives (1953–63), she demonstrated that she was willing to do the hard work and take the hard knocks associated with seeking and retaining high political office. Much of the credit for her success she shared with her husband, John W. Pfost, a master mechanic, whom she met after moving from Harrison, Arkansas, where she was born in 1906, to a farm in Boise Valley. Only 17 when they were married, Gracie Bowers Pfost combined housework, which she thoroughly disliked, with earning a diploma from Links Business University in Boise.

"Jack" Pfost died in 1961, but while he was alive she publicly acknowledged that her work in Congress was "more or less a joint venture with him" and that he spent "as many hours working on behalf of the First District of Idaho as any administrative aide on Capitol Hill—without a single cent of payment." When *Life* magazine reported that Jack Pfost had accompanied his wife on a junket to New York City in the company of members of a House Public Works subcommittee, she not only rose to his defense on the House floor ("He paid his own expenses") but also suggested that the Henry R. Luce "publishing empire" should concern itself "more with putting out an accurate, unbiased news journal rather than the thing that appears on our newsstands every week."

Part of her philosophy about a woman in politics was that "she must be willing to have her every motive challenged, her every move criticized . . . must submit to having her private life scrutinized under a microscope . . . and [being] the subject of devastating rumors every day." There were, of course, things that Congresswoman Pfost feared, but they were not those that usually terrify public officials. She was not afraid of dinner table gossip or of editorial writers. The *Idaho Daily Statesman,* an influential Independent-Republican daily published in Boise, intermittently upbraided her for the bill she introduced in 1953 calling for construction of the Hells Canyon dam, contending that it was "detrimental to Idaho." "I do not intend to be bluffed, bullied, or frightened by the private monopolies," was her stock rebuttal.

Other captious critics suggested that Gracie Pfost was not interested in the dam beyond the value it might have as a campaign issue in her district. Partisan politics aside, there is no evidence that she moved to get her bill out of the House Committee on Interior and Insular Affairs, of which she was a member. Moreover, her own county, where the farmers' first concern was irrigation water, voted overwhelmingly in favor of her Republican opponent as long as it appeared the dam might be built with federal funds.

As chairman of the Subcommittee on Public Lands, she was less controversial. To attract as much attention as possible to legislation designed "to establish a national wilderness preservation system for the permanent good of the whole people," she moved the hearings to the Far West, where, historically, opposition from die-hard commercial interests has been the strongest. On the occasion of passage of the Wilderness Act during the 88th Congress, Secretary of the Interior Stewart L. Udall credited her with having "added fresh momentum to the cause of conservation when decision hung in the balance."

By then, however, Gracie Pfost was no longer on Capitol Hill, having forsaken a relatively safe House seat to try for the U.S. Senate, only to lose. Her GOP opponent was Len B. Jordan, the Boise rancher and businessman who had been elected governor of Idaho in 1950, the year she made her unsuccessful bid for Congress. At stake was the seat left vacant by the death of Senator Henry C. Dworshak, to which Jordan had been appointed three months before the 1962 general election. Out of 257,677 votes cast, Gracie Pfost received 126,398, or 4,881 fewer than the incumbent. Had she carried her home county of Canyon and adjoining Ada, her political mortality could have been postponed.

"They don't go back to Pocatello," Oregon's Senator Richard L. Neuberger wrote in one of his books about politics. Gracie Pfost, having become enchanted with the nation's capital, accepted an appointment as special assistant for the elderly in the Federal Housing Administration. In 1965, she lost her untimely struggle with Hodgkin's disease and died. Of all the testimonials tendered by her former colleagues, she would have liked best the one from Idaho's Democratic Senator Frank Church: "She proved how much a good woman can contribute to public life."

Of Truth and Its Consequences

LEONOR K. SULLIVAN
DEMOCRAT OF MISSOURI

Leonor Sullivan is a consumer guardian—one of the best. It's not an easy life. Quiet, assiduous reformers arouse resentment, particularly if they say "No" to pork-barreling colleagues and refuse to compromise with either business or bureaucracy.

Deceptive packaging, harmful food additives, diseased meat and poultry, hidden finance charges, cosmetics that disfigure— Leonor Sullivan has crusaded against them all, and more. She has had no choice. Consumer guardians cannot select; they are governed by the awful law of Where-the-Exploitation-Is.

No wonder consumer guardians, especially those in Congress, get cramps in their souls. What keeps Leonor Sullivan going—witty, alert, patient to a fault? In her heart of hearts lies an unspoken hope: If she can just show consumers that their collective voice will be heeded—teach them that they are not powerless to change or make laws—she will have demonstrated that the government belongs to the people.

Although Leonor Sullivan's consumer-activism predated by years that of Ralph Nader, the acknowledged national consumer champion of the seventies, her name is not a household word—except in metropolitan St. Louis, from whence she hails. She is not known more widely for the same reason Nader tried to remain a private person. It is the need for time. Were the congresswoman to accept all of the invitations for public appearances that would lead to national prominence, there would be no time for congressional homework. It is one of her cardinal rules—one she has not broken since coming to Congress in 1953—that she never introduces a bill, never rises to speak on the floor unless she has done exhaustive research on the subject in question. While this kind of dedication to duty and responsibility may lead to a lonely life-style, it provides the credibility that is indispensable to winning legislative battles against consumer frauds.

Combined with her enormous appetite for work are other old-fashioned qualities, not the least of which is persistence. Once convinced of the propriety of a given piece of legislation, she will fight to the finish for passage, taking on all comers. A case in point is the measure popularly known as truth-in-lending.

Proposals for full disclosure by business of the true annual rate of interest to enable buyers to comparison-shop for credit date back to 1960, when Senator Paul H. Douglas of Illinois pioneered such legislation (cosponsored in the House by Representative Sullivan). The bill she introduced in 1967, after Douglas's defeat, was not only stronger than the one William Proxmire of Wisconsin finally pushed through the Senate by a vote of 92 to 0 but considerably broader than the one backed by the Johnson Administration. Not limited to the disclosure of finance charges by business, the Sullivan bill contained comprehensive credit protection for the consumer.

Determined not to permit the parliamentary skirmishing to degenerate into a morass of confusion, she made plain during the hearings that the opposition—mainly retail stores and mail-order houses—would not be permitted to thwart the will of those like herself who demanded a bill "with teeth in it." Reason ruled her rhetoric, but her adversaries drew little comfort from being told bluntly that their recalcitrant stand could be traced to the suspicion "they made more on what they took in through credit fees than on the merchandise itself."

Because the bill was on President Johnson's priority agenda, he joined the fray. Representative Sullivan was invited to the White House six times in less than six months—always in her official capacity as chairman of the Banking and Currency Subcommittee on Consumer Affairs. Johnson's reputation for getting others to do his bidding notwithstanding, the Lady from Missouri held out—again employing reasoned rhetoric—for her comprehensive measure.

By the time H.R. 11601 reached the floor early in 1968, the basic issues at stake were sharply etched. The battle, however,

was just beginning. Those on the side of business had succeeded in attaching several loophole amendments that would
not only give loan sharks a privileged sanctuary but also ex-
empt firms with revolving credit plans from revealing their
annual percentage rates.

"Now we come to the moment of truth in truth in lending," Leonor Sullivan told assembled colleagues. "Will we give
the consumer the whole truth in lending, or just part of the
truth?" Noting that the American Retail Federation "has had
seven straight years of victory" on the revolving credit issue,
"which is a very good batting average," she said flatly, "Enough
is enough."

Defeat of the crippling amendments was due as much to
the clearinghouse for information that she ran from her office
throughout the stormy period as to the unquestionable integrity and appropriateness she manifested on the House floor.
When President Lyndon B. Johnson signed the comprehensive Consumer Credit Protection Act in 1968, he paid special
tribute to "that able Congresswoman from Missouri" who fought
—"and I say 'fought'—for a strong and effective bill when
others would have settled for less."

There are those who suggest that a man would not have
drafted so politically explosive a law as Representative Sullivan's. Former Senator Douglas, in fact, admitted that he did
not dare advocate requirements with the scope of those contained in her bill. Moreover, the measure that passed so overwhelmingly in the 99 per cent–male Senate conveniently
omitted most of the controversial basic elements she had the
courage to include.

What all of this appears to indicate is what objective political
observers have been saying all along: Women can make a unique
contribution in Congress, particularly if they have gilt-edged
credentials, as Representative Sullivan does, of sensitivity, insight, and in-depth understanding of problems that exist in the
social and human areas.

Leonor Sullivan, while not disagreeing that women are tem-
peramentally well fitted for political leadership, maintains that
a woman's most important place is in the home. "I believe that
wholesome family life is the backbone of civilization," she declares. Fear that the legal effects of the Equal Rights Amendment (ERA) could "accelerate the breakup of home life"
prompted her to vote against it in the 92d Congress, the lone
congresswoman to do so. The ERA will abolish hundreds of
protective state statutes, she points out; "for example, it will

make it impossible for our courts to punish a deserting father for failure to at least provide support for his children."

While opposed to "sweeping legislation that would only open up a very large box of mischief," on consumer matters Leonor Sullivan favors an end to piecemeal legislation. On the opening day of the 87th Congress in 1961, she introduced a 41-page omnibus bill (H.R. 1235) covering *all* foods, drugs, and cosmetics. It represented eight years of accumulated grievances against what she calls the "blowout patch" approach to closing gaping loopholes in the Food, Drug, and Cosmetic Act of 1938, a law she complains is a "sieve of shortcomings, deliberately written special exemptions, and obsolete deficiencies."

She was warned by more senior members that if she tried to accomplish too much at one time she would "stir up the dogs" —get too many powerful interests united against her—and possibly lose congressional support for any legislation at all. But at the same time a thick file of carping letters apprised her of just how much discontent there was in the land over low-quality and hazardous goods.

There were the thousands of women suffering burns, rashes, skin eruptions, or loss of hair or even fingernails as a result of using various beauty aids, the instances of food or cosmetics containing chemicals "known to cause cancer in laboratory animals," and the 125 to 150 children under five killed annually by accidental ingestion of flavored aspirin.

Although the consumer-protection laws that Congress has passed since 1961—one at a time—are not the "package" she wants, the fact that some opposition to a consumer bill of rights has been overcome is a tribute to her pertinacity. Her rational rhetoric has brought into being such major consumer legislation as the banning of cancer-inducing agents in food, which led to the prohibition against cyclamates; compulsory federal inspection of poultry for wholesomeness; pretesting of all chemical additives used in or on foodstuffs; stricter controls over manufacture and sale of pep pills, barbiturates, and the like; and the Fair Credit Reporting Act, which protects consumers against arbitrary, erroneous, or malicious information disseminated by credit bureaus. Pretesting for safety and mandatory disclosure of the ingredients in cosmetics, however, remain outside the law—any law—as do many other provisions of her original H.R. 1235.

Undaunted, she has reintroduced into every Congress since the 89th this omnibus bill—the only measure in either the House or the Senate that would combine in one bill provisions for closing all major loopholes in an act passed nearly 35 years ago! In 1972 she repeated substantially what she had told Congress in 1962: "You are faced with an area of supreme importance to the lives and health and safety and well-being of the American people—all of the foods we eat, all of the drugs and devices we use for health purposes, all of the cosmetics used not only by women but in increasing numbers by men, as well."

As she talks about the past in the quiet, salon-like atmosphere of her very large office in the Rayburn Building, she sighs. It is but one of the telltale signs of frustration that can only be classified as normal in a legislator who has lived with an idea so long. Sometimes she looks through the windows into the courtyard, past walls adorned with autographed photographs and paintings of Presidents Truman, Kennedy, and Johnson, framed coins and silver medals (one commemorating the St. Louis Bicentennial). "I'm doing what I want to do" she says. She is fashionably dressed in a suit obviously chosen to enhance her blue-green eyes and graying brown hair. Her well-trained, well-modulated voice gives no hint of the fact that she had to conquer a deep-seated fear of speaking in public before she could even dare contemplate elective politics for herself.

Born Leonor Alice Kretzer in St. Louis in 1904, she inherited a certain optimism from her father, a second-generation German tailor who taught all of his nine children that under the American system everything is possible, provided one perseveres. Yet, because she did not have the opportunity to earn a college degree ("There was not much chance of a $35-a-month telephone-company clerk being able to finance a higher education"), she grew up lacking self-confidence.

Nevertheless, she persevered. From demonstrator of office machines, she rose to training director overseeing the education of as many as 2,000 business machine operators a year. During those terms when her husband, John Berchmans Sullivan, served in Congress, she worked closely with him, both as an unpaid (four years) and as a paid member of his staff. After his death in 1951, when the St. Louis Democratic Central Committee refused to nominate her to fill the vacancy, she got a job as administrative assistant to Representative Leonard Irving of the Missouri 4th District to earn enough money to finance her own primary campaign the following year. Meanwhile, to bolster her confidence, she enrolled in public-speaking courses at the downtown Washington YWCA, choosing "Politics" as the subject of her classroom orations.

Missouri does not encourage women to go into politics. The professionals, in fact, are downright discouraging. "Why not run as an Independent?" some friends suggested. She refused. "John was a Democrat from the 3d District and I am a Democrat," she said, hoping that the men would understand that she envisioned her role as a continuation of his "more than a thing apart."

"We have nothing against you, but a woman can't win" was what she heard from the politicians. During the 1952 primary, the party-endorsed candidate said, "I know Lee Sullivan, and if you'll elect me I'll give her the top position in my office." There were statements to the effect that she did not possess the qualities of leadership the Democrats would need in Congress if Republican Dwight D. Eisenhower won the Presidency.

She campaigned on the basis that she was "better qualified" than her opponents because of her experience on Capitol Hill. She also suggested that the voters needed a woman's voice in Washington—someone who thought as a woman, who would share ideas freely with other women. By a special ruling from the state attorney general, she was listed on the ballot as Mrs. John B. Sullivan. Although her plurality in the primary—against seven men—was a mere 2,965 votes, she garnered 107,428 in the general election, or almost twice as many as her GOP opponent, Claude Bakewell, the incumbent. In all the races since, she has faced opposition in only two primaries, and in the general elections, against eight different male Republican contenders, she has won by margins ranging from 65 per cent to 79 per cent.

Attributing her first election victory almost entirely to the fact that she was John B. Sullivan's widow, she recognized that she had to establish her own identity as a competent member of Congress. This she did as Leonor K. Sullivan. However, on the ballot and on her stationery, her name is printed "Leonor (Mrs. John B.) Sullivan."

Representative Sullivan's most successful legislation has grown out of give and take with the public and out of raising questions about how to meet unanswered needs. In her "Speaking From Washington" newsletters she prods constituents with a one- or two-line reminder that "the best help a Member of Congress can have in solving problems is to know the details of those problems as they affect the average family. So send your letter along: *I'll read it.*" The professional groups she addresses are also asked for "information, ideas, suggestions, comments, and criticism."

Dean of congresswomen since 1969 (after the defeat of Ohio veteran Frances Bolton), Leonor Sullivan, by virtue of being a senior member of the Banking and Currency Committee, the ranking member of its Subcommittee on Housing, and secretary of the Majority Caucus (and also a member of the Majority Steering Committee), is in a position to influence decisions on consumer issues not only in her subcommittee but in other House committees as well. Still, she is humble about her power. "I remember what it was like when I arrived," she says. "Those of us interested in consumer legislation could have caucused in an elevator."

Any member can establish the *need* for legislation, she explains. "Yet, getting Congress to act, even when the need is clear, takes a lot of pressure. In that respect, Congress is like the accelerator of a car; you make it go by putting your foot down."

There have been times when she has put her own foot down— hard. After a 5-year battle, her food stamp plan (replacing the hit-or-miss "dumping" of surplus food in cities) was included in the agriculture bill passed in 1959. It was a hollow victory, however, for Secretary of Agriculture Ezra Taft Benson, who had opposed food stamps on the ground that "People like to buy their food; they don't like to have it given to them," withheld operational funds.

To Depression-reared Leonor Sullivan, who is also an ecumenical Catholic in the tradition of Pope John XXIII, such "callous" disregard of the hungry and malnourished called for pressure tactics. Her letter to President-elect John F. Kennedy reminding him that as a senator he had supported her plan and now had a "chance to prove he meant it" reached the White House the day after he was inaugurated. Under his Administration a year-long pilot program in eight counties was instituted. A dozen more counties were added in 1962—in both rural and metropolitan areas with high unemployment. In 1964 she sponsored a Johnson Administration bill to expand the program nationwide. By 1971, the inadequate diets of 9 million low-income Americans were being supplemented through food stamps at a cost of approximately $2 billion a year.

No one who knows Leonor Sullivan is surprised by the imaginative and sometimes bold action she takes—even in matters outside of the consumer field. When the *Delta Queen*, last of America's overnight paddlewheel excursion riverboats, was headed for a forced retirement because of an official interpretation of the Safety at Sea Act (which she had helped enact primarily to ensure the seaworthiness of ocean-going vessels), she succeeded in pushing through legislation to allow the *Delta Queen* to operate until a replacement vessel could be built. After it was learned that prohibitive construction costs (estimated at $10 million) would preclude building a new sternwheeler, she found a way to bypass the Committee on Merchant Marine and Fisheries (on which she serves), whose chairman was opposed to extending the *Queen*'s life. By a majority vote in both Houses, one of the few remaining links to the Mark Twain era was preserved.

Leonor Sullivan is not universally loved for her efforts. Business sometimes accuses her of pitting buyers against sellers and tampering with the machinery of free competition. General Foods has complained that she is "playing politics in the pantry" by "pitching emotion-charged appeals" to consumers. Former board chairman Charles G. Mortimer included her among the "vote-conscious politicians" who, he said, indulge in "headline-making innuendos" in order to create the impression that America's food-marketing system "needs to be watched and regulated even more closely than it is."

Publicly pleading guilty to the food manufacturer's indictment that she is a "vote-conscious politician" who feels that supermarket customers in the United States need more effective government protection, Representative Sullivan at the same time challenges the allegation that there is something ominous or reprehensible about the role of "politics" in such an issue. "Instead," she says, "let's have more politics in the pantry—and all through the house."

Prescience is not one of the prerogatives that comes with membership in Congress. But, had Leonor Sullivan been able to envision the battling that nearly two decades would bring, would she have run for office? Yes. She would have done as her conscience dictated, as she believes every adult who calls himself a citizen should do. This is just one more reason why she goes on fighting for the consumer, by persuasion when she can, by clout when reasoned rhetoric fails.

Percentage Power

"Gov. Robert B. Crosby did the women of America as well as the women of Nebraska a great honor in appointing Mrs. Eva Bowring to the vacancy created by the death of Sen. Dwight Griswold."

These words from Senator Margaret Chase Smith's syndicated column, "Washington and You," though they appeared in April 1954, varied not at all, except in names and place, from those that appeared in scores of newspapers in 1922 when Rebecca Felton became the first woman named to the Senate—appointed by Georgia's Governor Thomas W. Hardwick. Similarly, even after 32 years, the political motives behind the interim appointment of a female senator remained the same. The passage of time had made only one significant difference: There would be no delay to Eva Bowring's being sworn in.

EVA BOWRING
REPUBLICAN OF NEBRASKA

Nebraska GOP leaders, aware of the precarious numerical balance in the Senate (47 Republicans to 48 Democrats, with Independent Wayne Morse of Oregon voting with the GOP on organizational matters), were so anxious for Governor Crosby's appointee to take the oath of office that they even offered to help "roundup" her affairs.

For Eva Bowring, a handsome, blue-eyed, witty woman of 62, "roundup" meant almost literally that. A widow and the owner of a 10,000-acre Hereford ranch near Merriman in the Sandhills of northwestern Nebraska, she laughingly told friends after a press conference in Lincoln that she was going back to the Bar-99 "to kiss the cattle goodbye," adding, "they are about the only ones interested in kissing me anymore." In a serious vein she told reporters that she considered herself "one of the boys —an extra ranch hand," explaining that she had "never believed in ordering anyone to do something you couldn't do yourself."

That meant arriving at quick buying and selling decisions that could make a difference of thousands of dollars in profits. It also meant riding through blizzards to rescue stray cattle. She had missed the annual Republican Founders Day celebration in Lincoln in February because she was rounding up calves to keep them from freezing on the snow-covered open range.

It was her ability to perform a man's work that elicited admiration for Mrs. Bowring, not only in the Cherry County cattle country but, as she became known on the political scene, throughout the state. Yet she could be thoroughly feminine, as any visitor to her rambling white house furnished with fine antiques could testify. In record and manner, she was a sensible type with a philosophical outlook: "I've not been one who thought the Lord should make life easy; I've just asked Him to make me strong."

Her charm and ready wit had made her a spokeswoman for Republicans within the state and an outstanding delegate to national party conventions. At the time she was chosen to be the first Nebraska woman to sit in the U.S. Congress, she was serving her eighth year as vice-chairman of the State Central Committee.

Politics and range-riding as a life-style were a combination she adopted after her marriage to homesteader Arthur Bowring in 1928. She had always exhibited an ability to juggle jobs. Born Eva Kelly in Nevada, Missouri, in 1892, she was married at 19 to Nebraskan Theodore Forester. After he died in 1924, she supported her three sons by taking over his sales route, driving an automobile over hundreds of miles of unpaved roads to solicit orders for feed and grain.

Marriage to Mr. Bowring had meant that she had to learn how to run the ranch, for he was often away in Lincoln serving in the State Legislature. From the outset, she divided what free time she had between politics and livestock. The first woman county GOP chairman in the state, she was also the first woman chairman of the Nebraska Stockgrowers Association Brand Committee.

Mrs. Bowring, who describes herself as a "forward-looking Republican," initially declined the honor of going to the Senate. Then she reminded herself that she had frequently told meetings of Republican women, "When a job is offered to you, take it. Men can refuse, but women are increasingly important in political life." She was not the only candidate for the position; nor was she the only woman considered (the late Senator Griswold's widow was viewed as a possible interim appointee); but she was the only person to whom the position was offered. Few would have argued with one reason Governor Crosby gave for his decision: "I think Mrs. Bowring's background and familiarity with affairs of government and ability as a thinker in that field [are] the best available, regardless of sex."

In Washington, after telling reporters, "Everybody calls me Eve, and that flatters me," she said she saw nothing unlucky in the fact that she was the 13th woman to join the 83d Congress —the highest number to serve during any one session. "Prepare yourself," she declared; "there will be more and more women."

Among those personally welcoming Senator Bowring—in addition to Margaret Chase Smith of Maine—were William F. Knowland of California, the GOP leader, and Lyndon B. Johnson of Texas, the Democratic leader. (At the time, the former was somewhat better known than the latter.) The press elicited from her the opinion that she expected "lenient" treatment from her colleagues, "since I'm just a grandmother from the cow country and will be here only a short time." She delighted Washington correspondents with such "cow-country" metaphors as "I'm going to have to ride the fence awhile until I find where the gates are." She also evoked chuckles when she said that she had already adjusted to "city ways," sleeping as late as 6 A.M. On the ranch her rising time was 4 A.M., and she usually retired early. She would amend that schedule, she said, to attend some Washington social affairs. "I like people and I expect to go to a few parties, but my main object in being here is not social. I came to be a senator."

How socially conscious (or cautious) some members of Congress can be was apparent the day she arrived on Capitol Hill. Her escort down the aisle to take the oath was, according to custom, the senior senator from the same state, Hugh Butler, 76. As they reached the front of the chamber, Vice President Richard Nixon declared, "Senator Butler has asked me to inform the Senate that no implication should be drawn from the fact that the senior Senator from Nebraska is a widower and the junior Senator is a widow."

On an hourly basis, Eva Bowring may have put in longer days during her six months in Washington than any woman senator ever had before. She was there during the midsummer talka-thon on the atomic energy bill and during the long day-and-night sessions in the closing days before the fall recess. True to her word ("If I'm silent, it'll be unusual for a woman—and especially unusual for Eve Bowring"), she did not observe the unwritten rule of silence followed by most new senators.

Eisenhower Republicans were pleased by her maiden speech. As one said, "When the outlook for passage of Ike's farm pro-gram was dark and most signs indicated that the farm bloc in Congress would have its way [continuation of high rigid sup-ports], she had the courage to stand up and be counted as one who supported the President." It would be an exaggeration to say that her arguments turned the tide, but she was the first senator to deliver a full-length address in defense of flexible price supports for basic farm crops. And coming when it did—in June—from a senator representing a major agricultural state, it carried weight. Late in August the Senate passed flexible price support legislation (after the House had acted), giving the Presi-dent one of his major first-term victories.

That Eva Bowring was one of only two women in the 96-member Senate automatically made her newsworthy. Almost ev-ery move she made was recorded. Asked by the Associated Press what she and "Ike" had talked about during her first visit to the White House, she replied, "Weapons. Shotguns, to be exact." When she emerged with Nebraska Representative Roman Hruska from the office of HEW Secretary Oveta Culp Hobby, the re-porters were waiting. It was duly recorded in the *Lincoln Eve-ning Journal* that the pair had presented Omaha's official bid for the proposed new Federal Social Security Division head-quarters.

"She's doing a fine job for us," said Mrs. Edna Donald, na-tional committeewoman from Nebraska. It is fair to say she was voicing a Republican consensus. The GOP leaders mapping cam-paign strategy for the off-year elections decided she should carry the party message to the farmland of central and eastern Ore-gon. As a member of the Labor and Public Welfare Committee, she was selected to go to Hawaii to review the veterans' educa-tion and training programs implemented under the Servicemen's Readjustment Act.

As her term came to an end, Senator Bowring was tapped by

the executive branch to serve as a member of the Mental Health Advisory Council of the National Institutes of Health. Later she was appointed to the Federal Bureau of Prisons Parole Board.

When Eva Bowring originally accepted her senatorial commission from Governor Crosby, she had remarked that she hoped to be back on her Merriman ranch "helping with the November roundup." She was.

HAZEL H. ABEL
REPUBLICAN OF NEBRASKA

Meanwhile, another footnote was being added to the Senate's statistical record book. For the first time in history, one woman succeeded another as U.S. senator. Hazel Abel of Lincoln had been elected to the officially designated "short term" in the Upper House. (This November-to-January vacancy is created by a state law stipulating that an appointee may serve only "until the next regular election" and that a candidate seeking the 6-year term may not run for the two remaining months of an unexpired term.)

Before the August primary, Nebraskans thought the whole idea a little silly. "After all," one citizen explained, "it looks like such an empty honor—electing somebody to fill a two-month term at a time when the Senate isn't even supposed to meet." Yet 16 Republicans (including Hazel Abel) and three Democrats (including Mabel Gillespie) made a full-scale race of it. Sixty-six-year-old Mrs. Abel, the primary winner, collected 18,-426 more votes than her nearest GOP competitor. During a whirlwind statewide campaign—with much time spent at the wheel of her air-conditioned Cadillac—she got tagged with the nickname "Hurricane Hazel,"and she lived up to it in November, when she defeated former state Democratic Chairman William Meier of Minden with a 60 per cent majority. She carried all but seven of the state's 93 counties.

"While Eve [Bowring] polishes her boots and saddles on the ranch, I'm going to be the receptionist for the 6-year senator [Cart T. Curtis]," Senator Abel jokingly told well-wishers. Her keen sense of humor was well known, but, for this woman of action, much action, her commitments were anything but casual. The major interests to which she was committed were youth and education. Her boundless energy went into everything from the PTA and the Camp Fire Girls to the YWCA and the American Association of University Women.

Mrs. Abel, like Eva Bowring, had supported her children by doing a man's job after she became a widow. Yet she did not have to scuffle up from the bottom of rural life. She stepped into the presidency of the Abel Construction Company after her husband died in 1937, and she relinquished the post only after her four daughters and one son had graduated from college. Fortunately, her own college degree was in mathematics and she had had five years' supervisory experience as a high school principal before her marriage. "These assets compensated somewhat for my lack of knowledge about cement-mixing," she once said.

Also like Eva Bowring, she had ardently supported Eisenhower for the Presidency and been outstanding in the GOP organization. When Mrs. Bowring resigned as vice-chairman of the Republican State Central Committee to go to Washington, it was Hazel Abel who took over the office.

"She has the courage and resourcefulness of her pioneering parents," her minister liked to point out. In the frontier town of Plattsmouth, where she was born in 1888, her mother had been a teacher and her father, a Burlington Railroad employee, was on the school board for many years. Hazel Pearl Hempel had to wait a year between high school graduation and college entrance because the University of Nebraska in 1903 would not admit 15-year-olds. The interval between her engagement to college classmate George P. Abel and marriage was even longer: 10 years.

She never forgot this period when they both worked (her salary as a beginning teacher was $65 a month) to save money to get married. Although noted for her philanthropic generosity later in life, she remained a thrifty person. On one of her campaign trips she saw a sign advertising eggs for 22 cents a dozen. Into the back seat of the Abel car went several cartons of eggs for home consumption.

The day she was sworn in was a historic one: Censure proceedings against Republican Senator Joseph McCarthy of Wisconsin were due to begin. Moreover, Mrs. Bowring returned especially to escort her successor to the Vice President's rostrum for the oath-taking. The entire Abel clan—from all over—was there to see it happen.

On the social circuit the next day, she became aware of how short-lived the dazzle of the national limelight can be in a city teeming with VIPs. She was temporarily removed from the guest line at a British Embassy reception for Queen Mother Elizabeth by a man wearing a white carnation who told her he doubted she was actually a senator. "I had to produce proof," she said. "It could never happen in Nebraska."

What the Senate was asked to do on November 10, 1954, was to display its confidence in the subcommittee that had been assigned the task of investigating McCarthy—on the grounds that he had lied when he had accused various people of treason and subversion while he was cloaked in the immunity from libel granted to legislators when they speak on the floor. One of the members of this subcommittee was Margaret Chase Smith, newly elected to her second term.

Before and during the debate over censure, Hazel Abel declined to discuss how she would vote. "I want to weigh the evidence before making up my mind," she said. So intent was she on hearing "every single minute" of the arguments for and against the motion that she missed not one of the 930,000 words of testimony. On the final day, which began at 10 A.M. and ended at 7:10 P.M., she never left the floor. The first senator to answer the roll call, she cast her vote with the majority (67 to 22) to condemn McCarthy's conduct.

In sixty days in office, she also mailed some three thousand government publications—maps, Agriculture Department home and garden leaflets, and farm yearbooks—to Nebraska schools, libraries, and farm organizations; appointed four Nebraska youths to the new Air Force Academy; attended briefings on defense and foreign aid; lunched twice with Mrs. Eisenhower and once with Vice President Nixon and conferred with President Eisenhower at the White House; and took a trip (as a member of the Interstate and Foreign Commerce Committee) to inspect, at her own expense, U.S. business operations in Germany, Italy, England, France, and Austria.

To give Senator-elect Curtis a seniority advantage over other senators elected November 2, Senator Abel resigned three days ahead of the expiration of her term. "To me it was more than a short term in the Senate," she told a *Newsweek* correspondent. "I wanted Nebraska voters to express their approval of a woman in government. I was sort of a guinea pig."

Hazel Abel went back to being a civic-political dynamo in Nebraska. But it was not the same. Exposure on Capitol Hill led inevitably to her being singled out for national assignments. She was sent as an observer to the NATO countries to study educational facilities for children of American military personnel. President Eisenhower appointed her to the Theodore Roosevelt Centennial Commission, which sparked the 1958 celebrations honoring the Rough Rider. She was chosen the American Mother of 1957 and invited to the Brussels International Exposition to deliver a message to Mothers of the World and to pay an official visit to Queen Juliana in Holland.

Age slowed down but did not stop her activity. At 72 she sought the Republican nomination for governor. She came in second, losing the primary to State Senator John Cooper of Humboldt.

In 1963, the former senator was awarded an honorary LL.D degree by her alma mater for, among other things, "her dedication to the cause of learning as essential to the strength of the state and vital to the dignity of the person." She was grateful, she said, that she had had the opportunity to be a citizen participant in "extending opportunity for the free pursuit of knowledge to the people." At the time of her death in 1966 she was doing exactly that.

In the Best Tradition

"If the gentlemen of the 84th Congress appear a little better shaved and a little better mannered than usual, there'll be a reason: women."

With these words, the International News Service told Americans on November 3, 1954, that 16 women, a record number at the time, had captured congressional seats. With the election of Kathryn Granahan, Democrat of Pennsylvania, to fill the vacancy created by the death of her husband in 1956, the total rose to 17.

Although there was no single overriding issue to bind the off-year races together, the Republicans worked, wheedled, and fought to retain the House and Senate majorities they had won two years earlier. Vice President Richard M. Nixon led the way, swinging a verbal mace with ferocity. His incessant cry was that the Democrats were senseless servants of Communist propaganda because they insisted that Soviet economic progress could pose new and grave challenges to the United States. President Eisenhower, to offset the "pocketbook nerve" reaction to unemployment in industrial centers, emphasized a "peace and prosperity" theme.

For all the high-level energy expended, GOP defeats lay all about. The Democrats, with the help of four women candidates, emerged in control of Congress. Of these female newcomers, three—Edith Green in Oregon, Martha Griffiths in Michigan, and Coya Knutson in Minnesota—ousted Republican incumbents. Iris Blitch hailed from the one-party state of Georgia.

The most gratifying aspect of the 1954 elections, from the feminist point of view, was that *all* the women incumbents— seven Republicans and five Democrats—were re-elected. In length of service, Edith Nourse Rogers, Massachusetts Republican, topped the list, winning her 16th term. Republican Margaret Chase Smith won her second Senate term in Maine's September runoff.

In 1956, another vintage year for incumbents, women voters turned out in unprecedented numbers. Only one new feminine voice, however, was addel to the 85th Congress (1957–59), that of Florence P. Dwyer of New Jersey, a Republican. Missing were Vera Buchanan, Pennsylvania Democrat who died in office, and Ruth Thompson, Michigan Republican who failed in her bid for renomination.

IRIS F. BLITCH
DEMOCRAT OF GEORGIA

The biggest hurdle for Iris Blitch in her quest for a House seat from southeastern Georgia was not the 1954 general election but the Democratic primary a month earlier. The 42-year-old state legislator startled party professionals by defeating W. M. Wheeler, then in his fourth term as 8th District representative. In a classic and successful grassroots campaign, she made Wheeler's "lack of party loyalty" and "absenteeism" the main issues. Although her victory margin was narrow (1,369 votes), she carried 13 of the district's 20 counties.

The political philosophy this dark-haired, drawling beauty brought to Washington was the legacy of a rural Southland. Born Iris Faircloth on a farm in Normantown, halfway between Macon and Savannah, she was orphaned at the age of nine and reared by two married sisters in the hinterlands of Frederick County, Maryland.

Her interest in politics was shared by Erwin Blitch, a Homerville, Georgia, druggist and farmer whom she met at the University of Georgia. They were married in 1929 and immediately confronted by the crisis of the Depression. "The farm was a lifesaver," she recalls. "And we worked hard. I've done everything there is to do in a drugstore." The national calamity aroused her concern. "Why has the government failed the people?" she wondered. In her spare time (there were two small children to care for), she studied the political records of candidates running for office and later campaigned for those she felt "best qualified."

In 1940, when she could not decide whom to support for the State Legislature, Erwin asked, "Why don't *you* run?" She did, but lost. Only 28, she launched a personal campaign to recruit a following. Active participation in civic and political groups helped her along, as did her high school debating experience. "At the drop of a hat," she recalls, "I spoke in favor of attracting new industry to the coastal plain and inland region from which both Negroes and whites were fleeing in large numbers."

When Iris Blitch finally reached the Statehouse in 1946, women were such a novelty that she was named "Queen of the Legislature." More satisfying to her was the fact that the bill she proposed to give women the right to serve on juries became law. Of the three terms she served in the legislature, two were spent in the Senate and one in the House.

Outspoken in defending interests in which both she and Georgia had a stake, Congresswoman Blitch generally voted with the South, except on economic issues that cut across sectional lines. She not only signed the 1956 Southern Manifesto against the Supreme Court's ruling on school desegregation but also opposed the so-called voting-rights amendment on the House floor as vehemently as any of her male colleagues. Calling the measure "iniquitous, infamous," and a "cancer of indecencies," she hurled "shame" at Congress, the press, social institutions, and the President for "destroying freedom in the United States of America."

A member of the Public Works Committee, she had equally pronounced persuasions about environmental protection in her district. Her one-woman crusade to save the incomparable Okefenokee Swamp "from disastrous drought and fire" resulted in appropriations for safeguards such as low-sill dams on the connecting waterways. She also successfully sponsored an amendment to the Watershed Protection and Flood Prevention Act that provided small property owners with federal financial assistance for water-conservation projects.

A worsening arthritic condition forced Congresswoman Blitch to retire from public life in 1963, at the end of her fourth term. Widowed four years later, she moved to one of the pristine Golden Isles off the Georgia coast. Still under a physician's care, she is able to travel part of each year, and she has attended several meetings of Former Members of Congress, Inc., in Washington, D.C.

Asked if Georgia governor James Earl Carter, Jr., spoke for her at his 1971 inaugural when he said that "the time for racial discrimination is over," she answered affirmatively. The classic Southern rhetoric of "never" is dead, she believes, because the population drain has been reversed. "The South," says Iris Blitch, "can grow while there is still time to protect the land from careless exploitation."

EDITH GREEN
DEMOCRAT OF OREGON

If there were such a title as Mrs. Education, it would go without serious opposition to Oregon representative Edith Green. She is practically the only member of Congress who has made a career out of worrying over the state of the nation's schools, particularly its colleges and universities. When she first ran for the House in 1954, one of her tenets was: "Education should be the Number One business in the country." Nothing has happened since to change her mind.

As a result of the orderly progression of the congressional seniority system, she became the second-ranking member of the Education and Labor Committee and the chairman of its Special Subcommittee on Education. Whichever hat she wore at a given time, her role in shaping a wide range of domestic social legislation has been a stellar one.

Under four Presidents she has presided over the conception and delivery of laws that have profoundly influenced federal aid to education. Her imprint initially appeared on the precedent-shattering National Defense Education Act of 1958. President Lyndon B. Johnson paid her a singular compliment when he called the Higher Education Facilities Act, which she authored in 1963, the "greatest step forward in the field since passage of the Land-Grant Act of 1862." Because of the "Green Amendments" (an accepted phrase in House jargon) to the 1965 Vocational Rehabilitation Act, urban youth are eligible for training opportunities once restricted to rural youngsters. Out of her continual pursuit of progress came the Higher Education Act of 1965 (amended in 1968), widely heralded as a breakthrough in the previously largely neglected area of student financial assistance.

Practically the only major legislative defeat she has suffered occurred in the wake of the riots that swept U.S. campuses during the late 1960s. Fearing that the full House might over-react to student violence and cut off all federal aid to colleges and universities, she drafted a moderate bill that offered higher-education officials a way to curb collegiate unrest. It would have denied government financial support only if administrators failed to file with the U.S. Office of Education a student code of conduct and a plan for handling disorders.

Committee liberals (Edith Green calls them "ultraliber-als"), arguing that her measure was "repressive and punitive," marshaled forces to defeat it. "What right does Congress have to require colleges to submit a behavior code and an anti-riot plan?" one adversary asked. "It is a foot in the door to-ward complete federal control of higher education," said an-other. By one vote—18 to 17—the liberals prevailed.

It was not the first time she had lost in committee, but in previous instances she had gone on to win on the floor. Her skill as a floor manager (the lawmaker who steers a bill through House debate to the critical roll-call stage) is legendary. When members of the Education and Labor Committee, reputedly the most liberal and contentious in the House, have turned a deaf ear to her carefully wrought legislative handiwork, she has opted to proceed by securing support from a so-called floating coalition.

As familiar—and acceptable—as the coalition has become in the House of Representatives, it is also a device that sets the stage for political collisions at both their rawest and most so-phisticated levels. The time when there was only one coalition ended with Republican Charles Halleck of Indiana and Demo-crat Howard W. ("Judge") Smith of Virginia. So many exist today that there are even coalitions of coalitions.

"It may be that the House is starting to prove to be what its founding fathers meant it to be—a legislative body that represents the American body politic as it may be disposed to declare itself every two years," *Los Angeles Times* Washing-ton correspondent Thomas J. Foley wrote in 1971. "The inde-pendence of the individual member from party control, or even group control, makes for a more democratic society."

This appraisal is one with which Edith Green heartily con-curs. By taking such a stand, however, she has not only elic-ited public denunciation from her liberal colleagues but Ad-ministration animosity as well. In 1967, when she lined up a majority of Republicans and Dixiecrats to pass an education funding plan giving the states control over certain federal school-aid grants, a thunderclap of outrage reverberated from both ends of Pennsylvania Avenue. Representative Charles S. Joelson, a liberal Democrat from New Jersey, dismissed her as the "drum majorette for the coalition bandwagon." A key White House staffer said, "If she doesn't get her own way, she takes out her hatchet and chops down trees just as they start to bloom."

Unwittingly, an angry aide in the Department of Health, Education, and Welfare came closest to the truth: "She is opposed to educational innovation that is stimulated from Washington." Her own brief explanation, quoted in *Newsweek,* was that she believes "the people in my state . . . know a great deal more about Oregon's problems than the Office of Education in Washington."

Edith Green has been espousing government decentralization ("Government has gotten so big, it's going to fall under its own weight")—and reorganization to achieve it—as long as she has been in Congress. But, until Graham Barden of North Carolina retired in 1960 as chairman of the Education and Labor Committee, she was powerless to do or say very much about it. Southern chivalry notwithstanding, Barden's iron-fisted rule over his committee extended to any woman serving on it.

Under the chairmanship of Adam Clayton Powell, Jr., speech was freer, but committee action was clouded by the declining political fortunes of that Harlem congressman. When Edith Green speaks of Powell's obsession with quantity of legislation over quality ("He rated personal success by how much of his office wall space could be covered with framed bills"), she does not do so to belittle the man. Professionally, they got along well together. Rather, she is lamenting a fact of legislative life that, unfortunately, she could not rectify.

The symbiotic relationship between Edith Green and Carl D. Perkins, chairman of the Education and Labor Committee since Powell's exclusion from the 90th Congress early in 1967, has been a wry one. Perkins is a Kentucky lawyer whose qualifications for coping with educational nuances and complexities rest primarily on his pre-Washington career as a legal representative for state highway interests. Consequently, the fashioning of laws concerning education is left to subalterns. One of the most expert, by virtue of her long association in the field, first as a teacher and then as a legislative lobbyist for Oregon education groups, is Edith Green.

While privately recognizing Representative Green's expertise, Perkins is loath to admit it publicly. Some say he feels threatened by the encyclopedic educational lore she has amassed. Others suggest that a masculine backlash is involved. "Like many men at the top of the prestige ladder, he is not going to give an inch to any movement founded on the principle that women need not be secondary to any man—even if that man happens to be in Congress," says a realistic observer of the scene.

Where does all of this leave a lady who came to Congress singularly dedicated to the proposition that "the multitudinous government education programs must function better"? As head of a subcommittee, Edith Green, while owing allegiance to the chairman, has considerable power of her own and considerable authority over those under her. She also has had backing for most of what she wanted to accomplish from a wide sector of the academic community (institutions from coast to coast have awarded her honorary degrees) and encouragement from such constituents as Gemma Adams of Portland, who wrote to praise Representative Green's censuring of "radicals who destroy campus property" and to say, "Thank you for giving so much of yourself for all of us." Representative Green's ultimate legislative weapon, of course, is the coalition.

Edith Green feels the country "has turned a corner." As reasons, she cites "cutbacks in the space program and winding down the war in Vietnam." (In 1965, she was one of six in the House—and the only woman—to vote against President Johnson's request for funds to escalate that war.) But she continues to emphasize the point on which she has been most vocal: the need "to decentralize Big Government." The inventory survey she initiated in 1962 provided the first information ever available on how much the federal bureaucracy spends on education, and for what. The rabbit-like growth of agency programs (125 in the U.S. Office of Education alone) and the dispersion of control over these programs through many congressional committees convinced her that new mechanisms of coordination must be instituted to eliminate wasteful duplication.

Her proposals, endorsed at the time by the prestigious American Association for the Advancement of Science, among others, included the creation within the executive branch of an Interagency Council on Education to coordinate the educational activities of all federal agencies and departments and the establishment of a nonlegislative Joint Congressional Committee on Education to provide Congress with an overall picture of federal educational activities.

Despite a rebuff by Perkins to her 1970 suggestion that a temporary study committee be established to take a broad look at the impact of federal programs "on the quality of education," she feels her proposal is still relevant. "There is bound to be a crisis in confidence when education programs are administered by 19 federal agencies scattered through eight Cabinet-level departments, and 14 House committees handle one or more school programs," she points out.

Liberals resent her proposition that "the Education and Labor Committee cannot sit as a National Board of Education claiming to have expertise on the problems and priorities in Beloit, Wisconsin and Portland, Oregon; in Tampa, Florida and Anchorage, Alaska; in Portland, Maine and Honolulu; in the rural areas of South Dakota and the ghetto districts of Chicago or New York or Watts."

But, to Edith Green, if the continuing proliferation of education programs means defying the committee leadership and seeking votes among liberal Republicans and conservative Democrats in the House, so be it. In her view bipartisan support for education is as worthy as "shifting more responsibility to the states."

Representative Green's "style" almost personifies her reform measures—articulate, reasonable, lucid. A good-natured woman of below-average height, with brown eyes and gray hair combed in precise waves, she tends to remind Green-watchers of their "civics teacher back home." Hers is neither a face nor a figure that would stand out in a crowd. But, on the House floor or in the committee hearing room, her position is imposing.

The inquisitorial aura she imparts to the hearings over which she presides is deliberate. The representative whose perennial campaign slogan is "You Get Straight Answers from Edith Green" expects her questions to be answered just as frankly. A U.S. Commissioner of Education is as likely to run into her verbal buzzsaw as a spokesman for the U.S. Chamber of Commerce.

Strong-willed, high-principled, and above all independent, Edith Green has always held her own in the struggle for accomplishment that so conspicuously grips the men in her official life. One of the reasons is that she is a tiger for work. The daughter of schoolteachers and for 14 years a schoolteacher herself, she knows well the worth of formal education. Had Edith Green, born Edith Starrett in South Dakota and taken to Oregon in 1916 at the age of six, not been dissuaded from the course of study she wanted to pursue in college, she would today be an electrical engineer. "Relatives told me not to be 'silly,' " she says. " 'Who,' they asked, 'would hire a woman engineer?' So I went to the University of Oregon and majored in English and education." Postgraduate courses in speech at Stanford led, after teaching, to a radio commentator's position in Portland. "Edith Green gives rousing speeches," says Yvonne Franklin, Washington correspondent for the Portland *Oregonian.* "They are the kind that keep members glued to their leather chairs in the House chamber." It is a compliment paid to few members of Congress, male or female.

Mrs. Green got into politics in 1952 when friends urged her to run for Oregon secretary of state. "Their persuasive power was mighty," she recalls. "The job didn't interest me. I wanted to oust an antieducation state senator." Although she lost in 1952, the Green name got statewide exposure, and two years later she won the 3d Congressional District seat by defeating the well-known TV newscaster (later governor) Tom McCall. It was her only close race. From a plurality of only 9,608 in 1954, her majority zoomed to 65,011 two years later. In the general elections since, she has never captured less than 63 per cent of the vote. In the 1970 May primary, with a college professor as her opponent, two former college professors (Senator Eugene McCarthy of Minnesota and former Senator Wayne Morse of Oregon) heading the speakers list, and a doorbell-ringing contingent of collegians, Edith Green clung steadfastly to her own brand of liberalism, which eschews militancy, and the voters responded by giving her a 70 per cent majority.

Her political power has been recognized as an asset by Democratic Presidential candidates since 1956, when Adlai E. Stevenson asked her to second his nomination at the national convention. She managed John F. Kennedy's victorious Oregon preferential primary campaign—against Morse and Minnesota Senator Hubert H. Humphrey—in 1960. While her efforts to garner Oregon Democratic support for Senator Robert F. Kennedy in 1968 and Senator Henry M. ("Scoop") Jackson from the neighboring state of Washington in 1972 were not successful, it nonetheless says something about her reputation for clout that these Presidential aspirants personally solicited her aid.

Had Edith Green not turned down three opportunities to run for the Senate, her prominence in politics might loom even larger than it does. Ironically, fellow Oregonian Morse influenced her decisions. As long as he was chairman of the Senate Subcommittee on Education, it was a foregone conclusion that, even if she was elected, she would not be appointed to that committee. There were other determinants, of course. The high cost of campaigning was a factor in 1966. "I will not get into anything where it will not be possible for me to be a free agent," she says, referring to the political fact of life that there would be "strings attached" to some of the $250,000 she would have needed for a Senate race. In refusing to be a candidate in 1972, she said that Democrats should nominate someone who could serve 24 or 30 years. At 62, she did not qualify.

There are women in the House with as much seniority as Edith Green, but none with more power. While demanding respect on the basis of ability, not sex, she has, characteristically, employed her congressional prestige to end discrimination against women. She cites as one of her three most important accomplishments the Equal Pay Act of 1963. "To get it passed took eight years," she says, "—eight years to persuade Congress that a woman doing identical work with a man ought to be paid the same salary!"

The statement she made to open the 1970 hearings on her omnibus higher-education bill left little doubt about her determination to force a showdown with Academe: "Many of us would like to think of educational institutions as being far from the madding crowd, where fair play is the rule of the game and everyone, including women, gets a fair roll of the dice. Let us not deceive ourselves—our educational institutions have proven to be no bastions of democracy." That colleges and universities are more democratic today is the result of a key provision in the 1972 Omnibus Higher Education Act. Institutions accepting federal financial support are prohibited from discriminating on the basis of sex.

Edith Green practices what she preaches. Her office staff is mostly female. In the congresswoman's Rayburn Building office there is an atmosphere of enthusiasm and camaraderie, devoid of backbiting, jockeying for position, and deference to the boss. To some degree, this is a tribute to Edith Green's gift for inspiring loyalty. But perhaps in a more important sense it is the product of her zest for meaningful legislative causes.

When Edith Green took the oath of office for the first time, in 1955, onlookers included her husband, Arthur, and her sons, James and Richard. "Few husbands will go as far as Mr. Green," a *Harper's* writer reported at the time. "He is moving his electrical heating business to Washington. Perhaps most callings are less mobile than electrical heating. But since the election of a married woman to national office usually involves uprooting or forfeiting a valued male, there is a chronic shortage of good female candidates."

Now divorced (but not because of her political career), Edith Green disagrees with *Harper's* assessment of the dearth of female office seekers. Women, she feels, are the victims of a form of psychological warfare, systematically waged by men who consider the political world their exclusive domain. "When I entered politics," she says, "a thousand and one times in a condescending tone, I heard: 'How did it ever happen that you [meaning a woman] are running for office?'"

As fervent as her hope is that "Congress will be increasingly preoccupied with legislation necessary to ensure equal rights, equal opportunities, and equal status for human beings of both sexes," she is also anxious for Congress to concern itself with some simple reforms that could enable it to represent more effectively the will of the electorate. She suggests, for example, that the House Education and Labor Committee be divided into two committees—one dealing with education; the other, with labor. She is not alone in favoring such a split. John Dellenback, her GOP colleague from Oregon's 4th District, also advocates it. Moreover, her proposal has received strong editorial endorsement: "There are few direct ties between education and labor legislation," the *Oregon Journal* has noted. "Therefore, it is an odd alignment at best. . . . Congressmen whose primary interest is education may not have similar expertise in labor, or vice versa. . . . If the House cannot make so minor, yet helpful, a change on the division of the Education and Labor Committee, there is little hope for the broader reform of the country's lawmaking branch of government."

This is a judgment that Edith Green does not really expect Chairman Perkins to share. Consequently, the collision of their wills undoubtedly will continue to play a significant role in coming battles over federal aid to education.

MARTHA W. GRIFFITHS
DEMOCRAT OF MICHIGAN

"My grandmother wanted to live long enough to vote for a woman president. I'll be satisfied if I live to see a woman go before the Supreme Court and hear the justices acknowledge, 'Gentlemen, she's human. She deserves the protection of our laws.'"

Congresswoman Martha Griffiths, a former municipal judge,

has lived to witness the making of constitutional history. The high court, for the first time in its 182-year existence, unanimously held in 1971 that a law was unconstitutional because of discrimination based on sex. Chief Justice Warren E. Burger, who spoke for the court as it struck down an Idaho law giving men preference over women in administering estates, found the preference for males "arbitrary" and in violation of the equal-protection clause of the 14th Amendment.

As delighted as Martha Griffiths is that the nine-man court has finally ruled "in favor of justice, not prejudice," she does not view the decision as a strong precedent. "The actual language is narrow," she points out. "It avoids enunciating a broad general principle." Because the court did not say that classifications by sex are inherently suspect, as are classifications based on race, she believes, as do other legal experts, that it could uphold such classifications whenever some kind of reasonable case can be made for them.

More significant, in Martha Griffiths's analysis, "the court's opinion is not a substitute" for the Equal Rights Amendment (ERA), which guarantees that "equality of rights under the law shall not be denied or abridged by the United States or by any State on account of sex." As the sponsor of this legislation and the one who shepherded it through the House—not once but twice—she speaks with authority.

Like the Woman Suffrage Amendment, which languished in congressional committees for more than 40 years before winning approval, the ERA, its text unchanged since 1943, had been introduced into every Congress for nearly half a century before being passed and sent to the states for ratification in 1972. "It is," said House Minority Leader Gerald Ford (also from Michigan), "a monument to Martha."

How was Martha Griffiths able to effect a turnaround in Congress after so many others had failed, including Katharine St. George (Republican of New York), a former colleague noted not only for strong leadership but for political shrewdness as well?

In Martha Griffiths's campaign arsenal to help her collect the requisite number of signatures for a discharge petition to remove the measure from the Judiciary Committee, her most effective weapons appear to have been a handful of political IOWs and a good pair of track shoes. "I didn't let anyone forget this one," she says. "I chased fellow congressmen ruthlessly. I'd even listen to roll call for the names of any who hadn't signed. Having spotted the face, I'd promptly corner him for his autograph. Louisiana's Hale Boggs, Democratic whip, was opposed to the amendment. But he promised to sign as Number 200, convinced that I would never make it. You may be sure than when I had Number 199 signed up, I rushed to his office, and Hale Boggs became Number 200." Although she set no speed record for collecting signatures, the necessary 218 were affixed to the petition within 40 days.

Timing was also a persuasive factor. The year 1970 was marked by the 50th anniversay of woman suffrage; it was also an election year. "Many a congressman might have voted differently did he not face an immediate accounting at the polls," editorialized the *Christian Science Monitor*. The swiftness with which the Women's Liberation Movement had captured public attention was certainly an asset, for some politicians were forced to re-evaluate their men-only philosophy.

Finally, Martha Griffiths's nine terms in the House have to be counted as a plus. As the *Monitor's* Marion Bell Wilhelm observed, "She had a working friendship with key committee chairman and the respect of those who, however reluctantly, admire the ability of a woman to compete in a man's world."

The only setback for Representative Griffiths occurred in the closing days of the 91st Congress. Whereas the House had passed the measure, by a resounding 350-to-15, the Senate, in one of those crude contradictions of politics, permitted it to die with adjournment. Starting anew the following year, she again secured passage in the House (354 to 23), then girded to do battle with recalcitrant senators. "Anyone not present and voting for my bill in the Senate," she warned early in 1972, "will be defeated." The tally late on the afternoon of March 22 was 84 to 8.

Having studied in microscopic detail the large and emotionally complex problem of women's rights, the Michigan congresswoman concludes that it originated with the men who wrote the Constitution. On a coast-to-coast telecast, "Our Rights and Our Freedoms," she was asked by panelist Dr. Paul M. Stevens, director of the Southern Baptist Radio and Television Commission, if "the framers of the Constitution intended and therefore wrote a document which would not allow women to be equals in this country?"

"I think they and the Senate judiciary never even thought about women . . . never even considered them," she replied. "When they said 'men' they really meant men. We've added women since."

Now that eligible women voters outnumber men by several

million, Martha Griffiths predicts that it soon will be impossible to elect any man President who does not take a firm stand on equity for women. "There might be one more election with a candidate who vacillates," she concedes, "but that will be the last. There's not going to be another President of the United States who considers women inferior people."

Her 18-year record in the House is studded with antidiscrimination bills she has sponsored or votes she has won for laws more equitable to both sexes. She is largely responsible for the fact that divorced women who have been married 20 years or more are eligible to draw on their former husbands' Social Security, that motherless children are eligible for Social Security benefits which widowers were unable to collect from their working wives' accounts, and that widowers are eligible for their wives' civil service pensions. It was at her insistence that the word "sex" was added to "race, color, religion, and national origin" in the Civil Rights Act of 1964. "Had 'sex' not been included," she says, "white women discriminated against by an employer could not have invoked the law." To substantiate this claim, she confronted her colleagues with a telling argument:

> It would be incredible to me that white men would be willing to place white women at such a disadvantage except that white men have done this before. When the 15th Amendment had become the law of the land, a brave woman named Virginia Minor, a native-born, free, white citizen of the United States and the State of Missouri, read the amendment and on the 15th of October 1872 appeared to register to vote. The registrar replied that the State of Missouri had a statute which said that only males could register to vote. Her reply, of course, was, "Why, the 14th Amendment says 'No State shall make or enforce any law which shall abridge the privileges or immunities of citizens of the United States.'"
>
> In October 1874 in 13 pages of tortured legal reasoning, the Supreme Court of the United States explained how the Missouri law prevailed, and finally said: "The amendment did not add to the privileges and immunities of a citizen. It simply furnished an additional guaranty for the protection of such as he already had."
>
> So, your great grandfathers were willing as prisoners of their own prejudice to permit ex-slaves to vote, but not their own white wives.

Because Martha Griffiths earned her law degree at the University of Michigan and has for so long been associated with the 17th Congressional District (mainly northwest Detroit), she is often thought of as an original product of the so-called Automobile Capital of the World. Actually, she was born (in 1912) and reared in Pierce City, a small town in the Missouri Ozarks notable in the childhood memory of Martha Wright for the "awful" fact it had no public library.

"School was the light of my life," she recalls. Before she enrolled at the University of Missouri to study English and economics, this postman's daughter and descendant of French and English pioneer women (some of whom held a job outside the home) had read every book on every shelf.

Money for college expenses was not readily available during the Depression. Miss Wright managed by obtaining a loan ("I paid back every cent") and by taking time out between her sophomore and junior years to teach in Pierce City. While attracting attention as a member of the university debating team, the popular brunette also attracted the attention of a fellow student, Hicks W. Griffiths of Schenectady, New York. Married in 1933, they burned the midnight oil together at law school in Ann Arbor and were admitted to the Michigan bar in 1941.

Like her romance with Hicks Griffiths, Martha's romance with politics did not begin on a love-at-first-sight basis. The thought of living in the nation's capital was depressing. "I remembered the frustrating four years during World War II when, as a negotiator of federal contracts for the Detroit Ordnance District, I had to cope with the red tape in the Pentagon," she says. "But Hicks convinced me I should run for Congress."

She had qualifications germane to the job: two terms in the State Legislature, where she helped codify public utility laws, served on the judiciary and conservation committees, and was acclaimed by the Capitol Press Corps as one of Michigan's 10 best legislators.

In 1952, however, the Democrats were powerless to stop the Eisenhower bandwagon, and she lost to GOP incumbent Charles G. Oakman by 10,597 votes. "But I won something, too," she says. "I talked to approximately 40,000 prospective voters, many of whom were lured to my house-trailer campaign headquarters by their children, curious to see what it was like inside." In 1954, with Hicks as her manager, she collected enough votes from these constituents and from others she met along the campaign trail to unseat Oakman. Despite redistricting, there have been no close elections since. Her plurality in 1970 was 80 per cent.

Day by day, working in the nation's capital is no less frustrating than it was during the 1940s, but Martha Griffiths has come to terms with it. "The reason I can do what I do," she says, "is because of Hicks' wonderful attitude and support." The couple spends almost every weekend together. When the pressure of business prevents her from flying to Detroit, he takes a plane to Washington. "If there was ever any question that my career was interfering with my husband's happiness and I had to make a choice, I definitely would give up my career."

Disciplined legal craftsman that she is, her legislative skill has worked in Congress because she has worked at being a good legislator. Recognition has come swiftly. Following two terms as a member of the committees on Banking and Currency and Government Operations, she was named to the Joint (House and Senate) Economic Committee, and a year later Wilbur Mills suggested she could become the first woman in history to "invade" the most prestigious committee of all, Ways, and Means, which he has chaired since 1957.

A woman on this 25-member committee charged with drafting legislation that provides the means for maintaining the Republic has a salutary effect, she believes. "A feminine voice removes a proverbial blind spot in the thinking of male lawmakers," she says. "Men think of women as wives or widows, but never as workers." That she is listened to is reflected in the legislative rhetoric which has emerged. "Surviving spouse" is gradually being substituted for "widow."

Whether dealing with fiscal policy, Medicare, tariffs, taxes, or welfare reform—all within the purview of Ways and Means— the Michigan representative is in strategic position to exert leadership and influence laws affecting women. Among the issues still on her agenda is sex discrimination in consumer credit. As she puts it, "Banks, savings and loan associations, credit-card companies, finance companies, insurance companies, retail stores, and even the federal government discriminate against women in extending credit."

Martha Griffiths is also still working for the Equal Rights Amendment, which, when enacted, will confirm her hopeful prediction that "the future policy of this country will be to judge every human being, black or white, or whatever color, or man or woman, as an individual and not as a class." She has visited more than a dozen states to urge support by the legislatures and plans to visit more. Aside from scattered antifeminist groups and some male legislators, certain labor unions (including the AFL-CIO) have been the most adamant opponents of the ERA. She has no patience with their continuing criticism. "Out of fear, hostility, and who knows what else, there are those who simply do not want to write women into the Constitution as persons, guaranteeing them the equal protection of the law," she says. "As for labor opposition, I think the leaders simply painted themselves into a corner 50 years ago and don't understand the paint is dry."

COYA KNUTSON
DEMOCRAT OF MINNESOTA

"Mark her well," a clairvoyant said of Minnesota Democratic congressional candidate Coya Knutson in 1954. "She is a woman on the eve of celebrity."

When celebrity came, Mrs. Knutson had a long day of it: a stormy dawn of campaign controversy, a high blaze of legislative success, a waning afternoon of trial by the threat of blackmail. Four years later dusk fell as she was foiled in her bid for re-election, the victim of a malicious conspiracy to which her allegedly alcoholic husband, Andrew, was a party.

This defeat marked the end of a decade of lawmaking for the 46-year-old, blue-eyed blonde from Oklee (population 499) in the Red River Valley—10 years during which she had been the standard-bearer of a movement to save family farms, first as a member of the State Legislature then of the U.S. Congress.

Now living in Bemidji where her adopted son, Terry, owns a travel agency, Mrs. Knutson says she is not bitter about the highly publicized "Coya come home" letter that terminated her promising Capitol Hill career. "God moves in mysterious ways," she says. "My solid Lutheran upbringing enabled me to maintain at least a semblance of courage during the trying ordeal."

When Coya Knutson won a House seat in a stunning upset over the six-term incumbent Harold C. Hagen in 1954, the husband she left behind to manage the five-room family hotel on the main street of Oklee was already addicted to alcohol. But prior to the announcement that she would seek a third term, he confined his drunken verbal abuse to the four walls of the couple's living quarters in Minnesota. Then, in a fit of anger, he wrote a letter picturing himself as a lonely, neglected castoff. "Our home life has deteriorated to the extent that it is practically nonexistent," he declared. Soon afterward he signed a press release accusing Coya of improprieties with handsome, young (30) Bill Kjeldahl, her administrative assistant, and threatened him with a $200,000 alienation of affections suit.

A letter of apology that Knutson said he wrote himself eventually made its way into Drew Pearson's syndicated column, but not before the newspapers had headlined "Andy's" grievances and 9th District voters had had the last word. "A woman shouldn't be running around," Mrs. Carl Ramstad gave as her reason for rejecting Coya at the polls. Another Oklee resident who voted against her said, "Woman's place is in the home, and her boy probably needed her; a teenager needs his mother most at that age."

The only Democratic incumbent in the country to be unseated by a Republican in 1958, Coya kept her silence until she appeared before the special House elections subcommittee to charge that she had been unfairly victimized by a cabal that exploited her domestic situation. The star witness, Andrew, testified that friends persuaded him to write the letter. Later he admitted that some of these "friends" were Coya's rivals in the Democratic primary. The press release, according to testimony, had been drafted by Maurice O. Nelson, campaign manager for the GOP winner, Odin Langen.

"This is very weird," Subcommittee Chairman Clifford Davis of Tennessee said before announcing that the investigating body had agreed unanimously that "the exploitation of the family life of Mrs. Knutson was a contributing cause to her defeat." But the subcommittee found "no direct evidence of a plot" and ruled that corrective action "must be left to the good taste of the electorate."

If there was a silver lining to the bizarre episode, the former congresswoman now believes that its exposure may have made some contributions to "clean politics and free elections." The incident also seems to have had a beneficial effect. In the years since the Knutsons' marriage was dissolved, other congresswomen have obtained divorces; yet their domestic troubles, unlike Coya's, have not become grist for the front pages. What columnist Doris Fleeson wrote at the time about the "political double standard" appears to have had a lasting impact:

> Many in Washington, not all of them women . . . feel that she [Coya Knutson] was marked down as 'fair game' simply because she was a woman and roughly treated in a manner that the men in her business are not. . . . There are many better stories here than *l'affaire* Knutson and they are about much more prominent people, but it is not considered cricket to use them as a political weapon.
>
> The lesson is that, as a practical matter, women are held to a far higher standard of accountability in politics than men are. Women clearly cannot count on the club spirit for protection.

Almost lost in the debris of slander and libel preceding Mrs. Knutson's 1958 defeat was her exemplary congressional record.

Near the top of the list of her accomplishments, certainly from the standpoint of the farmers who sent her to Washington, was her appointment to the Agriculture Committee, a first for a woman. When Chairman Harold Cooley of North Carolina protested to Speaker Sam Rayburn that he "didn't want a woman on his committee," Rayburn said: "She did the impossible of getting elected, and she's going to get her pick of committees." In time, Mrs. Knutson recalls, she and Cooley became "the best of friends."

Her strident criticism of GOP Agriculture Secretary Ezra Taft Benson's "big business farm policies," which filled pages in the *Congressional Record,* failed to secure the action she wanted "to rescue farmers from the mire into which they have been cast." It did, however, force subcommittee hearings on the family farm that produced grassroots testimony against "the heartless, unrealistic and expedient farm practices of the Eisenhower Administration." Comparing the 1950s with the present, she says: "We laid the groundwork for constructive legislation, yet even as the exodus from the plains has brought rural life to the edge of extinction, Congress continues to ignore the tragic plight of the small farmer."

Two legislative landmarks are credited to the Minnesota congresswoman. Title II of the National Defense Education Act of 1958 was her bill "to create a federal student loan fund." Years as a high school teacher (following graduation from Concordia College) in small towns in her native North Dakota and in northwest Minnesota motivated her, she says, "to find a way for poor country kids to go to college." She still gets letters from grateful graduates who write, "I couldn't have made it without the loan."

She also authored the bill which provided more than $1 million for cystic fibrosis research. A grant to the University of Minnesota Medical Research Department resulted in the perfection of a serum to counteract the disease.

Political defeat in 1958 did not deter this friendly, optimistic descendant of Norwegian immigrants, who had been born Cornelia Gjesdal, from trying again. "I ran in 1960 knowing that I couldn't possibly win," she says, "but as a candidate I had a platform from which to campaign for John Kennedy. And when all the ballots were counted, the 9th District was *the* one to put him over the top in Minnesota."

An appreciative President Kennedy appointed Coya Knutson to a congressional liaison post with the Office of Civilian Defense. "The job was a godsend," she remembers. "Defeat had left me $10,000 in debt."

KATHRYN E. GRANAHAN
DEMOCRAT OF PENNSYLVANIA

What amazed (and amused) Washington newsmen about the first congresswoman from Philadelphia, Kathryn Granahan, was not her obsession to have Good Friday declared a national holiday or her self-admission that she was a "mad hatter." The astonishing fact about Mrs. Granahan—to male reporters, at least —was that she held the title Ward Leader.

"Down the years the designation 'ward leader' has come to possess all the dignity and majesty of 'ward heeler,'" George Dixon wrote in the *Washington Post*. "There is widespread disposition to regard them as synonymous, to be used interchangeably. The very term 'ward leader' is more than likely to conjure up a picture of a fat, unsavory character talking around the side of a cigar."

Because of this traditional conception, Columnist Dixon did what he called a "double-gape" on being introduced to Representative Granahan and learning that she was the Democratic leader of the 52d Ward in West Philadelphia. Noting that she was "gracious, tastefully dressed and college educated," he asked if she represented a silk-stocking ward. "The opposite," she said. "It is poor and heavily integrated."

The freshman congresswoman also told George Dixon that she felt she had a sound reason for "doubling in brassy politics." Her late husband, William T. Granahan, held the same two posts when he died in May 1956. She was determined to "carry on." There would be some changes, however. She hoped to make the designation "ward leader" sound as respectable as "gentlewoman." Already she had made some headway she said: "The district committeemen no longer expect me to have a barrel of beer on tap at the ward meetings."

Mrs. Granahan's life-style was shaped by the provincial Catholicism of Easton, Pennsylvania, where she was born Kathryn Elizabeth O'Hay (circa 1900), and Mount St. Joseph College in well-to-do Chestnut Hill. William Granahan spotted her while she was supervisor of public assistance in the State Auditor General's Department. He was chief disbursing officer of the State Treasury. They were married in 1943 and two years later moved to the nation's capital.

In terms of political philosophy, Mrs. Granahan was a comrade, in purpose and temper, of the New Deal and Fair Deal. The bills she introduced were weighted on the side of civil rights, labor, and public works. She became identified with a number of reform measures dealing with immigration, health, Social Security, and housing. To that extent, she differed not at all from liberal Democratic colleagues who, like herself, found that few of their bold words could be turned into solid achievements as long as House Republicans and President Eisenhower called for deep cuts in federal expenditures.

Highly dedicated and personable, she won re-election with progressively larger margins in 1958 and 1960. Yet through 1958 her main political distinction lay in the fact that she was the only congresswoman who, in textbook terms, was a "machine politician."

In 1959, however, as chairman of the Subcommittee on Postal Operations of the Post Office and Civil Service Committee, she found herself propelled, somewhat to her surprise, onto the battleground of public morals. For two months the subcommittee conducted hearings—from the District of Columbia to San Francisco—dealing with the sending of obscene matter through the U.S. mail. Many witnesses were questioned, from police to purveyors. And necessarily, the group pored over a quantity of primary material.

Like a buoyant Irish nun, Kathryn Granahan issued exhortations and warnings: "A half-million dollars is realized annually in mail-order pornography and obscenity. . . . There is a direct relationship between the increase in smut made available to our youth and the increase in juvenile delinquency." Quoting Evangelist Clyde W. Taylor, she raised the question of America's image abroad: "The public should not be surprised if people overseas eventually get the idea that the United States is populated by multitudes of sex maniacs."

Naturally, the hearings provoked lively national debate. Conventional moralists praised her for denouncing the whole "manifest evil" of the "lewd, lascivious, indecent, filthy, vile nature of the material involved." Libertarians, on the other hand, called her "a puritanical killjoy" and accused her of promoting neo-Victorian repression. *The Nation* declared she was "a worthy successor" to Anthony Comstock, "the smut hound whose idea of suppressing vice was to ban books which the next generation regarded as great literature."

The subcommittee's report concluded that pornography was bad—unequivocally—for young, old, and in between and proposed measures to strengthen the hand of the Post Office Department restricting its distribution. The Granahan amendment earned paeans from both sides of the House, as well as awards and medals from a wide assortment of nonpolitical organizations.

Moreover, her crusade for decency did not go unnoticed in the Senate. Among the congratulatory letters she received was one from a young Massachusetts Democrat, John F. Kennedy.

After Kennedy became President, he followed a tradition initiated by Harry Truman in 1949 and named a woman to the post of Treasurer of the United States. Mrs. Granahan did not resign from Congress, but waited until her term expired on January 3, 1963 to accept the appointment. Following the onset of a serious illness in 1966, she submitted her resignation "with reluctance" to JFK's successor, Lyndon B. Johnson.

FLORENCE P. DWYER
REPUBLICAN OF NEW JERSEY

Democrats in Union County, New Jersey wound up at a wake instead of a victory celebration on election night in 1956 because President Eisenhower's coattails were long enough to help GOP congressional candidate Florence Dwyer score an upset. Incumbent Harrison A. ("Pete") Williams, Jr. (later elected to the Senate), whom she defeated by the slender margin of 4,399 votes, became the last Democrat to represent all of Union County. "They had to redistrict to get another Democratic congressman in at least part of the county," says Walter Ramsay, a one-time campaigner with College Students for Williams.

Ramsay smiles when he recalls the 1956 race. "Mrs. Dwyer's victory probably belonged to Eisenhower," he says, "but her subsequent triumphs have all been hers. Some of her re-election margins would have made Ike jealous." One of the top vote-getters in New Jersey history, she has scored in heavily Democratic cities as well as in Republican suburbs.

Florence Dwyer, called "Flo" by her friends, local newsmen, and many constituents, attributes her political popularity to the fact she's had "the courage to do what's right." It is with pride that she says, "I do not have a 100 per cent union or a 100 per cent Chamber of Commerce voting record."

Her relative independence has given her the chance to pursue those objectives she believes to be in the public interest. From her own reading and from reports prepared by her staff, she attempts to learn everything about every piece of legislation within her assigned jurisdiction on the Government Operations and the Banking and Currency committees. Though she cannot possibly achieve this goal, her careful scrutiny of the fine print has more than once uncovered attempts by House members to act other than in the national interest.

During hearings on the 1966 housing and urban development bill, she alone called attention to 52 nonqualifying special subsidies that had been slipped in without benefit of debate, most of them for auditoriums, civic centers, and convention halls—"all great monuments to a congressman's ability to 'do more' for his constituents," as *Life* pointed out, "but not much help in clearing up urban slums." Had these exemptions, estimated to cost $725 million, not been deleted, both urban renewal and the Model Cities program would have been "wiped out," according to then-Secretary of Housing and Urban Development Robert C. Weaver. Congresswoman Dwyer failed in her first three attempts to get the exemptions dropped, but she drew so much attention to the pork-barreling that the Banking and Currency Committee finally voted, 16-to-13, to eliminate them. Her admonition that "It's a common failing, I suppose, to take all you can get, but it's a failing people in public office should try to resist" was heeded by the whole House as well.

Feminists admire Florence Dwyer for the forceful way she has moved in such varied fields as consumer protection and equal pay for women, but most of all for her commitment to fight for human rights and for being willing to take political risks when confronted by an issue involving blatant sex discrimination. Helen Delich Bentley might never have been appointed chairman of the Federal Maritime Commission, a post promised her by President Nixon, had it not been for the intervention of Florence Dwyer. Peter Flanigan, White House patronage chief with a low opinion of women in government, had arbitrarily decreed that Mrs. Bentley would be bypassed. When this information reached Mrs. Dwyer, she elicited the support of three other Republican congresswomen and took the case to the Oval Office. Once alerted to the situation, Nixon overruled Flanigan.

Florence Dwyer herself has experienced little or no discrimination during the more than 20 years she has been in politics. "The first time a woman tries for elective office, it's true that if there is a choice between a man and a woman there is a tendency to favor the man," she once told *U.S. News & World Report*. "You do have to break a barrier. You have to convince the voters that you will serve as their representative. Some women who try for office say: 'Vote for me because I will be the first woman in the office.' That's an insult to women. Why should a woman appeal just to women?"

As for the treatment congresswomen receive from congressmen, she is convinced that "If you do your homework, know the facts and have sound arguments and then go to a man in a key spot—as you do have to—he will listen to you. I never try to stand on the fact I wear skirts."

Being a woman has not hampered the New Jersey representative in playing the self-appointed roles of legislative watchdog and devil's advocate or in taking the offensive to introduce and defend legislation designed to redeem congressional prestige and respect. She believes (and who can argue?) that "the people think there is something wrong with Congress." There is a lack of confidence, she says, "I have never seen before." What distinguishes her from the other, and mostly younger, national legislators who feel the same way is that she has been demanding internal reforms for years. In the 1960s she declared the key question to be "Will Congress continue to approach its responsibilities in the old, disordered ways . . . or will we all insist upon—and get—something better, a new beginning?"

Her contributions to a fresh start have had some far-reaching effects. As the organizer of a liberal Republican group in the House (nicknamed the "Saintly Seven"), she led the successful effort to enlarge the Rules Committee, thereby preventing the coalition of Southern Democrats and conservative Republicans from continuing the practice of keeping major social legislation from reaching the floor for debate. It was her amendment to the Legislative Reorganization Act of 1970 that provided for public disclosure of how members vote on teller votes. Previously they had simply walked down an aisle and were counted, but not listed by name. The first significant test of this new ruling followed debate on an appropriations bill dealing with the future of the supersonic transport (SST). Twice before the House had voted—by sizable margins—to continue the development of this controversial aircraft. In March 1971, however, by 215 to 204, the measure was defeated. "Of special importance," Mrs. Dwyer commented at the time, "was the fact that members could not take positions anonymously which were unsupportable publicly. I had not anticipated so dramatic and gratifying an effect so soon."

As the representative of one of the most densely populated areas in the country, in a state whose biggest environmental problem is wall-to-wall urbia, she has been in the forefront of legislative drives to create the National Commission on Population Growth and the American Future, as well as the Environmental Protection Agency. She was also one of the early proponents of federal support for mass transit and helped bring into being the Department of Transportation.

Mrs. Dwyer's strength comes more from program than from

personality. Her low-key, somewhat humorless manner is more typical of the legislative chairman of New Jersey Business and Professional Women's Clubs she once was than anything else. The four terms she served in the New Jersey State Assembly as a member of the policymaking committee and as assistant majority leader have given her a tactical advantage over less-experienced colleagues. Of her devotion to congressional business, a Capitol Hill aide says, "She demands no more from anyone else than she demands of herself, which is limitless." Every account of her work habits mentions the day-into-night schedule she has maintained for 16 years.

Pennsylvania-born Florence Price Dwyer is tall and has reddish hair styled in soft waves. Behind her gilt-framed glasses are a pair of intense blue eyes. She has been a widow since 1968 when her husband, M. Joseph Dwyer, a retired industrial relations executive, died. Although she does not view age as necessarily meaning senility and decline, several months before her 70th birthday (July 4, 1972) she announced she would not be a candidate for re-election.

"The time has come to rearrange my priorities—to spend more time with my family," she declared in her formal retirement statement, made, she said, "with some reluctance." It is difficult to imagine Congresswoman Dwyer in retirement, even with the companionship of her son, daughter-in-law, and grandchildren. For nearly half a century she has maintained a residence in Elizabeth, New Jersey, but her real home has been the U.S. House of Representatives.

The Up Side of Down

Leaders of both political parties had been saying for some time that, if and when women were elected to Congress in significant numbers, it would come about, not as an explosive shift in attitudes, but as an orderly evolution flowing from woman's enlarged experience and enhanced public status. As the fifties faded and the sixties began, it appeared that this orderly evolution was taking place. Nineteen women served in the 86th Congress (1959–61). Of the ones who tossed their hats into the ring in 1960—63 for the U.S. Senate and 26 for the House of Representatives—17, or nearly 60 per cent, were elected. Subsequent special elections raised the total in the 87th Congress to 20, an all-time high.

Forty years after ratification of the 19th Amendment, the "always fascinating, sometimes baffling, and ever-changing story" of women politicans was the subject of a *Time* cover story featuring Maine's Republican Senator Margaret Chase Smith and her Democratic opponent, Lucia Cormier. (To then, the only other congresswoman accorded *Time* cover honor had been Ruth Hanna McCormick, Illinois Republican elected to the House in 1928.)

Winning seats in the 86th Congress were three Republicans, Catherine May of Washington, Edna Simpson of Illinois, and Jessica Weis of New York, and two Democrats, Julia Hansen, also of Washington, and Maurine Neuberger of Oregon. Mrs. Neuberger succeeded her late husband in the Senate.

The roll call was answered in the 87th by three more new-comers, all widows of congressmen: Democrats Catherine D. Norrell of Arkansas and Corinne B. Riley of South Carolina and Republican Louise G. Reece of Tennessee. Of the record-setting total, Democrats outnumbered Republicans 12 to 8.

Among those missing in 1961 was the *doyenne* of congress-women, Edith Nourse Rogers, Republican of Massachusetts, who had served 35 years in the House, a record surpassed by no other woman and only nine men. When she died two days before the 1960 primary, she was unopposed for her 19th term.

CATHERINE MAY
REPUBLICAN OF WASHINGTON

Washington, the fourth state to satisfy the suffragists' demand for the vote (in 1910, with a gentle nudge from Jeannette Ran-kin), waited nearly half a century before sending a woman to Congress. When 44-year-old Catherine May, a Republican, made the break-through in 1958, she "made it big," one of her 4th District constituents says. The largely agricultural territory she wooed and won in southeastern Washington is huge—about 15,-000 square miles stretching from the Cascades in the west to the Idaho line.

How to cover this vast political ground on a slim budget was a critical problem for Mrs. May. Both the money and the message of her wealthy Democratic opponent, Frank LeRoux, were highly visible in the plethora of expensive billboards that blossomed across the landscape.

Well aware of her underdog odds, Mrs. May challenged Le-Roux to television debates. He ignored the invitation, under-standably nervous about going on the air opposite a lady whose longtime radio broadcasting career would give her the edge. Undaunted, she took the only other practical campaign ap-proach that would give her visibility: the grueling precinct-by-precinct road. "I went to the people," she says. In dots on the map like Dusty, "I visited in farmyards with individual families: mother, father, kids, grandfather, cousins—and the dog." To gain added exposure in cities, she relied on news-paper ads that dared LeRoux to "come out from behind those billboards."

Informal politicking suited Catherine May. A bouncy, solid person, her manner was genial, and she had the energy es-sential to a vote-getting search that meant six days and nights a week on the hand-shaking circuit. The main issue was the economy, and she communicated a credible "I'll-do-the-best-I-can" honesty.

Mrs. May won by a handsome margin in a year that saw a host of Democrats elected on a wave of recession discontent. A by-product of her victory was that it pumped new life into the run-down GOP organizational machinery in the 4th District. This revitalization saved her political skin in the anti-Goldwater year of 1964 when Democrats captured four seats previously held by GOP representatives in the seven-member Washington delegation. Only Thomas ("Tom") Pelly and Catherine May survived the rout.

Holding elective office was not a novelty to Mrs. May. "Up until about 1950," she says, "my husband and I, like so many citizens, spent a lot of time complaining about the state of the nation, yet did nothing about it. My dad spurred us to take some action. Shortly before his death we had a long philosophical discussion. He told us he was worried about the kind of world he was leaving. 'I can't give you the right answers,' he said, 'but I can urge you to strike out and find your own.' "

That was the beginning. They joined the Young Republicans, spoke out on local issues, and campaigned for GOP candidates, including Eisenhower and Nixon. "When the party was looking for new faces to run for the state legislature in 1952," she recalls, "my husband, Jim, persuaded me to file. 'I can't afford a big financial contribution,' he said, 'so I'll donate you!' "

Her three terms as a part-time lawmaker in Olympia were fruitful. "State housekeeping," she says, "requires the same skills every good housewife utilizes in her own home—making the most of what she has and improving the service while enforcing strict economy. I believe I got this message across to the men with whom I served on the appropriations committee."

Mrs. May believes that the political experience also enriched her family's life. There was a time, for example, when son James' third-grade class wrote a letter lobbying for a bill that would designate a section of a new state road the Lewis and Clark Highway. "After I read his letter in the House, the bill passed with no dissenting votes," she says. "I've never been so relieved in my life. That was the only lobby that ever had me scared."

By her own admission, Yakima-born Catherine Dean Barnes ("Billie" to her friends) did not have a specific career in mind when she matriculated at the junior college in her home town during the Depression year of 1932. But by the time she was graduated from the University of Washington four years later, with a major in English literature and a minor in speech, she knew she wanted to be a radio commentator. While searching for an opening, she taught English at Chehalis High School.

In 1942 she volunteered for the WAVES but was turned down because she wore glasses ("I'm near-sighted"). The next best thing to do to aid the war effort, she decided, was to work as a hostess at the local USO club. Here she met James O. May of Bloomfield, New Jersey, a regular army non-commissioned officer whose specialty was radar. They were married in 1943, and following his medical discharge in 1945, he stayed on in Yakima to help manage the Barnes real estate and insurance firm. Jim May considered going into business in the nation's capital after Catherine was elected to Congress, but ended up back in Yakima. "Jim really didn't like Washington, D.C.," she says. "He came East when he could, and of course I went home at least once a month."

Congresswoman May campaigned successfully for a seat on the House Agriculture Committee. It was a breakthrough of sorts, for Frank LeRoux had repeatedly told the voters that he was "the only person in the state who could get on the Agriculture Committee and had a telegram from Speaker Sam Rayburn to prove it." The details surrounding her appointment remain a secret, but her record as a member is in the public domain.

One of the unwritten rules of the House of Representatives is that no matter whose name is on a bill when it is referred to a committee, if it is reported out by that committee it will usually bear the name of the chairman or of a ranking majority member. As a Republican in Democratic Congresses, Catherine May did not see her name on many agriculture bills.

Her special contribution, according to Stephen T. Adams, who served as her research assistant, was in the role of mediator. "She performed a unique and sometimes critical service as a peacemaker," he says, "trying to find an acceptable middle ground between opposing points of view or working to resolve a basic clash of personalities. Her aura of reasonableness helped resolve many a legislative impasse and get important bills back on the track."

Both before and after her appointment to the Joint Committee on Atomic Energy, she battled to save the Hanford nuclear reactor from deactivation. The largest of its kind in the world, it was a source of electric power and jobs in the tri-cities of Richland, Kennewick, and Pasco. Environmentalists questioned the damage to aquatic life from radiation. The controversy ended in a draw. Plutonium production was cut back, but the relatively cheap production of steampower from uranium was allowed to continue.

Though Catherine May tagged herself a conservative, her legislative orientation revealed, more than anything else, a total loyalty to the branch of Republicanism being espoused by the party leader, be he in or out of the White House. Publicly and privately she adhered to the centrist philosophies of both Eisenhower and Nixon.

A little-known facet of her political life—only because the press paid it little heed—is that in the mid-1960s, when Spiro T. Agnew was a political unknown except in his native Maryland, she was booming the kind of positional diatribes at the television networks that later made the Vice President famous (some would say infamous). Urging the industry "to make the voice of business as loud as the voice of government and labor," she declared: "If you aren't embarrassed by selling underarm deodorants, I can't see why you're embarrassed about selling the business point of view." To the National Association of Broadcasters she quoted a toothpaste commercial: "You wonder where the yellow went; more of you had better be concerned with where the freedom went." Although Mrs. May has never been in favor of government policing of the airwaves (other than through the Federal Communications Commission), she reminded the broadcasters, "Unless you in your industry meet your responsibilities, you dull the weapons of your congressional friends who must fight on the front lines against pressures from people who don't understand the basic law."

Catherine May, unlike Spiro Agnew, has never been asked by the media to lower her voice—not even during the 1968 Presidential campaign when she delivered any number of her homilies on issues roiling the national temper. She was speaking for herself as a candidate for re-election, but she was also speaking as a member of a select task force advising GOP nominee Nixon. He lost Washington State to Hubert Humphrey by 27,527 votes, but carried her 4th District. It was, in fact, the only one in the state to give him a plurality.

Two years later the issues at the midterm elections did not turn on specific legislation but on such worries and fears as the youth revolution, slackening moral standards, disrespect for the law, rocketing crime rates, and drug addiction. The Democrats made their central charge the economy, blaming the Republicans for recession and unemployment.

The sluggish state of the economy was not the sole reason Catherine May missed being re-elected to a seventh term by only 6,876 votes. But in a state whose jobless were increasing at an alarming rate, it contributed significantly to terminating her congressional career. "Everywhere I went," she says, "I heard, 'You've been in Washington 12 years and haven't done a thing about inflation.' Of course no one remembered that Nixon had inherited runaway prices from his predecessor." The President later conceded that the economy had without doubt hurt GOP candidates.

In hindsight, does she think her divorce (granted in May 1970) might have contributed to her political downfall? "No," she replies, without hesitation. "It was an amicable parting. Jim still lives in Yakima. There was no scandal. We'd been separated for six years. It seemed the civilized thing to do."

Mrs. May's fierce loyalty to the party has never gone unnoticed. Nixon, recognizing her efforts on behalf of his legislative program, sent her a "Dear Catherine" letter to express his appreciation. Not long after her defeat there was the promise of a Presidential appointment—to the board of incorporators of the National Railroad Passenger Corporation (Amtrak), the quasi-governmental agency created to turn the railroads into a modern if diminished mode of travel.

When confirmation came, she was in Morocco—on her honeymoon. "Don [new husband Donald W. Bedell, a management consultant] and I were dining at our hotel in Marrakech," she says, "when the waiter informed us that there was a call from the White House in Washington—'for Mr. Bedell.'

"He watched in utter disbelief as I walked to the phone," Catherine May Bedell remembers. "Morocco is clearly a man's world. Would a woman be summoned to the phone from the palace in Rabat?"

A more prestigious reward was yet to come. In mid-July 1971 Mrs. Bedell became the first woman chairman of the U.S. Tariff Commission. Nominated by President Nixon and confirmed by the Senate, she succeeded Chester L. Mize, a former congressman from Kansas, as head of the six-member bipartisan federal agency.

The fact that she has risen as high as she has in so short a time has its advantages. One of them is that she can answer with credibility a question very prevalent in the seventies:

What, specifically, can politicized women do? "Demand more of themselves," she says "—and of their daughters. Above all, pay close attention to a father's advice, particularly if his message is 'to go out and fight for the things you believe in.' "

EDNA SIMPSON

REPUBLICAN OF ILLINOIS

Victory was overshadowed by sadness for stately, white-haired, 67-year-old Edna Simpson, elected to the 86th Congress from downstate Illinois. The Carrollton native, widowed just nine days before the November 4 election, reluctantly agreed to permit her name to go on the ballot in place of her late husband, an eight-term GOP representative from the 20th Congressional District.

Neighborly sympathy for Mrs. Simpson was reflected at the ballot box. People who didn't know her and had never seen her (she did not campaign) nevertheless voted for her. Henry W. Pollock, the Democratic contender, didn't have a chance. She carried all but two of the fourteen rural counties fanning out to the west from Springfield. The Simpson name evoked memories of fair and just representation in Washington. (The official tally revealed that more than 400 votes were cast for the dead congressman, Sid Simpson.)

To assist Mrs. Simpson on Capitol Hill, Janet, one of her two daughters, went on the office payroll. A George Washington University graduate, she had previously worked for her father, and for one year during the Eisenhower Administration was a secretary to Assistant to the President Sherman Adams. Although Edna Simpson earned what her colleague from Illinois, Marguerite Stitt Church, called "an admirable record of service" on two committees, House Administration and Interior and Insular Affairs, she was such a private person that she was virtually unknown to most members of Congress. She served a full two-year term without once addressing either the Speaker or fellow members of the House.

As far as anybody knows, the only time she used her official voice was in the House clerk's office. Over his objection, her name was printed on congressional stationery—not as he wanted it and as it appears in the *Biographical Directory of the American Congress* ("Edna Oakes Simpson"—Oakes was the name of her first husband) but as she preferred: "Edna (Mrs. Sid) Simpson."

JESSICA McCULLOUGH WEIS

REPUBLICAN OF NEW YORK

"Woman in politics have more talent than mobility. I have said for years that women cannot pick up and leave their families and come to Washington."

Jessica Weis of Rochester, New York, did not speak these lines (Katie Louchheim did—when she was director of Women's Activities for the Democratic National Committee), but she fully understood them. Her husband believed in the so-called natural order of things: women should be concerned first and foremost with child care, husband care, and home care. Only after their three children were grown and she was a widow could she consider running for elective office.

Despite the restrictions imposed by Charles W. Weis, Jr., a corporate executive, "Judy" Weis arrived in Congress in 1959 with credentials in areas other than lawmaking that, for a woman, were rare. For 15 years she had stood near the center of power within the hierarchy of the Republican Party, and before that hers was an official voice in the Monroe County GOP organization and on the New York State Executive Committee.

Her base of operations from 1935 on was her Rochester home, which she described as "just like the party symbol, a big ungainly gray elephant" of a frame house. When she left it to organize Presidential motorcades (boosting the 1936 candidacy of Alfred M. Landon) or to speak at rallies, she was never away "for long"—except for the one remarkable time she was on the hustings for 41 days and slept in 40 different cities. Toward the end of that whirlwind tour she said: "I felt like little flags were coming out of my head."

Some people would say that Judy Weis was made to hold office. Affable, gregarious, well-read, well-informed, hard-working, vibrant, slender, with gray eyes and gray hair, she never seemed harried or unsure of herself. Like New York's first congresswoman Ruth Baker Pratt, whom she succeeded as Republican National Committeewoman in 1943, Mrs. Weis viewed political life with the partisan professionalism of a James Farley. Characteristically she was at her vocal best when constructively analyzing the health of the Republican Party, talking about "stepping up the selling campaign for our own product" and the need to explain clearly "what's basically wrong with our competitor's product," constant in her attack on "the inflationary big government philosophy that is motivating a great majority of the opposition."

Judy Weis's background was one of affluence. She was born in Chicago in 1901 and educated at Miss Wright's School in Bryn Mawr, Pennsylvania and at Madame Reiffel's School in Manhattan. Her father, Charles H. McCullough, Jr., at the time of his death in 1920 was president of the Lackawanna Steel Company in Buffalo. Following her marriage in 1921, she joined the Rochester Junior League and did charity work. Personal opposition to the New Deal convinced her to take an active role in strengthening her own party.

When Representative Kenneth B. Keating resigned his House seat to run for the Senate in 1958, Mrs. Weis opted for the vacancy. Wresting the nomination from three men ambitious to represent the 38th District proved more difficult than defeating the Democratic contender, attorney Alphonse L. Cassetti.

"It took a bit of doing," she said following her election, "especially in an industrialized city like Rochester." She conducted what she called a "people-to-people" campaign. To cover the grape-growing areas and dairy country in nearby Wayne County, she traveled in a land cruiser equipped with bunks and a kitchenette. Tipping the scales on the side of her victory was the fact she was well known in Monroe County and had the backing of a well-knit women's organization that she had nurtured over a period of years.

As a freshman in the House without previous legislative experience, Mrs. Weis spent the better part of her first term feeling her way along unfamiliar legislative ground. In the fashion of any member of Congress who plans to seek re-election, she remained an assiduous campaigner, returning to her district frequently to appear on local television and radio programs and to deliver speeches. An annual celebration she never missed was the one honoring Susan B. Anthony at the suffrage leader's Rochester home, which Mrs. Weis had helped restore. She used the occasion to encourage more women to take a more active part in politics, whether as a volunteer or as an office-holder.

"By 1960," says Helen B. Gladwell, who served as her administrative assistant, "she had firmly established a reputation for diligent service to the people she represented. Sincere and conscientious, she retained a sharp wit and keen sense of humor which kept her very 'human' in an atmosphere where egos often assume disproportionate emphasis."

One of the highlights of her second term was being assigned to the newest House Committee, Science and Astronautics. According to Mrs. Gladwell, it was typical of Judy Weis to want to be associated with the exciting challenge to place a man on the moon in the decade of the sixties.

Unhappily, Congresswoman Weis did not live long enough to witness the manned space program. Early in her second term she learned that she had terminal cancer. With what Helen Gladwell describes as "indomitable courage," she continued to work every day as long as she could. She died in May 1963. Before returning to Rochester, Judy Weis donated her congressional papers to The Women's Archives at Radcliffe College.

JULIA BUTLER HANSEN
DEMOCRAT OF WASHINGTON

Capitol Hill abounds with lawmakers who for one political reason or another claim they were concerned about ecology long before it became a household word. Few, however, can appear in public and truthfully say, as Representative Julia Butler Hansen did early in the 92d Congress: "This committee has had a deep interest in the environment long before it was fashionable."

She referred to the subcommittee of the House Appropriations Commitee that oversees the funding of the Department of the Interior and related agencies, the number of which varies, and she was speaking in her official capacity as its chairman— the first woman to head a key appropriations subcommittee.

"I've always had a great sense of identification with the land," Mrs. Hansen says. "It's packed into my genes. My father was a woodsman, and my grandparents homesteaded in the Washington Territory. We lived an uncomplicated life on the edge of a vast, unspoiled wilderness that was ours for the hiking." In 1935, when she was 28 and had finished college, she wrote a prize-winning book about the untamed wildness of the Pacific Northwest. *Singing Paddles* is the story of pioneer life in her hometown, Cathlamet, situated on the banks of the Columbia River at the edge of foothills which rise northward in Wahkiakum County.

Julia Butler Hansen's 33-year marriage to working lumberman Henry A. Hansen, now retired (they have one son, David), spans approximately the same years as her political career. She holds the record for continuous length of service by a woman in a state legislature west of the Mississippi: two months short of 22 years. A Democrat, she has since 1960 represented the

3d Congressional District in southwestern Washington, replacing the late Republican Representative Russell V. Mack.

She campaigned for a seat on the House Public Works Committee, but accepted a place on Interior and Insular Affairs to placate Arizona Congressman Morris Udall, an intimate of President John F. Kennedy. The makeup of this committee has come under attack from conservationists who say it is weighted with Westerners "whose constituents have been extracting income from public land for generations." She was also appointed to the Education and Labor Committee, not because she had chaired the education committee in the Washington Legislature but because a Democratic vacancy existed and she was an available newcomer. Her resignation from these committees in 1963 was in compliance with the House rule that prohibits anyone on the 55-member Appropriations Committee from serving on any other.

The key to Mrs. Hansen's reputation as a legislator is dedication. "Even some of the older members who have been hard-bitten about women as members of Congress changed their tune after working with her," says Joseph McCaffrey, Washington, D.C., radio and television congressional correspondent. "They found she not only could hold her own in committee work, but that she was fair, her word was her bond, and she had the willingness to stay with an issue until it was resolved."

As chairman of her subcommittee, Julia Hansen, a full-figured, pleasant-looking woman with silver-white hair, presides, with help from seven male members from as many different states, over a whopping annual budget of over $2 billion, half of which is returned to the U.S. Treasury in the form of revenue derived from fees for use of public land. "It is truly a nationwide committee," she points out. "We fund activities from Alaska to Maine and from the Great Lakes to the Trust Territories. The problems are many and varied. It is a tremendous responsibility."

Although Representative Hansen's subcommittee has nothing whatsoever to say about legislation governing national land policies, it is accountable for parceling out the dollars and cents in such a manner that the taxpayer gets the best possible return for his investment in the nation's land, now recognized by conservationists and exploiters alike as finite. The implications are enormous. Public land includes national forests (187 million acres), national parks (23 million), and the so-called public domain—federal land not classified for forest, parks, or other special purpose. Its 470 million acres consist largely of the high, sage-covered plains of the intermountain West and the roadless bulk of Alaska.

The political tightrope on which Mrs. Hansen and her colleagues must balance lies between the ecologists who plead for increased funding for "protection" and those who are interested in "management" and "yield"—for minerals, lumber, and wool as well as recreation space. The tug-of-war between these two special-interest groups is never more highly visible than during the budget hearings, held in the spring of each year.

On one side are the Friends of the Earth, insisting that the subcommittee could realize major savings if the National Park Service would not propose "roads that neither the visitors want, nor the local citizens have asked for." On the other are representatives from McLean Trails requesting the subcommittee to "allocate funds to build the Potomac Heritage Trail in Virginia, from Burling Park to Mount Vernon, consistent with the intent of the National Trails Act of 1968."

Mrs. Hansen bristles somewhat when a witness appears overly hostile. "I don't know what you are going to do about fighting forest fires if you have no roads and trails," she told George Alderson, legislative director of Friends of the Earth, one of the more than 150 witnesses who testified before the committee during hearings on the 1972 budget. "I have to say that, having lived in the forest country all my life."

"Madam Chairman," Mr. Alderson answered: "I was born in Ellensburg and grew up in Portland and was all over the Northwest myself. The Forest Service's justification for the road program has not generally, in my experience, been on the basis of increased fire protection."

Madam Chairman had the last word: "You haven't grown up in an area of real bad forest fires, years before there weren't any roads in these forests. It was very bad."

If Mrs. Hansen's subcommittee had its way, there would be more money for the preservation and orderly development of natural resources, pollution abatement, and research. But, as she has told the whole House, "I am not going to say what a chairman usually does, 'This is a good bill,' because it could be better. Under the circumstances, however, it is the best that can be done."

To a certain extent, Congresswoman Hansen has been placed on the political defensive by the growing clout of the ecological forces. But she is not one easily given to discouragement. Public pulse-taking, she believes, has proved she is "on the right track" with regard to the environment. Answers to a questionnaire circulated among her constituents in mid-1971 revealed that 68 per cent are "willing to pay increased taxes to support strong governmental pollution control."

Residents of the 3d District, an 11-county area between the Pacific Ocean and the Cascade Mountains, rely on agriculture, shipping, and such natural resources as timber and fish for their livelihood. That so many agree to bear a fair share of the cost of anti-pollution devices to control industry's outpouring of noxious wastes is, in Mrs. Hansen's view, significant.

The Washington State legislator's concern for "the quality of life" extends by law and by personal interest to nearly half a million American Indians. Over the years she has collected considerable firsthand information about Indian customs among remnants of western Washington tribes bearing such unique names as Skokomish, Quinault, and Muckleshoot. "I have five shorthand books filled with legends told me by an Indian woman who passed away over 25 years ago," she says, "and I'm waiting for the day I have time to transcribe them." Julia Hansen is the first to admit government shortcomings in accomplishments for the Indian people. Noting that she has visited "most of the Indian schools from Alaska to Philadelphia, Mississippi," she acknowledges that "money has not always been the problem with Indian development." Her questioning of witnesses from the Bureau of Indian Affairs is sharp and relentless. If they don't have the answers, she sends them back to do their homework. She has no patience with bureaucratic sinners. "Let us rearrange our bureaucracy," she admonishes them, "to recognize that children are human beings and that it is not nearly so important to ensure the security of a bureaucrat as it is the well-being of a child."

For all the impatience with which she reacts to bureaucracy, Mrs. Hansen appears to enjoy herself immensely in the nation's capital. She seems to have no trouble turning off the job and resorting to other challenges, among them adding to her knowledge of history by visiting the Civil War battlefields in the surrounding area. The zoo lured her in the months not long after she arrived. But now that she reviews the yearly appropriations for the National Zoo, she doesn't visit it any more. The lack of federal funds to improve the condition of the pens and create a proper habitat for the animals depresses her.

Labeled liberal by the press, Mrs. Hansen's branch of politics is quite palatable to many Democratic archconservatives. On a whirlwind trip through Mississippi to inspect the Natchez

Trace Parkway and other Interior Department projects, she drew rave notices for her address before the State Legislature. Syndicated columnist John Perkins called her "a gracious and intelligent woman who has convictions that voters in a state or congressional district have a right to elect the representative (or senator) of their choice."

Although the main thrust of her speech was the need to protect the environment and enhance natural resources, she hinted rather broadly that she doesn't think much of the idea that elected representatives of the people should be challenged and denied their rightful voice in Congress. According to Perkins, it was the kind of political philosophy that delighted her Democratic colleagues from the Magnolia State, "particularly in light of the recent effort by a Mississippi faction to unfrock the congressional delegation of rights and privileges of seniority in the Democratic Party."

While Lyndon B. Johnson was in the White House, the Washington congresswoman occasionally found herself in disagreement with his fiscal policies, but said nothing publicly. With a Republican in charge of the country, she has no need to conceal her anguish over attempts by the Office of Management and Budget (OMB) to block Bureau of Land Management funds. Less than a month before her subcommittee met to review the 1972 Interior budget, she called for a congressional investigation of OMB, claiming that executive orders had held up authorized funds in violation of the Constitution. A colleague on the subcommittee, Oregon's Wendell Wyatt, expressed "delight" during the hearings that the timber-sharing formula showed no signs of having been tampered with. Most of the credit, he said, was due to Mrs. Hansen's "active assistance" in preserving a form of government whereby "Congress legislates, not the Bureau of the Budget."

CATHERINE D. NORRELL
DEMOCRAT OF ARKANSAS

Large advertisements in a score of southeastern Arkansas newspapers urged voters to "Keep Your Congressional Power Up! Elect Mrs. W. F. ("Bill") Norrell as your Representative in the 6th District . . . the only candidate already prepared to step in."

Normally, the election of a congressman's widow in the South turns on little more than this kind of honest, low-key wooing of the electorate. The spring of 1961 was not a politically normal time in Arkansas, however. The 6th District race carried implications that could seriously affect the long-term economic and political integrity of the southeast section of the state.

The one aspect of this special election that set it apart from others was the redistricting plan (widely labeled as gerrymandering) adopted by the State Legislature. Arkansas's population decline, verified by the 1960 census, dictated that the House delegation be reduced from six to four. The 6th District was slated for oblivion. Its counties were to be incorporated into two other districts with the majority (11 out of 13) being combined with Oren Harris's 4th District in southwestern Arkansas.

The successor to the late Congressman Norrell would, therefore, either have to retire at the end of the 87th Congress (1961–63) or oppose Harris, a veteran of 20 years on Capitol Hill. His political worth to the state can best be illustrated by the fact he was chairman of the important House Interstate and Foreign Commerce Committee. Concern for the vested interests of 6th District residents was raised in a *Pine Bluff Commercial* editorial: "We can't think that Southeast Arkansans will be eager to send anyone to Congress who is not pledged to run the good race against Harris in 1962."

No such pledge was forthcoming from any of the four men who entered the race against Catherine Norrell. She, too, avoided the issue. But intimates knew that if she could finance a full-scale campaign, she would joust with Harris. "What we couldn't afford," says her daughter Judy, who took time out from law studies at George Washington University to manage her mother's 1961 effort, "was a contest of bank accounts."

Ironically, the question of finances became an issue sooner than anyone expected. Candidate John Harris Jones, a 39-year-old attorney from Pine Bluff, brought up the subject a week before the special election. "Mrs. Norrell doesn't need the salary of a congressional office," he said in a televised speech. Citing the fact that the 61-year-old widow was entitled to her late husband's pension and one of her own based on the salary she had earned as a member of his staff, Jones's strategy was to snare some of the sympathy votes which automatically go to a congressman's widow.

His scheme backfired. The voters went along with Mrs. Norrell's self-proclaimed contention that she was "fully prepared to take up where Bill Norrell had been forced to leave off." She collected almost twice as many votes as did Harris, the runner-up.

The new member's credentials in lawmaking were sketchy at best, so some members of the small but powerful Arkansas delegation were initially skeptical of her ability to perform under the demanding pressures of congressional service. It may have been reassuring to them to hear her admit—in answer to a question President Kennedy posed during a White House coffee hour— that the problems of running a legislative office look a lot different from the inside than from the outside. "Having the responsibility squarely on your own shoulders," she said, "is not quite the same as watching someone else do it." Kennedy agreed.

Finding herself on the national political scene was something Catherine Norrell had not even imagined as the daughter of a poor Baptist minister and his wife. Born Catherine Dorris in Camden, Arkansas, she spent her childhood in half a dozen different parsonages in Texas, Tennessee, and Ozark towns before settling in Monticello. She studied music at Ouachita Baptist College in Arkadelphia and at the University of Arkansas in Fayetteville, then taught music in the public schools. It was while serving as director of the music department at Arkansas A. & M. College that she met a new lawyer in town, Bill Norrell. They were married in 1922, and twelve years later she was introduced to politics when he ran successfully for the State Senate.

When the Norrells arrived in Washington in 1939, Hattie Caraway, a personal friend, was the senior senator from the state. Wilbur Mills of Kensett was waiting in the wings for an appointment to the House Ways and Means Committee, and Lyndon Baines Johnson of Texas was beginning his second term in the House. Over the next 22 years, Catherine Norrell, as a member and eventually president of the Congressional Club, was on a first-name basis with Lady Bird Johnson, Polly Mills, and a host of other wives of distinguished members of Congress.

Predictably, Congresswoman Norrell's 20 months as a legislator followed the unspectacular but effective course Bill Norrell had pursued. The Pine Bluff Arsenal and the Arkansas River were among his deepest interests. She continued to safeguard the one and press for development of the other.

Among the New Year's predictions recorded for 1962 was one in the *Dumas Clarion* to the effect that "Catherine D. Norrell and Oren Harris will run against each other, with Mrs. Norrell carrying the vote in her district counties and Mr. Harris taking his district counties. How heavy the vote will determine the outcome."

Had the dignified Monticello matron, known for her engaging smile and politically conservative voting record, not been dissuaded from seeking re-election, the *Clarion* might have been vindicated. But four days before the filing deadline (her timing was criticized), she announced she would not be a candidate. Publicly, she gave no reason. Privately, she said that the campaign price tag was too high. Citing the growing dominance of television, she said that politics had become "a rich person's game."

Within days following the expiration of the 87th Congress, she was sworn in as a Deputy Assistant Secretary of State for Educational and Cultural Affairs, a Kennedy appointee. She learned of his assassination later that year while on an official trip to the Middle East. Homeward bound aboard the U.S.S. *Constitution,* she was present when a wreath of red roses was dropped off the stern in memory of the late President.

Catherine Norrell retired from government service in the mid-1960s. Now living in Honolulu, she has resumed the career that was interrupted by marriage and politics. Says the former congresswoman turned church musician: "Like Shakespeare's wheel, I have come full circle."

LOUISE GOFF REECE

REPUBLICAN OF TENNESSEE

While Louise Goff Reece served in the 86th Congress, members of the House put aside legislative business one afternoon in August 1961 to commemmorate the 41st anniversary of the ratification of the 19th amendment to the Constitution. Mrs. Reece, a woman of few words, directed her remarks to the heart of the matter: the fact that the Tennessee Legislature in her adopted state had been the "all-important thirty-sixth" to ratify the amendment.

Had Louise Goff not been overseas in 1920 driving an ambulance for the Committee to Help France, she undoubtedly would have been a suffragette. Though too young to vote (even if women had been permitted to do so) when her grandfather, Nathan Goff, ran successfully for the U.S. Senate from West Virginia in 1912, she was aware that neither her mother nor her grandmother could go to the polls on his behalf.

Ironically, she was prevented from voting for her father, Guy D. Goff, when he was elected to the Senate (also from West Virginia) in 1924, but solely because she was then a legal resident of Tennessee, having become the wife of B. Carroll Reece, a second-term representative from Johnson City in the heavily Republican 1st Congressional District.

What Mrs. Reece, a graduate of Miss Spence's School in Manhattan, missed politically as a youth, she more than compensated for in adult life. Her husband was a Capitol Hill veteran in the most literal sense, serving 34 years in the House. Because he did not drive a car, she was pressed into service as a chauffeur during many of his campaigns for re-election. "They were a team," says daughter Louise Marthens, a licensed pilot who was at the controls of the plane that transported her father in the late 1940s. Recalls Doris Kirkman, onetime Reece office staff member: "Most East Tennesseans thought of them as Mr. and Mrs. Republican."

In the May special election held following Reece's death of cancer in 1961, silver-haired Mrs. Reece had no trouble defeating Democrat William W. Faw by an almost two-to-one margin. "I thought of a lot of back roads my husband had forgotten," she said afterwards.

She ran for the seat, she said at the time, because "I am certain Carroll would have wanted me to." A conservative and a member of the Public Works Committee, she concentrated on legislation pertaining to juvenile delinquency and school construction.

The onset of a severe and painful arthritic condition forced Louise Reece to decline to stand for re-election. She turned to the historical facet of politics, cataloguing the couple's legislative papers for deposit in the Carroll Reece Museum on the campus of East Tennessee State College. It was dedicated in 1965, the former congresswoman cutting the ribbon as her grandchildren looked on. Before her death five years later, at age 71, she had succeeded her husband as a member of the Republican National Committee.

CORINNE BOYD RILEY

DEMOCRAT OF SOUTH CAROLINA

Past experience had convinced Democratic leaders in the 2d South Carolina District that the strongest congressional candidate they could put forward, on short notice, was a member of the family of the deceased congressman. Thus, when Representative John Jacob Riley of Sumter died on New Year's Day in 1962, they persuaded his widow, Corinne Boyd Riley, to file for the office.

What Mrs. Riley and the party hierarchy failed to consider was that another woman, better qualified from the standpoint of having held elective office, would challenge all the old traditions—of party discipline, support for a congressman's widow, and particularly a recently bereaved one. State Representative Martha Thomas Fitzgerald of Columbia put the politicians on notice that their calculated strategy might not work. This was awkward for them, but good for the electorate.

Whereas Mrs. Riley had the political power structure behind her, Mrs. Fitzgerald had the credentials. Not only had she been re-elected five successive times to the South Carolina Legislature following her breakthrough in 1950, but she had established a reputation as an able lawmaker. In most other respects, the ladies' backgrounds were similar. Both were college graduates; both had been school teachers; both had been reared in the patriotic traditions of the Confederate South.

Among the voters, the campaign became a debate, but never a race. Mrs. Riley, in mourning, did not appear in public, thereby denying "Mattie" Fitzgerald even the semblance of a confrontation. The turnout for the February primary was light, only 14,-884 going to the polls out of a registration of approximately 125,-000. Corinne Riley won by a large margin, almost three to one. Her victory confirmed the judgment of political experts.

Unopposed in the special election on April 10, Mrs. Riley became the fourth woman (all widows of congressmen) from South Carolina to go to the U.S. House of Representatives, and the second, after Willa Lybrand Fulmer in 1944, to represent the 2d District.

To the surprise of everyone on Capitol Hill, including friends of her late husband, Congresswoman Riley turned down, one at a time, appointments to two lower-echelon committees (Post Office and Civil Service and Education and Labor) and convinced House leaders John McCormack and Carl Albert that she should serve on one "more useful" to her constituency. She said "Yes" to their offer of a place on Science and Astronautics, delighted that "it might mean a trip to Europe." It did.

Neither Mrs. Riley's daughter nor her son, who work and live in Sumter, has ever evinced an interest in politics. About her own eight months in office, the former congresswoman, as she approached her eightieth birthday, said, "It was a pleasant interlude."

Family Affair

MAURINE B. NEUBERGER
DEMOCRAT OF OREGON

Sometimes in politics the name *is* the game. Perhaps no one knows this political fact of life better than Oregon's Maurine Neuberger. The right last name helped her take over her late husband's U.S. Senate seat in 1960. Six years and a new husband later, Maurine Solomon chose not to seek re-election, aware that without the Neuberger name she would find herself seriously handicapped.

The subtle irony of Mrs. Neuberger's entrance-exit saga is that it belies her own much-publicized theory about the special problems that exist for women in politics. "The hardest thing about being a woman senator," she contends, "is getting elected in the first place."

While equality of the sexes in political elections is not yet in sight in Oregon, women of ability seeking national office have fared better there than in most other Western states. Wyoming, for example, which as a territory pioneered in political equality by granting women the right to vote in 1869 and vowed to remain out of the Union rather than come in without suffrage, has never been represented in Congress by a woman.

The two women who have gone to the U.S. House of Representatives from Oregon encountered more difficulty because of party affiliation than because of gender. Both Nan Wood Honeyman, who served one term during the Rooseveltian era, and

Edith Green, first elected in 1954, sought the office as Democrats in one of the nation's most consistently Republican states.

The fact that Richard L. Neuberger, an avowed liberal, won the 1954 Senate race was something of a milestone. No other Oregon Democrat had done it in 40 years.

The quandary that Dick Neuberger's widow faced immediately following his sudden death only two days before the March 11 filing deadline in 1960 was not whether she could win but if she should enter the race.

"I couldn't think of anything except going back to Washington and getting Muffet, our cat, closing the office and moving out of our apartment," Maurine told Robert Cahn of the *Saturday Evening Post*. "But as I thought more about it, I began to realize I was probably as qualified as any other potential candidate. And, above all, I knew in my heart that Dick would have wanted me to run."

Several thousand Oregonians signed petitions to put her name on the ballot. GOP Governor Mark Hatfield, required by state law to appoint a member of the deceased's party, announced he would not name an interim appointee until the filing deadline had passed. By long-distance, Democratic National Committee Vice-Chairman Katie Louchheim and Republican Senator Margaret Chase Smith urged her to run. Senator Hubert Humphrey sent a telegram: I CANNOT IMAGINE THE SENATE OF THE UNITED STATES WITHOUT A NEUBERGER IN IT.

At first glance, such gestures of encouragement would seem to provide sufficient reassurance to even the most hesitant of candidates. Yet Mrs. Neuberger's decision to file troubled her. "It could not be delayed," she said. "I only hope I did the right thing."

By temperament a fiercely independent human being, she wanted to become a senator strictly on her own. It was one thing for Dick Neuberger to have earned the right to represent fellow Oregonians in the Senate. If she were to follow him, she wanted to work her own passage. From the outset of the campaign, she made it clear that she hoped the voters would put sentiment aside—memories, too—and base their choice on "What kind of a lawmaker will *Maurine* make?"

The electorate in the most populous county, Multnomah, already knew, for Mrs. Neuberger had been Representative Neuberger for two terms in the State Legislature (1951–55), serving concurrently with her husband, a state senator. "Maurine wowed the state as a representative," Dick once said. "She also taught the people of Oregon—and her husband—a lot about what a woman could accomplish in government."

Before Maurine arrived on the state legislative scene, no one had ever dared challenge the almost sacrosanct dairy interests. To dramatize her crusade to remove the long-standing ban against colored margarine, she appeared before the agriculture committee carrying a mixing bowl and wooden spoon. Donning an apron, she demonstrated the tedious and messy task confronting any housewife who tried to combine color pellets with a white block of oleo. The "stunt" received widespread in-state press coverage. Legislators were deluged with mail from aroused homemakers. Colored margarine has been sold legally in the state ever since.

When she introduced a bill that would entitle working mothers to subtract from their income tax money spent on child care, the tax committee pigeonholed the measure. She bided her time, meanwhile sorting the letters that arrived by the mailbagful. Just before the end of the session, she approached tax committee members with a polite request: "Perhaps you can advise me about replying to this mail; I don't quite know how to tell these women that the baby-sitting bill has been bottled up in committee." She also reminded the gentlemen that some of the letters from irate mothers came from their home districts. They got the point. Before adjournment, Oregon became the first state in the nation to grant working mothers a tax deduction for money "paid for the care of dependent children."

It was this kind of record—plus a platform supporting such Oregon interests as additional recreation facilities in U.S. Forest Service lands (though not at the expense of wilderness areas), low-cost federal power, and an end to tight money policies that had slowed home-building and in turn the lumber industry— that she took to the voters. As a campaigner, she was impressive. One lifelong Republican, Alice Ingalls Wallace of Corvallis, remembers that she had "charm, warmth, spontaneity, and a friendly open manner—none of the dogmatic bombast that politicians sometimes feel is called for." In a magazine article entitled "My Wife Put Me in the Senate," Dick wrote: "Wherever I went campaigning with Maurine, I did much better at the polls than where I stumped the countryside alone. There is not a doubt in my mind she could win any office the state has to offer, including the one which I occupy."

She proved him right. In the May primary she won the nomination over four male contenders. In November, bucking a Republican tide that gave the state to Richard Nixon by a 37,000-vote margin, she defeated former GOP governor Elmo Smith, by a plurality of almost 70,000 votes.

Maurine Brown Neuberger's pithy speech, her penchant for thrift were characteristics derived from her Western girlhood, and typical of the small towns like Cloverdale, where she was born in 1907, that dot the northern Oregon coastline, a sandy stretch constantly exposed to the shifting mists and chill winds that whip across the Pacific. A second-generation Oregonian, she was the great-granddaughter of the covered-wagon pioneer Amos Harvey, who in 1846 established in Amity the first Disciples of Christ church west of the Continental Divide. Her father, Dr. Walter T. Brown, was a general practitioner, and her mother, a graduate of the State Normal School at Drain, taught classes there. A rule in the Brown household was that spending money had to be earned. Maurine picked fruit, helped harvest peas and beans, and had a paper route. One of the first things she "saved up for" was a camera.

She was a good student, though not outstanding. Following in her mother's footsteps, she was graduated from a state normal school and entered the teaching profession. After four years as a high school instructor of physical education and modern dance, she enrolled at the University of Oregon to earn a B.A. degree. It was while teaching English at Portland's Lincoln High School that her path crossed that of Dick Neuberger. He was a free-lance writer with a reputation as a firebrand, earned at the University of Oregon during his undergraduate days when he led a drive to abolish ROTC.

Maurine remembers that the first question he asked her was: "Are you a Republican?" Their romance and Dick's first term in the Oregon Legislature were interrupted by his World War II army service in Alaska and Washington, D.C. During part of this same period she was pressed into duty as a dairymaid on the family farm, sometimes milking 20 cows a day when the hired man was working at the shipyards. Just before Christmas in 1945—in Missoula, Montana—Maurine and Dick were married. The arrangements were courtesy of Montana Representative Mike Mansfield.

The following year she helped her husband campaign for a State Senate seat, which he lost in the Republican landslide. Their income at the time came from magazine articles they wrote about the Pacific Northwest and from the photographs she took to illustrate them. From 1948, the year Dick was successful in winning a four-year term in the Oregon Senate, until his death in 1960, their life was wrapped up in being a political team.

As a Senate wife in the nation's capital, Mrs. Neuberger created quite a stir when she modeled a swim suit at a political fund-raising style show. Her slender figure and long legs did not go unnoticed by Washington's photographers, and her picture in a one-piece bathing suit was splashed across newspapers from coast to coast. It amused Maurine when she thought about the furor the incident caused. "Didn't anyone know that Oregon is the longtime home of Jantzen Knitting Mills?" A reporter covering her 1960 campaign asked how she felt about the criticism. The forthright answer came quickly: "What do people think a senator's wife wears when she goes swimming? And why should a senator's wife be different from anyone else? We're only people."

As Dick's nonsalaried assistant in Washington, she performed as a second pair of ears and eyes. To her fell such tasks as sitting in on committee hearings that he did not have time to attend and ferreting out legislative data he needed from the Library of Congress. Together they scripted his weekly radio program for Oregon stations and wrote the monthly newsletter directed to voters back home. Their photographs appeared side by side on the masthead.

Her close identification with Dick Neuberger's job led the pro-Republican Portland *Oregonian* to accuse her of being "created" politically by her husband. "There is some doubt in our mind that Mrs. Neuberger will be able to take up where her husband left off," the paper editorialized when she was running for office. "It is not enough to go to the Senate with an inherited program."

Such criticism backfired, as she knew it would. And when she returned to Washington alone, it was evident that her legislative focus would be distinctly her own. Two weeks after her election she flew to Paris to be briefed on U.S. defense strategy as a member of the Senate advisory delegation to NATO.

During most of the 87th Congress, the 53-year-old freshman senator out of the Far West settled quietly into the Democratic majority, conforming to the unwritten rule that a new member of the club should be seen but not heard. She ceased to be just another backbencher the day late in 1962 when she delivered a four-and-one-half hour speech against the Administration bill to set up a corporation to develop and operate communications systems that utilize space satellites. By far the longest speech ever vented by a woman member of the U.S. Senate, it was her way of aiding and abetting the filibuster launched by Oregon's senior Senator Wayne Morse, the maverick who had once called the filibuster a "disgraceful and contemptible procedure."

The unaffected, flat, and somewhat rasping Neuberger voice was henceforth heard on a variety of compelling topics. Though not necessarily less controversial than the communications satellite bill, they reflected her determination to create a positive image—to get some laws on the books that would obtain practical results.

She helped sponsor—with success—an extension of the antibillboard provision in the federal interstate highway program. As a member of the Commerce Committee, she cosponsored a truth-in-packaging bill to force cosmetics makers, among others, to list ingredients on the labels of their products. It was her contention that two-thirds of the cost of cosmetics "goes into packaging, advertising, and promotion, while very little is spent on the beauty aids themselves."

As she had demonstrated in the Oregon Legislature, Mrs. Neuberger was not afraid to take on touchy political causes. The nationwide antismoking campaign she initiated was bound to outrage the tobacco industry. And since it pre-empted the Surgeon General's report linking tobacco with lung cancer, she stole a march on her elders, who had been hesitant about committing themselves to such a nettlesome issue. Congress did not authorize all that she wanted, but it did give the Federal Trade Commission the authority to regulate cigarette advertising and labeling and allocated funds to establish a National Clearinghouse for Smoking and Health. Some of the education front she covered herself. Her 1963 book, *Smoke Screen: Tobacco and the Public Welfare,* called attention to the hazards of smoking, and her articles in *The PTA Magazine* were designed to awaken the parents of teenagers ("If present trends continue, lung cancer will claim the lives of 1 million children now in school").

Senator Neuberger used her last months in office to hold hearings, as chairman of a subcommittee of the Special Committee on Aging, on up-to-date ways to improve the nation's health. Press coverage was guaranteed when she announced that a mobile medical unit equipped with the newest automated and semi-automated devices for detecting chronic diseases would be located outside the New Senate Office Building and that she would personally undergo a health-screening. It was her belief that preventive medicine would save up to $93 billion a year in medical bills and lost wages.

The junior Senator from Oregon arrived at her decision to ask Congress to "turn the corner from treatment to prevention" by way of personal experience. Early diagnosis had given both Neubergers a new lease on life following successful cancer surgery.

Oregonians were in general agreement that most of Senator Neuberger's legislative programs, while unspectacular, had merit. However, there were those—and not all of them Republicans—who raised the question of how good a job she was doing for her constituency.

On a number of issues Mrs. Neuberger was vulnerable, politically. Her vote to choke off the hearings on the Bobby Baker case was galling to a large segment of the electorate who wanted the Senate to investigate Baker's dealings with his congressional mentors. "We wonder," editorialized the *Albany Democrat-Herald*, "if Mrs. Neuberger has ever thought of the inconsistency of one's shielding Democratic senators from possible exposure for wrong-doing while loudly accusing industries of mislabeling packages, without benefit of investigation?"

When a storm of criticism erupted after she had lent the Oregon flag to marchers in the Selma-to-Montgomery civil rights march, she defended the action on the basis that since the flag was her "own personal property" she did not "need to apologize to anyone" for the manner in which she decided it was to be used. "It seemed to me that Oregonians had long ago indicated their support for the full enfranchisement of all American citizens," she said. "The presence of our state flag in the historic march was offered by me as symbolic evidence of that support."

Being on the defensive is a grave disadvantage. The more time Mrs. Neuberger had to spend answering charges, the less she had to devote to Senate business. Fuel was added to the fire when, following her marriage to Boston psychiatrist Philip Solomon, she sold her home in Portland, set up housekeeping in Newton Centre, Massachusetts, and announced she would "spend as much time as I can speaking in the East."

Her campaign statements about not wanting to be mortgaged to the past came back to haunt her. "In the cold light of political logic, it appears that she will continue to trade on the name of her late husband, Richard Neuberger," was the sentiment expressed by the *Klamath Falls Herald and News*. "Otherwise, why does she continue to call herself Senator Neuberger when her real name is Solomon?"

Before her 1964 marriage, the Lady from Oregon confided to close friends that she did not want to run for re-election. They dissuaded her from announcing the decision on the grounds that it would make her a lame-duck senator too soon. So it was not until November 1965 that she publicly bowed out, revealing that she intended to become plain Mrs. Solomon once her term expired.

"After 25 years in public service, I am willing to pick up a new life," she told the Women's National Press Club. "As a senator, you find yourself subject to the pressures of selfish groups. But I've found it easier to stand up to those pressures because I know politics is not my whole life."

Displaying the refreshingly casual attitude toward herself that some unsentimental observers felt had been indispensable to her political popularity, she said she believed she was a better person as a result of having served in the Senate: "less selfish, less obstinate." She also confessed that she had "learned to compromise and to realize that sometimes the other fellow might be right."

Senator Neuberger refused to say she would "never again run for elective office," but promised that she would "always be out on the stump talking about the importance of the issues for which I've battled as a professional."

As long as the Democrats were in the White House, she served as chairman of the Citizens' Advisory Council on the Status of Women. She also went back to being a teacher, lecturing on government at Radcliffe, and has remained active in the American Cancer Society's ongoing campaign against smoking. "I'm too busy to work," she told Gordon Macnab of the Associated Press in 1971.

Now divorced from Dr. Solomon, she is again Maurine Neuberger and calls Portland "home." At 65, she crisscrosses the country, addressing a younger generation. Whatever their politics, campus audiences are won over by her engaging smile and by the debate that her arguments spark. "Consumer protection and lobbying," she says, "are popular topics nowadays. So is inflation."

Now and then she pauses long enough to question the process that elected her to the Senate. One of the compelling reasons for her voluntary resignation, she says, was the high cost of campaigning. "The price in 1960 was just under $90,000," she recalls. "In 1966 I would have had to spend at least $250,000. I wanted to be free from that financial obligation."

She feels that it is the system which is essentially wrong, not individual people. What Dick Neuberger wrote in his book, *Adventures in Politics*, she subscribes to:

> There will not be truly free government in America—at the state, national, or local level—until campaign spending is rigidly controlled. In fact, why should a politician ever take a bribe when a donation to his next race for office is so much simpler—and so much more legal?

On the Wane

The sixties were barely half over when the *Chicago Tribune* raised the provocative question, "Are lady lawmakers facing extinction?" and in a word answered it: "Possibly."

From a record high of 20 in 1962, the number of congresswomen decreased each successive election year of the decade. By 1969 there were only 11—the fewest since 1951.

"There are three times as many whooping cranes as congresswomen," bemoaned one female member of the House. "While many things are being done to protect the rare, long-legged bird, nobody seems concerned about our being an endangered species."

"Politicians aren't sure if it's faint heart or fading interest that's causing a decline in the number of women running for Congress nowadays," wrote Associated Press staffer Frances Lewine. Another Capitol Hill correspondent, Willard Edwards, suggested that the paucity might be due to "the apathy, if not the hostility, of women voters toward women candidates."

It would be a rash mind indeed that could confidently explain the phenomenon. But the names and reputations of the men being challenged would seem to account for women's failure to gain political ground. The enormous advantage that a popular incumbent almost always enjoys over a challenger is a formidable obstacle. Although the polls gave Pennsylvania Secretary of Internal Affairs Genevieve Blatt a "fighting chance" against Republican Senator Hugh Scott in 1964, she failed to score an upset. Lopsided from the start were two other Senate races: former Assistant GOP National Chairman Elly Peterson versus Michigan's Philip A. Hart (1964) and WAC Lieutenant Colonel Ruth M. Briggs against Claiborne Pell of Rhode Island (1966). In House contests incumbency also proved to be the biggest handicap. Among the losers were Eleanor Clark French (vs. John V. Lindsay of New York); Frances McGovern (vs. William H. Ayres, Ohio); Ruth U. Swayze (vs. Cornelius E. Gallagher, New Jersey); Mary Gravina (vs. Abraham J. Multer, New York; Dorothy R. Powers (vs. Thomas S. Foley, Washington); and Elizabeth Bowen (vs. James Kee, West Virginia).

The era that heralded the first nomination of a woman Presidential candidate by a major party—Senator Margaret Chase Smith, Republican of Maine—was not entirely bereft of heartening signs for would-be female policymakers, however. With only two exceptions, incumbent congresswomen were regularly re-elected by substantial margins (Katherine St. George of New York was a victim of the Democratic landslide in the anti-Goldwater year of 1964, while 83-year-old Frances Bolton of Ohio was a casualty primarily of congressional redistricting in 1966). Another encouraging aspect was the breakthrough scored by female members of racial minorities. A Japanese-American and a Negro were elected to the House. Geographically, the roster of victorious women spanned the nation, from Honolulu to Brooklyn.

The six new feminine faces in the House between 1963 and 1969 belonged to Republicans Charlotte T. Reid of Illinois and Irene B. Baker of Tennessee, elected to the 88th Congress; Democrats Patsy Takemoto Mink of Hawaii and Lera M. Thomas of Texas, the 89th; Margaret Heckler, Republican of Massachusetts, the 90th; and Shirley Chisholm, Democrat of New York, the 91st.

CHARLOTTE T. REID
REPUBLICAN OF ILLINOIS

How does a congresswoman respond to the President of the United States when he asks her to accept an Executive appointment? "The same way a congressman does," says Charlotte Reid of Illinois: "With an unequivocal 'Yes, Mr. President.'"

It was with mixed feelings, however, that Mrs. Reid left Capitol Hill in October 1971 to move downtown to the headquarters of the Federal Communications Commission (FCC). During nine years in the House of Representatives she had attracted a large and loyal following in the 15th District west of Chicago. She had climbed, rung by rung, up the congressional seniority ladder to a coveted place on the House Appropriations Committee. Her diligence and legislative judgment were widely respected by colleagues on both sides of the aisle.

Somewhat paradoxically, her qualifications for the FCC are of the genre that drew criticism when she first ran for the House in 1962, following the sudden death of her husband, the Republican nominee. The opposition faulted her then because her only business had been show biz. A professional singer, she had entertained millions of radio listeners during the late thirties (under the name Annette King) as the featured vocalist on Don McNeill's nationally acclaimed "Breakfast Club."

The only child of musically gifted parents, Charlotte Thompson had to forego formal voice training with the onset of the Depression. "I enrolled at Illinois College in Jacksonville to earn a teaching certificate," she recalls, "but never gave up the hope of singing professionally. In my free time I knocked on the door of almost every radio station in Chicago. I was told I had talent but needed experience," she says. Louise Gilbert, voice coach of movie stars, gave her free lessons ("I had no money") at odd hours. Sometimes she sang on local programs without pay. Her highest salary—for singing commercials—was $5 a week. The turning point came in a dramatic way in 1936. From more than 100 other hopefuls at a National Broadcasting Company audition, she was chosen for the "Breakfast Club" role.

Among the program's regular fans was former Congressman Frank R. Reid, Sr., who told his son, an Aurora attorney, that he had heard a local girl on the radio with whom he ought to become acquainted. Recalls the former Miss Thompson, "Marriage and, eventually, motherhood replaced my singing career."

Twenty-three years later, with wholehearted support from her four children, Charlotte Reid, 49, entered politics. When she was sworn in at the beginning of the 88th Congress (1963–65), the *Chicago Tribune* reported that "the gallants of the House observed primarily that she was beautiful." As the months went by and she demonstrated that she possessed many attributes of a good lawmaker, they were impressed by her ability as well.

Charlotte Reid's winning ways were so apparent that, despite her freshman status in 1964, she received 19 invitations to campaign for Republican candidates. Engrossed in her own re-election campaign, she declined all but two. "It would have been a breach of protocol," she says, "to refuse House GOP Leader Charles Halleck of Indiana and Minority Whip Leslie Arends of my home state."

Although the 15th District, a five-county section in north-central Illinois, which includes some of the state's richest cornland as well as sprawling factories, had long been pro-Republican, Mrs. Reid viewed her 1964 race against Poppy X. (for Xenophen) Mitchell as a serious challenge. Forty-six-year-old Mrs. Mitchell, a college graduate and mother of one daughter, had never run for political office but had had plenty of experience as a platform speaker. She went door to door dispensing coffee, sometimes from a converted mail truck and sometimes from a second-hand Brink's armored car, both painted white and labeled "Poppy Wagon." "Mrs. Reid," she said, was "unconcerned" about such vital issues as federal aid to education and medical care for the aged.

Charlotte Reid emphasized her conservative philosophy: economy in government ("I may be old-fashioned, but I don't believe in spending more than we take in") and less federal control ("The freedom you save may be your own"). She also stressed the necessity of maintaining a strong military force to achieve "peace with honor" in Vietnam.

Poppy Mitchell carried her home county, LaSalle, by 687 votes, but Mrs. Reid won re-election with a 58 per cent majority, a stunning victory considering that Republican Charles H. Percy (later elected to the U.S. Senate) failed in his bid for the Illinois governorship and the GOP archconservative Presidential nominee, Barry M. Goldwater, lost all but six states, including Illinois, to Lyndon B. Johnson.

Less than a year later, Charlotte Reid, after announcing she would go to Vietnam at her own expense, became the first member of Congress to be cleared by the Defense Department to visit the war zone. American intervention to prevent a Communist takeover of South Vietnam had become the subject of bitter controversy early in 1965 after President Johnson ordered U.S. bombing attacks on North Vietnam. The full-scale antiwar movement that would force verbal battle lines to be drawn all across the nation had not yet been launched, but peace vigils and the burning of draft cards were not uncommon. In the 15th District of Illinois, where patriotism runs deep, there was widespread concern about the effect such protests might have on the morale of U.S. combat troops.

"I want to reassure our fighting men that the overwhelming majority of loyal Americans stands back of them 100 per cent," Mrs. Reid said before leaving for Saigon. With her, she took the names of GIs from her constituency who were serving in South Vietnam and a petition supporting the U.S. effort there signed by more than 2,000 residents.

When the four-day visit ended, she was satisfied she had not been overprotected. She flew over the jungle treetops in an open helicopter with a Marine machine-gunner at each elbow; observed the aftermath of a Vietcong ambush on Hill 22 near Da Nang; talked with the wounded being brought into a mobile Army surgical hospital in the Bien Hoa area; toured such outposts as Monkey Mountain, and boarded the aircraft carrier *Ticonderoga* as it plied the South China Sea. She also visited the recently liberated villages of Cong My, Le My, and Hoa Loc.

"Needless to say," she wrote in a report to her constituents, "I was surprised that the men ended up thanking me for making the effort to come to see them." When she telephoned the families, it was possible, she says, "to honestly reassure them that their sons and husbands felt it was their duty to be there and were determined to secure a lasting victory over Communist aggression."

To bridge the information gap between Washington and north-central Illinois, Congresswoman Reid periodically mailed questionnaires to registered voters. Answers to a list of carefully prepared questions, she believes, are better indicators of public sentiment than primaries. "Once the returns had been tabulated, it was up to me," she says, "to act."

When 82 per cent of her constituents responded that they favored "a constitutional amendment which would allow prayer and Bible readings on a voluntary basis in public schools," she sponsored a resolution to rescind the Supreme Court decision outlawing public school prayers. In a plea for passage on the House floor, she offered a cogent argument:

There are a great many contradictions in our country, and some of them simply do not make sense. The matter of prohibiting a prayer time for children in our public schools is one of them. Each day when the House convenes, the Speaker gavels for order and then says: "The Chaplain will offer prayers." Chaplains of the House and Senate, whose salaries are paid from public funds, offer their prayers in a public building built from public funds. When the distinguished Justices of the Supreme Court of the United States are announced by the Court Crier, he asks God to "save this honorable court." But the court has ruled that prayers by and for children in public schools are prohibited.

"Those who disagreed with me at home were quick with their rebuttal," she remembers. An editorial in the *Elburn Herald* considered "the problems which would arise in the future" to illustrate "how risky it would be to breech *[sic]* the wall separating church and state: The School Board members are of different faiths. Which would write the prayer? Would each teacher decide? Or would 'Springfield' [the state capital] do it, or Washington?" Noting "Mrs. Reid's comparatively sheltered background," the editor suggested she had "underestimated the explosive character of the issue."

Charlotte Reid is a woman of exceedingly gentle disposition, but she does become impatient with people who fail to see the association between religion and government. "Our government is more than just a set of laws," she says, "and religion is more than a mere set of rules to live by—it is a way of life. Therefore, it is a primary source of ideals for our country and our democracy. How can we have a moral government without a moral 'We The People'?"

The tall photogenic brunette from Illinois does not consider herself a feminist, yet she has often demonstrated her opposition to discrimination based on sex. After receiving a routine bulletin announcing a calisthenics class for members of the House, she was one of three congresswomen to appear at the door of the men's gym—to the embarrassment of a startled attendant who stammered, "It's just for members of Congress." The story was front-page news in papers as far away as Paris. She again made headlines when she arrived on the House floor wearing a black wool, bell-bottomed pantsuit, high fashion in 1969. "Yet no one paid much attention," she recalls, "to my speech on behalf of the Equal Rights Amendment sponsored by Martha Griffiths [Democrat of Michigan]."

Charlotte Reid had initially thought that being a woman might be a handicap in Congress. But such was not the case. She was appointed to the Interior and Insular Affairs Committee because the chairman thought a woman's view was needed. "Men respect our opinions and ideas," she frequently stated, during her congressional years. "Small as our numbers are, we create a needed balance in the complicated business of adapt-

ing our governmental processes to the requirements of a changing society."

Believe it or not, says Mrs. Reid, there have been times when
the men actually thanked God that there were ladies in the
House. "After members took up a collection to buy a wedding gift for the President's daughter, Tricia, and fiance Edward Finch Cox," she remembers, "there was no debate over
who would count the money and make the purchase. The
Speaker designated a bipartisan committee of two—two wom-
en. Mrs. Nixon indicated that Tricia would like a pair of silver
candelabra, so that is what Leonor Sullivan [Democrat of Mis-
souri] and I selected."

Speculation that Congresswoman Reid would be appointed
to the FCC appeared in print as early as May 1970 when the
Washington Star predicted that "our girl Charlotte will move
onstage." She and Richard Nixon have been good friends since
she won her first political race and received a "Dear Charlotte"
letter on stationery bearing the Broad Street address of his
Manhattan law firm. "Pat joins me in sending our congratula-
tions and very best wishes," he wrote on a day in which news
of Republican congressional successes was, in his words, "pretty thin."

In accepting the seven-year FCC appointment, she became
the second woman to serve on the seven-member commission,
and the first since 1948. Taking the $38,000 job meant a cut in
her $42,500 salary.

With campaigning behind her, she has begun what she calls
a "new challenge." Even before being confirmed by the Senate, she announced that she felt her past experience, both in
Congress and in broadcasting, would give her "a good understanding and a balanced view of some of the problems of the
communications industry, as well as the public need." At a time
when many difficult decisions confront the FCC, she is pleased
"that the President feels I can make a meaningful contribution."

IRENE B. BAKER
REPUBLICAN OF TENNESSEE

The nine-county East Tennessee 2d District which Irene
Baker was elected to represent is unusual in that the men it
has sent to Congress have usually held the job for life. When
Representative Howard H. Baker died on January 7, 1964, it

had been served for most of the century by only three men, all Republicans.

The decision by GOP leaders to nominate Mrs. Baker, 62, "for the remainder of the term" was made quickly and unanimously. Predictably, it achieved the desired effect. The coterie of hopefuls who had been expected to toss their hats into the ring bowed out temporarily, thus postponing a wide-open, probably acrimonious squabble within the Republican Party.

Initially it appeared that her selection might also eliminate Democratic opposition. One high-ranking Democrat told Mike Miller, Washington correspondent for the *Knoxville News-Sentinel,* that he didn't think the party "should even field a candidate against Mrs. Baker." His opinion was not shared, however. Democrat Willard Yarborough, a reporter on the same newspaper, waged an intensive campaign and collected 31,763 votes. It was a good showing, but nearly 9,000 short of victory. He had little chance of winning in a strong Republican district against a well-known and respected widow who proved to be an unusually effective campaigner. Mrs. Baker's personal party credentials further strengthened her candidacy. A GOP national committeewoman, she was also chairman of the Grass Roots Organization of Republican Women (GROW), a statewide committee seeking new ways to reach women voters.

Witty and attractive, Mrs. Baker became involved in politics, she says, because of "loyalty to my party and to friends." The former Irene Bailey of Sevierville, she was a young widow employed as an abstractor of titles by the Tennessee Valley Authority in the early 1930s when she met Baker, a widower with two small children, Howard H., Jr., and Mary Elizabeth. They were married in 1935, and a daughter, Beverly, was born two years later. Beginning in 1938, when Baker ran unsuccessfully for governor, through 1962, when he won his sixth consecutive term in the U.S. House of Representatives, she played a major part in every campaign. In Washington she worked in his office but was not on the payroll. During the nearly 10 months she was a member of the 88th Congress, a colleague who served with her on the Government Operations Committee remembers that she was known "for doing her work without fanfare but doing it well."

Still sprightly and on-the-go despite her 71 years, she commutes daily during the week from her home overlooking Fort Loudon Lake to downtown Knoxville where she is city welfare director. Although she lives intensely in the present, political history fills the lakeside house. Among the many mementos in the oak-paneled library is a piece of sandstone from the original U.S. Capitol, *circa* 1793.

The Baker name resumed its prominence in Washington in 1967 when Howard H. Baker, Jr., took the oath as a U.S. senator. Three years earlier he had been mentioned as a possible candidate for the congressional seat left vacant by his father's death—but only if Irene Baker refused to run.

PATSY T. MINK

DEMOCRAT OF HAWAII

In physical appearance Patsy Mink reflects her Japanese ancestry: she is petite, her facial features porcelain-like. In temperament she is tart yet profoundly humanistic. She abhors bigotry, cherishes candor, and wholly reveres independence. At once intellectual and optimistic, she possesses an anti-Establishment image shared by most liberal activist Democrats. One thing she does not have is an identity crisis. "Patsy was a liberated woman long before the movement had a name," says a former member of Oahu Young Democrats, an organization Mrs. Mink revitalized in 1954.

Although Hawaii has a tradition of beloved female rulers, discrimination against women policymakers in the 50th state is as prevalent as it is on the mainland. Even Patsy Mink's parents did not initially support her political ambitions. "Like most natives, they are quiet and retiring," she says, "and therefore were fearful of the publicity—for themselves and for me. Only after my election to the Territorial House in 1956 were they able to understand that I no longer needed to be protected from anything."

A political career was not on Mrs. Mink's agenda when she returned to Hawaii in the early 1950s with a husband, a baby daughter, and a law degree from the University of Chicago. "My ambition was simply to be a practicing attorney—one of the best," she says. As the second woman of Oriental ancestry to be admitted to the Hawaii bar, she hoped to join a Honolulu law firm, but none of those to which she applied would hire her. " 'Stay home and take care of your child,' I was told. So I opened my own office, renting space for $50 a month." While waiting for clients, she became involved with the community, the Democratic Party, and the drive for statehood, all of which led to seeking political office for herself.

From the House, she moved to the Territorial Senate. Although she lost her bid for the U.S. House in 1959, the year

Hawaii was admitted to the Union, she tried again in 1964 and, at 36, became the first woman from the 50th state to be elected to Congress. Patsy Mink celebrated by observing the old Japanese custom of painting in the missing eye on her *daruma* doll. (Considered a good luck symbol, the doll is purchased without eyes. One is painted in at the beginning of a new venture, the other when the owner achieves success.)

Congresswoman Mink, originally elected at large, has since 1971 represented the 2d Congressional District: the windward and leeward sides of Oahu, plus Hawaii, Maui, Molokai, Kauai, Lanai, and Niihau. Nearly 60 per cent of her constituents are nonwhite, with Japanese Americans comprising one-third of the population. Ethnically, she identifies with the latter. The granddaughter of Japanese who migrated in the 1880s to work in the sugar cane fields, she was born in Paia, a village on Maui Island, in 1927. Her father, Suematsu Takemoto, was one of the first natives of Japanese descent to earn a degree in civil engineering at the University of Hawaii. Five of her Nisei relatives served with distinction in World War II.

As Patsy Takemoto, she was introduced to politics while attending Maui High School, where she was elected student body president. Valedictorian of the 1944 graduating class, she enrolled in premedicine at the University of Hawaii, then studied at Wilson College in Chambersburg, Pennsylvania, and subsequently at the University of Nebraska. "Our family physician had been one of my heroes," she explains. After earning a bachelor's degree in zoology and chemistry at the University of Hawaii, she decided that law, not science, would enable her to be more independent. It was "a lucky accident," she recalls, "to be admitted to the University of Chicago Law School. A quota for foreigners existed, and some idiot there thought Hawaii was a foreign country, so I was accepted."

In 1964 the decision to move as a family to Washington, Mrs. Mink says, was a joint one—"made by John, Gwendolyn and me." John Francis Mink, a World War II Air Force hero from Pennsylvania who is as well known in his field of specialization, hydrology, as his wife is in hers, serves as her campaign manager. "As a geologist, he has much more flexibility than most husbands," she explains. "In the capital he opened his own business as a consultant in water supply." Not quite jokingly, she adds, "If I wasn't already in Congress, I think he'd be a candidate."

Does he mind being listed on social protocol lists as "congressman's spouse"? "Not really," he says. "She's simply John

Mink's wife in my professional groups." He views his political role as that of a confidential adviser. "We discuss the issues, take positions, have differences of opinion, and eventually come to some sort of consensus. The final decision in any vote in Congress, though, is Patsy's."

Representative Mink arrived on Capitol Hill just as President Lyndon Johnson was escalating U.S. military involvement in Vietnam. The conflict itself had not been a point of controversy during her campaign, but she early committed herself unequivocally to the antiwar faction in Congress. When peace efforts failed, her measured tone turned strident. Nixon's war policy was compared to Hitler's atrocities. "It is just as immoral to intervene with a virtual genocide in Vietnam as it was for the Aryan 'pure' race in Germany to slaughter six million Jews" became a standard line in her speeches, which also advocated amnesty for men who had evaded the draft and Executive clemency for those whose protests while in uniform resulted in a less-than-honorable discharge.

Mrs. Mink's opposition to the war over the years has cost her some votes in the 2d District, where major military installations are vital to the economy. Her GOP opponent in 1968 depicted her as a "friend of Hanoi." Speaking as "a person of Asian descent," she ignored the epithet and charged that "any justification of the war reflects a racist policy which approves the continued slaughter of Asians by Asians. Unless our people can be made to understand the magnitude of the error in Vietnam, and why it happened," she declared, "the malignancy in our national mentality will continue."

> Throughout our brief history, we have pretended that the civilization of Western Europe was the sole guiding force of human destiny. . . . We need to know that there has been culture in Asia, and science and art, going back for thousands of years. The Caucasian race alone cannot lay claim to all the triumphs of human ingenuity. . . . Oriental life is no less valuable than European life.

Combining the populist vision of Senator George McGovern of South Dakota with the reform concept of Wisconsin senator William Proxmire, Patsy Mink attracts voters to whom the state of the nation is a pressing concern. She emphasizes that:

> *People,* young and old, are the principal purpose for the existence of any government. I believe we can turn this country around and generate a prosperity which enriches our soul: full employment; more schools, more teachers; more food for the hungry; more

technology for a cleaner and purer environment; more mass transportation; more open spaces, parks, and recreational facilities;
more housing for the poor; a health care program which guarantees every human being free hospitalization as a matter of right;
a child care program for children of all ages.

Nothing better illustrates her feisty persistence than the
course of action she has followed in pursuit of equality of opportunity for members of her own sex. When President Nixon
nominated George Harrold Carswell to be an associate justice
of the Supreme Court, Mrs. Mink was the first opposition witness and the only member of Congress to ask the Senate Judiciary Committee to reject Carswell on the ground that his
confirmation would constitute "an affront to the women of America." Citing Carswell's refusal, while a judge of the 5th U.S.
Circuit Court of Appeals, to reconsider a woman's claim that
she was denied a job because she had children of preschool
age (*Ida Phillips* vs. *Martin Marietta Corporation*), Representative Mink said that he "demonstrated a total lack of understanding of the concept of equality . . . and the right of wom-
en to be treated equally and fairly under the law."

By exposing Carswell's alleged bias, Patsy Mink set off a chain
of events rarely witnessed in new or old times in government. The Nixon Administration entered the case on the side
of Mrs. Phillips, the mother refused employment as an assembly trainee, and the Justice Department asked the Supreme
Court to hear her appeal. Back in Hawaii both houses of the
State Legislature passed anti-Carswell resolutions citing his "in-
sensitivity to the delicate issues of equal treatment regardless
of race and sex." In turn, Republican Senator Hiram L. Fong,
a member of the Judiciary Committee who had voted for the
nominee and whose vote Nixon needed on the Senate floor,
called a news conference two days before the crucial roll call
to reveal he had changed his mind and would "vote against
confirmation."

Patsy Mink believes that she "had something to do" with
Carswell being defeated by a 51-to-45 vote. But she categori-
cally denies the role which author Richard Harris accorded her
in his book, *Decision*; namely, that "she told several audiences
she might be compelled to run against Fong when he came up
for re-election the following fall" if he did not vote against
Carswell. The congresswoman would have liked to make the
Senate race and had received encouragement to pursue her
ambition, but almost a week before Fong announced his turn-

about she had declared publicly her decision "to defer making the move at this time." Funding a senatorial campaign, she pointed out, would not have been a problem. "I would have raised the money as I had always done—through small amounts from literally thousands of people."

Money—or the lack of it—makes a difference to Mrs. Mink only when the high cost of commuting between Washington and Honolulu is added up. Because she likes to see her constituents often, it has been necessary to spend some of her $42,500 annual salary on airline tickets. "I use the travel time [10½ hours each way] to advantage," she says. On those weekends that she is airborne, she manages to "get in a full day of reading."

Representative Mink's dedication to equality and reform led to her decision in 1971 to accept an invitation from a group of Oregonians to enter the 1972 May Presidential primary in that state. While a Gallup poll had indicated that 66 per cent of the American public would support a qualified female candidate for President, she made it clear in seven weekend visits to Oregon that she was not in the race solely to advance the cause of women. "I'm running for two reasons," she said:

> Without a woman contending for the Presidency, the concept of *absolute equality* will continue to be placed on the backburner as warmed-over lip service.
>
> My candidacy offers a real and tangible [political] alternative, based—if any one word can be singled out—on humanism.

Although she garnered only 2 per cent of the vote in the only preferential primary in which all contenders for the Democratic nomination were represented, she feels she did not "waste time and energy." The experience convinced her that "there'll be a woman Vice President sooner than might otherwise have been the case."

As a native of a multiracial archipelago admired for its high degree of harmony and assimilation, she would prefer that her equal rights objectives (not to be confused with those of the Women's Liberation Movement) could be achieved without angry rhetoric—or at least with a minimum of waspish debate. But while arguing before the Democratic National Priorities Committee that the right of women to be policymakers should be at or near the top of the party's list, she discovered that it sometimes takes an outward display to drive home an inward lesson.

One committee member, Edgar F. Berman, who was also former Vice President Hubert Humphrey's personal physician, took exception to her proposition. "Physical and psychological inhibitants," Dr. Berman declared, particularly "the raging hormonal influences" of the menstrual cycle and menopause, limit women's potential in the executive spheres of business and politics. "Suppose," he speculated, "that we had a menopausal woman President who had to make the decision on the Bay of Pigs or the Russian contretemps with Cuba at the time?" She might be "subject to the curious mental aberrations of that age group."

Startled and angry, Mrs. Mink, by letter, demanded Berman's ouster from the committee. He was guilty, she wrote, "of the basest sort of prejudice against women." His "use of the menstrual cycle and menopause was to ridicule woman and to caricature all women as neurotic and emotionally unbalanced." Such "a disgusting performance," she contended "was as indefensible and as astonishing as those who still believe, let alone dare state, that the Negro is physiologically inferior."

The upshot of the widely publicized brouhaha, headlined in *Time* as "Hormones in the White House," was Dr. Berman's resignation. In bowing out, however, he fired a parting salvo at Mrs. Mink, claiming that he had been crucified on the cross of liberation. Her anger, he stated, was in itself "a typical example of an ordinarily controlled woman under the raging hormonal imbalance of the periodic lunar cycle."

About 500 cases involving discrimination based on sex are received in her office each year, and often she is able to resolve them. When, for example, she learned that Post Office regulations barred women from positions as postal inspectors, she protested to then Postmaster General Winton M. Blount. Two weeks later applications for women postal inspectors were being accepted. One incidence of discrimination which she was powerless to change, however, concerned her own daughter, who, though qualified, was refused admittance to Stanford University. "The admissions office told her in a rejection letter that under its quota system only 40 per cent of the students could be women, no matter what their qualifications," Mrs. Mink says.

As a member of the Education and Labor Committee, an appointment Patsy Mink secured, in her own words, "only after the hardest and most intense campaign of my life," she has been able to draft legislation designed to eliminate sex discrimination at all educational levels. The women's education bill she sponsored in 1972 calls for specific changes in curriculum to do away with the role-conditioning to which girls are subjected in the public schools. She is also using personal persuasion to convince major textbook publishers to produce texts which portray women in other than traditional roles.

Although Congresswoman Mink has ruled out seeking national office again in 1976, she has made no such statement concerning the Senate. Whatever happens politically, it is certain that few will agree when it comes to adding her up. Some will call her—in fact, do call her—an opportunist. Others will praise her as a militant liberal who never relaxes in battling for human rights, civil liberties, and social progress. She does not find the dichotomy of opinion surprising. "We in the minority have suffered more," she says, "and are therefore willing to fight more."

LERA M. THOMAS
DEMOCRAT OF TEXAS

Texas is a state where a widow's dreams, like everything else, come big. In the 1966 congressional election year, Houston spawned, even by its own outsize standards, an overly ambitious political scheme. The central figure was 64-year-old Lera Millard Thomas, widow of a congressman who during his 29 years on Capitol Hill became one of the dozen most powerful men in the House of Representatives. Poor boy, close friend and valued ally of Democratic Presidents, member of the Appropriations Committee who steered Houston into the space age, man aboard Air Force One at Love Field in Dallas when Lyndon Baines Johnson was sworn in as Chief Executive, Albert Thomas in death left a widow who had spent nearly 44 years backstage in the role of mother (two daughters) and willing member of a political team.

It is doubtful whether Nacogdoches-born Mrs. Thomas could have become an overnight political celebrity in any other place but Texas. The state's election laws then in effect were bizarre. If a candidate died after the filing deadline (Thomas had paid his $3,500 filing fee prior to the February 7 cutoff date), his name remained on the first primary ballot and the votes cast for him were counted and credited to him. In the event a deceased candidate received a majority, the party hierarchy (in this case, the Harris County Democratic Executive

Committee) was required to choose a successor, whose name appeared on the general election ballot.

"It is possible that Thomas' name on the May 7 Democratic Primary ballot for the term commencing January 3, 1967 would receive a majority of the votes," the *Houston Post* reported on February 19, the day he was buried. "This would then make it possible for the Harris County Democratic Executive Committee to choose Mrs. Thomas as the nominee in the November election."

Even as Lera Thomas, like her husband a paradoxical mixture of humility and pride, won the right in a special March election to serve out the remainder of Thomas's unexpired term, a movement got under way in that part of northern Harris County described as the shops, docks, and yards of Houston to persuade the electorate to place an X opposite the dead congressman's name. The gist of the argument advanced by those who wanted Mrs. Thomas to be re-elected to the full term was that she was knowledgeable concerning the needs of the 8th Congressional District. "We see in her," one proponent said, "the modesty and integrity personified by her late husband." The voters, however, opted to send State Representative Bob Eckhardt to the 90th Congress.

Considering that Lera Thomas's term in the House lasted but nine months, her performance satisfied constituents. Being appointed to the Merchant Marine and Fisheries Committee helped. "I was able," she says, "to keep an eye on the Houston Ship Channel, one of Albert's concrete accomplishments."

Following a trip in December 1966 to South Korea and South Vietnam, where she personally delivered letters from Texas families to relatives and friends on duty there, she returned to Washington and served briefly as a consultant on manpower information in the Vietnam Bureau of the Agency for International Development.

Her vocabulary does not include the word retirement. Although in her early seventies, she leads a peripatetic life. The energy she once had for folksy-type political campaigning is channeled into overseeing a farm on which she raises cattle, restoring and furnishing 19th-century homes (including two log houses once inhabited by forebears), operating the Texana Museum she founded, and roaming the world in search of items to stock Millard's Crossing Antiques, the shop she owns in Nacogdoches. "Proceeds from guided tours through the restored 'village,'" she says proudly, "are donated to the Albert Thomas Scholarship Fund at Stephen F. Austin University."

MARGARET M. HECKLER

REPUBLICAN OF MASSACHUSETTS

Prior to the start of the $1.5 million 1972 Republican Convention in Miami Beach, political pundits predicted that the platform would be a Nixon document outlining what the White House envisioned to be the key issues of the fall campaign. Day care centers were not on the list, one reason being that the President had vetoed a child care bill on the ground it favored a communal approach "over against the family-centered approach."

Had Nixon read the *Congressional Record,* in particular the remarks of GOP Congresswoman Margaret Heckler of Massachusetts urging the House to override his veto, he could have anticipated a challenge from a not-unexpected source: a petite and peppery redhead who answers to the nickname Peggy.

Even as the White House offered stubborn but diminishing resistance to her platform plank advocating federally sponsored day care centers, a *Time* reporter at the convention noted that "Peggy worked over a staggering total of 96 drafts on child care. For two hours she argued for the inclusion of a single word: quality. During the tedious wrangling, she left the impression she was willing to walk out." Admitting that she would not take no for an answer, Mrs. Heckler suggested that "there should be a higher level of consciousness at the White House." Before the session ended, the Platform Committee endorsed a plank for child care, and she received a promise from Representative John Rhodes of Arizona, the committee chairman, to cosponsor a day care measure with her in the 93d Congress.

For the only Republican congresswoman from the most politically liberal state in the nation to challenge her own President is firm reinforcement of the importance she attaches to her constituents. "If there's anything that's number one with her," says a staffer, "it's serving the 10th Congressional District." Says Margaret Heckler: "I never intend to forget the people who put me here." Thus, it was for the working mothers in industrial Taunton and Fall River at the southern end of the district where, she says, "the need for day care is very real," that she fought the White House to a standoff.

Although Mrs. Heckler's biography is a matter of public record, hardly anyone who knows her in Massachusetts remembers that she was not born there. The only child of John and Alice O'Shaughnessy, who emigrated from Ireland to Long Island, she grew up in Flushing. John Heckler entered her life in the campus political arena. "He was a Yale freshman and I was running for the speakership of the Connecticut Intercollegiate Student Legislature. Up to that time all I had ever dreamed about was being a concert pianist. But after he helped me win, I knew I wanted to go into government through law." From Albertus Magnus, a small parochial women's college in New Haven (1953) she went on to Boston College Law School (1956), where the dean was Robert Drinan, a Jesuit and a Democrat who later ran successfully for Congress. Ten years of private law practice followed, then an apprenticeship with the Wellesley Republican Town Committee (1958–66) and the eight-member Massachusetts Governor's Council (1963–66).

Peggy Heckler's independence of mind, her refusal to conform to party lines or to Administration policy have made her appear unpredictable, if not undependable. Yet were she not of the precise temperament that she has manifested on Capitol Hill, she would never have had the courage in 1966 to challenge former GOP House Speaker Joseph W. Martin, Jr., who, at 81, had represented the 10th District (Bristol, Middlesex, Norfolk, and Plymouth counties) for 42 years.

"What right does *she* have to his seat?" fumed a partisan of the grand old man of the Grand Old Party. "Hasn't he pledged that this will be the last time he'll run?"

He had. But in Mrs. Heckler's view—and in that of other Republicans who would admit the truth—1966 was the year to change the *status quo*. The GOP had a strong ticket headed by Governor John A. Volpe, and State Attorney General Edward W. Brooke was favored to win a Senate seat. "Two years from now," she argued at the time, "the only statewide race will be for President, and another strong [Lyndon B.] Johnson win could hand the district to the Democrats."

For a complex of reasons, certainly including male chauvinism, the implacable 34-year-old Margaret Heckler of Wellesley Hills did not receive official backing from the GOP in her 1966 congressional race. Even Volpe, for whom she had campaigned vigorously, stated publicly that Martin should be returned to Capitol Hill. Volpe shrewdly avoided mentioning that the voice of the octogenarian was being heard at fewer than 50 per cent of House roll call votes.

Mrs. Heckler made only oblique references to Martin's age and loss of vigor. "We all respect what he has done in the past," she told a group of women at a coffee klatch in Newton, "but can the district afford to wait to have its voice recorded on the crucial issues? We can respect the past without forfeiting the present and the future."

Enough voters agreed they needed a full-time representative to enable her to win the primary by 3,223 votes. Compared to the nomination, the election campaign was even more difficult. Many Republicans were embittered over the way Martin's career had been terminated. A star-studded cast of Democrats—Vice President Hubert Humphrey, Postmaster General Lawrence O'Brien, and the Kennedy brothers, Robert and Edward—stumped for her opponent, Patrick Harrington, Jr., a popular attorney. Finally, the 10th District, once a GOP stronghold, was gradually going Democratic. There were 81,000 registered Democrats and 90,000 Independents to 68,000 Republicans.

The many housewives who had rallied to the slogan "You Need a Heckler on the Governor's Council" went into action again, and the candidate herself shook a thousand hands a day. No gathering was too small for her attention. "The men kept saying I couldn't make it," she recalls, "but the women convinced them that a woman, even if she was the underdog, deserved their backing." By winning the second and decisive round, she went to Washington in 1967 owing no political favors. She was free to be a "Heckler in Congress."

Despite a drastic redrawing of the 10th District lines in 1968, she handily defeated District Attorney Edmund Dinis, a 44-year-old native of Portuguese ancestry (the largest ethnic group in the area) who would later achieve national prominence as prosecutor of the case involving the death by drowning of Senator Edward Kennedy's female companion at Chappaquidick. Two years later, when the Democrats nationwide increased their House majority by nine, Margaret Heckler was not among those they unseated. As a Republican, she has proved that a charismatic person with a facile mind, a dramatic sense of timing, a drive to be on the cutting edge of change, and a willingness to speak out on behalf of constituents can attract and hold an enthusiastic following—even in a Democratic stronghold.

No one is prouder of Margaret Heckler's sucess in politics than her husband John and their three children: Belinda, 15; Alison, 13, and John, Jr., 12. When the Hecklers' son announced that his ambition was to be President, Alison, obviously impressed by her mother's government role, replied: "You can't. You're a boy." Because John Heckler's investment business keeps him in Massachusetts during the week, the couple takes turns traveling to and from McLean, Virginia, and Boston.

The male-dominated U.S. Congress, like the U.S. Army, appears to enjoy placing square pegs in round holes. But at least there was tradition behind Margaret Heckler's appointment as a freshman, not to the Judiciary Committee she requested, but to Veterans' Affairs. The first congresswoman from Massachusetts, Edith Nourse Rogers, had risen in seniority to chair this committee during two Republican-controlled congresses. Since 1969 Representative Heckler has also served on Banking and Currency, chaired by Wright Patman of Texas.

During the 1972 Presidential campaign when Representative Patman revealed over prime-time television that he had authorized a staff investigation of "the mysterious and complicated route of $700,000 collected in Texas for the Republicans by officials of the Pennzoil Corporation," viewers were treated to an unrehearsed verbal confrontation between the elderly Patman and Margaret Heckler, one of the committee's most junior members. Uninvited and unannounced, she appeared beside him in front of TV network microphones, where, in an articulate and forceful manner, she requested the names of the investigators. "The committee members have not been kept informed," she said. Of her assault on Patman's credibility, ABC news editor Robert R. Roy said later: "That took guts, but she made her point."

The legal investigator in Margaret Heckler has also emerged on the Hill. Her sleuth-playing during the 91st Congress uncovered the fact that 80 per cent of all body armor being shipped to U.S. troops in Vietnam was defective. In the face of Defense Department complacency ("Defective armor is better than no armor at all"), she called the $16 million contract to the attention of the General Accounting Office, the independent watchdog arm of Congress. Comptroller General Elmer B. Staats replied in typical government bureaucratese:

> We share your concern over the possible defects which may be occurring in the production of these items, and we are hopeful that the action taken by our Office in directing that proper consideration be given to the question as to the propriety of exercising the option provided for in the specification and/or test procedures which may be employed in future procurements of this vital item.

The Pentagon subsequently improved the specifications for body armor, and the congresswoman had the assurance not only of more careful attention to procurement procedures in the future but of increased surveillance during the testing stages.

On at least one occasion she has broken precedent to secure effective legislation. In the spring of 1971 a large Soviet fishing fleet off the coast of Massachusetts, while harassing American lobster boats, destroyed gear valued at $250,000. The State Department, hoping to prevent further incidents, arranged a meeting aboard the Russian mother ship between the Soviet fleet commander and U.S. officials. No firm agreement was reached, however. The only deterrent to Russian encroachment, the lobstermen told Mrs. Heckler, was round-the-clock presence of Coast Guard cutters. When she learned that a shortage of funds and manpower would not permit their presence 24 hours a day, she went to the House floor and won an additional $1 million for the Coast Guard, earmarked specifically for lobster boat surveillance. Appropriations bills are rarely amended on the floor, and in making an exception in this case, the House hierarchy clearly bowed to the legislative finesse of the Gentlewoman from Massachusetts.

In Margaret Heckler Congress has acquired a member with high hopes. She not only wants the House to be restored to its former pre-eminence but will work for certain reforms. In place of the present seniority system, she advocates that committee chairmen be elected by secret ballots cast by the five most senior members of each committee. She also proposes that the length of House terms be lengthened from two to four years, that the franking privilege be suspended during the last month prior to an election "to give nonincumbents less of a handicap," and that there will be a follow-through on congressional effort to discipline the use of money in politics. Finally, she says, "we should elect the President in the same way we elect all other officials, by direct vote of his constituents, with the high man winning." A tall order, but in her view, "necessary—if we are going to make government workable and politics responsible again."

Against the System

SHIRLEY CHISHOLM

DEMOCRAT OF NEW YORK

Upon occasion Shirley Chisholm has been called headstrong, pugnacious, egotistical, overbearing, expedient, power-hungry, brazen, peevish, and pushy. True enough. At one time or another this 100-pound black congresswoman whom aides call "Chizzy" has no doubt deserved each of these epithets. She also has been described as purposeful, magnetic, bright, amazing, courageous, spunky, dynamic, and forthright. This irrepressible and exasperating Brooklynite, quixotic and impulsive, has always been what the title of her autobiography suggests: *Unbought and Unbossed.* To black male politicians she is an everlasting problem child. Her fonts of tears and laughter lie very close together. No one knows, upon encountering her in political exchange, whether to expect a kiss or a dirk—or both. Almost anything can happen when this maverick is up and about, but whatever it is, it won't be dull.

And the fireworks, which everyone thought ended with Mrs. Chisholm's unsuccessful attempt to forge a coalition of her race, her sex, and all other disgruntled minorities that would culminate in the 1972 Democratic nomination for President of the United States, may have just begun. Supporters, proud of the 151.95 delegate votes she received for the Presidency, are urging her to enter the 1974 New York Senate contest. In the meantime she continues as "a shaker-upper of the system," the self-ascribed role she has been playing in politics for more than 20 years.

Shirley Chisholm was *not,* as she said repeatedly prior to the Miami Beach convention in July 1972 "the first woman to seriously seek the Presidency." In 1964 Senator Margaret Chase Smith of Maine entered two primaries, was nominated at the GOP National Convention, and received 27 delegate votes on the first ballot. But to those who followed the Brooklyn congresswoman along a new "Chisholm Trail" for nearly eight months, she *seemed* to be the first female candidate for the highest office in the land. "Even Senator Hubert Humphrey [one of the contenders] was amazed by the showing Chisholm made in the Florida primary," according to *Ms.* editor Gloria Steinem, "and said often that, with a little money and organization, 'she might have defeated us all.'"

What made Shirley run? Critics in the media and elsewhere have offered varied opinions:

"To gain publicity."—Douglas Kiker, NBC News

"It was a vehicle for her ego."—Pete Hamill, *New York Post*

"To enhance her lecture income."—A Democratic assemblyman from the Bedford-Stuyvesant section of Brooklyn who requested that he not be identified by name

"To be a power broker and a kingmaker."—Vernon Jarrett, *Chicago Tribune*

"Like everybody else in politics, [because she's] selfish, practical, political, and playing the money game."—Alcee Hastings, a black Fort Lauderdale lawyer

Congresswoman Chisholm's own explanation is a mixture of apparent naïveté and impressive bravado. In announcing her candidacy, she said she wanted "to repudiate the ridiculous notion that the American people will not vote for a qualified candidate simply because he is not white or because she is not male." As to her qualifications, she emphasized her "near-genius IQ," placing the figure variously at 160 and 170. "I have four college degrees [a bachelor's, a master's, and two education certificates for additional graduate work]. I'm 10 credits from a Ph.D. I'm the only candidate who speaks Spanish fluently. What else do you want?"

For one thing, would-be supporters wanted a potential winner. "It's unrealistic to back Shirley Chisholm," said Coretta King, widow of assassinated civil rights leader Dr. Martin Luther King, Jr. "It will be another four or eight years before a black woman has a chance." "She knows where it's at," proclaimed a Miami nightclubber, "but I'm voting for John Lindsay because the country won't support a woman." Minorites also wanted something else: a positive, workable platform. Although she sometimes talked about the traditional Democratic bread-and-butter questions of inflation, unemployment, and high taxes, more often she spoke with intellectual arrogance—either *against* President Nixon, accusing him of being guilty of the "big lie" in general and of "deliberate conniving deception" concerning the Vietnam War negotiations, or *for* Shirley Chisholm: "I'm not going to be modest; I'm the best thing going. I am the only fresh new voice. I am the only unique candidate, and the only dark horse, literally and figuratively." Midway into the campaign the prize-winning *Washington Star* columnist Mary McGrory wrote: "Her program is Shirley Chisholm."

The congresswoman's predisposition toward self-styled political activism can be traced more to her sex than to her color. "I've suffered worse discrimination as a woman than as a black," she says. A faithful dreamer of the American dream "borne up," in her words, "by Almighty God," she decided early in her adult life "to overcome." The pragmatic place to begin, she reasoned, was in the schoolroom ("Where else could a black woman start?"). As a nursery school teacher and later as supervisor of 10 New York City day care centers she had time during off-duty hours to search for a better base from which to shake the foundations of prejudicial thinking.

The longer she studied the indifference displayed toward black women by the all-white male bosses who in the 1940s and 1950s ruled the 17th Assembly District in Bedford-Stuyvesant where she lived, the more convinced she became that the political process offered the best hope for changing the *status quo.* Her personal thrust determined, she took the next step: open defiance of the autocratic system. It worked. Within a decade, this rebel with a mission rose from the lowly ranks of the Unity Democratic Club to the lofty heights of the U.S. Congress.

She explains her meteoric ascent this way: "I'm a consistent fighter. I've been a person who has never turned down a challenge."

Through long years of toil in the political vineyards of Brooklyn, Shirley Chisholm became a well-known personality. On Capitol Hill, however, despite the fanfare stemming from her uniqueness (not only was she the first black woman ever elected to Congress but in 1969 the *only* new feminine face), she was merely one neophyte among the 243-member Democratic majority.

"I've been beating the odds all my life," she said in obvious reference to the cynical view she took of playing by the rules. "I have no intention of just sitting quietly and observing. I intend to speak out immediately in order to focus attention on the nation's problems." The voice was as strident as the slight lisp of her West Indian accent could force it to be. During the first session of the 91st Congress she used it to challenge the hierarchy. In A-B-C order, she listed her committee preferences: Education and Labor ("I would bring a lot of know-how and expertise to that assignment"), Post Office and Civil Service (she would look into promotion policies governing minorities), and Foreign Affairs ("I happen to feel that the future of black people in America is linked to the future of Africa").

The logic behind her appointment to the Agriculture Committee and to its subcommittees on family farms, rural development, and forests has never been made public. The old saw about "a tree grows in Brooklyn" aside, an assignment less relevant to the vertical concrete reservation she represents would be difficult to imagine. Mrs. Chisholm's written request to have her name removed from the Agriculture Committee roster was not without precedent, even among female newcomers to Congress. The first to reject a committee assignment was Republican Florence Prag Kahn of San Francisco, whose 1925 objection to being placed on the Indian Affairs Committee was similar to that raised by Shirley Chisholm 44 years later: namely, that a House member from an urban congressional district is not qualified to represent a rural constituency. The mistake that the congresswoman from Brooklyn made—from the standpoint of older members—was her inept, melodramatic handling of the situation.

Bypassing Wilbur Mills of Arkansas, chairman of the Democratic selection committee, she took her complaint directly to House Speaker John McCormack of Massachusetts. If he did not reassign her to another committee, she threatend "to do her own thing." A pattern of hostility between those who held the appointive reins and the upstart from Bedford-Stuyvesant was set—destined to endure. She was, however, transferred —not to one of the committees of her choice, but to the Veterans' Affairs Committee.

The fearless facet in Shirley Chisholm's makeup is not, as might be presumed, based on street reality but on heritage.

Brooklyn-born (1924) but reared on her maternal grandmother's farm in Barbados from age three to nine, Shirley Anita St. Hill early manifested characteristics not normally associated with a child who is both impoverished and undersized: she was precocious and dauntless. "Even Mother was almost afraid of me," she boasts. She approached adolescence equipped with a British-style education that adhered rigidly to the "spare-the-rod-spoil-the-child" maxim and a militant sense of black pride, transmitted primarily by her father, a native of British Guiana (now Guyana) who became a factory worker in Brooklyn and a disciple of Marcus Garvey, the Jamaican immigrant noted in the United States for his evangelicism on behalf of black separatism.

The eldest of four girls, Shirley's private hell in Brooklyn was not the cold, the ill-fitting clothes from the Welfare Department, or even the substandard diet, but an overprotective mother. Mrs. Ruby Seale St. Hill, a seamstress who also worked as a domestic, often left the impression that her primary family function was to mete out discipline. In her first-born, it sowed seeds of rebellion.

Had her parents not been poor, Shirley would have accepted one of the scholarships (Vassar, Oberlin) she was offered while attending Girls' High School; instead, she commuted by subway to Brooklyn College, a free-tuition municipal institution. Blacks were welcome, but in the early 1940s few could meet the entrance requirement of a "B" average; consequently, they made up only 2 per cent of the student body. While earning a *cum laude* degree in sociology (a minor in Spanish), she also became involved with the issues of minority rights. They were debated in the Political Science Society, in the Urban League settlement house where she worked as a volunteer, and in the Brooklyn chapter of the NAACP (National Association for the Advancement of Colored People). She recalls that she "sat through more meetings and discussions than I ever want to remember" and saw "very little get done." She vowed then that one day she "would tell the world how things were" as she saw them. In the meantime, she found a job with the Mt. Calvary Child Care Center in Harlem and enrolled in the evening division of Columbia University to earn a master's degree in early childhood education.

Conrad Chisholm, her husband since 1949, has been, she says, a distinct asset to her political career. Eight years her senior, he has a similar background. In Jamaica, where he was born, his father used a whip when necessary to enforce discipline; he observed politics at the grassroots level as secretary to his councilman father and struggled up the economic ladder—from cook to private investigator (insurance claims). When his wife ran for Congress and for the Presidency he took a leave of absence from his job with the New York City Bureau of Medical Services to be her chauffeur, research her speeches, and "see that she eats on time." He told Myra McPherson of the *Washington Post* that he considers himself a reassuring force for Shirley, whom he describes as "a thin bundle of nerves" and "my beautiful little star."

At a time in American history when the black man is nurturing his own new-found strength and pride, the black woman's role is particularly sensitive and complex. Conrad Chisholm believes—unlike certain black politicians in Brooklyn and Washington who have openly accused his wife of "castrating them" —that she has much to offer and should be encouraged. "Let's look at it this way," he has said: "If we're to get on an even keel, this country needs its best brains—whether it be man or woman, black or white."

Shirley Chisholm served her apprenticeship for Congress in the New York State Assembly (1965–68), the second Negro female to be elected to this body and the first from Brooklyn. While in Albany she was credited with legislation instituting the SEEK program that enables poor youngsters to go to college and with bills to extend prekindergarten programs, expand day care centers, provide domestics with unemployment insurance coverage, and permit teachers whose careers are interrupted by pregnancy to retain tenure rights.

Her decision to run for Congress when she did was prompted, she says, "by a black welfare mother who came to my house and told me that she and her friends wanted me to seek the office. She gave me a dirty envelope containing $9.62 in nickels, dimes and quarters and promised that if I ran, a group would sponsor fund-raising affairs every Friday night to help finance my campaign. Her gesture moved me to tears."

Prior to 1968, the district that would send her to Capitol Hill had for many years been divided like a pie among Brooklyn's all-white delegation (Representatives Frank Brasco, Emanuel Celler, Edna Kelly, and John Rooney)—a fact that galled blacks who resented not having a congressional voice of their own. Once Shirley Chisholm had defeated the Democratic organization candidate, William C. Thompson, in the June primary and had been named a national committeewoman, she figured she would have no trouble winning the general election. She did, that is, until James Farmer, founder of CORE (Congress of Racial Equality), was nominated by both the Republican and Liberal parties and she was forced to absent herself from the campaign for three weeks to recuperate from major surgery.

The area she sought to represent had an ethnic breakdown of 70 per cent Negro and Puerto Rican and 30 per cent white. At its heart lay mostly black Bedford-Stuyvesant. On the fringes to the north were Puerto Ricans in Williamsburg and Italians in the Bushwick section; to the south, Jews in Crown Heights. If the black vote were to splinter, the election would be decided by the white ethnic and Jewish electorate. From the standpoint of party registration, Mrs. Chisholm held an overwhelming advantage: the roughly 91,000 registered voters were 80 per cent Democratic.

While she fumed with impatience from her hospital bed about losing precious exposure, Farmer, sound trucks blaring, cruised the territory. Over and over he hammered away on a single theme: Because "racists and bigots" would hold positions of strength in the upcoming Congress, the blacks would need "strong, experienced representatives who could command national attention to stand up to them." Now and then he would ask, "Where's Mrs. Chisholm?"

When she reappeared, Farmer shifted his emphasis. In an undisguised appeal to black males, he introduced the issue of "matriarchal dominance"—the premise that "women have been in the driver's seat" in black communities for too long. His literature, stamped with the slogan "Vote Farmer First," stressed the need for "a strong male image" and "a man's voice in Washington."

Shirley Chisholm, calling "discrimination against women in politics particularly unjust," initiated a strategy calculated to attract the female vote, a tactic she had heretofore deliberately eschewed. She sought out feminine leaders of social groups, civic clubs, and the PTA, asking for united support.

When the returns were in, she was the winner, with 34,-885 votes or 67 per cent, while Farmer collected only 13,777. "If someone tries to use my sex against me," she said following her victory, "I delight in being able to turn the tables on him." There is no way to ascertain how many women voted for Mrs. Chisholm, but the fact she carried the Puerto Rican sections proved that her fluency in Spanish had been an asset.

A congratulatory telephone call from the defeated Presidential nominee, Hubert Humphrey ("Shirley, I'm sorry I won't be there to work with you") added fillip to her triumph, and a three-week vacation in Jamaica restored her health. She arrived in Washington to be greeted by a noisy group of followers who urged her to "Sock it to 'em, Shirley."

Over her years in public life she has frequently told audiences that "one thing people are afraid of in Shirley Chisholm is *her mouth*." She had promised her constituents that she would use it in the House "as an instrument of power" on their behalf. Obviously the majority believed her. But what kind of bills has she introduced or cosponsored? Only two bear her name: a comprehensive bill to establish day care facilities at a cost the first year of $5 billion and a bill to establish a memorial to Mary McLeod Bethune, founder and first president of Bethune-Cookman College in Florida. The child care proposal was vetoed by President Nixon, the other measure was tabled. Her name appears as a cosponsor of legislation to create a Martin Luther King national holiday, to abolish the House Un-American Activities Committee (now the Internal Security Committee), to establish a Cabinet-level Department of Consumer Affairs, to institute tax reforms, and so on. With the exception of the day care bill, none of her legislative activity has dealt specifically with the desperate problems in what has been called "the worst ghetto in the United States."

During her first term she said in a floor speech that she intended "to vote 'No' on every money bill that comes before this House that provides any funds for the Department of Defense." As one who has often mocked the "unmet promises" of "politics-as-usual politicans," she stumbled into the same pitfall when she subsequently cast an "Aye" on a number of defense appropriations bills.

In Brooklyn, where she returns almost every weekend, her popularity has remained high among those who delight in watching anyone stick a moral stiletto into the pompous consciousness of lawmakers far removed from rats and roaches. Others, however, have been highly critical of some of her congressional priorities. Black women have accused her of "plotting genocide" by advocating abortion reform. Assemblyman Thomas Fortune says that she spends "so much time with women's lib and gay lib that she has forgotten all about black lib in Bedford-Stuyvesant." "All we ever read in the newspapers about Shirley Chisholm," another constituent complains, "is what she does for the District of Columbia."

In hindsight, Mrs. Chisholm acknowledges that she allotted a disproportionate amount of time to "public relations endeavors" during her first term, but defends the aid she has rendered to the District of Columbia, the population of which is predominantly Negro. "I did not seek out D.C.—D.C. almost drove me 'nuts' when I came here. What is one who is committed to the underdog to do when help is being sought?" Ironically, it was the non-voting congressional delegate from the District of Columbia, Walter Fauntroy, who prevented her from entering the Presidential primary in the nation's capital. He planned to enter as a favorite son and promised that he would release his delegates to her on the second ballot. When party reform ruled out favorite-son candidates, he delivered the D.C. votes to McGovern. "I had been skeptical [about his promise]," she said later, "but he recalled to me he was a minister, so I went along—to find out that a minister can be no different from anybody else when it comes to power."

"Perhaps the sorest point in the relationship between Mrs. Chisholm and black males in general," Tom Buckley of the *New York Times* says, "is her commitment to the Women's Liberation Movement. They regard it as iniquitous that she should be devoting a considerable part of her energies to the cause of women, most of them middle class and white, when the great majority of black men are still scuffling for a place in the sun." The fact that the Chisholms, who are childless, are extremely well off in comparison with their Bedford-Stuyvesant neighbors is another point of contention. "Shirley can afford to be above the battle," one of the local Democratic leaders says. "She doesn't have six kids at home, all needing shoes at the same time." The most recent Chisholm acquisition is, in her words, "a fabulous hilltop home in the Virgin Islands."

Despite the mounting criticism, it is generally agreed that Mrs. Chisholm is the only personality with a broad following in the Brooklyn black community. She was re-elected in 1970 by 82 per cent. Such vote-getting strength would tend to disprove Pete Hamill's opinion that "her district has people in it who just want to make it through the night and don't care about Shirley Chisholm's position in history."

The congresswoman, says legislative aide Shirley Downs, "operates on a crisis-to-crisis basis" with respect to her district (reshaped in 1972), beset with such explosive problems as slum housing, high unemployment, crime—everything related to poverty. And although she continues to ply the lecture circuit ("I am $50,000 in debt as a result of the Presidential race"), she has raised her attendance record at House roll call votes—from 55 per cent in the 91st Congress (1969–71) to 72 per cent in the first session of the 92d. Moreover, she has been instrumental in securing essential grants for the 12th District: $1,147,000 for the Charles Drew Neighborhood Health Center; $150,000 for the Brooklyn Local Economic Development Corporation, and $450,000 for the Consumer Action Program in Bedford-Stuyvesant. She also helped launch the Cheetah Charter Bus Service Company, a minority enterprise, and obtained funds for the Afro-American Teachers Association, an organization that grants scholarships to minority students and helps place them in jobs.

For all of her thrust-and-cut militancy, Shirley Chisholm appears to have become at least a part-time practitioner of compromise. "She voted for two Southerners—Hale Boggs for majority leader and Joe D. Waggonner, Jr., for a choice Rules Committee spot—and so got a better committee assignment [Education and Labor, her first choice] for herself," *Newsweek* reported in the wake of the convening of the 92d Congress. When Sam Donaldson asked her during the nationally televised ABC program "Issues and Answers" if she had bargained for the post, she refused to answer directly, saying only, "There's nothing wrong with a pragmatic approach." Later she amplified this remark with a question of her own: "Why should black politicians be any different from white politicians?"

Congresswoman Chisholm has said that she will make no decision about her political future until 1974, when the Senate term of New York Republican Jacob Javits expires. In her autobiography she has stated, "It is likely I won't last as long in Congress as some. . . . I have had a feeling all along that I will probably do my thing for six or eight years at most." But as a result of her Presidential bid, which she declares "opened the door for women and blacks," there are indications she may have had second thoughts. "I'm a catalyst for change, don't forget, and I intend to shake up this system until it begins to turn itself around."

Profit and Loss

To a 1970 Gallup Poll question—"If your party nominated a woman to run for Congress from your district, would you vote for her if she were qualified for that job?"—most Americans (84 per cent) replied in the affirmative. Was it empty rhetoric or unvarnished truth? The election results implied that the answer lay somewhere in between.

As the poll indicated, public opinion concerning women's political rights had changed dramatically over the half century since ratification of the 19th Amendment. With the advent of the Women's Liberation Movement, the idea of woman's equality apparently had caught at last in the national mind.

Although 1970 was not the Year of the Woman, women did return to the political lists in force. Nearly a score, including the 10 House incumbents, campaigned for Congress. Individually, they acknowledged that they were heartened by the results of George Gallup's survey, specifically by the reasons cited by those receptive to the idea of more women becoming involved in politics: "Women are just as capable as men; the number of men and women in government should be about equal; women would bring a fresh, sincere approach; women are more efficient."

While not discounting opposition viewpoints—"Women lack the background or experience; politics is a man's world; men stand up better under pressure"—serious women politicians were not deterred by these or other vestiges of discrimination. Author and historian Catherine Drinker Bowen spoke for them when she told members of the League of Women Voters: "The things women believe in and want done will not be done until women are in elective office."

The congressional race that attracted the most attention nationwide starred Lenore Romney of Michigan and two-term Democratic Senator Philip A. Hart. "I'm running," said the 61-year-old wife of Housing and Urban Development Secretary George Romney, "because this country is in a terrible mess in every area, and the times demand new leadership." The majority of Michigan voters, however, many of whom asked, "You mean you have the nerve to challenge a United States Senator?" did not agree. Mrs. Romney, who feels her campaign was "doomed by the myth of male superiority," says that the "rawest example of prejudice came from a farmer who told me, 'Ma'am, we don't vote for women or niggers in this county.' "

In House contests, which traditionally have produced more female winners, at least five losers, including one incumbent, had a valid reason to question the credibility of the Gallup Poll. Twelve-year veteran Catherine May, Republican of Washington, was defeated for re-election, while four highly qualified first-time candidates failed to make it all the way to Washington: Los Angeles Democrat Myrlie B. Evers, 37, widow of murdered civil rights leader Medgar Evers; Antonina P. Uccello, 47, Republican mayor of Hartford, Connecticut; Phyllis Schlafly, fortyish, Illinois author of "A Choice Not an Echo," the pamphlet that sounded the theme for Barry Goldwater's 1964 Presidential campaign; and Kathleen Z. Williams, 50, former career editor of *Glamour* magazine, an Indiana Democrat.

When all the statistics were in, only three of the 62 newcomers elected to the 92d Congress (1971–73) were women. A trio of very different individuals, Bella S. Abzug of New York, Ella T. Grasso of Connecticut, and Louise Day Hicks of Massachusetts nevertheless had several things in common. Democrats all, they shared middle age, motherhood, and, by their own admission, overweight.

The prospect that women would regain some of the political ground lost during the 1960s was reflected in the fact that the total number in the 92d Congress rose to 15. In 1972 Elizabeth Andrews, Democrat of Alabama, won a special election to fill the vacancy resulting from the death of her husband, and Elaine Edwards, a Louisiana Democrat, was appointed to a short term in the Senate.

BELLA S. ABZUG

DEMOCRAT OF NEW YORK

Not since the turn of the century, when Carry Nation's saloon-smashing rampage forced the Kansas Legislature into special session, has the performance of a truculent female crusader provoked such astonishment and outrage. By refusing to hedge her radical opinions or follow congressional protocol, Bella Abzug hones the cutting edge of her will to dominate. She does not merely walk into the well of the House; she takes possession of it. She has the reputation of being a volcanic congresswoman in continual eruption and sometimes goes out of her way to live up to it.

"Abzugian" was introduced into the political lexicon on the opening day of the 92d Congress, when Ms. (her preference) Abzug, after being officially sworn in, took a second, or "people's oath" on the Capitol steps. It was administered by her friend and colleague from Brooklyn, Shirley Chisholm, before a crowd of cheering Manhattan constituents. In no less unconventional a gesture, she introduced her first bill on the opening day of the first session—a measure demanding withdrawal of American troops from Vietnam within six months. At the initial meeting of the Government Operations Committee, to which she had been assigned, she defied the chairman by voting against his proposal to exclude the press. The media were barred, but that did not prevent the freshman member from giving reporters a blow-by-blow description of what had transpired.

In her 1972 autobiography, which the *Washington Monthly* called the "emptiest ego trip since *I, a Woman*," she introduces herself as having been

> . . . described as a tough and noisy woman, a prizefighter, a man-hater, you name it. They call me Battling Bella, Mother Courage, and a Jewish mother with more complaints than Portnoy. There are those who say I'm impatient, impetuous, uppity, rude, profane, brash, and overbearing. Whether I'm any of these things, or all of them, you can decide for yourself. But whatever I am—and this ought to be made very clear at the outset—I am a very serious woman.

She has been given high marks for intent, but her critics believe that some of her methods have been counterproductive to the long-range interest of her constituents. "She comes on so strong," says a leading Democratic liberal, "that she loses votes before she's very far into her message." Republicans are more caustic: "She's irresponsible," according to an old-timer from New York. "She's been that way all her life, and been successful at it. She'll flout any convention, any custom to get attention."

Although Bella Abzug would be the first to disagree, her scattershot House record can be readily identified as having originated in the mind of a bellicose maverick. One of the most flagrant examples was her drive to muster support for the Abzug abortion-rights bill. Upon her request, the *Congressional Record* published 136 pages of material, mainly court decisions favoring legalized abortion, at a cost to the taxpayer of $150 per page, or approximately $20,000. Retaliation was swift. The Joint Committee on Printing reinstated a rule requiring any member of Congress wishing to insert more than two pages in the *Record* to include a cost estimate as part of the request for consent. Representative Abzug, who had on occasion downgraded the *Record* as "busy work for legislative aides trying to make it look as if congressmen—who are on the town—are on the House floor debating a vital issue," called the rule "onerous."

As the six-page biography available from Bella's office attests, "The energy which [she] and her passionate commitment to progressive causes brought to Congress [was] always evident in her life and activities before her election." Bronx-born (1920) Bella Savitzky, daughter of the proprietor of the Live and Let Live Meat Market on New York City's Ninth Avenue, where, she is fond of saying, "We plucked one chicken at a time," credits her grandfather, an orthodox Jew who emigrated from Russia, with instilling in her a "strong feeling for justice." Collecting pennies on street corners for the Zionist cause as a child was merely the first step in a 30-year precongressional career of legal activism on behalf of civil rights and civil liberties. "Fight" has been her key word whether in the vanguard of the defense of Willie McGee, a Mississippi Negro accused of raping a white woman (he was executed in 1951); for people accused of subversive activities; for military deserters; or for anyone else she believes to be "on the outside of power."

This graduate of Hunter College and Columbia University Law School came to Congress by way of the anti–Vietnam War wave that washed over the 19th District during the late 1960s. A founder of Women's Strike for Peace, she rallied reform Democrats behind the so-called dump Johnson movement. Her influence grew. "I decided," she says, "it was time to send someone to Washington who really would do the things they said, and so, who else?"

From the Statue of Liberty to the fringes of Harlem—almost the entire length of West Side Manhattan—she went into the streets to campaign. Her "Hi! I'm Bella" was heard in Little Italy, the Bowery, Greenwich Village and all points in between. To get attention she wore a wide-brimmed hat and used the booming voice that, Norman Mailer says, "could boil the fat off a taxi driver's neck." Instead of trying to finesse the seat away from incumbent Leonard Farbstein, Ms. Abzug employed what Joe Flaherty described in the *Village Voice* as a "straight ahead, two-fisted assault." The primary race was close; so was the general election—against Barry Farber, a Manhattan radio interviewer endorsed by both the Republican and the Liberal parties—which she won with a total of 52 per cent of the vote.

When her 82-year-old mother was told of the victory, she said, "I'm not surprised. Bella always did her homework without being told." Her husband, Martin, a stockbroker and sometime novelist, and the couple's two daughters had similar reactions. "She's a tremendous leader," Martin says. "Not only that, but, as soon as she became a candidate, she made a commitment not to practice law. How many do that? She's a great brain; she tells it like it is; she has charisma."

Bella also has an earthy vocabulary. While she admits having used three-letter words, she denies employing the four-letter variety "to the extent [the media] say I do, and *never* in Congress." If she means on the floor of the House, there is no argument. In her office, on the telephone, and in certain speeches, however, President Nixon is a "bastard" and fellow liberals who oppose her and columnists who criticize her are tagged with epithets that would not pass the censor of anything except an X-rated movie.

The New York congresswoman's outspokenness may have won her few friends in Washington, but it has made her a fixture on the college and women's-rights lecture circuits. Charging an average of $1,000 per appearance, she earned $13,280 in honoraria during 1971. She considers speaking engagements one of the few legitimate activities open to a lawmaker who needs outside income, and she claims she is in this category because she helps supplement the Old Age Assistance and Medicaid payments her invalid mother receives.

While Ms. Abzug dutifully commuted between her office in the Longworth Building and the two she maintains in the 19th District and chalked up an impressive 92 per cent congressional voting record, the Republican-controlled New York State Legislature, in compliance with the one-man–one-vote rule, handed down a reapportionment plan reflecting Manhattan island's loss of population. The 19th was abolished and split among three congressmen, thus turning Bella into a political orphan. She made a difficult judgment and opted to oppose 10-year veteran William ("Bill") Fitts Ryan, 49, a Reform Democrat like herself whose record on precisely those issues that Bella had championed not only was as principled as hers but predated it.

"The liberals lined up, left and left," in the words of *Life* magazine. Bella, howling "discrimination," went back to the subway stops, park benches, and delicatessens to tell the voters in the new 20th District that they now had a chance to choose the "greater of two goods." Said Ryan, "I'm disappointed in her. When the real enemy [conservatives in neighboring districts] is elsewhere, it makes very little sense to run against a friend."

Before it was over, the Abzug-Ryan race generated more animosity, dissension, and psychic distress than New York's reform-minded Democrats would have predicted they could tolerate. One ploy that backfired was a whispering campaign by Bella's supporters about Ryan's health. Although he had undergone surgery for the removal of a malignant tumor in his throat, he claimed that "except for my voice, I am fully recovered."

Because the new 20th incorporated nearly all of Ryan's former district and only a third of Ms. Abzug's (including the family duplex on Bank Street), most of the electorate regarded him as the incumbent and her as the insurgent. When the June primary votes were counted, the size of Representative Ryan's victory margin was the real surprise. Both sides admitted that his 2-to-1 win was unexpectedly large.

Eight weeks before the November election, Bill Ryan died. When the Democrats began to argue about a replacement, the acrimony started all over again. "I wouldn't even let Bella live in the district, if it were up to me," a longtime Ryan supporter said. "She killed Bill Ryan." Irving Faust, who had also backed Ryan, declared in *New York Magazine* that "her preoccupation with the vertical pronoun" will always be a stumbling block in the way of political effectiveness. When the Democratic County Committee nominated Bella, the Liberal Party announced that its candidate would be Ryan's widow, Priscilla, and bitter discord over an Abzug-Ryan race erupted for a second time.

Other than having gained a national significance far beyond that of most first-term members of Congress, what has Bella Abzug accomplished? She has been instrumental in forcing land-lords to roll back rent increases; she has saved some housing from destruction; she obtained funds to give elderly tenants in a high-crime section Housing Authority police protection. Aides point also to a traffic light on Rivington and Columbia and a mobile food stamp-registration service for indigents too proud to ask for government assistance. Representative Abzug herself mentions the sex-discrimination amendment she managed to add to the Public Works Acceleration Act. Also high on her list is the formation of the National Women's Political Caucus, which she helped found. "It will enable an increasing number of women to enter Congress and the state legislatures," she says, "where they have been underrepresented for far too long." Would she do anything differently? "No, I'd do the same—only better."

ELLA T. GRASSO

DEMOCRAT OF CONNECTICUT

She was not quite a year old when the 19th Amendment be-came law, but Ella Grasso has had a political career that makes her sound like a suffragist's dream come true. Her training ground for politics was the League of Women Voters, successor to the American Woman Suffrage Association, and her political portfolio was assembled according to guidelines issued by Car-rie Chapman Catt: inside of a political party.

Ella Grasso's political sensitivities have been in tune since 1952, when she campaigned successfully for a seat in the Connecticut House of Representatives. Re-elected two years later, she be-came the first woman floor leader. With time out to serve as a Democratic national committeewoman and to chair the Demo-cratic State Platform Committee (another first for a Connecti-cut woman), she was elected secretary of state in 1958. The es-teem in which Connecticut holds this office is evident in the facts that the job title is "Secretary of *the* State" and the incumbent's personal automobile carries license plate number 3.

Mrs. Grasso soared like a comet through three terms in the Hartford Capitol, into the outer reaches of national Democratic politics: member of the Platform Drafting Committee at the 1960 National Convention and cochairman of the Resolutions Committee at the 1964 and 1968 conventions. The party leader to whom she reported in Chicago was Carl Albert of Oklahoma. He became Speaker of the House the year she was sworn in as the representative from the 6th District, in northwestern Con-necticut.

Her campaign (against Republican Richard C. Kilbourn, a Bristol radio-station manager) was folksy: a maximum of informal glad-handing on village greens, in city streets, in living rooms, and factories, and a minimum of formal speeches and TV appearances. The style suited her friendly, outgoing personality.

The only child of James Tambussi (now deceased), a baker, and his wife, Maria Oliva, both native Italians, she was born and reared in Windsor Locks. Bilingual Ella was a bright student who excelled in history and, after her graduation from Mount Holyoke College (Phi Beta Kappa and *magna cum laude*), she worked as a teaching assistant while earning a master's degree in economics and sciology. In 1942 she married Thomas H. Grasso, a schoolteacher who later acquired a doctorate and became principal of the Center School in East Hartford.

Had Ella Grasso not entered Congress with an abundance of home-grown assets, she could not have coped as well as she has with what is described as a "cancer of real depression" spreading through the industrial cities of her district. By mid-1971, when unemployment nationwide soared to a nine-year high of slightly more than 6 per cent, the jobless in New Britain and Torrington had risen to 14 per cent. In Bristol, the proportion was a critical 24 per cent. The defense-oriented industries (fuses, ball bearings, rolled steel) that two years earlier had employed 25,000 in Bristol had laid off nearly 7,000 highly skilled men and women. "The harshest of our laws," says Ella Grasso, "is the law of supply and demand."

That the great, creaking machinery of government turns slowly is of small comfort to constituents who are "going downhill each week" and for whom "next year seems an interminable wait," she points out. "There have been times when I wanted to take President Nixon and have him walk down the streets with me." It may be a cliché, but Ella Grasso uses it: "How amazing that this country can put a man on the moon yet can't get rid of unemployment!"

After the Administration imposed controls on prices and wages, plus a 10 per cent import surcharge, there was an upsurge of confidence in the northwest corner of Connecticut, but the unemployment picture did not change appreciably, and the number of families on welfare increased. "When you are priming a pump, it takes a little while, especially when there has been a long drought," the congresswoman explains. Consequently, her chief and abiding concern continues to be the economic plight of the 6th District.

The people back home are informed about each move she makes on their behalf, no matter how insignificant it seems. Thus they have learned that, after calling Nixon's summer-jobs program request a "wooden nickel," she succeeded in obtaining congressional action to increase the 1971 appropriation for youth; that she wrote to the President about the two thousand jobs that could be saved if the engines for the Lockheed TriStar super jet were built by East Hartford's Pratt and Whitney instead of England's Rolls-Royce Corporation; that Bristol, New Britain, and Torrington could qualify for public service jobs under the Emergency Employment Act of 1971; and that a toll-free telephone service to assist people seeking federal jobs had been established in the state.

Her cramped quarters on the top floor of the Cannon Office Building, like the spacious offices she occupied for 12 years on the first floor of the Connecticut Capitol, have been turned into an informal "people's lobby." Here, aided by mostly young staffers, the capable Ella Grasso, a short, mature-looking woman with serious, wide-apart brown eyes and closely cropped light-brown hair, goes about the business of drafting bills (one to preserve the American ball-bearing industry from unfair foreign competition has been placed in the legislative hopper), signing letters, writing speeches, and meeting with a constant stream of visitors.

Two-way communication lines are kept open at all times. Installed in her New Britain courthouse office is the toll-free Ella-Phone which provides around-the-clock service for residents in the 47 towns and cities of her district. "It's my way," she says, "of bringing government closer to the people and the people closer to the government."

Weekends find the congresswoman on Olive Street in Windsor Locks with her mother, her husband, and sometimes their children, Susane (an art teacher) and James (a student at the University of Connecticut). Her entire family "thoroughly approves of my being in politics," she says. Once asked how she managed to run for office while her children were small, she replied, "I have an Italian mother."

In varying degrees, most of the 435 members of the House have had to face frustration. Although Ella Grasso, in confronting the economic adversity of her constituents, has more reasons than many of her Hill colleagues to feel fettered, she still believes that "public service—working for the people—is the noblest profession."

LOUISE DAY HICKS
DEMOCRAT OF MASSACHUSETTS

A 1970 pre-election poll in the Massachusetts 9th Congressional District showed that all but 1 per cent of the voters knew who Louise Day Hicks was. The sampling further indicated that 81 per cent knew "quite a lot" about her. So Mrs. Hicks, who had zoomed to prominence as a vociferous opponent of school busing while chairman of the Boston School Committee, relied on a low-key campaign. Instead of participating in public forums, she concentrated on coffee klatches. In November she captured the Democratic seat held by House Speaker John McCormack, 78, who had announced his retirement.

With this victory, it was generally assumed that the 51-year-old widow from South Boston had fulfilled her political ambitions. She even said as much, vowing she could "do more for Boston on the federal level" and promising to "give the middle American the courageous voice he so desperately needs in Washington."

But, as other freshman members, notably Bella Abzug, defied tradition and spoke whenever they wanted to be heard, the Gentlewoman from Massachusetts maintained a stony silence. Except to confess to David Schoumacher on the CBS Evening News that she missed Boston, "even being away for a few days," Louise Hicks waited five months before uttering a single public word in the Capitol. And when she finally did rise on the House floor, her remarks could hardly be construed as courageous. She merely joined the ultraconservative chorus advocating censure of colleagues who had stood under a Viet Cong flag while addressing peace demonstrators.

"What is most baffling about Mrs. Hicks," a longtime Hill-watcher said, "is a certain amateur adventurism about Congress, as if she doesn't expect to go far." Intimates saw nothing puzzling about her behavior. "Being mayor of Boston is the only job she's ever wanted," a friend said. That statement is revealing. It explains the absence of zeal among her mostly male staff, as well as her own lackluster performance. It also explains why this daughter of the late Judge William J. Day of South Boston District Court and mother of two sons had, while in her 30s, gone back to college, earned a law degree from Boston University, and entered private practice. Her consuming preoccupation, even while a land-court examiner and a counsel for the juvenile court, was with getting through the preliminaries quickly so she could move into city hall with, in her words, the "power to make decisions."

It was during the last of her three terms on the school committee that Mrs. Hicks discovered the political mileage to be gained from opposing busing as a tool for desegregation. Events gave her pro-neighborhood-schools stand a dimension that she herself probably had not envisioned. Overnight she became a heroine to the thousands of white parents panicked by the thought of an increase in the proportion of blacks in their children's schools. Seen by these constituents as the goodhearted lady who stood for traditional values, she won a host of sympathetic followers.

In 1967 she was the favorite to become mayor of Boston, and most of her allies considered Kevin White's 12,000-vote majority a fluke. Their opinion was later reinforced when Mrs. Hicks easily won first place in the City Council race and defeated a former GOP representative, Laurence Curtis, and Vietnam veteran Daniel J. Houton, an Independent, for Congress. In both compaigns she ran on a strong law-and-order platform, working the rich vein of voter discontent over crime in the streets.

Less than six months after being sworn in as a congresswoman, she formally challenged White to a rematch, declaring, "I care enough to come back." As "Louise Day Hicks for Mayor" posters appeared on flagpoles dotting the front yards of the triple-decker wooden houses and smaller ones of brick in Boston's heavily Irish, blue-collar neighborhoods, the candidate became a part-time congresswoman and campaigned rigorously, even debating on television, something she had previously refused to do. The only thing she did not change was her 10-year-old slogan: "You Know Where I Stand."

"Exactly what she meant wasn't all that important," Robert Brigham noted in *Life*.

> It was the perfect political phrase because it allowed any voter to read into it all his fears. Some whites who opposed busing because, at bottom, they hate and fear blacks, can choose to believe that Louise Hicks is as racist as they are. She is not. But what she is, or what she stands for, it not that clear either. In her all-purpose speech, she seems to invoke a past when there were no municipal problems and Boston's maze of minorities lived happily walled into their own neighborhoods. The market for that kind of vision is shrinking.

As the mayoralty campaign went down to the wire, the threat of higher property taxes eclipsed the busing issue, and the incumbent, whose fiscal responsibility was a known quantity, won.

Said a Democratic official, "This defeat puts Louise on the brink of political oblivion."

He miscalculated. The full impact of busing was yet to come. In the fall of 1971 the number of court rulings calling for integration of schools increased, particularly in the North, and mountains of irate constituent mail produced overwhelming congressional support for an antibusing measure. It contained two key features that Louise Hicks, as a member of the House Education and Labor Committee, wholeheartedly supported: protection of the neighborhood school and a ban on busing across school-district lines. President Nixon signed the bill in mid-1972.

What about the "only job she's ever wanted?" Understandably reluctant to commit herself to a mayoralty race that won't take place until 1975, all she will say is, "My name is still on the door of my brother's law firm in Boston."

ELIZABETH B. ANDREWS
DEMOCRAT OF ALABAMA

So negligible were the costs of winning the uncontested 1972 special election for the 3d Alabama Congressional District seat left vacant by the death of George W. Andrews that the first act of his widow and successor, Elizabeth, was to return all political contributions. Although it was a year when everyone seemed to be talking more openly about campaign financing than ever before, Mrs. Andrews's admirable gesture went unreported. "No reflection on the press," said one constituent, "but certainly an insight into her character. She's never aspired to personal gain."

If there was no suspense in the April 4 election that assured Elizabeth Andrews, 61, the opportunity to fill the unexpired nine months then remaining of her late husband's term, the same could not be said of the political events leading up to it. While there were rumors immediately following Andrews's death on Christmas Day 1971 that his widow might be a willing candidate, it was well known that a number of male politicians in the 12-county largely rural area were interested in the job and would be acceptable to the State Democratic Executive Committee, the leadership of which tended to be more liberal in outlook than the conservative-minded Mrs. Andrews. "There probably would be a dozen or more running in a special election," Tex Middlebrooks wrote in the *Enterpriser*, "if it were not for reapportionment." His reference was to the fact that as a result of the 1970 census, the number of House seats in Alabama had been decreased from eight to seven, and that the boundaries most radically affected by the State Legislature reapportionment plan were those of the 3d District.

"I had no idea of running for George's office," Congresswoman Andrews said after being sworn in on April 10, "until friends encouraged me to do so." Actually, it was one friend in particular, former Congresswoman Lera M. Thomas of Texas, whose late husband had served on the Appropriations Committee with Representative Andrews, who "planted the seed," says Elizabeth Andrews. "Following the funeral, Lera rather pointedly suggested, 'Don't rule out going to Capitol Hill yourself. You know more about his plans than any other living person, and I personally know what it will mean to the constituency.' "

Endorsed by Alabama Governor George C. Wallace, whose hometown, Clayton, is in the 3d District, and the unanimous choice of 13 members of the State Executive Committee representing the district, Mrs. Andrews's nomination appeared assured. "Not so," said Democratic Party Chairman Robert S. Vance. "Most party leaders seem reluctant to nominate someone . . . who's unwilling to seek the subsequent full two-year term, and Mrs. Andrews has said she would not be a candidate in the November general election." "A case of hard-core politics competing with sentimentality," editorialized the *Opelika-Auburn News*.

"After looking at the attitude of the Executive Committee," said Vera G. Howell of Greensboro, "it seems to me that the only possible reason for not choosing Mrs. Andrews is that she is a woman. I do not belong to Women's Lib, but if she is not given this nomination I will certainly consider joining." "Womanhood per se," says Mrs. Andrews, "was never an issue. In Alabama today if a woman is qualified and capable, she can obtain political support." Nor did the Republicans pose a threat; the GOP hierarchy chose not to field a candidate against her. Opposition came only from so-called "loyalist" Democrats, including the black members of the State Executive Committee. What eventually swung the committee nomination in her favor, by a vote of 72 to 17, according to Don F. Wasson of the *Montgomery Advertiser*, was that "Governor Wallace let it be known that if [anyone else] was chosen, he personally would back Mrs. Andrews as an independent candidate."

Alabama's first female member of the U.S. House is a native of Geneva, in the southeastern part of the state, where her father, Charles Gillespie Bullock, was a businessman. Following graduation from Alabama College (now the University of

Montevallo) with a major in home economics, she taught one year in Livingston, where she earned $20 a month and paid $18 for room and board. "The Depression," she recalls, "was difficult." Fortunately she was offered a better-paying position in Union Springs. "There I met George Andrews, then district attorney. We were married in 1936." His 1944 decision, while serving with the Navy at Pearl Harbor, to run for Congress *in absentia* placed Mrs. Andrews in the political arena as a member of his campaign team. "I had a young daughter, but I found time to do whatever needed doing," she remembers. One of his campaign managers was the father of Winton M. Blount, Jr., who served as President Nixon's Postmaster General and ran unsuccessfully for the Senate on the GOP ticket in 1972. Ironically, Elizabeth Andrews was barred, as a Democratic officeholder, from supporting Blount, her longtime friend.

Another ironic twist peripheral to Mrs. Andrews's short-lived political career was the Capitol Hill office she occupied. The Clerk of the House assigned her the only available space in the Longworth Building. It was Room 1724, the same quarters George Andrews had occupied from 1950–64. Both the congress-woman and her staff, all of whom had worked for the late congressman and whom she retained, were pleased. "When I told Jane and George, Jr.," Mrs. Andrews said, "their response was: 'That's where we grew up.' "

During the political skirmishing early in 1972, the *Union Springs Herald* was among the many newspapers that argued Mrs. Andrews's political case editorially. "By naming her to fill the unexpired term of her late husband," the paper declared, "the Democratic Committee would be doing a good day's work. She would be in a position to carry through some of her late husband's plans for such things in Alabama as waterways and the cancer and heart research centers at Birmingham. So, make no mistake about it, we are not, as a few have suggested, doing Mrs. Andrews a favor; she is doing Alabama a favor."

While in office she did not, by her own admission, accomplish all she had hoped. But as the thousands of letters of appreciation she received from constituents testify, she did do many favors for Alabama. The theme running through all of the letters —grateful acknowledgment for services rendered—belies Ralph Nader's study-of-Congress conclusion that "Congressmen waste time by providing personal services to their constituents." Were Elizabeth Andrews to change her mind about staying in politics, she has the assurance of a built-in constituency.

Promises to Keep

ELAINE S. EDWARDS

DEMOCRAT OF LOUISIANA

While most U.S. senators can concentrate their energies on their own careers, Louisiana's Elaine Edwards always had to reserve some to promote the political interests of the Democratic governor who appointed her. Lest this be construed as sex exploitation, it should be noted that the governor in question was also her husband.

Edwin W. Edwards, a Cajun publicly committed to ending discrimination against women, called the August 1, 1972 appointment of his wife to the U.S. Senate "a meaningful gesture." In a state traditionally old-style Dixie conservative on matters of politics, there was an element of truth in his pronouncement. Just how meaningful the gesture was, however, the governor revealed in subsequent statements. One key factor, he said, in naming Mrs. Edwards to complete the unexpired term of the late Allen J. Ellender (elected in 1936 to succeed Louisiana's first woman senator, Rose McConnell Long) was that "the appointee must be willing to resign following the November election of Senator Ellender's successor." But the main reason for selecting his diminutive, dark-haired 43-year-old wife, Edwards conceded, was that she met another essential requirement: she "would not in the future seek the office or use the appointment to further personal or political gain."

"Edwards had other things in mind when he made his surprising selection," *Time* commented. "Too many other Louisi-

346

anans coveted the job, and it was politically perilous to choose among them. Beyond that, three of Edward's top financial backers [of his 1971–72 gubernatorial campaign] sought the post— not to mention his two brothers. Elaine was the only out."

If Governor Edwards had needed a precedent for resolving his dilemma the way he did, there was one, albeit highly controversial. On an August day 35 years earlier, Alabama Governor Bibb Graves had named his wife, Dixie, to fill the Senate vacancy created by Hugo L. Black's appointment to the Supreme Court. Although Edwards escaped the invective heaped upon Graves in 1937 (the *Birmingham News* accused Graves, among other things, of "cheapening a great deliberative body in favor of maudlin sentimentality"), the Louisiana governor's nepotism became the subject of polite but probing comment. "Whether Mrs. Edwards can perform well in her new assignment is a question no one will answer yet," Joan Kent wrote in the *New Orleans States-Item.* "Will she think for herself or will she be a puppet for her husband?"

Although eschewing the word "puppet," Senator Edwards provided ample evidence during her brief term of office that she was acting not on her own, but as the governor's agent. She could not have done otherwise—nor was she expected to try.

Coping with the antiquated procedures and musty mechanisms of the U.S. Senate requires the broadest possible legislative background, particlarly during the chaotic, debate- and deal-filled days of a Presidential election year when Congress is goaded into sustained action. The aggregate of Elaine Edwards's political experience, other than serving as a charming and decorous campaign partner for her husband, was as a recorder of messages from constituents. While Edwards was a member of the U.S. House of Representatives, a second telephone was installed in the family home in Crowley. She listened attentively to callers' requests or complaints ("mainly problems about Social Security") and at the end of each day dutifully relayed them to the congressman's Washington office.

It was the telephone, ironically, that became the dominant instrument in her Senate life. Although the offhand remark by a critic that "The senator doesn't go to the bathroom without calling the governor" was grossly exaggerated, there was a standing order to aides to place a call to his Baton Rouge office prior to every floor vote. When asked about the "hot line" to Louisiana, she offered the explanation that "Edwin and I both want what's best for our state—to move it forward in a positive direction."

Without her husband's achievement-oriented drive, which carried him from smalltown attorney to city councilman to state senator to U.S. representative to governor, Elaine Schwartzenburg Edwards undoubtedly would have remained in the role she had always preferred: a homebody. "I've never wanted to be liberated from sewing, cooking, or even gardening," she once said. "As for my children [two girls, two boys], I *enjoy* them. As thrilling as anything in my life is the close relationship we share." Gray eyes misty, but her soft voice carefully controlled, she frequently attested to a mother's pride by recalling that son Stephen, 18, withdrew $400 of his savings, without parental knowledge, to get out the youth vote that helped put his father in the state capitol.

Once ensconced in the million-dollar governor's mansion, with its staff of 40, the Edwards' family lived comfortably on the $28,-750 a year that Louisiana pays its chief of state. When the first lady also became the junior U.S. senator, a job in the $42,500 salary bracket, an inevitable question concerned the reaction of a Southern belle to earning more than her husband. "I haven't thought about it," was her answer. "But since we don't need my salary, I'm putting it in a trust fund, to be divided equally among the children when David, now 13, starts to college."

Though never poor, neither Elaine Schwartzenburg nor Edwin Edwards grew up in affluent circumstances. They were both natives of Marksville—she the only daughter of a grocery store owner, he a farmer's son. They met as teenagers at a birthday party and did most of their courting under a walnut tree in the Schwartzenburg backyard. Following graduation from high school, she worked a year as a secretary in Dallas while waiting for Edwin to finish law school. They were married in 1949.

Plainly insecure in her role as a senator, her conversation frequently clothed in vexing wisps of self-doubt, Mrs. Edwards nevertheless demonstrated a sincere willingness to conscientiously perform the duties required of her, whether taking a turn in the presiding officer's chair or donning a chef's hat to serve Louisiana creole gumbo, an entree added to the Senate restaurant menu in memory of Ellender. Like Rose Long, whose son Russell could be counted on for advice, she found committee work to her liking. "My proudest moment," she confessed, "was convincing members of the Public Works Committee to vote funds for a north-south highway to connect the two east-west interstates in Louisiana. Now the prospects are very real that we can lure much-needed industry to the central part of the state."

Despite Elaine Edwards's loyalty to home and family, she respects the views of women liberationists and expresses the hope that more levers of legislative power will be placed in female hands. Feminists are not impressed. In the so-called Year of the Woman Candidate—a year marked by the most significant political advancement of women since ratification of the 19th Amendment in 1920—liberationists viewed her appointment with wry bemusement. She did not exemplify their ideal woman politician—one who is willing to wage war "against sexism, racism, institutionalized violence and poverty."

In fairness to the 11th woman to occupy a seat in the U.S. Senate, a branch of Congress in which women have made a discouragingly small showing, it must be pointed out that certain sections of the country, notably the South, have been more reluctant than others to permit distaffers to share in political decision-making, power, and credit. Geography aside, it is the Senate itself that, 52 years following suffrage, remains the most formidable barrier to women candidates. No one knew this better than Senator Elaine Edwards, whose welcome to membership from GOP Leader Hugh Scott of Pennsylvania reflected the sentiment of his 97 male colleagues. Speaking from the floor on the day she was sworn in, he said: "I agree with those who argue that there should be more women in the Senate. It is fine with me as long as they do not occupy this particular seat."

Postscript: November 7, 1972

Although arbitrary discrimination against women congressional candidates was on the wane in 1972 and the political woods were alive with the sound of a record number of ambitious hopefuls, the election results told an all-too-familiar story: The male-female ratio in Congress would remain substantially unchanged. As usual, local personalities and local issues were pivotal. In fact they accounted for the most serious setback to feminine political progress in a quarter of a century: not a single woman was elected to the Senate.

Leaders of the National Women's Political Caucus (NWPC), the multipartisan organization whose aim is to raise women's standing in American politics, had never expected that the approximately two dozen women making their first try for Congress on major party tickets would win. But they seriously believed that a net gain of 10 in the House was possible. Instead, the total was five: Republican Marjorie Holt of Maryland and Democrats Yvonne Brathwaite Burke of California, Elizabeth Holtzman of New York, Barbara Jordan of Texas, and Patricia Schroeder of Colorado.

In general, voters were remarkably kind to incumbents, regardless of party. Of the 11 women seeking re-election, only two were retired: Louise Day Hicks, Democrat of Massachusetts, and Republican Senator Margaret Chase Smith of Maine. Mrs. Hicks was primarily a victim of redistricting. A lifelong urbanite, she failed to attract meaningful support in the seven Boston suburbs that had been added to the 9th District.

Senator Smith's unexpected defeat for a fifth term was due to a combination of circumstances, not the least of which was her age. "At 74, Mrs. Smith can no longer possibly have the stamina necessary to keep pace with the grueling daily schedule demanded of a U.S. senator," editorialized her hometown newspaper, the *Somerset Reporter*. It was not a year for seniority. From coast to coast younger contenders were able to exploit what *Time* called "the contrast between vigor and venerability." Another reason Senator Smith was unseated was that in contradistinction to her opponent, William D. Hathaway, 48, who stumped the state for a year in search of votes and visited each town at least twice, she followed her traditional pattern of taking to the hustings only when the Senate was not in session. But more than anything else, what weakened the Maine electorate's well-known resistance to change was the economic plight of the state itself. While she stressed her lengthy record in Congress and ignored Maine's pockets of poverty and high unemployment rate, Hathaway, a four-term representative, set forth specific programs to revitalize the economy and promised to work for them.

The political significance of Margaret Chase Smith's departure from the Senate was underscored in a statement she made early in the campaign. "I was thinking seriously of retiring this year," she told Susan Nelson of the *Chicago Tribune*. "But I hate to leave when there is no indication another qualified woman is coming in. We've built a place here for quality service. If I leave and there's a long lapse, the next woman will have to rebuild entirely."

In the House races, which female incumbents traditionally win by larger margins than do male incumbents, 1972 was a vintage year for women. Their pluralities ranged from 60.6 to 87 per cent. Re-elected were Republican Margaret Heckler of Massachusetts, who was unopposed, and Democrats Bella Abzug of New York and Patsy Mink of Hawaii, each of whom defeated a GOP female contender; also, Shirley Chisholm (New York), Ella Grasso (Connecticut), Edith Green (Oregon), Martha Griffiths (Michigan), Julia Butler Hansen (Washington), and Leonor K. Sullivan (Missouri). Mrs. Sullivan, ranking member of the Merchant Marine and Fisheries Committee since 1966, moved up to chair this committee, succeeding Maryland Democrat Edward A. Garmatz, who did not seek re-election. She is the fifth congresswoman ever to head a standing committee. Representative Green relinquished her seat on the Education and Labor Committee to accept an appointment to the Appropriations Committee and its Subcommittee on Labor–Health, Education, and Welfare.

Whether, as *Life* suggested, women newcomers in the 93d Congress (1973–75), together with their male counterparts, "have a chance, and the will, to help a venerable and arteriosclerotic institution revive and reassert itself" will depend on many intangibles. The one certainty is that the newly elected quintet, on the basis of past performance, has the potential for leadership. Lawyers all, each has either held elective office at the county or state level or served as legal counsel for a statewide organization. Their support of the NWPC motto, "Women! Make policy not coffee," is unanimous. Because they are relatively young (average age: 38), if they remain in office, the path to congressional power and prestige should not be difficult to tread, particularly if the seniority system remains in effect.

YVONNE BRATHWAITE BURKE

DEMOCRAT OF CALIFORNIA

When the largest state gained five congressional districts as a result of reapportionment, the one encompassing southwest Los Angeles and part of Watts appeared tailor-made for a black politician. That was all the encouragement third-term State Assemblywoman Yvonne Brathwaite (she was married to businessman William A. Burke, 33, during the campaign) needed to file as a candidate in the 37th District. As vice-chairman of the Democratic National Convention in July, she attracted nationwide attention via television with her fairness, firmness, good looks, and sunny disposition. These same qualities, plus her record as chairman of the committee on urban development in the State Assembly, proved unbeatable. Against attorney Gregg Tria, an antibusing, antiabortion opponent who lacked political experience, this 39-year-old daughter of a janitor at MGM's movie studios won handily.

MARJORIE HOLT

REPUBLICAN OF MARYLAND

The combination of a conservative ideology, hard campaigning, and the landslide victory of President Richard Nixon—in that order—won the new Maryland 4th District (Anne Arundel and southern Prince Georges counties) for County Circuit

Court Clerk Marjorie Sewell Holt of Severna Park. The wife of Duncan M. Holt, a Westinghouse engineer, mother of three, and a grandmother, Mrs. Holt, 51, is a longtime GOP worker who in 1968 served as state cochairman of the Nixon-Agnew ticket. Vice President Spiro T. Agnew, a former governor of Maryland, repaid this political IOU by conducting a timely rally on her behalf.

Birmingham-born Marjorie Holt, who welcomes the description "law-and-order advocate," has earned a deserved reputation as a legal reformer. Among her accomplishments is the widely praised streamlining and modernizing of the Anne Arundel County Court system to eliminate the criminal-case backlog. "My whole pitch during the campaign," she said following her victory, "was for less government." That was what Republicans and some Democrats wanted to hear, and they gave her an impressive 59 per cent of the vote over Werner A. Fornos, 38, a former state representative.

ELIZABETH HOLTZMAN

DEMOCRAT OF NEW YORK

By unseating Emanuel Celler, 84, who had represented the 16th District in Brooklyn for 50 years and was chairman of the House Judiciary Committee, Elizabeth ("Liz") Holtzman, 31 (the youngest woman elected to Congress to date), scored one of the biggest political upsets of 1972. *Time* dubbed her "Liz the Lion Killer." Actually, Celler set the stage for his own defeat by failing to remain in touch with his constituents (he did not even maintain an office in Brooklyn). "My victory," Liz Holtzman declared, "says that no political figure, no matter how powerful, can forget about the people he was elected to serve."

A former civil rights worker, a onetime assistant to New York Mayor John Lindsay, and, since 1970, a Democratic state committeewoman, Miss Holtzman faced only one handicap: money, or the lack of it. Although both her parents work (her father is a lawyer, her mother a member of the Hunter College faculty) and she earned a regular salary as a practicing attorney, she could not hope to raise the $100,000 that a campaign against Celler was estimated to cost. During the eight months of campaigning she spent slightly less than $50,000, most of which came in small amounts from voters espousing her own liberal causes. "Thank God for *The Godfather!*" she said after winning. The lines outside the theaters where the movie was playing were an ideal place to introduce herself. She also rang doorbells and shook hands in supermarkets and laundromats. "Shoe leather," she maintains, "is cheaper than television spots."

BARBARA JORDAN
DEMOCRAT OF TEXAS

More than a year before the 1972 elections, Texans on Capitol Hill were publicly predicting that State Senator Barbara Jordan of Houston would be the first black congresswoman from the South since Reconstruction. She held so many "firsts" that her move to the federal level appeared inevitable. The first woman elected to the Texas Senate and the first black since 1882, she was the first woman to serve as president pro tem of the Senate and the first black ever to serve as governor of the state (for a day).

Like Representative Burke, Miss Jordon, 36, won in a newly carved, largely black section of her hometown. Ironically, the creation of the new 18th District eliminated her State Senate seat, and critics have accused her of making "a tradeoff with the Establishment" in order to go to Washington. These same critics do not, however, deny that she is brilliant and politically shrewd. As a state legislator she concentrated on bills to extend workmen's compensation benefits, give Texas its first minimum-wage law, and establish a department for community affairs designed primarily to solve problems of urban minorities. Tall (5 feet, 8 inches) and dignified, she has a deep, resonant voice that has been a political asset. Since leaving the family home in a low-income neighborhood (her late father was a Baptist minister), Miss Jordan has striven, in her words, "to be something unusual" and to spur other members of her race to set the same goal. "Do not call for black power or green power," she tells them. "Call for brain power."

PATRICIA SCHROEDER
DEMOCRAT OF COLORADO

The state that granted voting rights to women in 1893 had to wait 79 years before a woman emerged as a serious candidate for Congress. Paradoxically, Patricia ("Pat") Schroeder, 32, of Denver captured the 1st District partly because opponent James ("Mike") McKevitt, 44, a conservative Republican incumbent, did not take her seriously until it was too late. Another explanation for Mrs. Schroeder's come-from-behind victory was her active support of Citizens for Colorado's Future, a volunteer group opposed, mainly on environmental grounds, to holding the 1976 Winter Olympics in Denver. (Coloradans, by a 3-to-2 margin, passed a public referendum cutting off all state funds for the Games.) What persuaded the wife of attorney James Schroeder and mother of two young children to trade her promising career as counsel for Planned Parenthood of Colorado and hearing officer with the State Personnel Board for national office? "Among other things," says Pat Schroeder, "the need for honesty in government. It's an issue that women can speak best to—and more should be given the chance."

Appendix

Alphabetical List of Women in the U.S. Congress, 1917-73

(Asterisk next to name indicates membership in Senate.)

Name	Political Party	State Represented	Election/Appointment Dates	Expiration of Term or Terms
ABEL,* Hazel H.	Rep.	Nebraska	Elected Nov. 2, 1954, to fill vacancy in term ending Jan. 3, 1955. Resigned effective Dec. 31, 1954.	Dec. 31, 1954
ABZUG, Bella S.	Dem.	New York	Elected Nov. 3, 1970. Re-elected to 93d Congress.	Jan. 3, 1975
ANDREWS, Elizabeth B.	Dem.	Alabama	Elected April 4, 1972, to fill vacancy in term ending Jan. 3, 1973.	Jan. 3, 1973
BAKER, Irene B.	Rep.	Tennessee	Elected March 10, 1964, to fill vacancy in term ending Jan. 3, 1965.	Jan. 3, 1965
BLITCH, Iris F.	Dem.	Georgia	Elected Nov. 2, 1954. Re-elected to 85th through 87th Congresses.	Jan. 3, 1963
BOLAND, Veronica B.	Dem.	Pennsylvania	Elected Nov. 3, 1942, to fill vacancy in term ending Jan. 3, 1943.	Jan. 3, 1943

Name	Party	State	Service	End
BOLTON, Frances P.	Rep.	Ohio	Elected Feb. 27, 1940, to fill vacancy in term ending Jan. 3, 1941. Re-elected to 77th through 90th Congresses.	Jan. 3, 1969
BOSONE, Reva Beck	Dem.	Utah	Elected Nov. 2, 1948. Re-elected to 82d Congress.	Jan. 3, 1953
BOWRING,* Eva	Rep.	Nebraska	Appointed April 16, 1954, by governor to fill vacancy.	Nov. 7, 1954
BUCHANAN, Vera D.	Dem.	Pennsylvania	Elected July 24, 1951, to fill vacancy in term ending Jan. 3, 1953. Re-elected to 83d and 84th Congresses. Died Nov. 26, 1955.	Jan. 3, 1957
BURKE, Yvonne Brathwaite	Dem.	California	Elected Nov. 7, 1972.	Jan. 3, 1975
BUSHFIELD,* Vera C.	Rep.	South Dakota	Appointed Oct. 6, 1948, by governor to fill vacancy. Resigned Dec. 26, 1948.	Dec. 26, 1948
BYRON, Katharine E.	Dem.	Maryland	Elected May 27, 1941, to fill vacancy in term ending Jan. 3, 1943.	Jan. 3, 1943
CARAWAY,* Hattie W.	Dem.	Arkansas	Appointed Nov. 13, 1931, by governor to fill vacancy. Elected Jan. 12, 1932, to continue to fill vacancy in term ending March 4, 1933. Re-elected Nov. 8, 1932, and Nov. 8, 1938, to six-year terms.	Jan. 3, 1945
CHISHOLM, Shirley	Dem.	New York	Elected Nov. 5, 1968. Re-elected to 92d and 93d Congresses.	Jan. 3, 1975
CHURCH, Marguerite Stitt	Rep.	Illinois	Elected Nov. 8, 1950. Re-elected to 83d through 87th Congresses.	Jan. 3, 1963

Name	Political Party	State Represented	Election/Appointment Dates	Expiration of Term or Terms
CLARKE, Marian W.	Rep.	New York	Elected Dec. 28, 1933, to fill vacancy in term ending Jan. 3, 1935.	Jan. 3, 1935
DOUGLAS, Emily Taft	Dem.	Illinois	Elected Nov. 7, 1944.	Jan. 3, 1947
DOUGLAS, Helen Gahagan	Dem.	California	Elected Nov. 7, 1944. Re-elected to 80th and 81st Congresses.	Jan. 3, 1951
DWYER, Florence P.	Rep.	New Jersey	Elected Nov. 6, 1956. Re-elected to 86th through 92d Congresses.	Jan. 3, 1973
EDWARDS,* Elaine S.	Dem.	Louisiana	Appointed Aug. 1, 1972, by governor to fill vacancy in term ending Jan. 3, 1973. Resigned Nov. 13, 1972.	Nov. 13, 1972
ESLICK, Willa B.	Dem.	Tennessee	Elected Aug. 4, 1932, to fill vacancy in term ending March 4, 1933.	March 4, 1933
FELTON,* Rebecca Latimer	Dem.	Georgia	Appointed Oct. 3, 1922, by governor to fill vacancy.	Nov. 22, 1922
FULMER, Willa L.	Dem.	South Carolina	Elected Nov. 7, 1944, to fill vacancy in term ending Jan. 3, 1945.	Jan. 3, 1945
GASQUE, Elizabeth H.	Dem.	South Carolina	Elected Sept. 13, 1938, to fill vacancy in term ending Jan. 3, 1939.	Jan. 3, 1939
GIBBS, Florence Reville	Dem.	Georgia	Elected Oct. 1, 1940, to fill vacancy in term ending Jan. 3, 1941.	Jan. 3, 1941
GRANAHAN, Kathryn E.	Dem.	Pennsylvania	Elected Nov. 6, 1956, to fill vacancy in term ending Jan. 3, 1957, and to ensuing two-year term. Re-elected to 86th and 87th Congresses.	Jan. 3, 1963
GRASSO, Ella T.	Dem.	Connecticut	Elected Nov. 3, 1970. Re-elected to 93d Congress.	Jan. 3, 1975

Name	State	Party	Remarks	Date
GRAVES,* Dixie Bibb	Alabama	Dem.	Appointed Aug. 18, 1937, by governor to fill vacancy. Resigned Jan. 10, 1938.	Jan. 10, 1938
GREEN, Edith	Oregon	Dem.	Elected Nov. 2, 1954. Re-elected to 85th through 93d Congresses.	Jan. 3, 1975
GREENWAY, Isabella	Arizona	Dem.	Elected Oct. 3, 1933, to fill vacancy in term ending Jan. 3, 1935. Re-elected to 74th Congress.	Jan. 3, 1937
GRIFFITHS, Martha W.	Michigan	Dem.	Elected Nov. 2, 1954. Re-elected to 85th through 93d Congresses.	Jan. 3, 1975
HANSEN, Julia Butler	Washington	Dem.	Elected Nov. 8, 1960, to fill vacancy in term ending Jan. 3, 1961, and to ensuing two-year term. Re-elected to 88th through 93d Congresses.	Jan. 3, 1975
HARDEN, Cecil M.	Indiana	Rep.	Elected Nov. 2, 1948. Re-elected to 82d through 85th Congresses.	Jan. 3, 1959
HECKLER, Margaret M.	Massachusetts	Rep.	Elected Nov. 8, 1966. Re-elected to 91st through 93d Congresses.	Jan. 3, 1975
HICKS, Louise Day	Massachusetts	Dem.	Elected Nov. 3, 1970.	Jan. 3, 1973
HOLT, Marjorie	Maryland	Rep.	Elected Nov. 7, 1972.	Jan. 3, 1975
HOLTZMAN, Elizabeth	New York	Dem.	Elected Nov. 7, 1972.	Jan. 3, 1975
HONEYMAN, Nan Wood	Oregon	Dem.	Elected Nov. 3, 1936.	Jan. 3, 1939
HUCK, Wimifred Mason	Illinois	Rep.	Elected Nov. 7, 1922, to fill vacancy in term ending March 4, 1923.	March 4, 1923
JENCKES, Virginia E.	Indiana	Dem.	Elected Nov. 8, 1932. Re-elected to 74th and 75th Congresses.	Jan. 3, 1939

Name	Political Party	State Represented	Election/Appointment Dates	Expiration of Term or Terms
JORDAN, Barbara	Dem.	Texas	Elected Nov. 7, 1972.	Jan. 3, 1975
KAHN, Florence P.	Rep.	California	Elected Feb. 17, 1925, to fill vacancy in term ending March 4, 1927. Re-elected to 70th through 74th Congresses.	Jan. 3, 1937
KEE, Elizabeth	Dem.	West Virginia	Elected July 16, 1951, to fill vacancy in term ending Jan. 3, 1953. Re-elected to 83d through 88th Congresses.	Jan. 3, 1965
KELLY, Edna F.	Dem.	New York	Elected Nov. 8, 1949, to fill vacancy in term ending Jan. 3, 1951. Re-elected to 82d through 90th Congresses.	Jan. 3, 1969
KNUTSON, Coya	Dem.	Minnesota	Elected Nov. 2, 1954. Re-elected to 85th Congress.	Jan. 3, 1959
LANGLEY, Katherine	Rep.	Kentucky	Elected Nov. 2, 1926. Re-elected to 71st Congress.	March 4, 1931
LONG,* Rose McConnell	Dem.	Louisiana	Appointed Jan. 31, 1936, by governor to fill vacancy. Elected April 21, 1936, to continue to fill vacancy in term ending Jan. 3, 1937.	Jan. 3, 1937
LUCE, Clare Boothe	Rep.	Connecticut	Elected Nov. 3, 1942. Re-elected to 79th Congress.	Jan. 3, 1947
LUSK, Georgia L.	Dem.	New Mexico	Elected Nov. 5, 1946.	Jan. 3, 1949
McCARTHY, Kathryn O'Loughlin	Dem.	Kansas	Elected Nov. 8, 1932.	Jan. 3, 1935
McCORMICK, Ruth Hanna	Rep.	Illinois	Elected Nov. 6, 1928.	March 4, 1931
McMILLAN, Clara G.	Dem.	South Carolina	Elected Nov. 7, 1939, to fill vacancy in term ending Jan. 3, 1941.	Jan. 3, 1941
MANKIN, Helen Douglas	Dem.	Georgia	Elected Feb. 12, 1946, to fill vacancy in term ending Jan. 3, 1947.	Jan. 3, 1947

Name	Party	State		Date
MAY, Catherine	Rep.	Washington	Elected Nov. 4, 1958. Re-elected to 87th through 91st Congresses.	Jan. 3, 1971
MINK, Patsy T.	Dem.	Hawaii	Elected Nov. 3, 1964. Re-elected to 90th through 93d Congresses.	Jan. 3, 1975
NEUBERGER,* Maurine B.	Dem.	Oregon	Elected Nov. 8, 1960, to fill vacancy in term ending Jan. 3, 1961, and to ensuing six-year term.	Jan. 3, 1967
NOLAN, Mae E.	Rep.	California	Elected Jan. 23, 1923, to fill vacancy in term ending March 4, 1923, and to ensuing two-year term.	March 4, 1925
NORRELL, Catherine D.	Dem.	Arkansas	Elected April 18, 1961, to fill vacancy in term ending Jan. 3, 1963.	Jan. 3, 1963
NORTON, Mary T.	Dem.	New Jersey	Elected Nov. 4, 1924. Re-elected to 70th through 81st Congresses.	Jan. 3, 1951
O'DAY, Caroline	Dem.	New York	Elected Nov. 6, 1934. Re-elected to 75th through 77th Congresses.	Jan. 3, 1943
OLDFIELD, Pearl Peden	Dem.	Arkansas	Elected Jan. 9, 1929, to fill vacancy in term ending March 4, 1929, and to ensuing two-year term.	March 4, 1931
OWEN, Ruth Bryan	Dem.	Florida	Elected Nov. 6, 1928. Re-elected to 72d Congress.	March 4, 1933
PFOST, Gracie	Dem.	Idaho	Elected Nov. 4, 1952. Re-elected to 84th through 87th Congresses.	Jan. 3, 1963
PRATT, (Eliza) Jane	Dem.	North Carolina	Elected May 25, 1946, to fill vacancy in term ending Jan. 3, 1947.	Jan. 3, 1947
PRATT, Ruth Baker	Rep.	New York	Elected Nov. 6, 1928. Re-elected to 72d Congress.	March 4, 1933

Name	Political Party	State Represented	Election/Appointment Dates	Expiration of Term or Terms
PYLE,* Gladys	Rep.	South Dakota	Elected Nov. 8, 1938.	Jan. 3, 1939
RANKIN, Jeannette	Rep.	Montana	Elected Nov. 7, 1916. Elected Nov. 5, 1940.	March 4, 1919 Jan. 3, 1943
REECE, Louise Goff	Rep.	Tennessee	Elected May 16, 1961, to fill vacancy in term ending Jan. 3, 1963.	Jan. 3, 1963
REID, Charlotte T.	Rep.	Illinois	Elected Nov. 6, 1962. Re-elected to 89th through 92d Congresses. Resigned Oct. 1, 1971.	Jan. 3, 1973
RILEY, Corinne Boyd	Dem.	South Carolina	Elected April 10, 1962, to fill vacancy in term ending Jan. 3, 1963.	Jan. 3, 1963
ROBERTSON, Alice M.	Rep.	Oklahoma	Elected Nov. 2, 1920.	March 4, 1923
ROGERS, Edith Nourse	Rep.	Massachusetts	Elected June 30, 1925, to fill vacancy in term ending March 4, 1927. Re-elected to 70th through 86th Congresses. Died Sept. 10, 1960.	Jan. 3, 1961
ST. GEORGE, Katharine	Rep.	New York	Elected Nov. 5, 1946. Re-elected to 81st through 88th Congresses.	Jan. 3, 1965
SCHROEDER, Patricia	Dem.	Colorado	Elected Nov. 7, 1972.	Jan. 3, 1975
SIMPSON, Edna	Rep.	Illinois	Elected Nov. 4, 1958.	Jan. 3, 1961
SMITH, Margaret Chase	Rep.	Maine	Elected June 3, 1940, to fill vacancy in term ending Jan. 3, 1941. Re-elected to 77th through 80th Congresses.	Jan. 3, 1949
SMITH,* Margaret Chase	Rep.	Maine	Elected Sept. 13, 1948. Re-elected in 1954, 1960, and 1966 to six-year terms.	Jan. 3, 1973
STANLEY, Winifred C.	Rep.	New York	Elected Nov. 3, 1942.	Jan. 3, 1945
SULLIVAN, Leonor K.	Dem.	Missouri	Elected Nov. 4, 1952. Re-elected to 84th through 93d Congresses.	Jan. 3, 1975

Name	Party	State		Date
SUMNER, Jessie	Rep.	Illinois	Elected Nov. 8, 1938. Re-elected to 77th through 79th Congresses.	Jan. 3, 1947
THOMAS, Lera M.	Dem.	Texas	Elected March 26, 1966, to fill vacancy in term ending Jan. 3, 1967.	Jan. 3, 1967
THOMPSON, Ruth	Rep.	Michigan	Elected Nov. 8, 1950. Re-elected to 83d and 84th Congresses.	Jan. 3, 1957
WEIS, Jessica McCullough	Rep.	New York	Elected Nov. 4, 1958. Re-elected to 87th Congress.	Jan. 3, 1963
WINGO, Effiegene L.	Dem.	Arkansas	Elected Nov. 4, 1930, to fill vacancy in term ending March 4, 1931, and to ensuing two-year term.	March 4, 1933
WOODHOUSE, Chase Going	Dem.	Connecticut	Elected Nov. 7, 1944. Elected Nov. 2, 1948.	Jan. 3, 1947 Jan. 3, 1951

Index

Abel, George P., 245
Abel, Hazel H., 219, 244–47
Abzug, Bella S., 333–38, 341, 351
Abzug, Martin, 336
Acheson, Dean, 133, 185
Adams, Stephen T., 276
Adkins, Homer, 94–95
Administration Committee (House), 53, 279
AFL-CIO, 263
Africa, House Subcommittee on, 133
Aging, Special Committee on (Senate), 297
Agnew, Spiro T., 277, 353
Agricultural Adjustment Act (AAA), 102, 103
Agriculture, U.S., Department of, 95, 195, 246
Agriculture and Forestry Committee (Senate), 93
Agriculture Committee (House), 98, 101, 163, 205, 266, 276, 325
Aiken, George D., 147
Airman, Duncan, 107
Alabama College, 344
Albert, Carl, 291, 339
Albertus Magnus College, 318
Alderson, George, 284
Alien Property, U.S., Office of, 195
Allen, O. K., 118
American Academy of Dramatic Art, 178
American Association of University Women, 244
American Conservatory of Music, 126
American Federation of Labor (A.F. of L.), 81
American Jewish Conference on Soviet Jewry, 216
American Labor Party, 185

American Red Cross, 12, 53, 58, 84, 125, 130, 158, 176
American Woman Suffrage Association, 338
American Women's Voluntary Service, 52, 107
American Women's War Relief Fund, 75
Anderson, Marian, 111, 170
Andrews, Elizabeth B., 333, 343–45
Andrews, George W., 343, 344, 345
Andrews, George W., Jr., 345
Angell, Homer D., 114
Anthony, Susan B., 281
Appleseed Farm (Douglas), 179
Appropriations Committee (House), 49 224, 283, 303, 344, 352; (Senate), 315
Arends, Leslie C., 304
Arkansas, University of, 95, 288
Arkansas A. & M. College, 288
Arkansas College, 66
Armed Services Committee (House), 141, 156, 205, 224; (Senate), 145
Army School of Nursing, U.S., 130
Arnall, Ellis, 191, 192
Associated Press, 78, 243, 299, 301
Astor, Nancy, 41, 42
Atlanta Law School, 192
Atomic Energy, Joint Committee on, 276
Austin, Albert E., 166, 168
Ayres, William H., 302

Baker Beverly, 308
Baker, Bobby, 298
Baker, Howard H., 307, 308
Baker, Howard H., Jr., 308, 309
Baker, Irene B., 302, 307–9
Baker, Mary Elizabeth, 308
Baker, Newton D., 130, 132